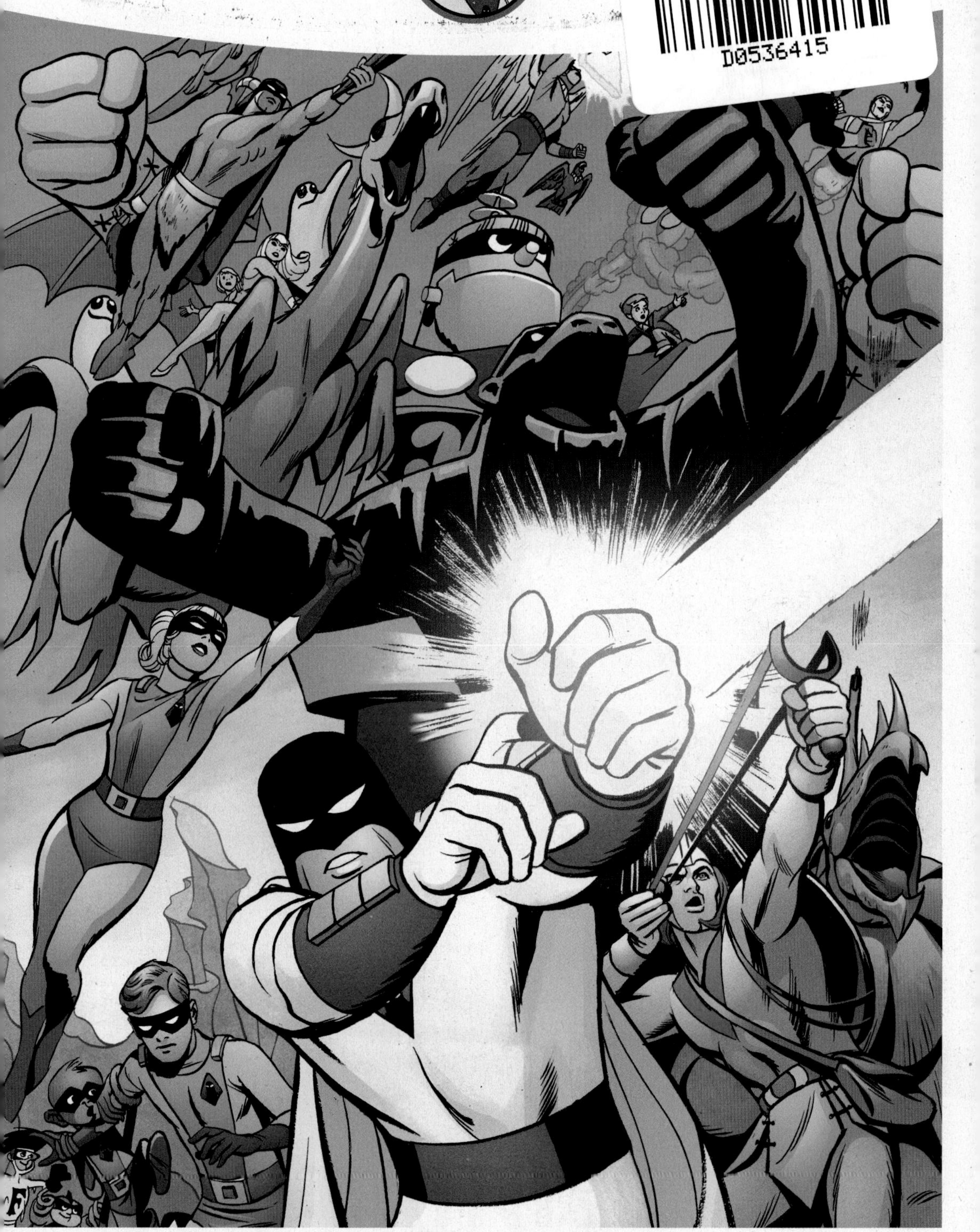

FUTURE QUEST
VOL.1

FUTURE QUEST
VOL.1

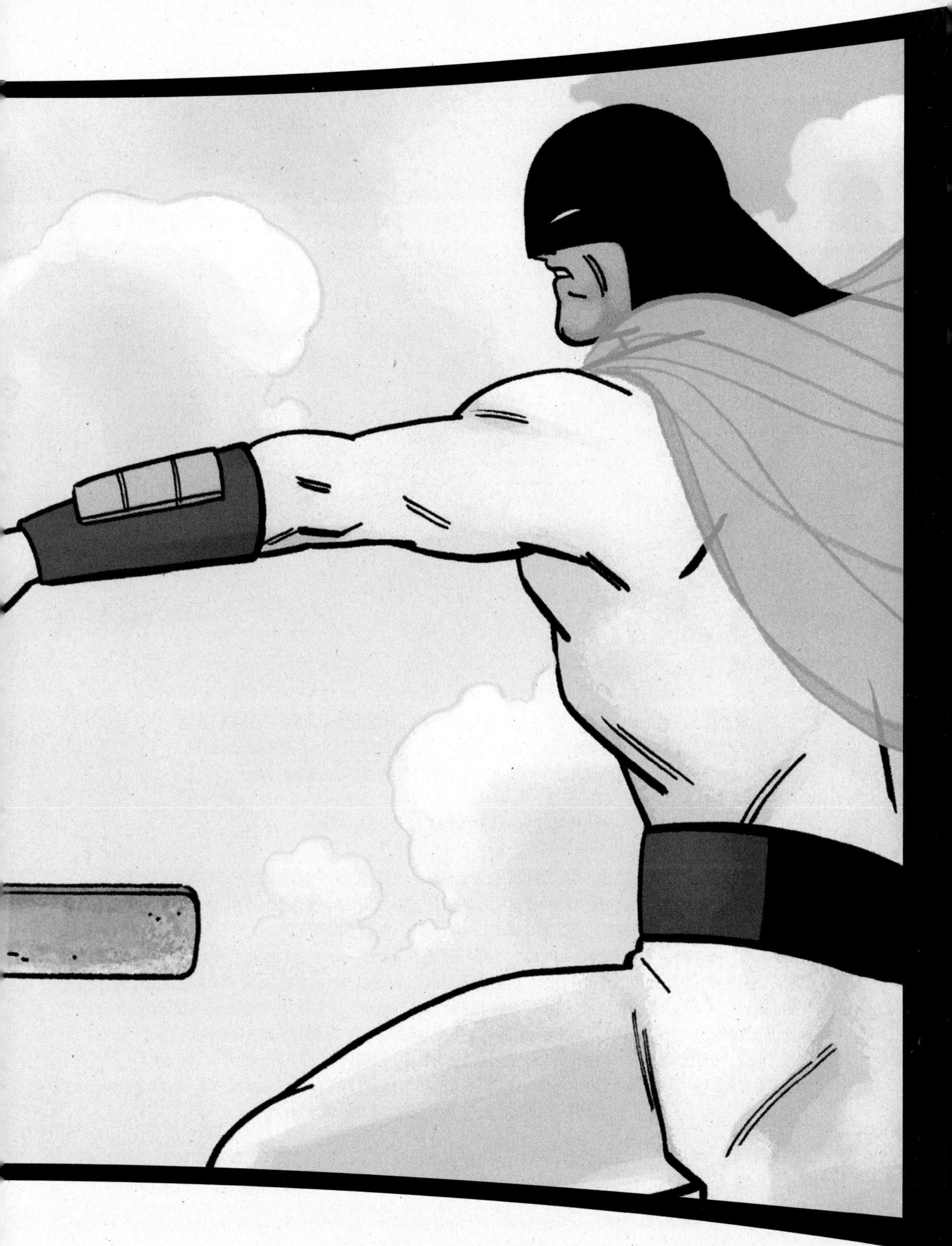

JEFF PARKER writer
EVAN SHANER STEVE RUDE RON RANDALL JEFF PARKER
JONATHAN CASE AARON LOPRESTI KARL KESEL CRAIG ROUSSEAU artists
JORDIE BELLAIRE STEVE BUCCELLATO HI-FI
JEREMY LAWSON VERONICA GANDINI colorists
DAVE LANPHEAR letterer **EVAN SHANER** collection cover artist
Special thanks to **DARWYN COOKE**

MARIE JAVINS Editor - Original Series BRITTANY HOLZHERR Assistant Editor - Original Series
JEB WOODARD Group Editor - Collected Editions ERIKA ROTHBERG Editor - Collected Edition
STEVE COOK Design Director - Books CURTIS KING JR. Publication Design

BOB HARRAS Senior VP - Editor-in-Chief, DC Comics

DIANE NELSON President DAN DiDIO Publisher JIM LEE Publisher GEOFF JOHNS President & Chief Creative Officer
AMIT DESAI Executive VP - Business & Marketing Strategy, Direct to Consumer & Global Franchise Management
SAM ADES Senior VP - Direct to Consumer BOBBIE CHASE VP - Talent Development MARK CHIARELLO Senior VP - Art, Design & Collected Editions
JOHN CUNNINGHAM Senior VP - Sales & Trade Marketing ANNE DePIES Senior VP - Business Strategy, Finance & Administration
DON FALLETTI VP - Manufacturing Operations LAWRENCE GANEM VP - Editorial Administration & Talent Relations
ALISON GILL Senior VP - Manufacturing & Operations HANK KANALZ Senior VP - Editorial Strategy & Administration
JAY KOGAN VP - Legal Affairs THOMAS LOFTUS VP - Business Affairs JACK MAHAN VP - Business Affairs
NICK J. NAPOLITANO VP - Manufacturing Administration EDDIE SCANNELL VP - Consumer Marketing
COURTNEY SIMMONS Senior VP - Publicity & Communications JIM (SKI) SOKOLOWSKI VP - Comic Book Specialty Sales & Trade Marketing
NANCY SPEARS VP - Mass, Book, Digital Sales & Trade Marketing

FUTURE QUEST VOL. 1

Published by DC Comics. Compilation and all new material Copyright © 2017 Hanna-Barbera. All Rights Reserved. Originally published in single magazine form
in FUTURE QUEST 1-6. Copyright © 2016 Hanna-Barbera. All Rights Reserved. All characters, their distinctive likenesses and related elements featured in this publication
are trademarks of Hanna-Barbera. The stories, characters and incidents featured in this publication are entirely fictional. DC Comics does not read or accept
unsolicited submissions of ideas, stories or artwork.

DC Comics, 2900 West Alameda Ave., Burbank, CA 91505
Printed by Solisco Printers, Scott, QC, Canada. 1/13/17. First Printing.
ISBN: 978-1-4012-6807-7

Library of Congress Cataloging-in-Publication Data is available.

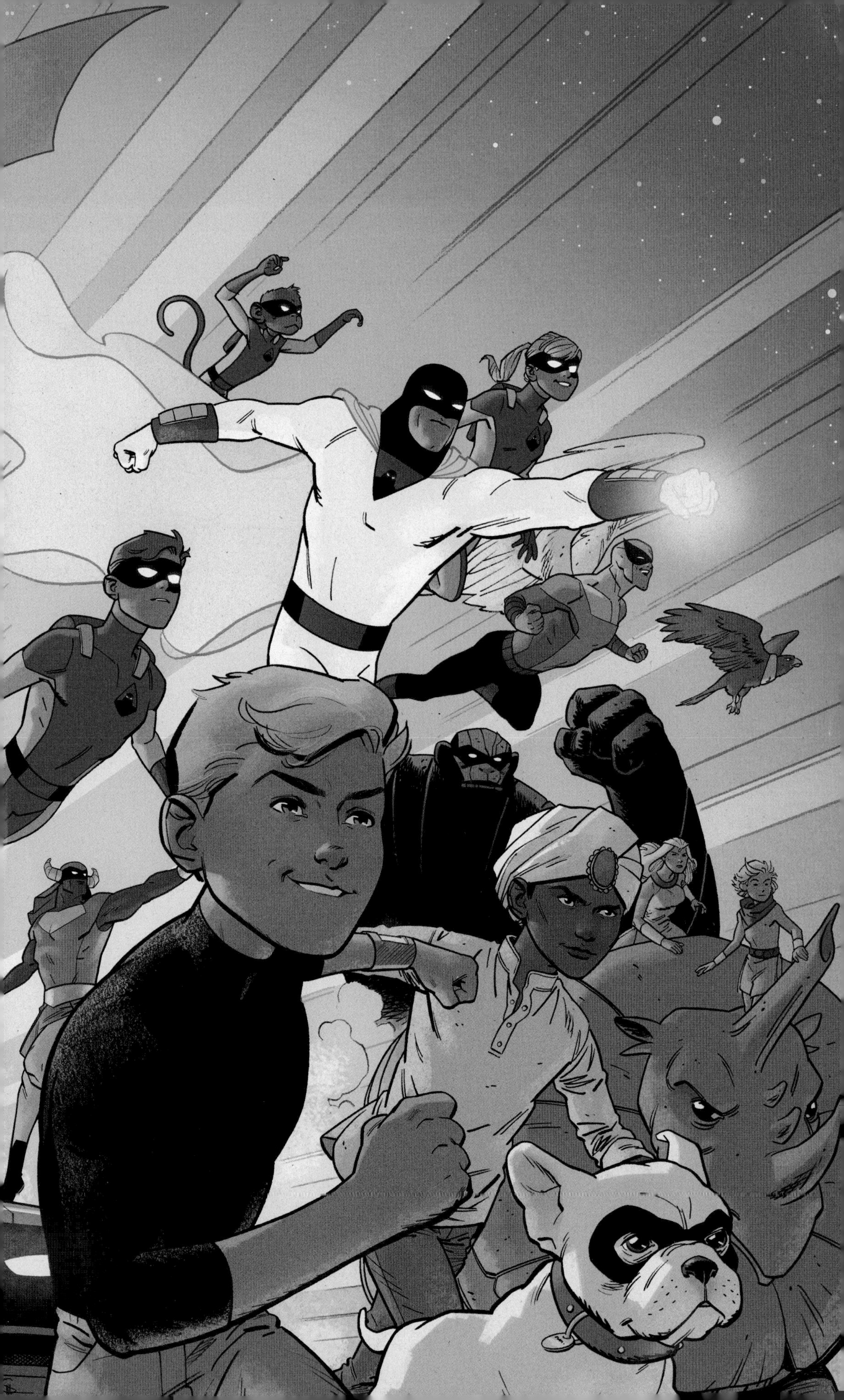

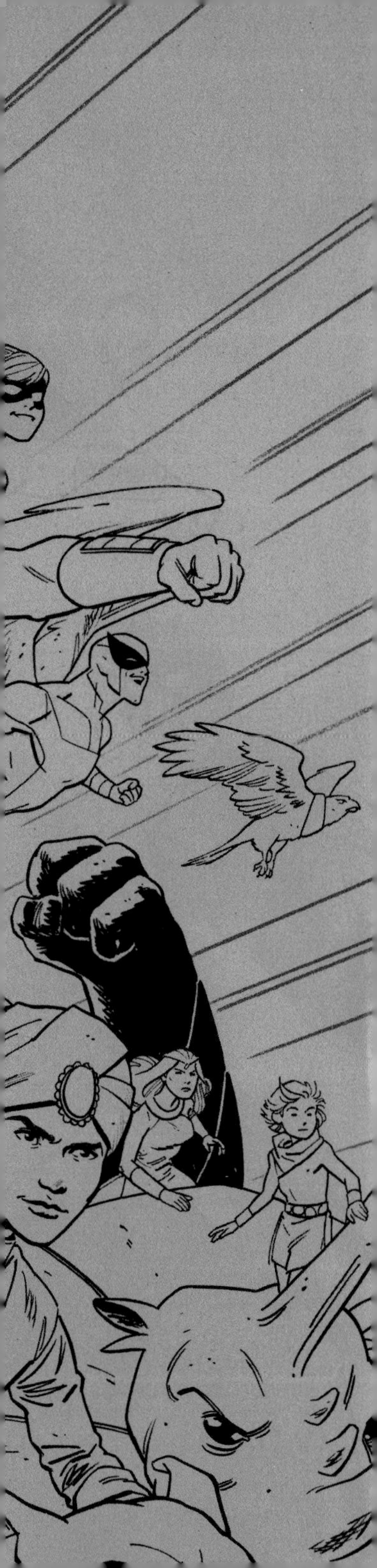

DCC037201

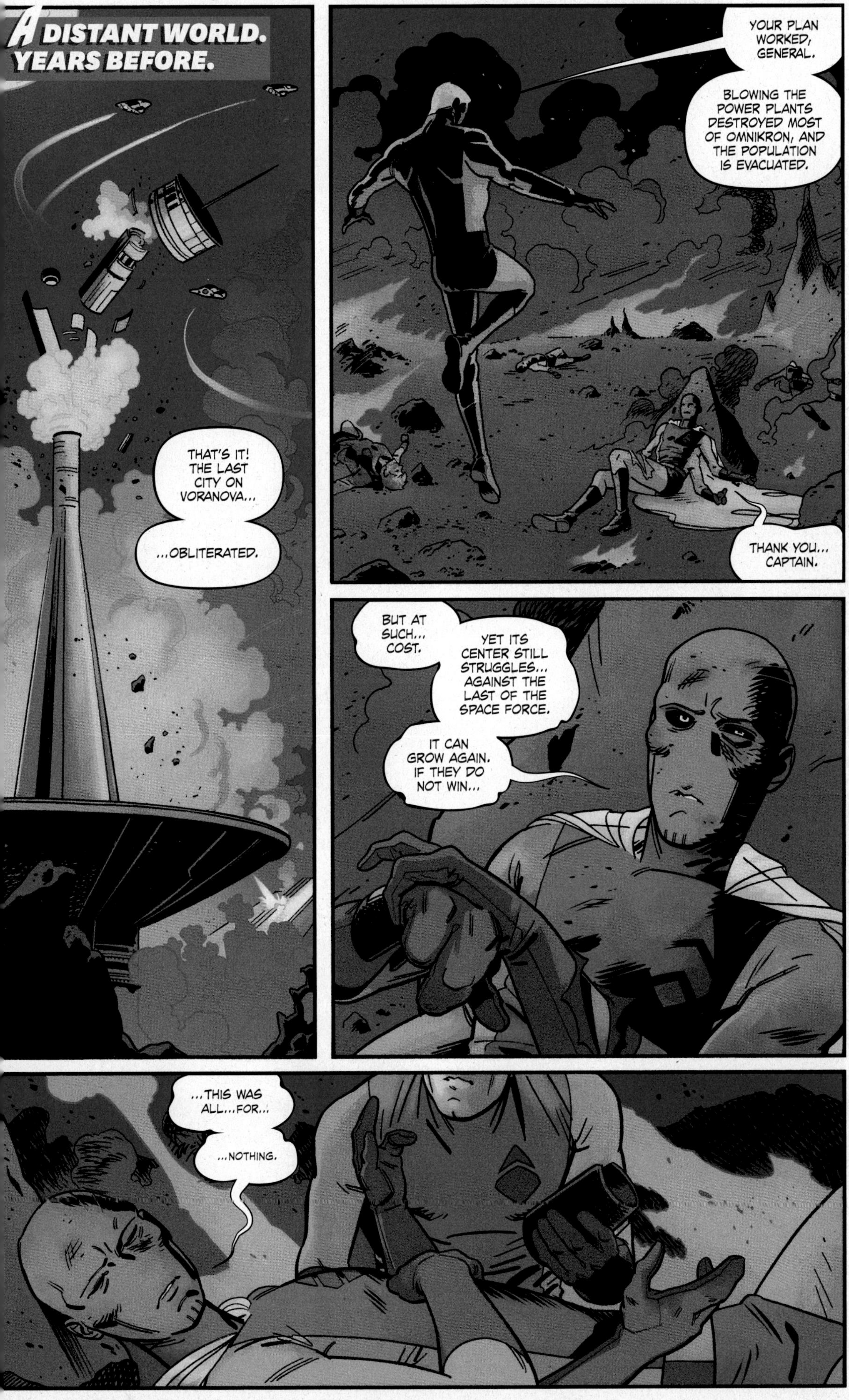
A DISTANT WORLD. YEARS BEFORE.
THAT'S IT! THE LAST CITY ON VORANOVA...
...OBLITERATED.
YOUR PLAN WORKED, GENERAL.
BLOWING THE POWER PLANTS DESTROYED MOST OF OMNIKRON, AND THE POPULATION IS EVACUATED.
THANK YOU... CAPTAIN.
BUT AT SUCH... COST.
YET ITS CENTER STILL STRUGGLES... AGAINST THE LAST OF THE SPACE FORCE.
IT CAN GROW AGAIN. IF THEY DO NOT WIN...
...THIS WAS ALL...FOR...
...NOTHING.

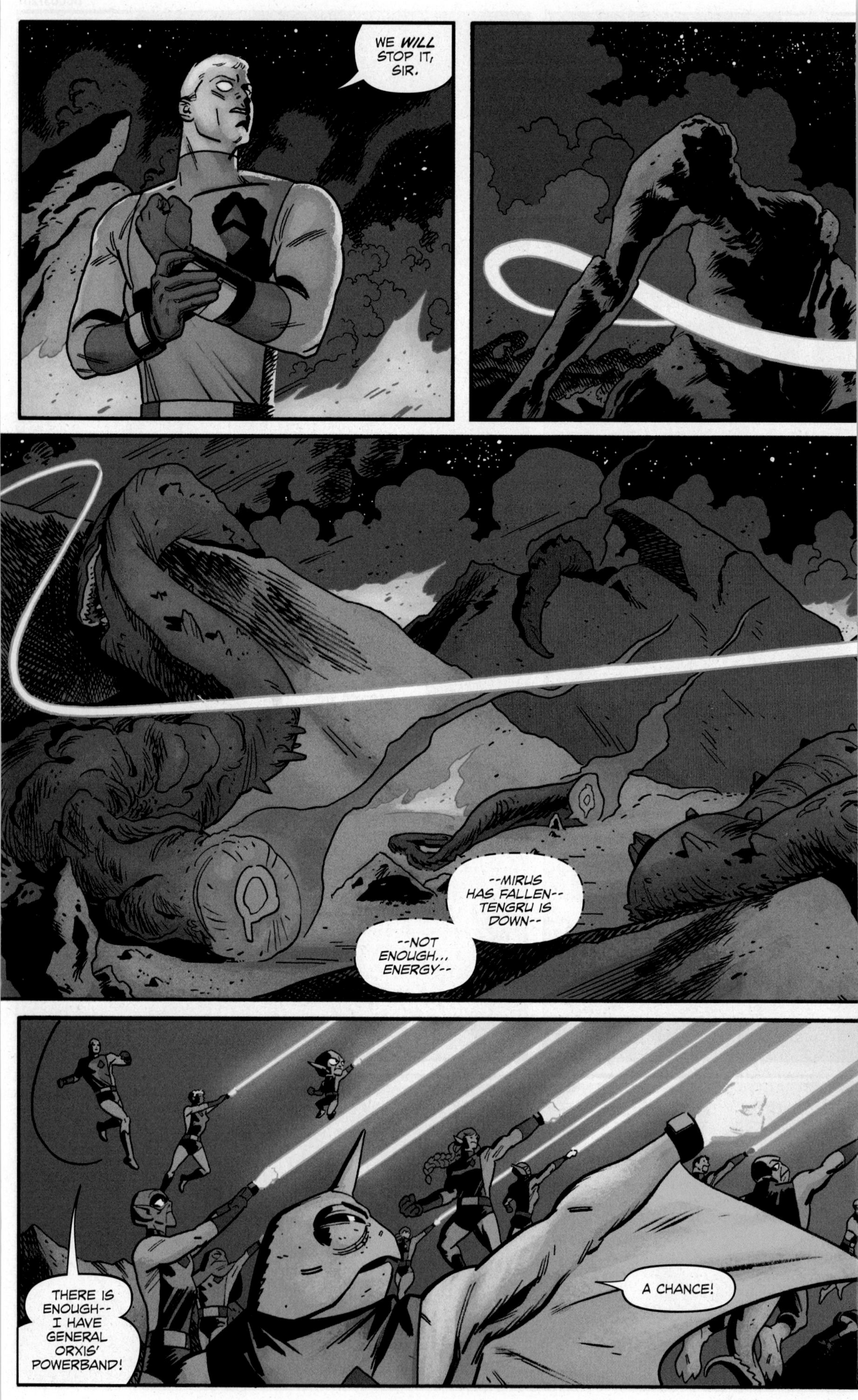
WE WILL STOP IT, SIR.
--MIRUS HAS FALLEN-- TENGRU IS DOWN--
--NOT ENOUGH... ENERGY--
THERE IS ENOUGH-- I HAVE GENERAL ORXIS' POWERBAND!
A CHANCE!

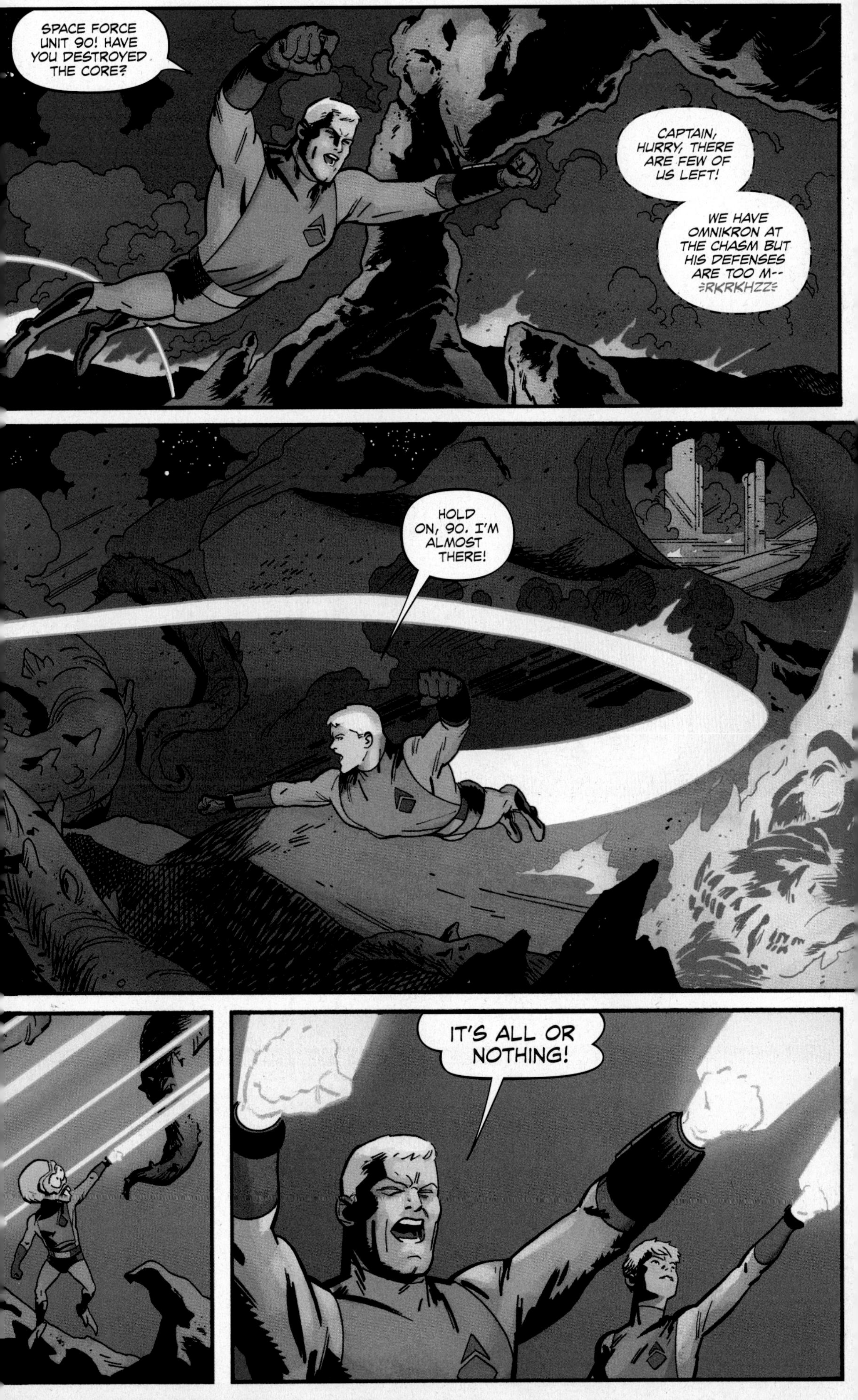
SPACE FORCE UNIT 90! HAVE YOU DESTROYED THE CORE?
CAPTAIN, HURRY, THERE ARE FEW OF US LEFT!
WE HAVE OMNIKRON AT THE CHASM BUT HIS DEFENSES ARE TOO M-- =RKRKHZZ=
HOLD ON, 90. I'M ALMOST THERE!
IT'S ALL OR NOTHING!

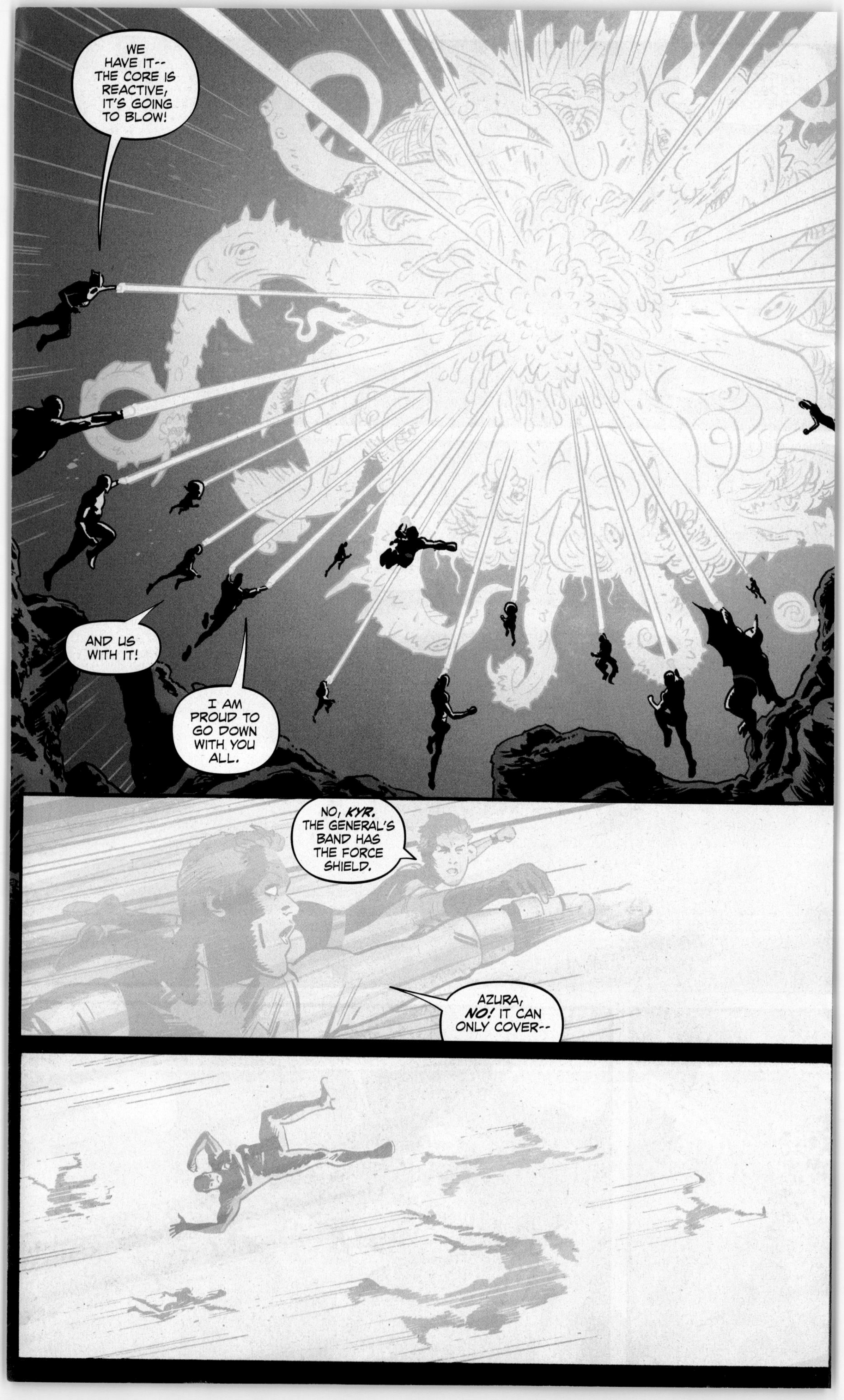
WE HAVE IT-- THE CORE IS REACTIVE, IT'S GOING TO BLOW!
AND US WITH IT!
I AM PROUD TO GO DOWN WITH YOU ALL.
NO, KYR. THE GENERAL'S BAND HAS THE FORCE SHIELD.
AZURA, NO! IT CAN ONLY COVER--

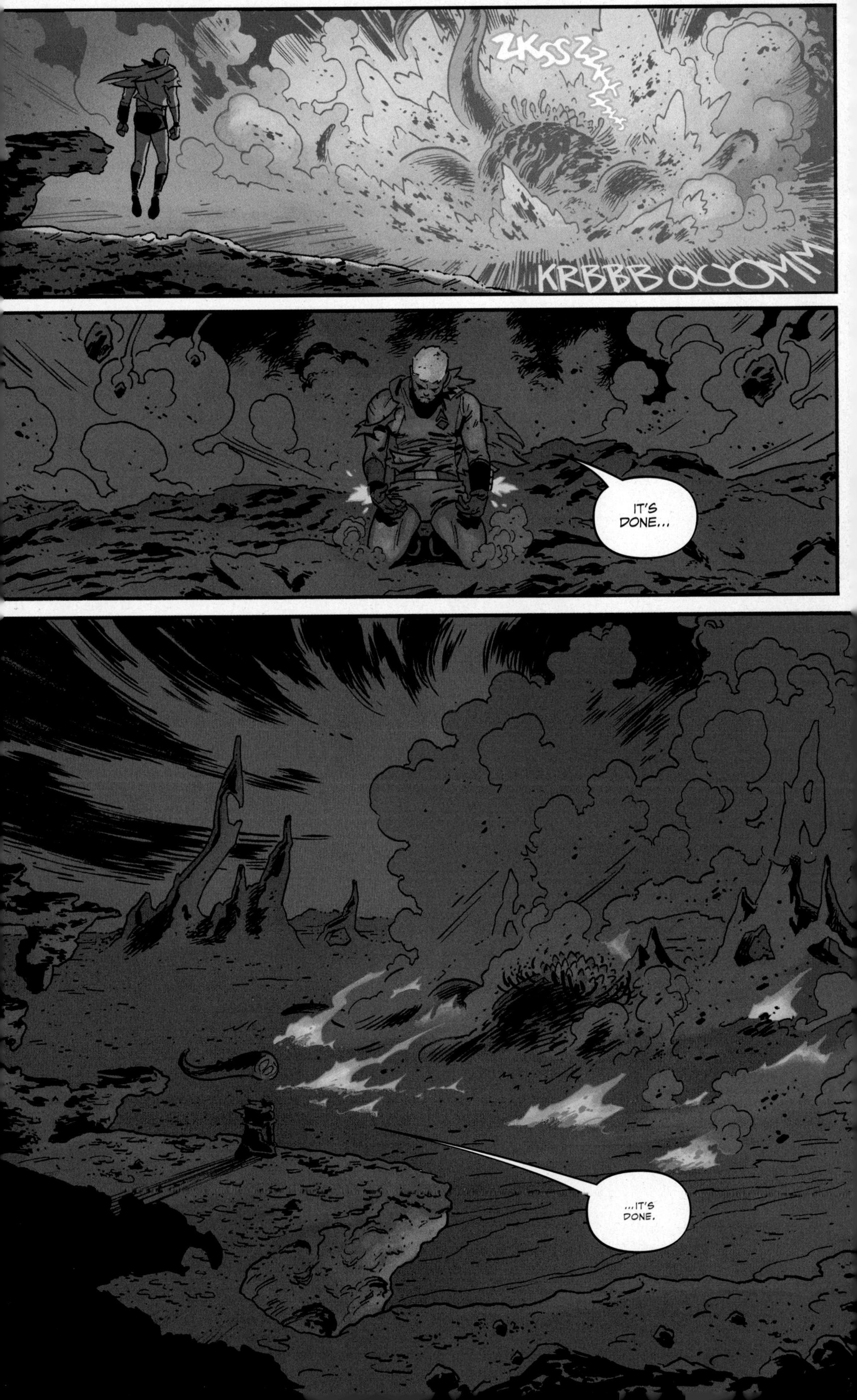
ZKSS
KRBBBOOOMM
IT'S DONE...
...IT'S DONE.

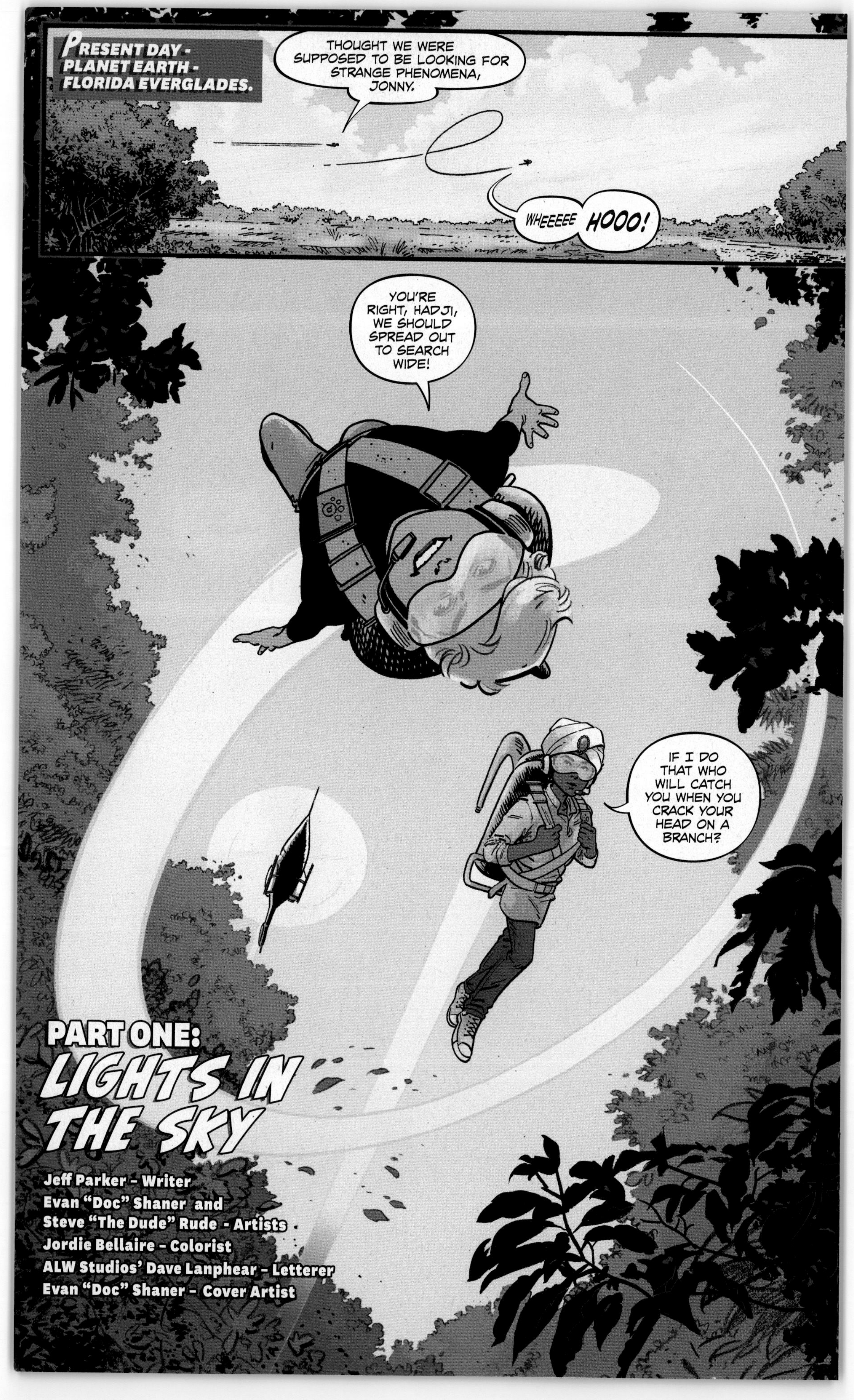

PRESENT DAY - PLANET EARTH - FLORIDA EVERGLADES.
THOUGHT WE WERE SUPPOSED TO BE LOOKING FOR STRANGE PHENOMENA, JONNY.
WHEEEEE HOOO!
YOU'RE RIGHT, HADJI, WE SHOULD SPREAD OUT TO SEARCH WIDE!
IF I DO THAT WHO WILL CATCH YOU WHEN YOU CRACK YOUR HEAD ON A BRANCH?
PART ONE:
LIGHTS IN THE SKY
Jeff Parker - Writer
Evan "Doc" Shaner and
Steve "The Dude" Rude - Artists
Jordie Bellaire - Colorist
ALW Studios' Dave Lanphear - Letterer
Evan "Doc" Shaner - Cover Artist

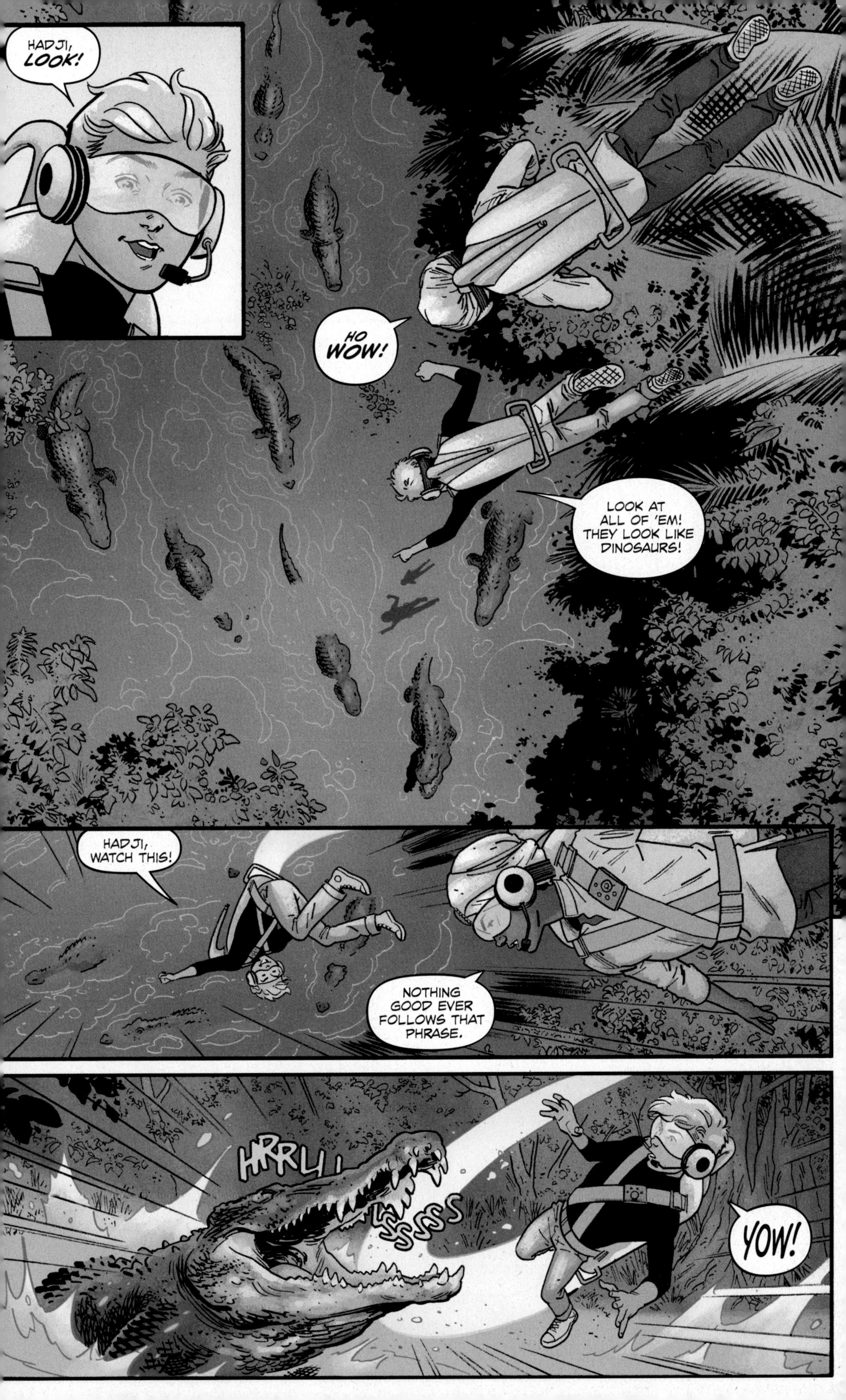
HADJI, LOOK!
HO WOW!
LOOK AT ALL OF 'EM! THEY LOOK LIKE DINOSAURS!
HADJI, WATCH THIS!
NOTHING GOOD EVER FOLLOWS THAT PHRASE.
HRRLLL
SSSSS
YOW!

...FATHER MEANT BY GOI... CLOSE FOR OBSERVAT... QUEST.

THIS IS RECONNAISSANCE, JONNY--WE'RE HERE TO OBSERVE.

DR. QUEST PREDICTS THERE'S GOING TO BE ANOTHER LIGHT SHOW TODAY AND HE NEEDS SCANS OF IT.

≋SNFFF≋

≋SNFFF≋

≋SNFFF≋

SORRY, RACE. I'LL FOCUS.

WHAT IF WE FIND A VORTEX LIKE THE LAST TIME, WITH THOSE KILLER PLANTS?!

THEN YOU BUG OUT AND LET *ME* HANDLE IT.

NOT ... TELL OUT H EARLY THE DO TAKE A IN T

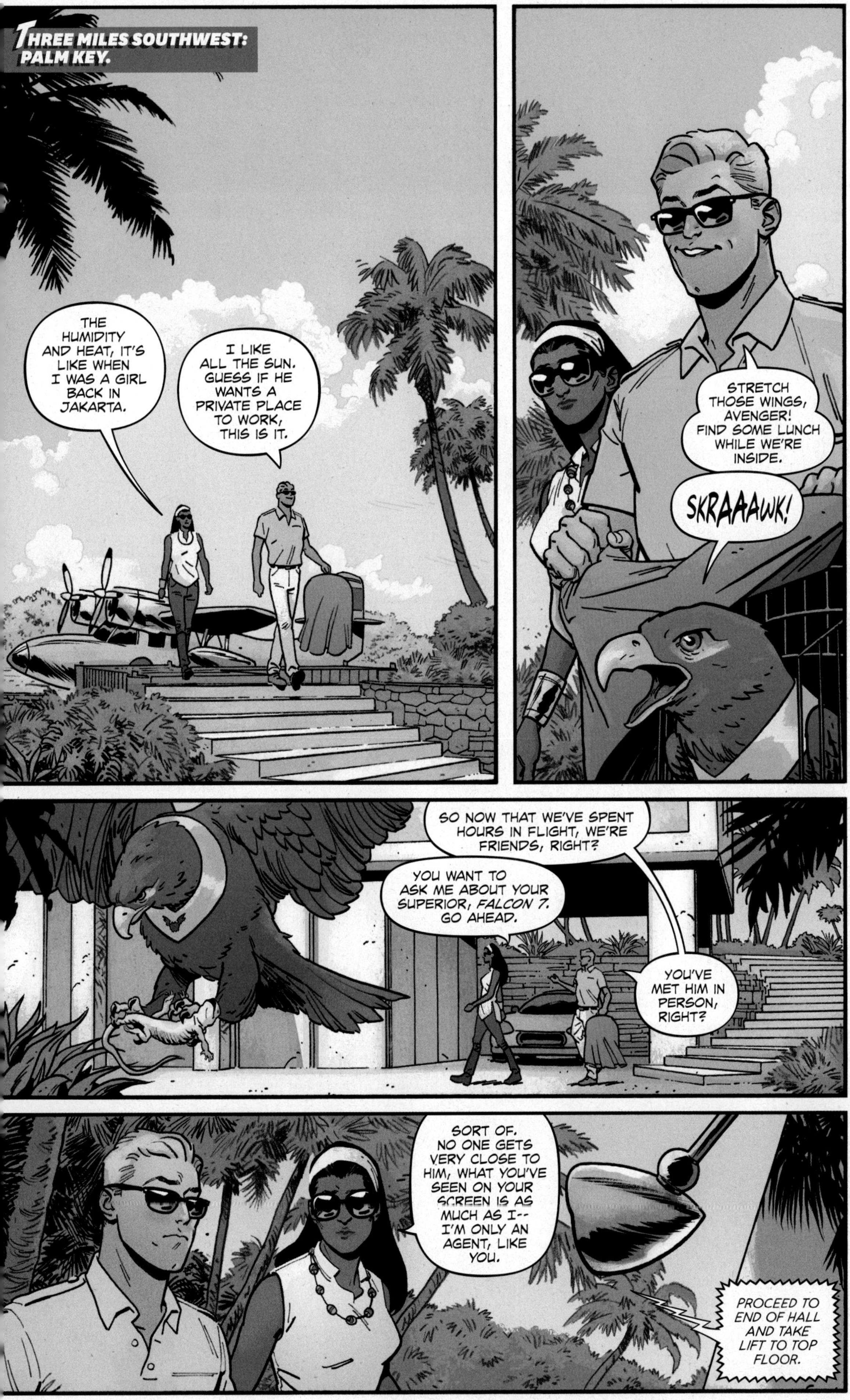
THREE MILES SOUTHWEST: PALM KEY.
THE HUMIDITY AND HEAT, IT'S LIKE WHEN I WAS A GIRL BACK IN JAKARTA.
I LIKE ALL THE SUN. GUESS IF HE WANTS A PRIVATE PLACE TO WORK, THIS IS IT.
STRETCH THOSE WINGS, AVENGER! FIND SOME LUNCH WHILE WE'RE INSIDE.
SKRAAAWK!
SO NOW THAT WE'VE SPENT HOURS IN FLIGHT, WE'RE FRIENDS, RIGHT?
YOU WANT TO ASK ME ABOUT YOUR SUPERIOR, FALCON 7. GO AHEAD.
YOU'VE MET HIM IN PERSON, RIGHT?
SORT OF. NO ONE GETS VERY CLOSE TO HIM. WHAT YOU'VE SEEN ON YOUR SCREEN IS AS MUCH AS I-- I'M ONLY AN AGENT, LIKE YOU.
PROCEED TO END OF HALL AND TAKE LIFT TO TOP FLOOR.

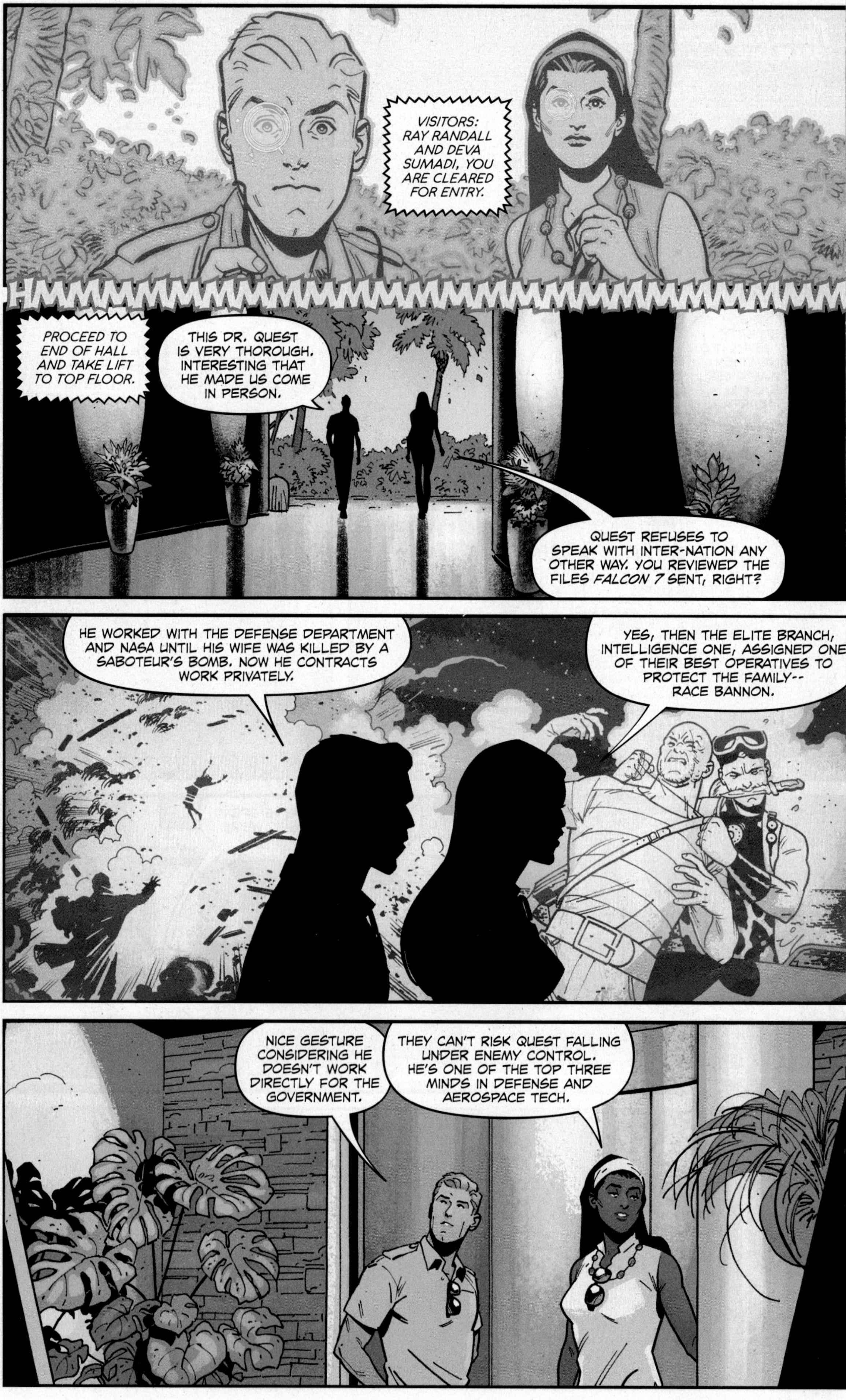
VISITORS: RAY RANDALL AND DEVA SUMADI, YOU ARE CLEARED FOR ENTRY.
HMMMMMMMMMMMMMMMMMMMMMMMMMMMMMMMM
PROCEED TO END OF HALL AND TAKE LIFT TO TOP FLOOR.
THIS DR. QUEST IS VERY THOROUGH. INTERESTING THAT HE MADE US COME IN PERSON.
QUEST REFUSES TO SPEAK WITH INTER-NATION ANY OTHER WAY. YOU REVIEWED THE FILES FALCON 7 SENT, RIGHT?
HE WORKED WITH THE DEFENSE DEPARTMENT AND NASA UNTIL HIS WIFE WAS KILLED BY A SABOTEUR'S BOMB. NOW HE CONTRACTS WORK PRIVATELY.
YES, THEN THE ELITE BRANCH, INTELLIGENCE ONE, ASSIGNED ONE OF THEIR BEST OPERATIVES TO PROTECT THE FAMILY-- RACE BANNON.
NICE GESTURE CONSIDERING HE DOESN'T WORK DIRECTLY FOR THE GOVERNMENT.
THEY CAN'T RISK QUEST FALLING UNDER ENEMY CONTROL. HE'S ONE OF THE TOP THREE MINDS IN DEFENSE AND AEROSPACE TECH.

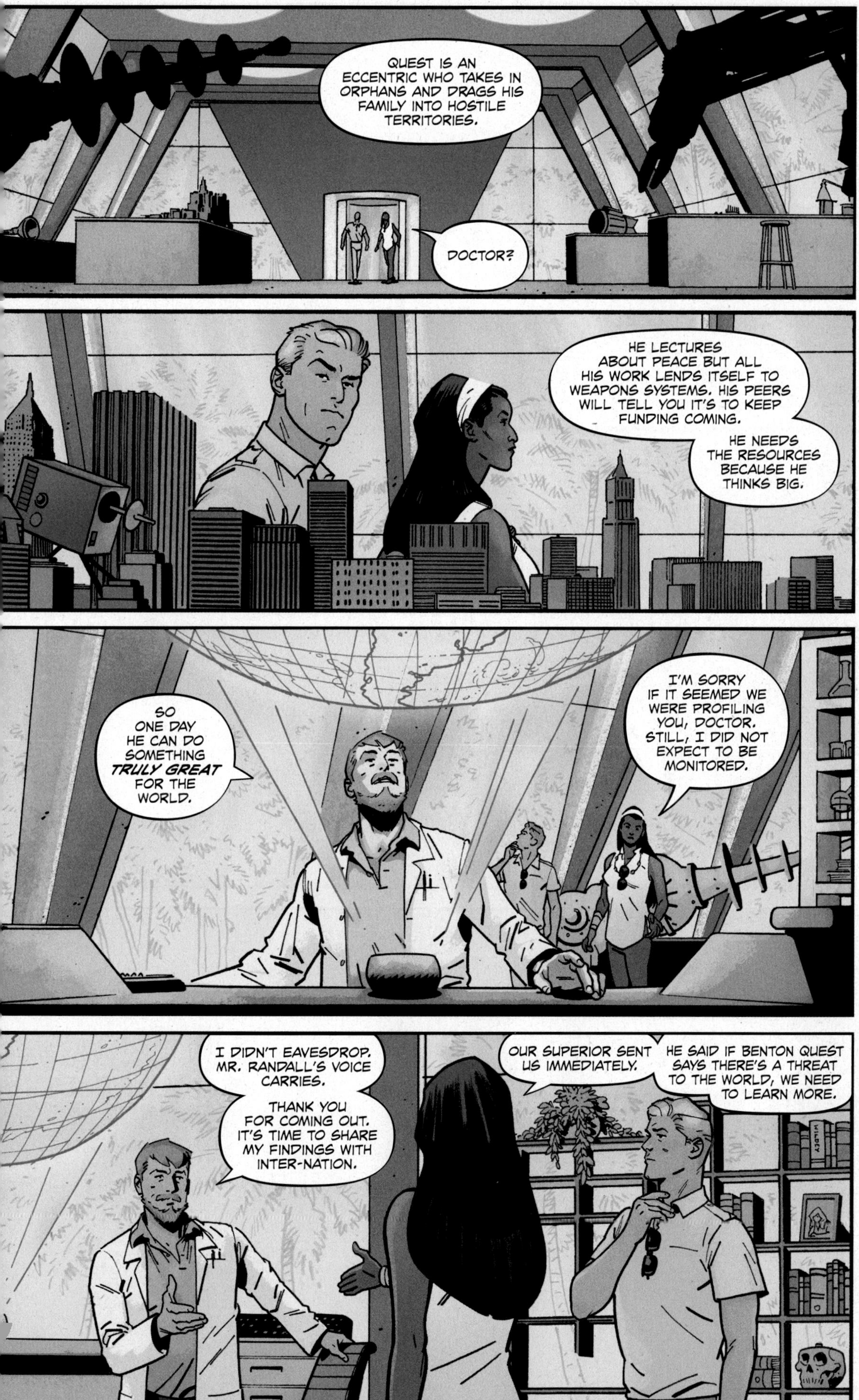
QUEST IS AN ECCENTRIC WHO TAKES IN ORPHANS AND DRAGS HIS FAMILY INTO HOSTILE TERRITORIES.
DOCTOR?
HE LECTURES ABOUT PEACE BUT ALL HIS WORK LENDS ITSELF TO WEAPONS SYSTEMS. HIS PEERS WILL TELL YOU IT'S TO KEEP FUNDING COMING.
HE NEEDS THE RESOURCES BECAUSE HE THINKS BIG.
SO ONE DAY HE CAN DO SOMETHING TRULY GREAT FOR THE WORLD.
I'M SORRY IF IT SEEMED WE WERE PROFILING YOU, DOCTOR. STILL, I DID NOT EXPECT TO BE MONITORED.
I DIDN'T EAVESDROP. MR. RANDALL'S VOICE CARRIES.
THANK YOU FOR COMING OUT. IT'S TIME TO SHARE MY FINDINGS WITH INTER-NATION.
OUR SUPERIOR SENT US IMMEDIATELY.
HE SAID IF BENTON QUEST SAYS THERE'S A THREAT TO THE WORLD, WE NEED TO LEARN MORE.

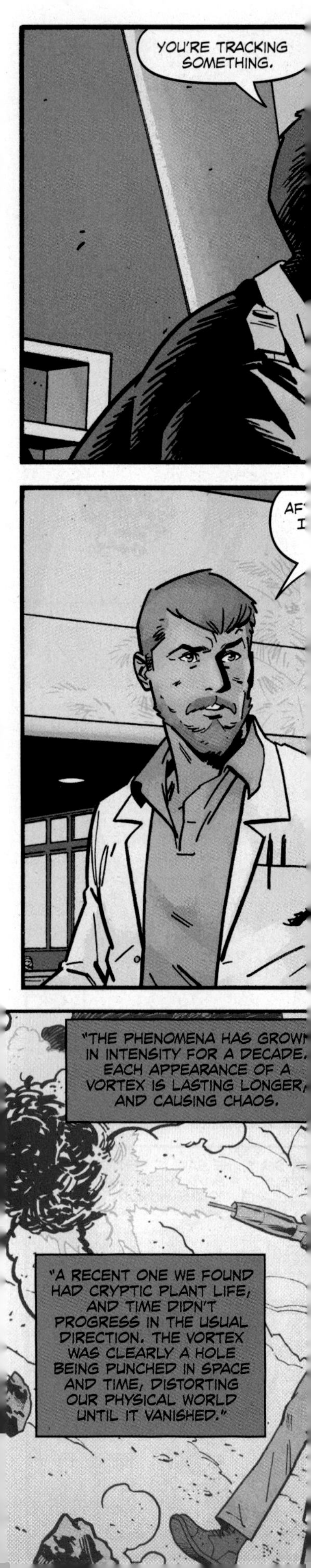
YOU'RE TRACKING SOMETHING.
"THE PHENOMENA HAS GROW IN INTENSITY FOR A DECADE. EACH APPEARANCE OF A VORTEX IS LASTING LONGER, AND CAUSING CHAOS.
"A RECENT ONE WE FOUND HAD CRYPTIC PLANT LIFE, AND TIME DIDN'T PROGRESS IN THE USUAL DIRECTION. THE VORTEX WAS CLEARLY A HOLE BEING PUNCHED IN SPACE AND TIME, DISTORTING OUR PHYSICAL WORLD UNTIL IT VANISHED."

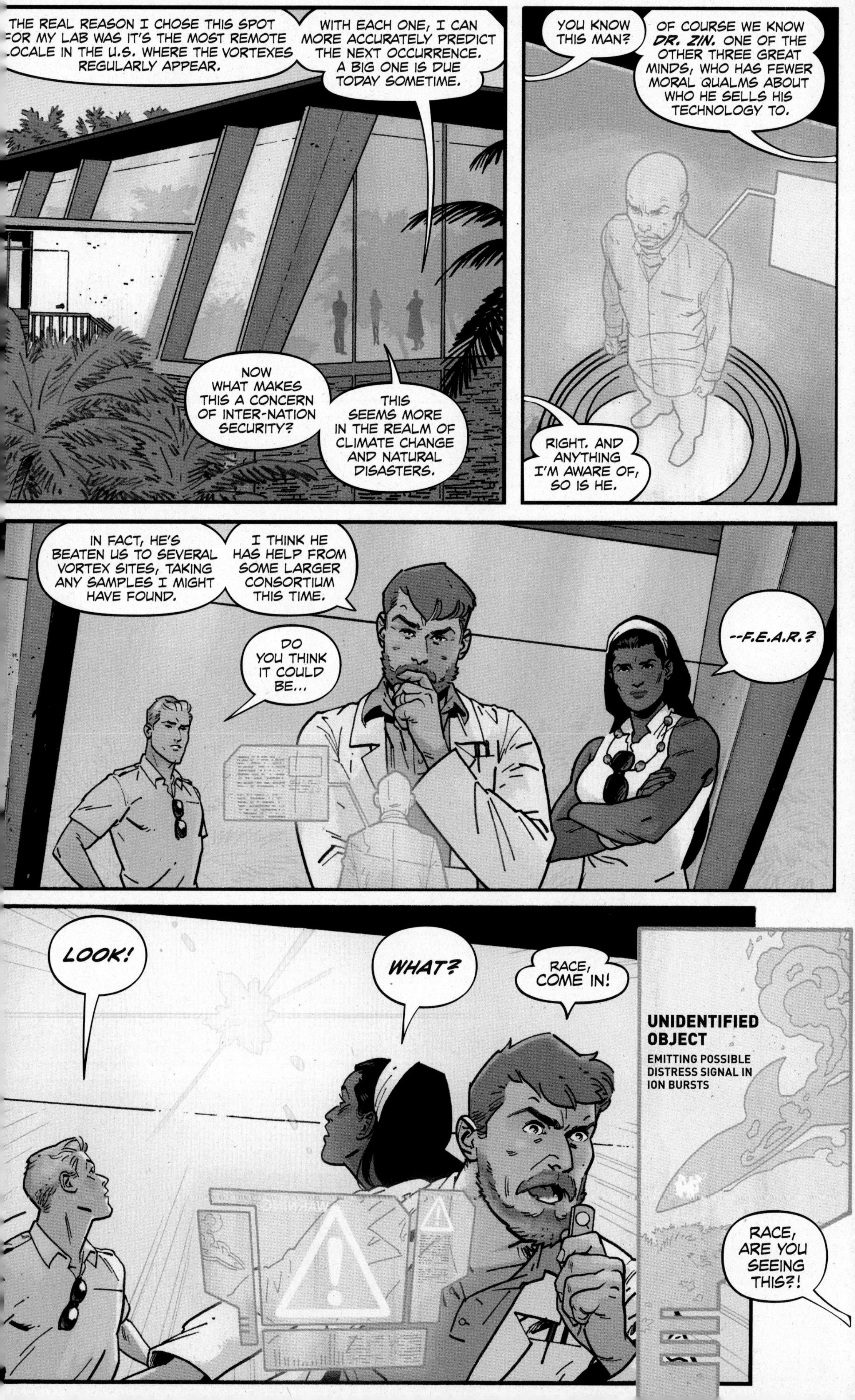

THE REAL REASON I CHOSE THIS SPOT FOR MY LAB WAS IT'S THE MOST REMOTE LOCALE IN THE U.S. WHERE THE VORTEXES REGULARLY APPEAR.
WITH EACH ONE, I CAN MORE ACCURATELY PREDICT THE NEXT OCCURRENCE. A BIG ONE IS DUE TODAY SOMETIME.
NOW WHAT MAKES THIS A CONCERN OF INTER-NATION SECURITY?
THIS SEEMS MORE IN THE REALM OF CLIMATE CHANGE AND NATURAL DISASTERS.
YOU KNOW THIS MAN?
OF COURSE WE KNOW DR. ZIN. ONE OF THE OTHER THREE GREAT MINDS, WHO HAS FEWER MORAL QUALMS ABOUT WHO HE SELLS HIS TECHNOLOGY TO.
RIGHT. AND ANYTHING I'M AWARE OF, SO IS HE.
IN FACT, HE'S BEATEN US TO SEVERAL VORTEX SITES, TAKING ANY SAMPLES I MIGHT HAVE FOUND.
I THINK HE HAS HELP FROM SOME LARGER CONSORTIUM THIS TIME.
DO YOU THINK IT COULD BE...
--F.E.A.R.?
LOOK!
WHAT?
RACE, COME IN!
UNIDENTIFIED OBJECT
EMITTING POSSIBLE DISTRESS SIGNAL IN ION BURSTS
RACE, ARE YOU SEEING THIS?!

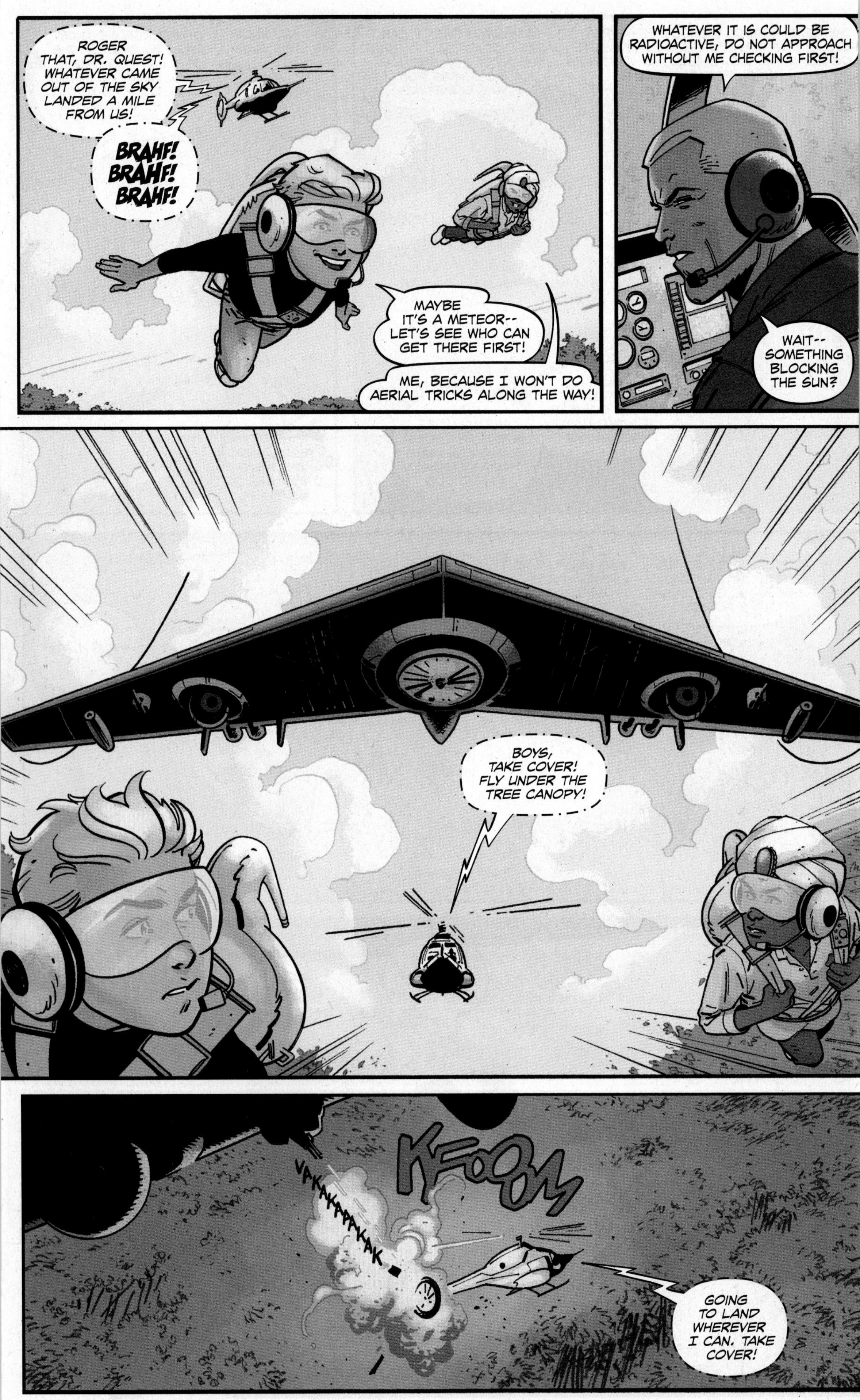
ROGER THAT, DR. QUEST! WHATEVER CAME OUT OF THE SKY LANDED A MILE FROM US!
BRAHF! BRAHF! BRAHF!
MAYBE IT'S A METEOR-- LET'S SEE WHO CAN GET THERE FIRST!
ME, BECAUSE I WON'T DO AERIAL TRICKS ALONG THE WAY!
WHATEVER IT IS COULD BE RADIOACTIVE, DO NOT APPROACH WITHOUT ME CHECKING FIRST!
WAIT-- SOMETHING BLOCKING THE SUN?
BOYS, TAKE COVER! FLY UNDER THE TREE CANOPY!
KFOOOM
VAKAKAPPAKAK
GOING TO LAND WHEREVER I CAN. TAKE COVER!

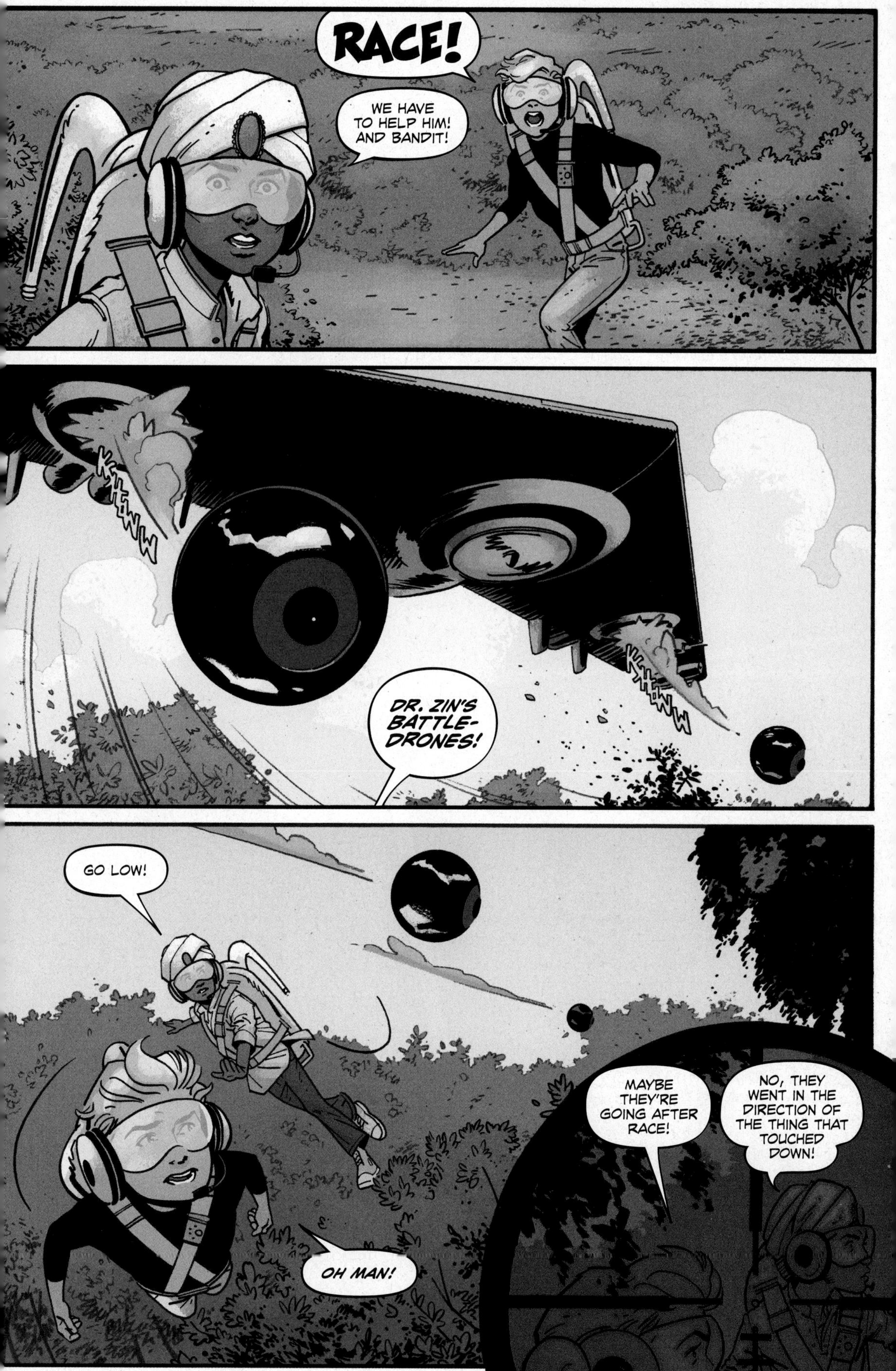
RACE!
WE HAVE TO HELP HIM! AND BANDIT!
KSHEWW
DR. ZIN'S BATTLE-DRONES!
KSHEWW
GO LOW!
OH MAN!
MAYBE THEY'RE GOING AFTER RACE!
NO, THEY WENT IN THE DIRECTION OF THE THING THAT TOUCHED DOWN!

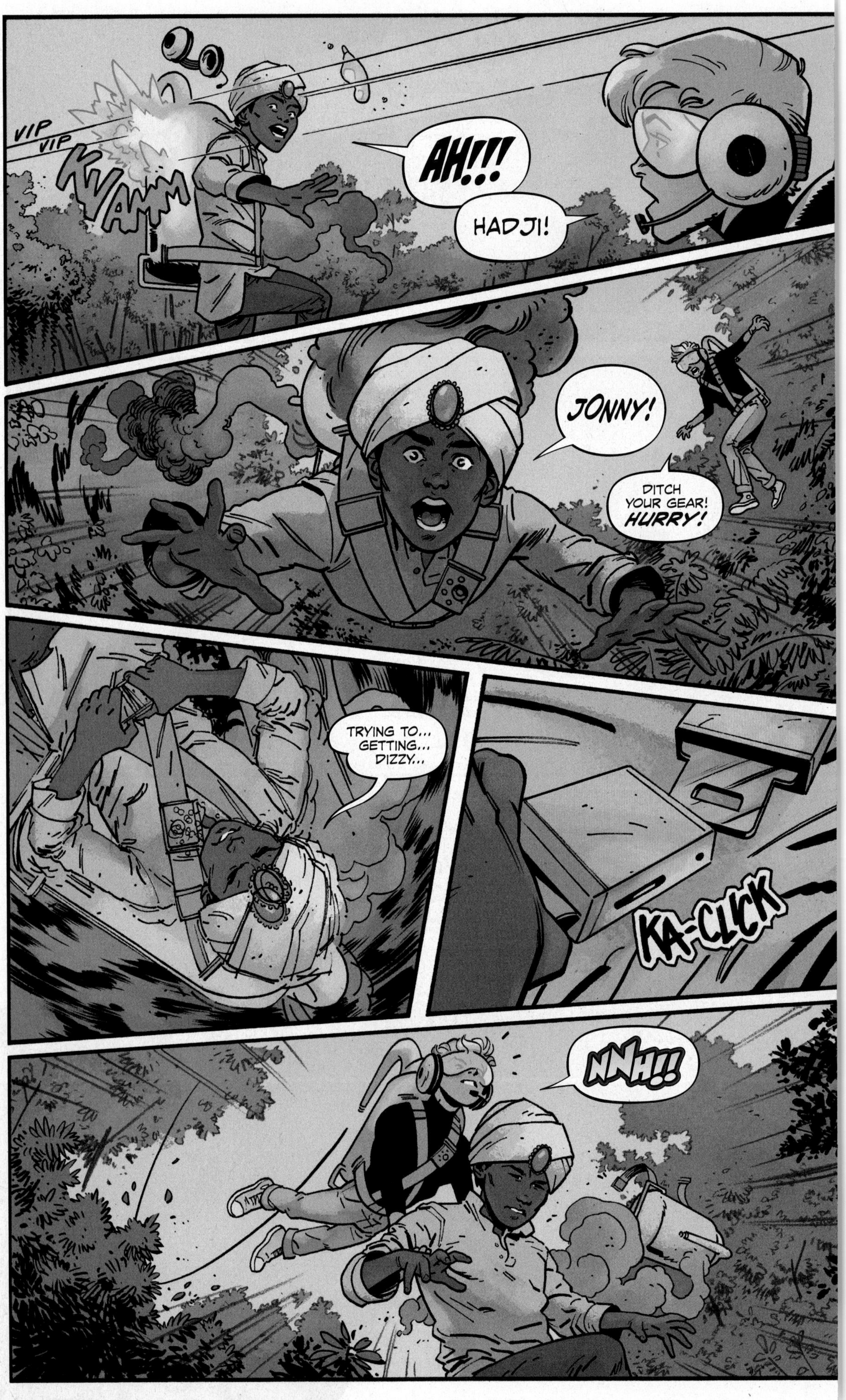
VIP
VIP
KVAMM
AH!!!
HADJI!
JONNY!
DITCH YOUR GEAR! HURRY!
TRYING TO... GETTING... DIZZY...
KA-CLCK
NNH!!

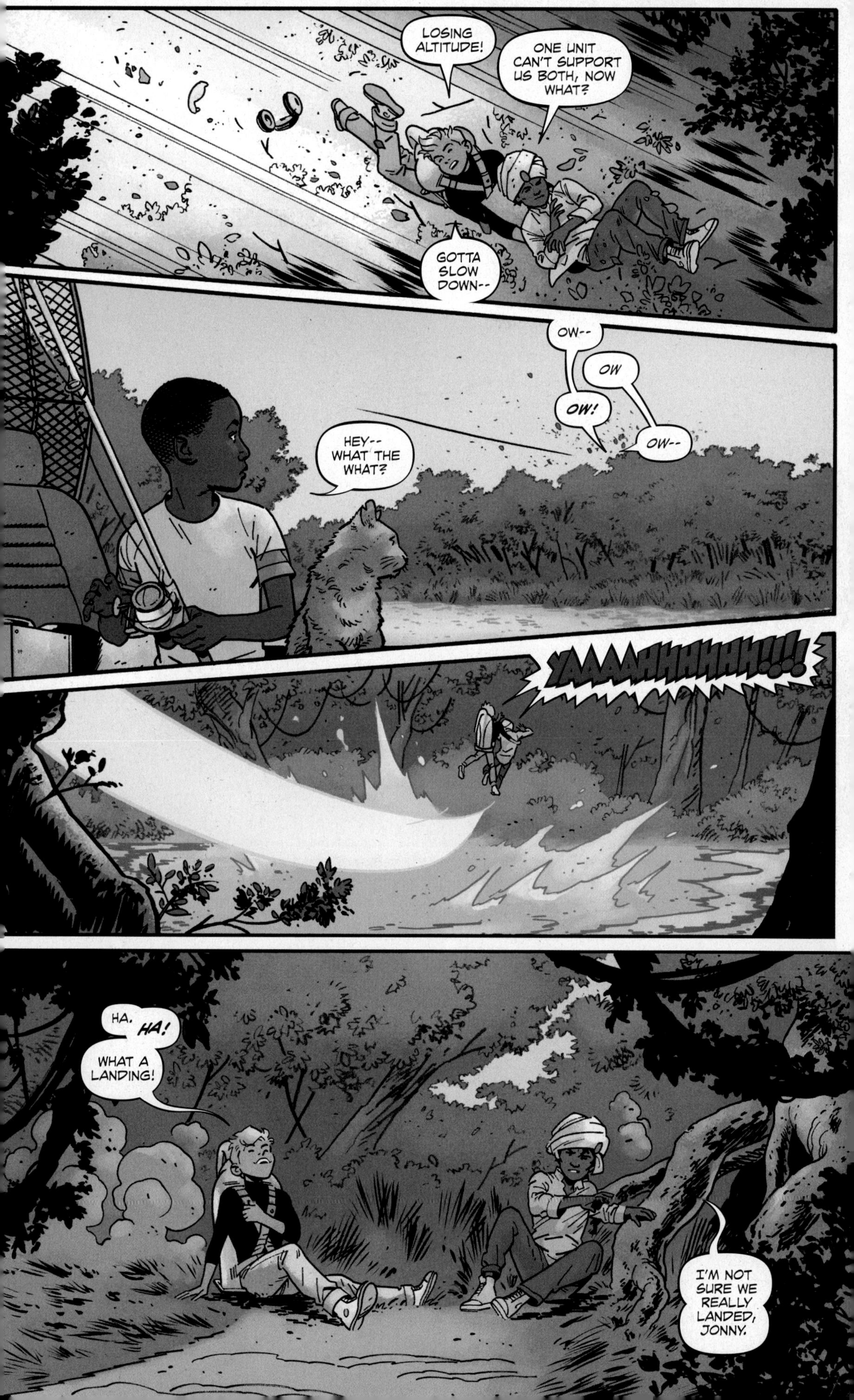
LOSING ALTITUDE!
ONE UNIT CAN'T SUPPORT US BOTH, NOW WHAT?
GOTTA SLOW DOWN--
OW--
OW
OW!
OW--
HEY-- WHAT THE WHAT?
YAAAAHHHHHH!!!!
HA. HA!
WHAT A LANDING!
I'M NOT SURE WE REALLY LANDED, JONNY.

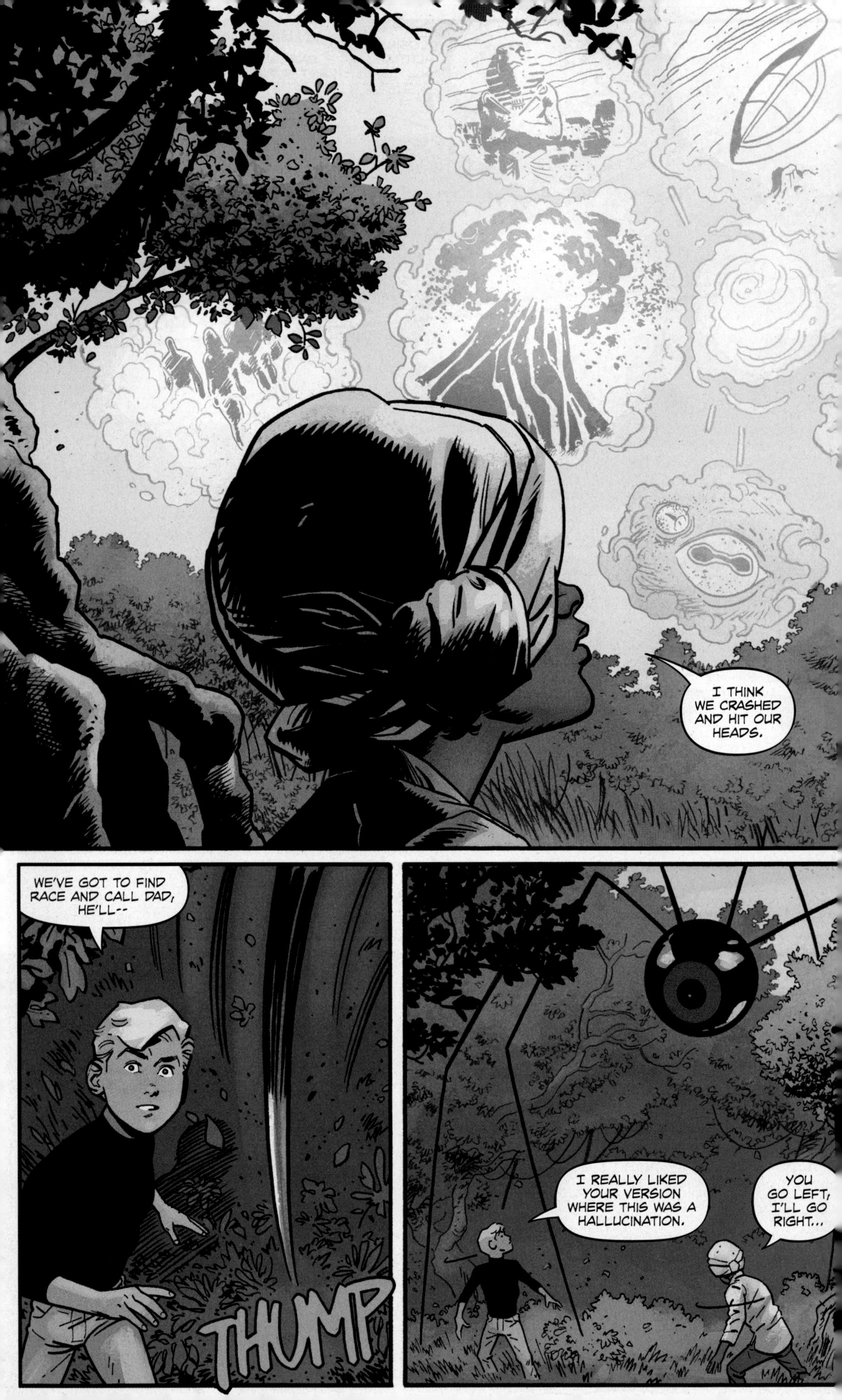
I THINK WE CRASHED AND HIT OUR HEADS.
WE'VE GOT TO FIND RACE AND CALL DAD, HE'LL--
THUMP
I REALLY LIKED YOUR VERSION WHERE THIS WAS A HALLUCINATION.
YOU GO LEFT, I'LL GO RIGHT...

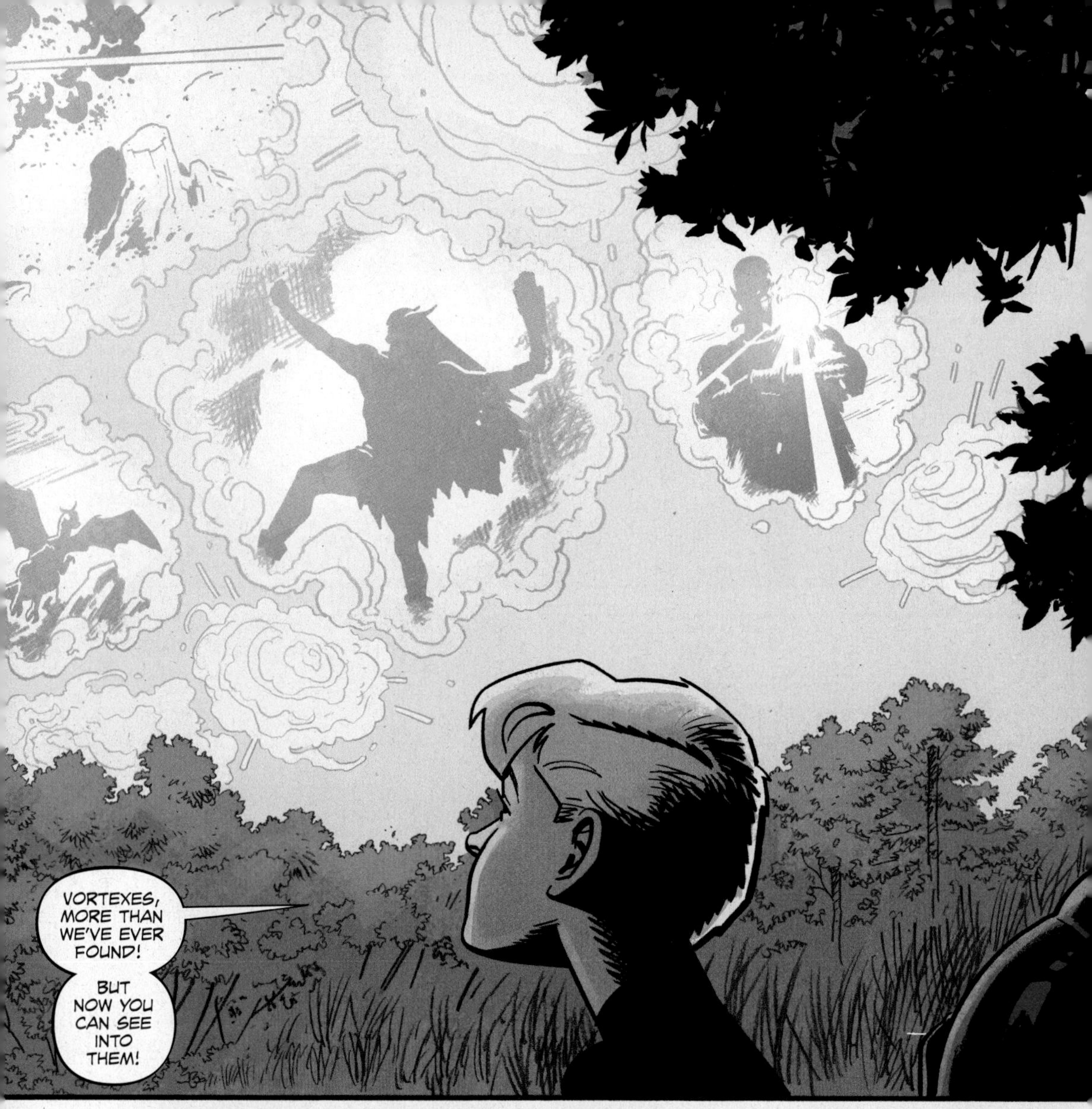
VORTEXES, MORE THAN WE'VE EVER FOUND!
BUT NOW YOU CAN SEE INTO THEM!

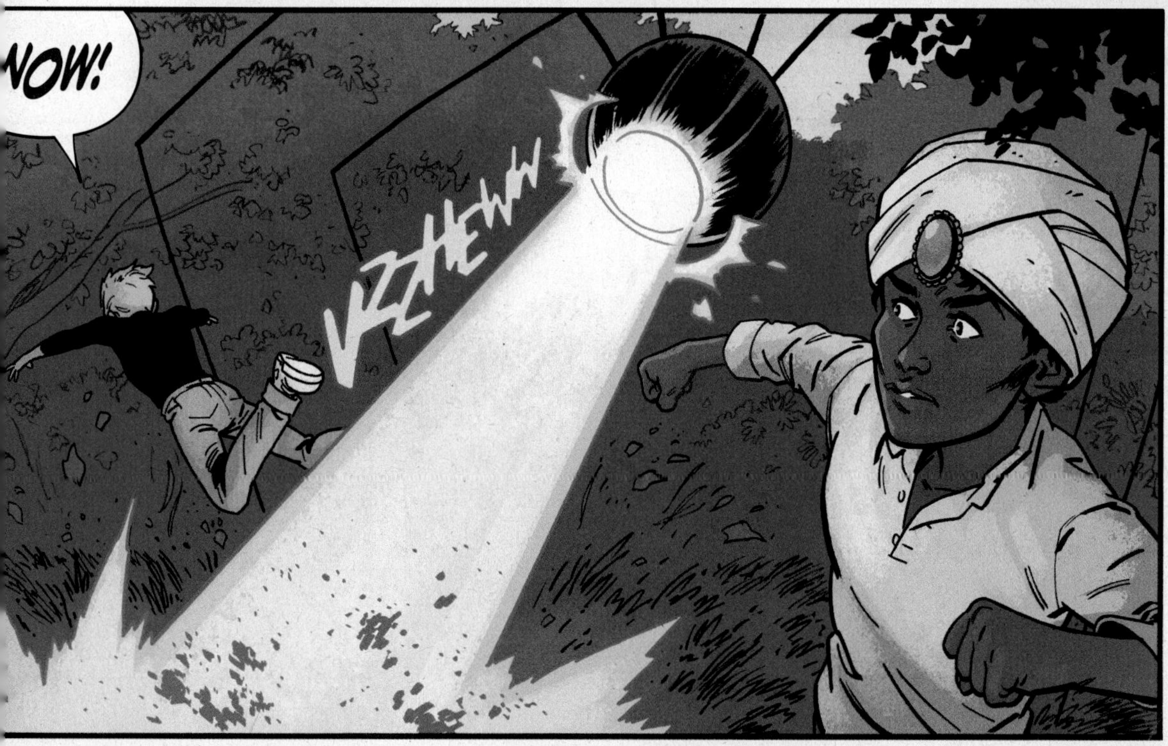
NOW!
VZZHEWW

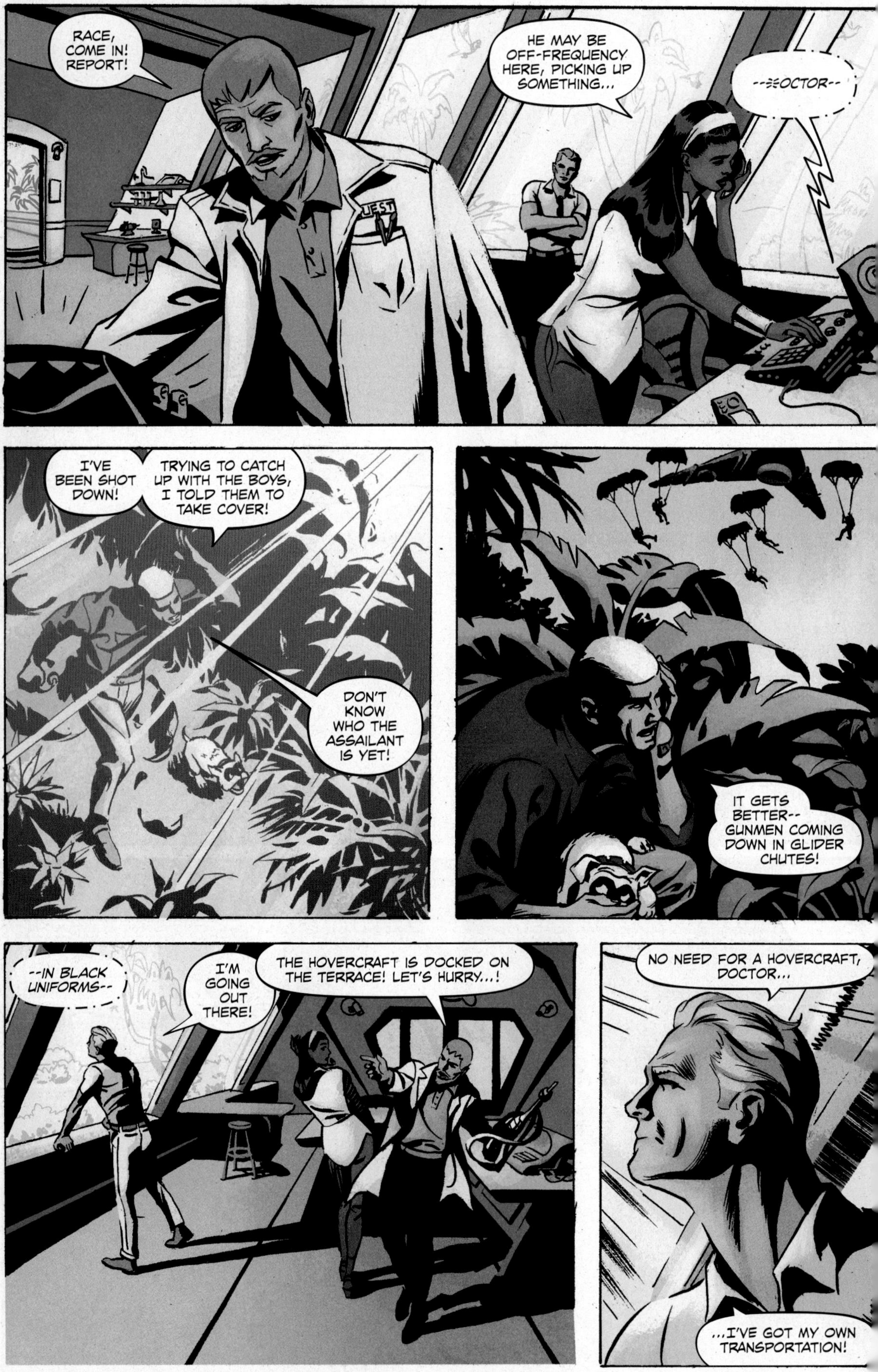
RACE, COME IN! REPORT!
HE MAY BE OFF-FREQUENCY HERE, PICKING UP SOMETHING...
--=OCTOR--
I'VE BEEN SHOT DOWN!
TRYING TO CATCH UP WITH THE BOYS, I TOLD THEM TO TAKE COVER!
DON'T KNOW WHO THE ASSAILANT IS YET!
IT GETS BETTER-- GUNMEN COMING DOWN IN GLIDER CHUTES!
--IN BLACK UNIFORMS--
I'M GOING OUT THERE!
THE HOVERCRAFT IS DOCKED ON THE TERRACE! LET'S HURRY...!
NO NEED FOR A HOVERCRAFT, DOCTOR...
...I'VE GOT MY OWN TRANSPORTATION!

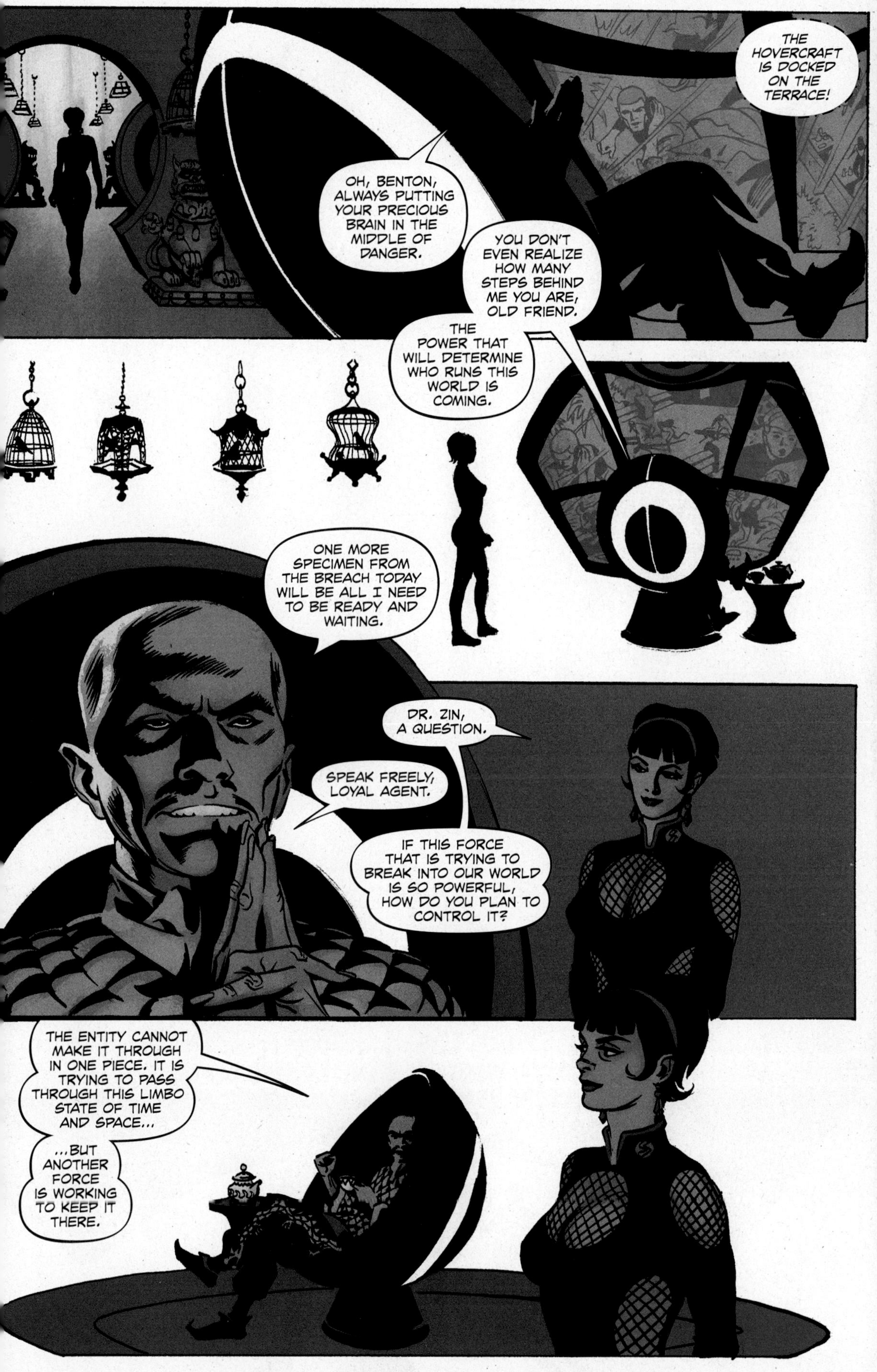
THE HOVERCRAFT IS DOCKED ON THE TERRACE!
OH, BENTON, ALWAYS PUTTING YOUR PRECIOUS BRAIN IN THE MIDDLE OF DANGER.
YOU DON'T EVEN REALIZE HOW MANY STEPS BEHIND ME YOU ARE, OLD FRIEND.
THE POWER THAT WILL DETERMINE WHO RUNS THIS WORLD IS COMING.
ONE MORE SPECIMEN FROM THE BREACH TODAY WILL BE ALL I NEED TO BE READY AND WAITING.
DR. ZIN, A QUESTION.
SPEAK FREELY, LOYAL AGENT.
IF THIS FORCE THAT IS TRYING TO BREAK INTO OUR WORLD IS SO POWERFUL, HOW DO YOU PLAN TO CONTROL IT?
THE ENTITY CANNOT MAKE IT THROUGH IN ONE PIECE. IT IS TRYING TO PASS THROUGH THIS LIMBO STATE OF TIME AND SPACE...
...BUT ANOTHER FORCE IS WORKING TO KEEP IT THERE.

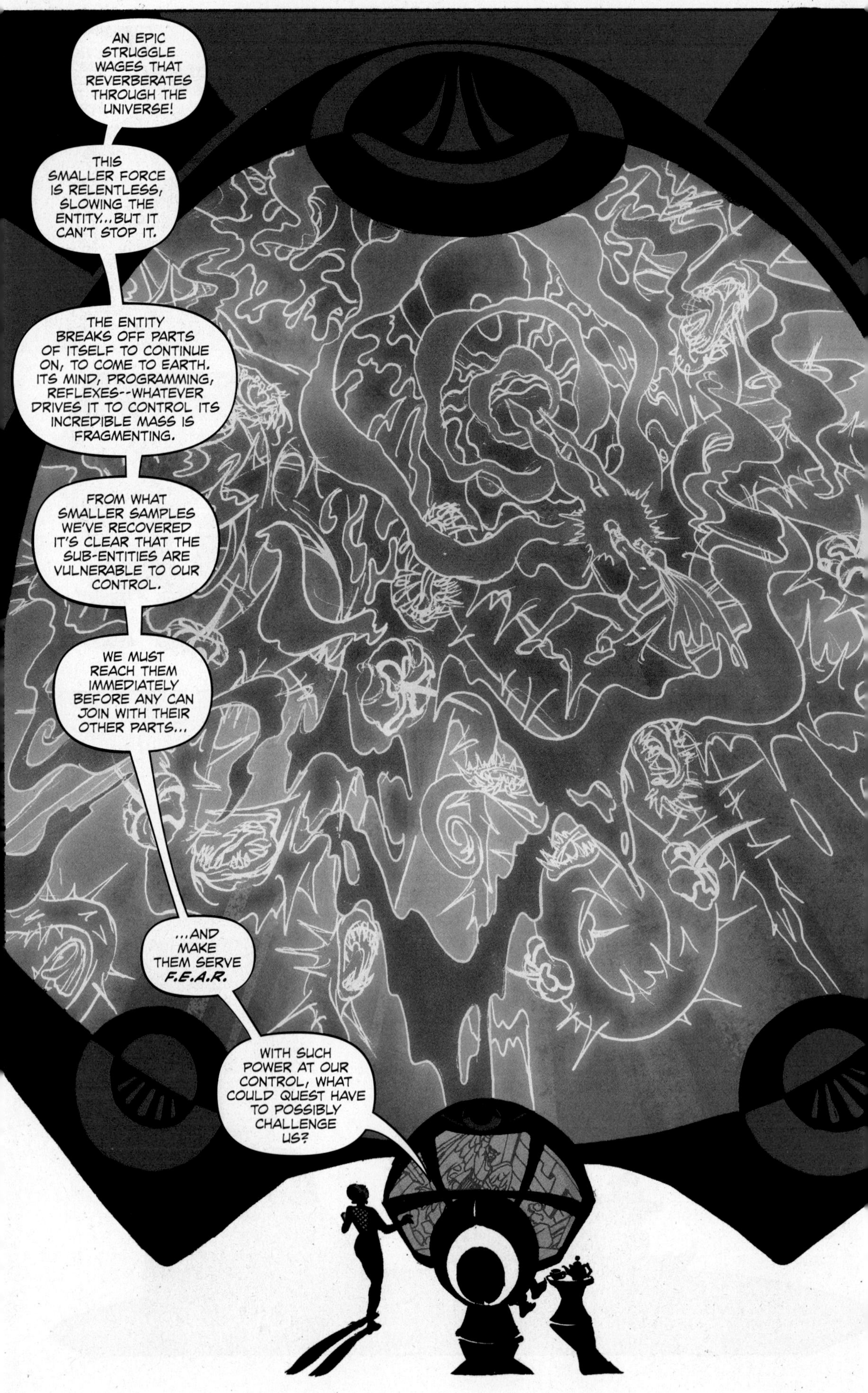
AN EPIC STRUGGLE WAGES THAT REVERBERATES THROUGH THE UNIVERSE!
THIS SMALLER FORCE IS RELENTLESS, SLOWING THE ENTITY...BUT IT CAN'T STOP IT.
THE ENTITY BREAKS OFF PARTS OF ITSELF TO CONTINUE ON, TO COME TO EARTH. ITS MIND, PROGRAMMING, REFLEXES--WHATEVER DRIVES IT TO CONTROL ITS INCREDIBLE MASS IS FRAGMENTING.
FROM WHAT SMALLER SAMPLES WE'VE RECOVERED IT'S CLEAR THAT THE SUB-ENTITIES ARE VULNERABLE TO OUR CONTROL.
WE MUST REACH THEM IMMEDIATELY BEFORE ANY CAN JOIN WITH THEIR OTHER PARTS...
...AND MAKE THEM SERVE *F.E.A.R.*
WITH SUCH POWER AT OUR CONTROL, WHAT COULD QUEST HAVE TO POSSIBLY CHALLENGE US?

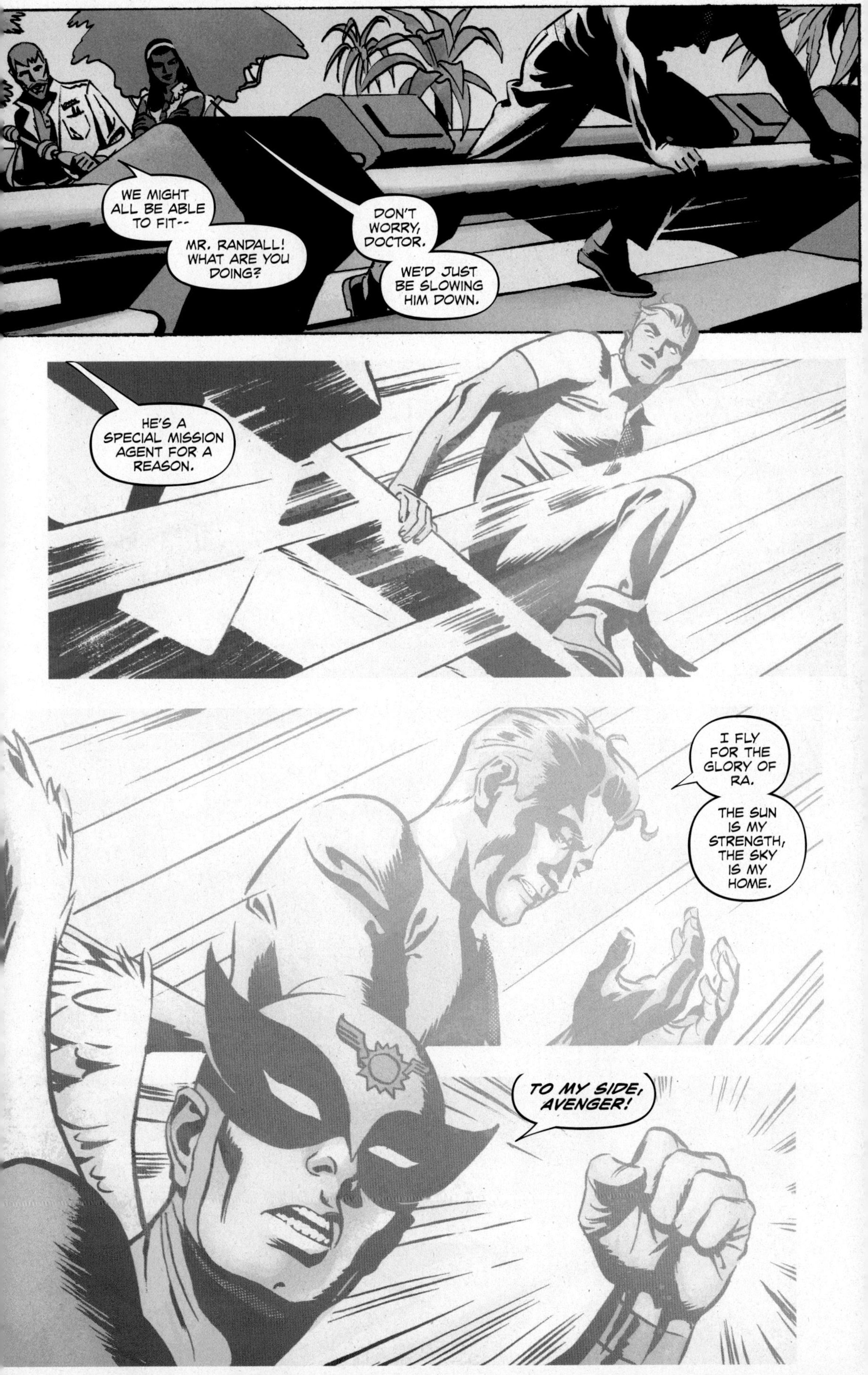
WE MIGHT ALL BE ABLE TO FIT--
MR. RANDALL! WHAT ARE YOU DOING?
DON'T WORRY, DOCTOR.
WE'D JUST BE SLOWING HIM DOWN.
HE'S A SPECIAL MISSION AGENT FOR A REASON.
I FLY FOR THE GLORY OF RA.
THE SUN IS MY STRENGTH, THE SKY IS MY HOME.
TO MY SIDE, AVENGER!

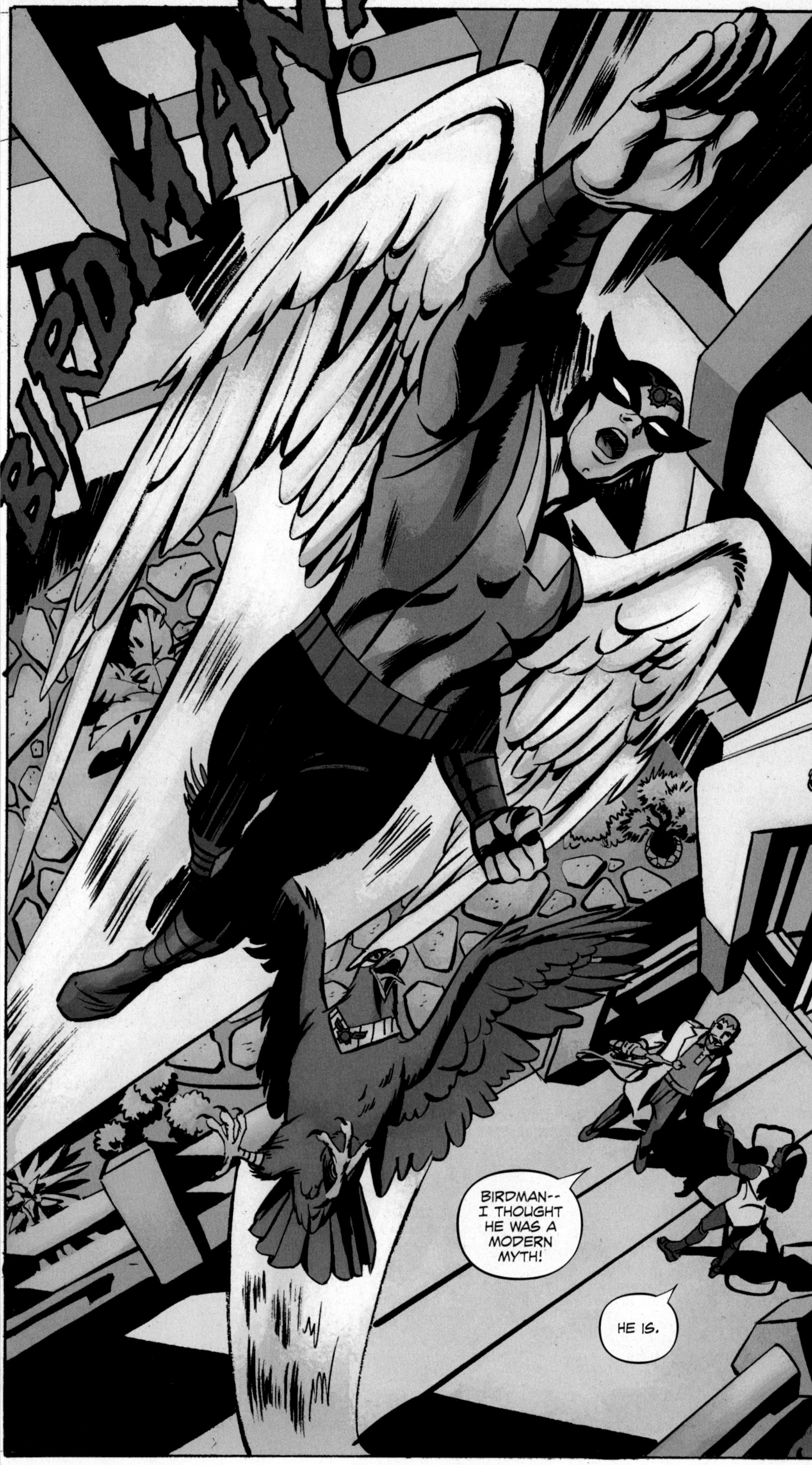
BIRDMAN!
BIRDMAN-- I THOUGHT HE WAS A MODERN MYTH!
HE IS.

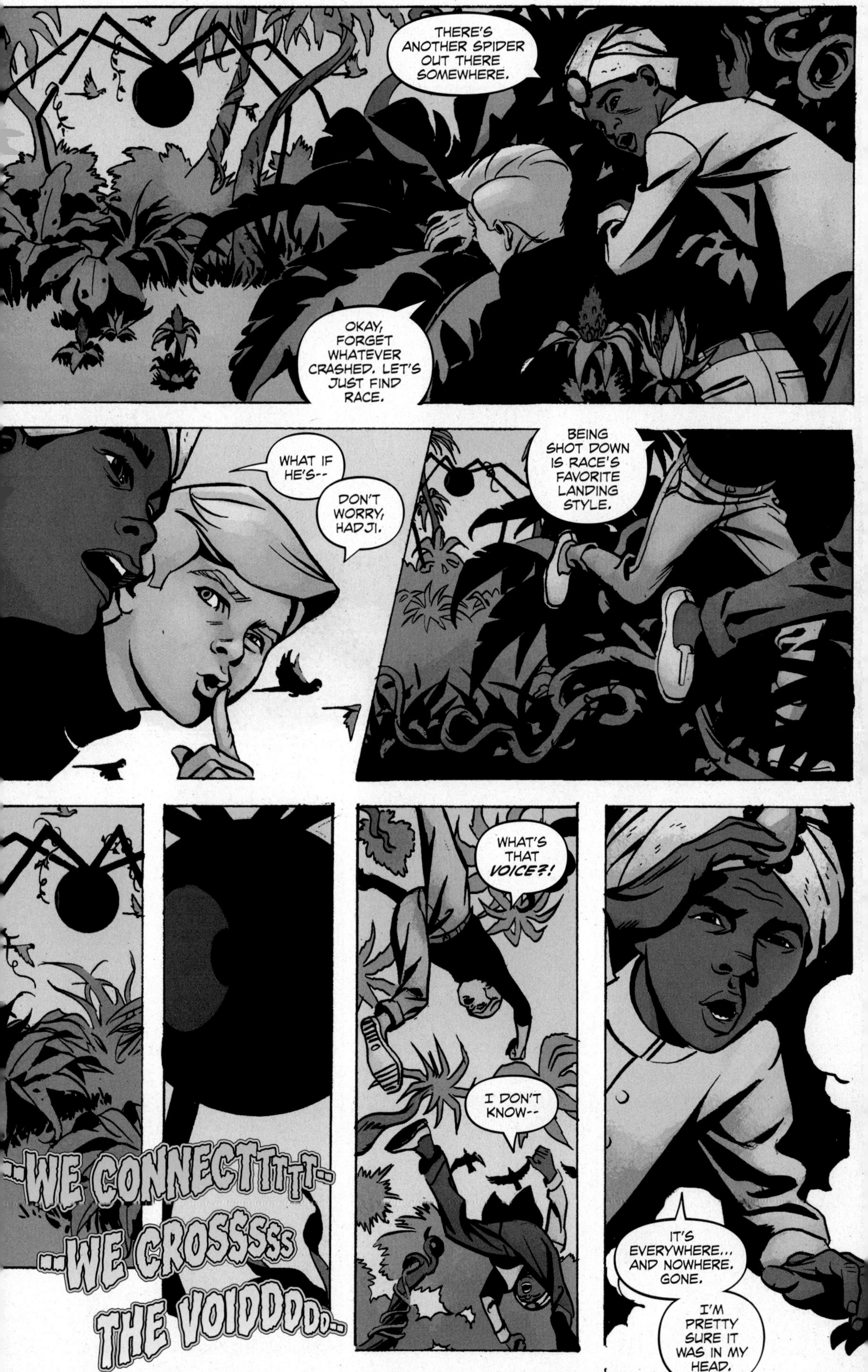
THERE'S ANOTHER SPIDER OUT THERE SOMEWHERE.
OKAY, FORGET WHATEVER CRASHED. LET'S JUST FIND RACE.
WHAT IF HE'S--
DON'T WORRY, HADJI.
BEING SHOT DOWN IS RACE'S FAVORITE LANDING STYLE.
--WE CONNECTTTTT-
--WE CROSSSSS THE VOIDDDDD--
WHAT'S THAT *VOICE?!*
I DON'T KNOW--
IT'S EVERYWHERE... AND NOWHERE. GONE.
I'M PRETTY SURE IT WAS IN MY HEAD.

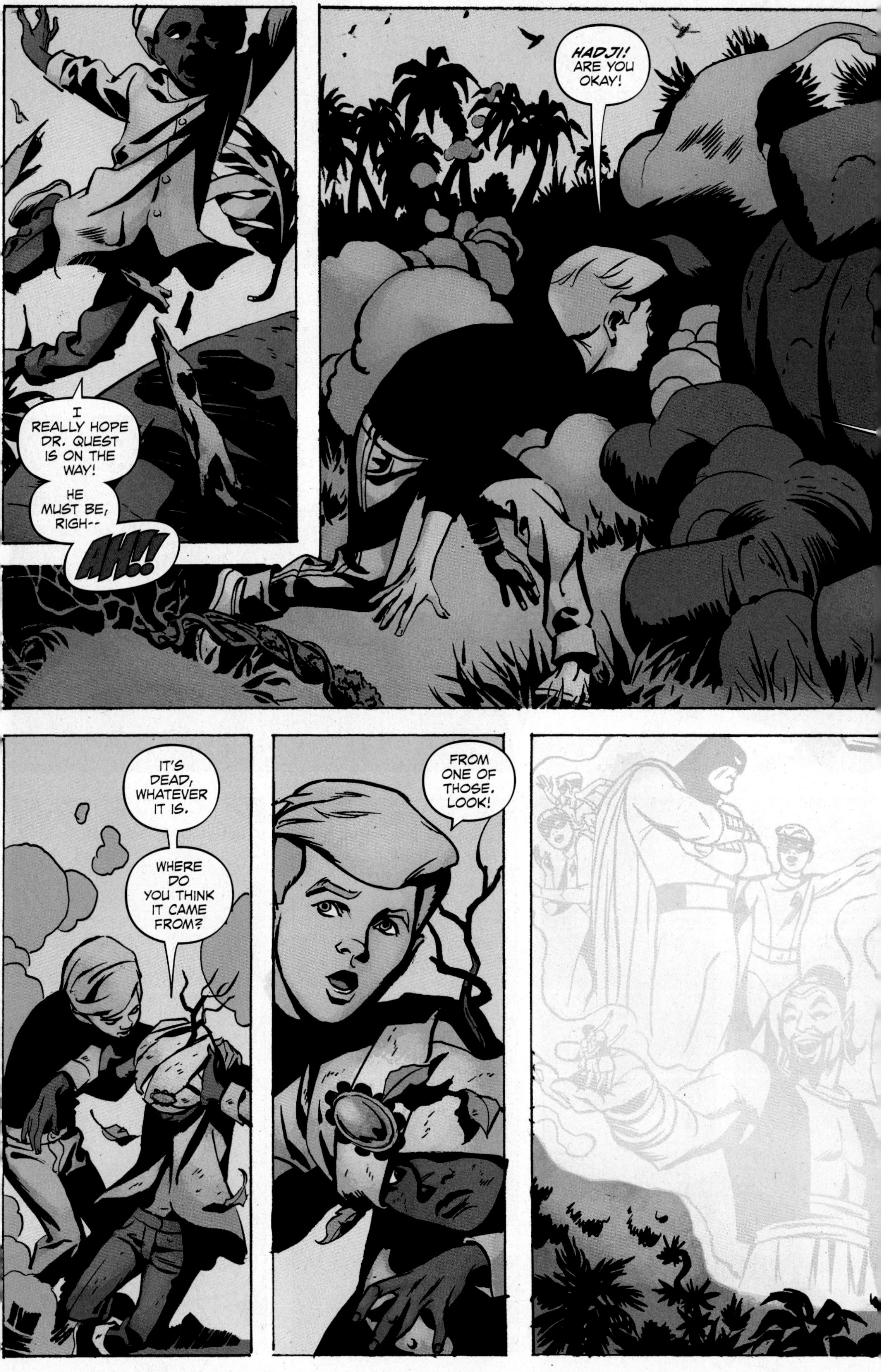
HADJI! ARE YOU OKAY!
I REALLY HOPE DR. QUEST IS ON THE WAY!
HE MUST BE, RIGH--
AH!!
IT'S DEAD, WHATEVER IT IS.
WHERE DO YOU THINK IT CAME FROM?
FROM ONE OF THOSE. LOOK!

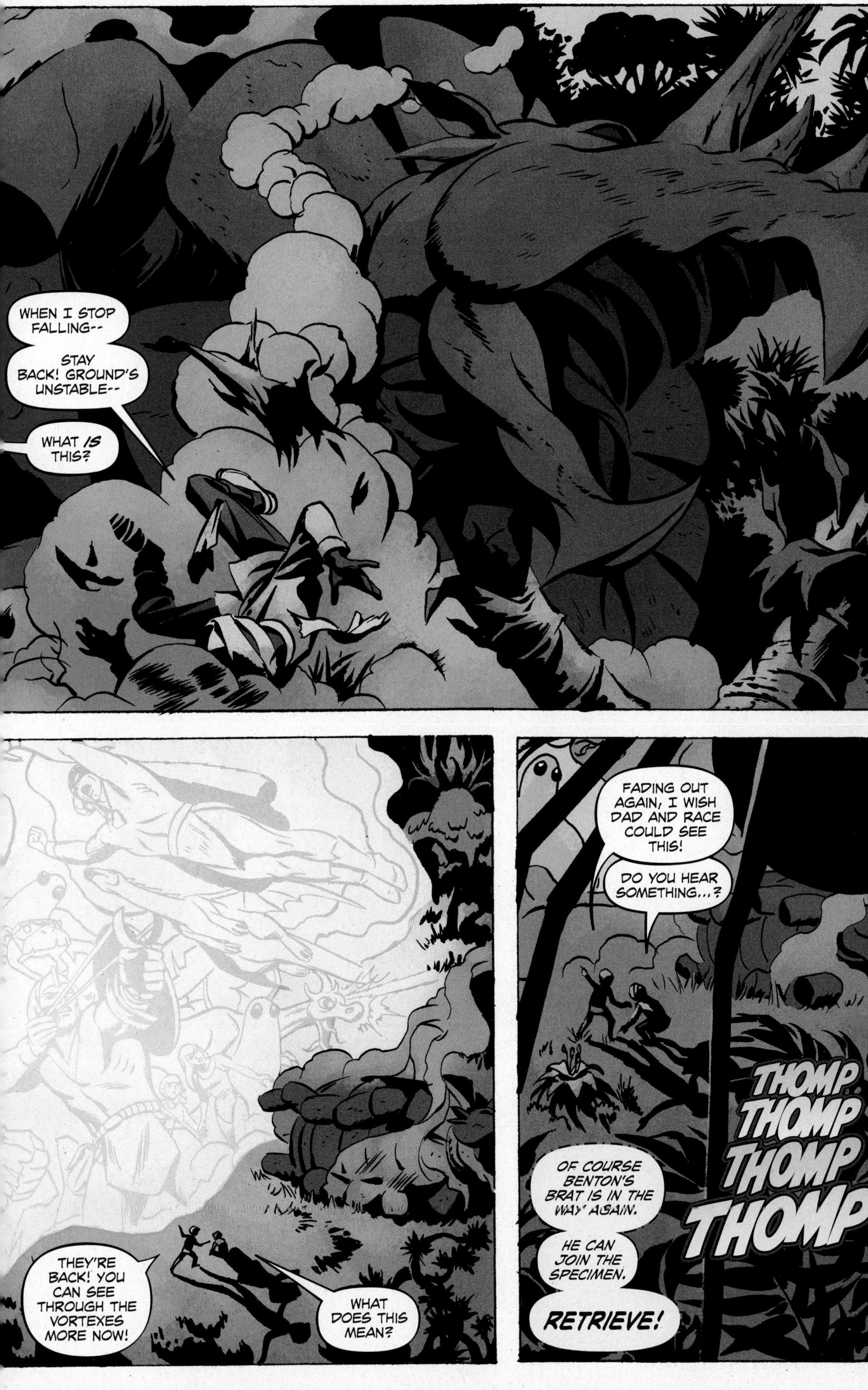
WHEN I STOP FALLING--
STAY BACK! GROUND'S UNSTABLE--
WHAT IS THIS?
THEY'RE BACK! YOU CAN SEE THROUGH THE VORTEXES MORE NOW!
WHAT DOES THIS MEAN?
FADING OUT AGAIN, I WISH DAD AND RACE COULD SEE THIS!
DO YOU HEAR SOMETHING...?
THOMP THOMP THOMP THOMP
OF COURSE BENTON'S BRAT IS IN THE WAY AGAIN.
HE CAN JOIN THE SPECIMEN.
RETRIEVE!

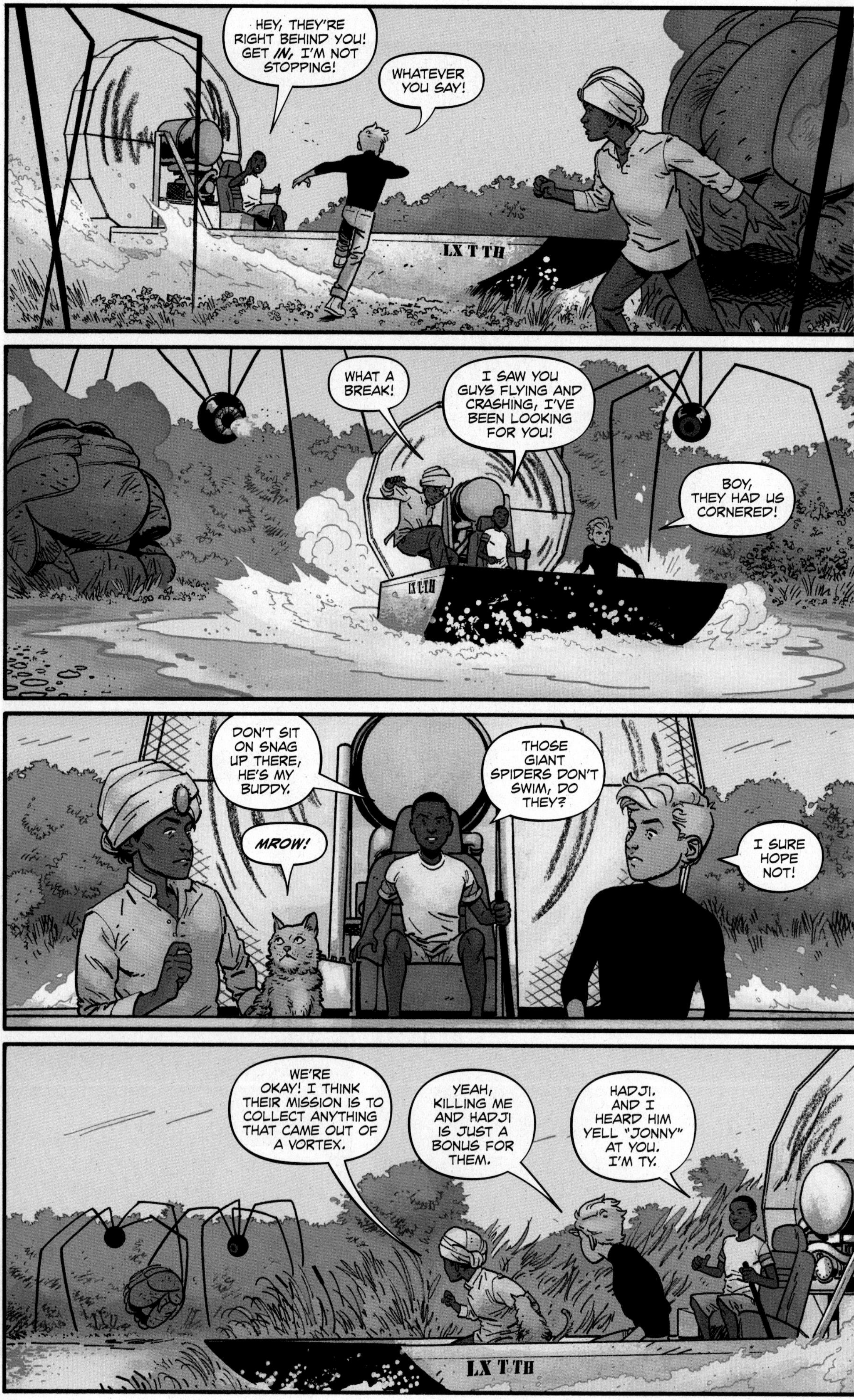
HEY, THEY'RE RIGHT BEHIND YOU! GET IN, I'M NOT STOPPING!
WHATEVER YOU SAY!
LX T TH
WHAT A BREAK!
I SAW YOU GUYS FLYING AND CRASHING, I'VE BEEN LOOKING FOR YOU!
BOY, THEY HAD US CORNERED!
LX T·TH
DON'T SIT ON SNAG UP THERE, HE'S MY BUDDY.
MROW!
THOSE GIANT SPIDERS DON'T SWIM, DO THEY?
I SURE HOPE NOT!
WE'RE OKAY! I THINK THEIR MISSION IS TO COLLECT ANYTHING THAT CAME OUT OF A VORTEX.
YEAH, KILLING ME AND HADJI IS JUST A BONUS FOR THEM.
HADJI. AND I HEARD HIM YELL "JONNY" AT YOU. I'M TY.
LX T·TH

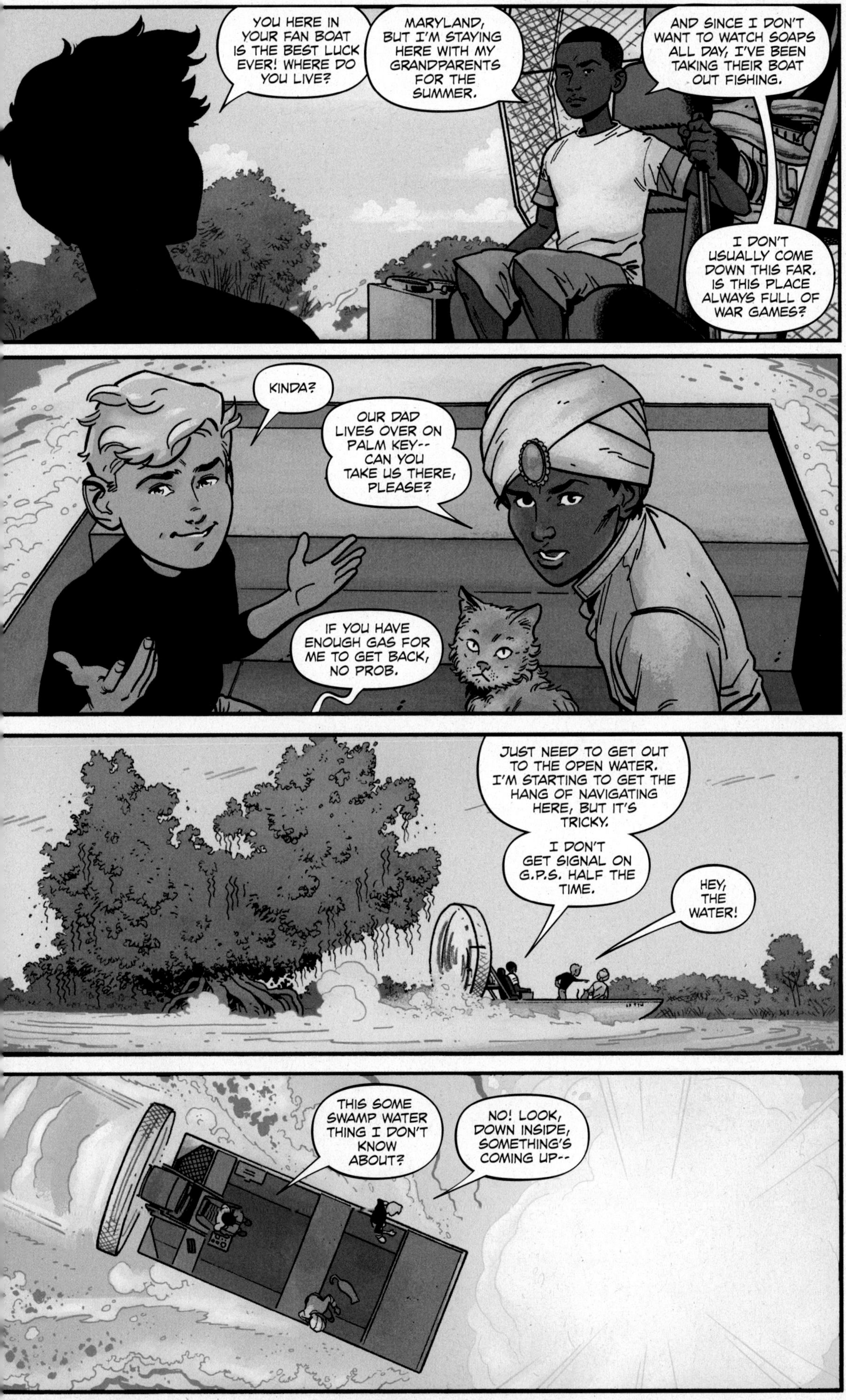
YOU HERE IN YOUR FAN BOAT IS THE BEST LUCK EVER! WHERE DO YOU LIVE?
MARYLAND, BUT I'M STAYING HERE WITH MY GRANDPARENTS FOR THE SUMMER.
AND SINCE I DON'T WANT TO WATCH SOAPS ALL DAY, I'VE BEEN TAKING THEIR BOAT OUT FISHING.
I DON'T USUALLY COME DOWN THIS FAR. IS THIS PLACE ALWAYS FULL OF WAR GAMES?
KINDA?
OUR DAD LIVES OVER ON PALM KEY-- CAN YOU TAKE US THERE, PLEASE?
IF YOU HAVE ENOUGH GAS FOR ME TO GET BACK, NO PROB.
JUST NEED TO GET OUT TO THE OPEN WATER. I'M STARTING TO GET THE HANG OF NAVIGATING HERE, BUT IT'S TRICKY.
I DON'T GET SIGNAL ON G.P.S. HALF THE TIME.
HEY, THE WATER!
THIS SOME SWAMP WATER THING I DON'T KNOW ABOUT?
NO! LOOK, DOWN INSIDE, SOMETHING'S COMING UP--

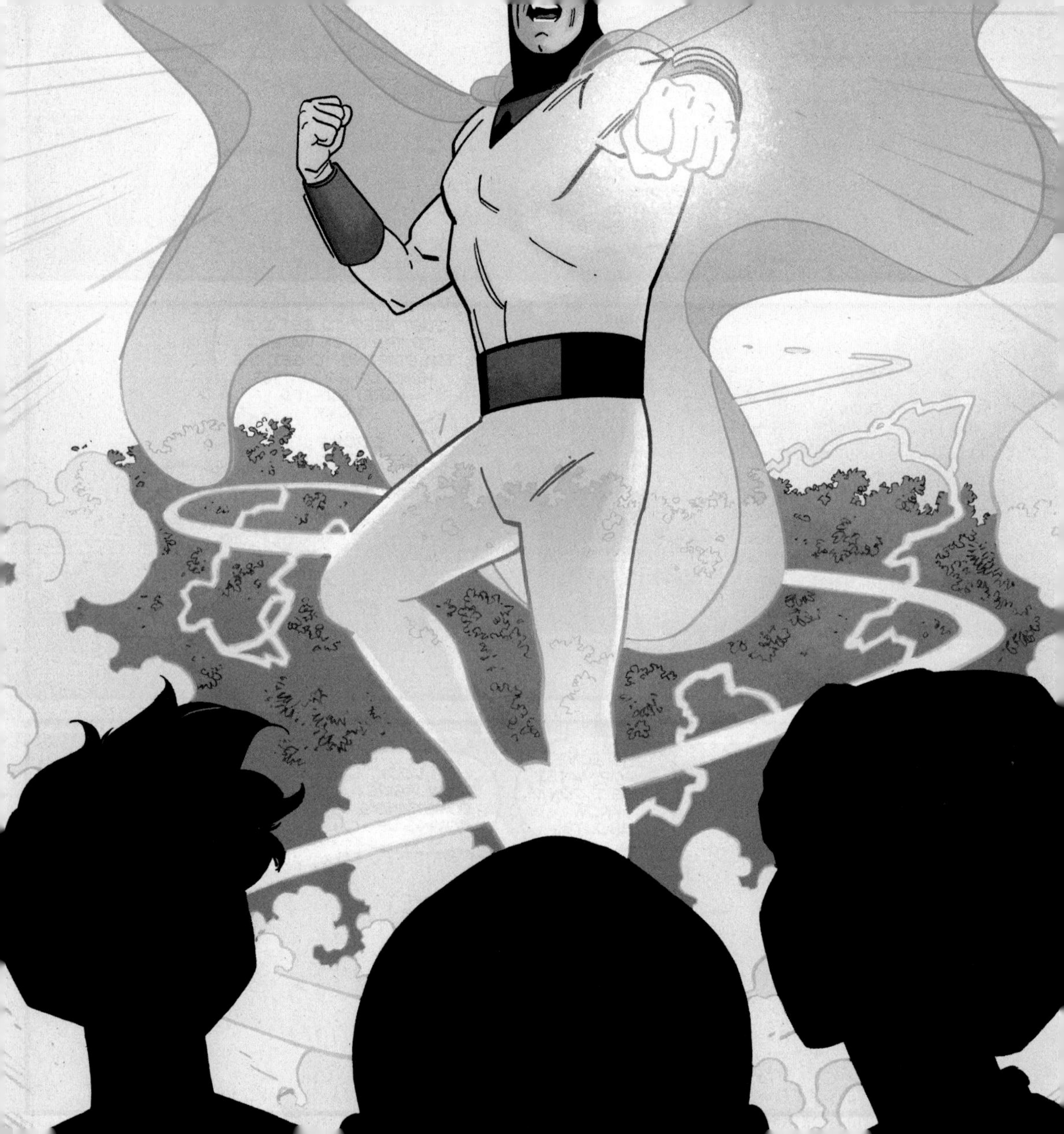

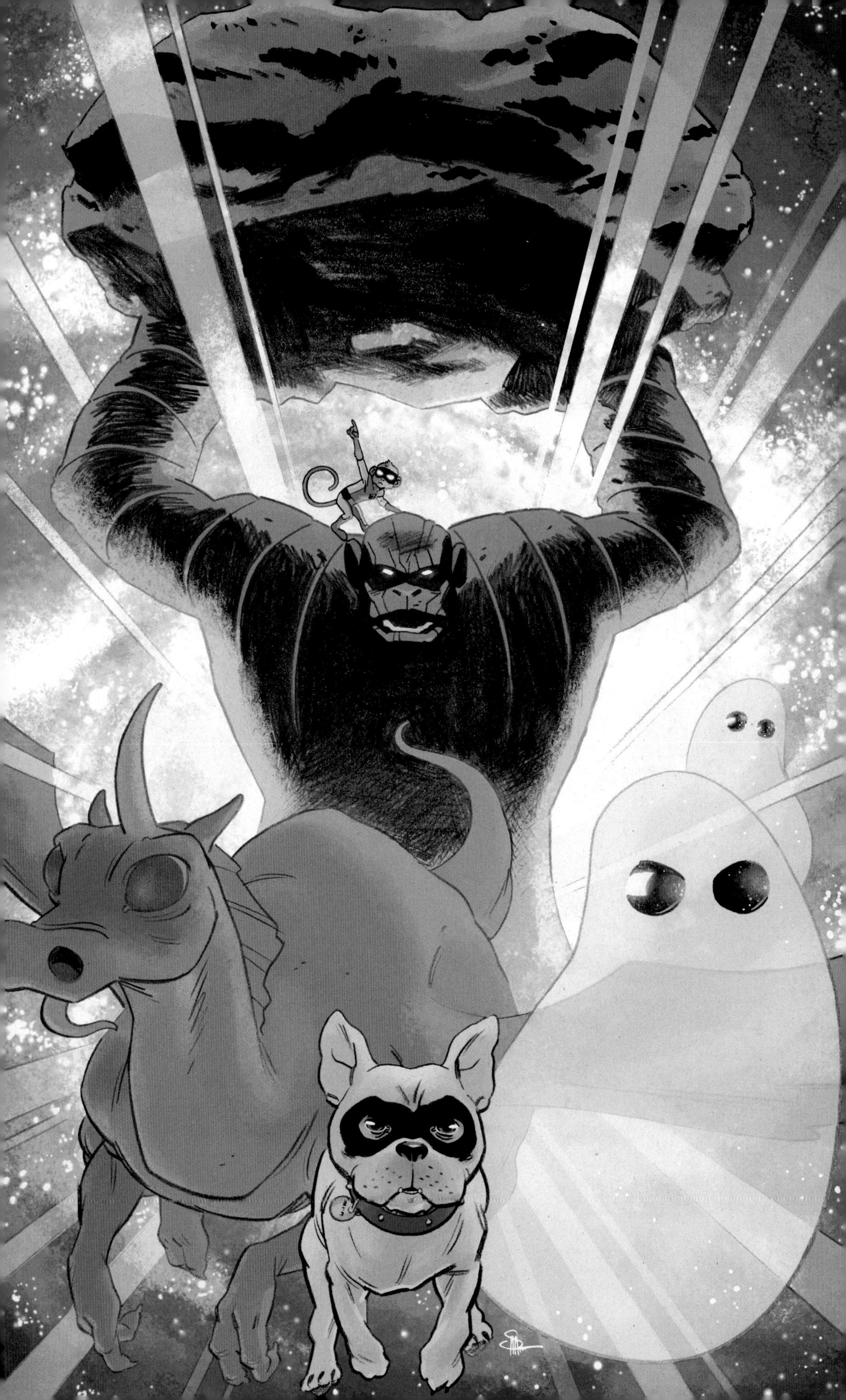

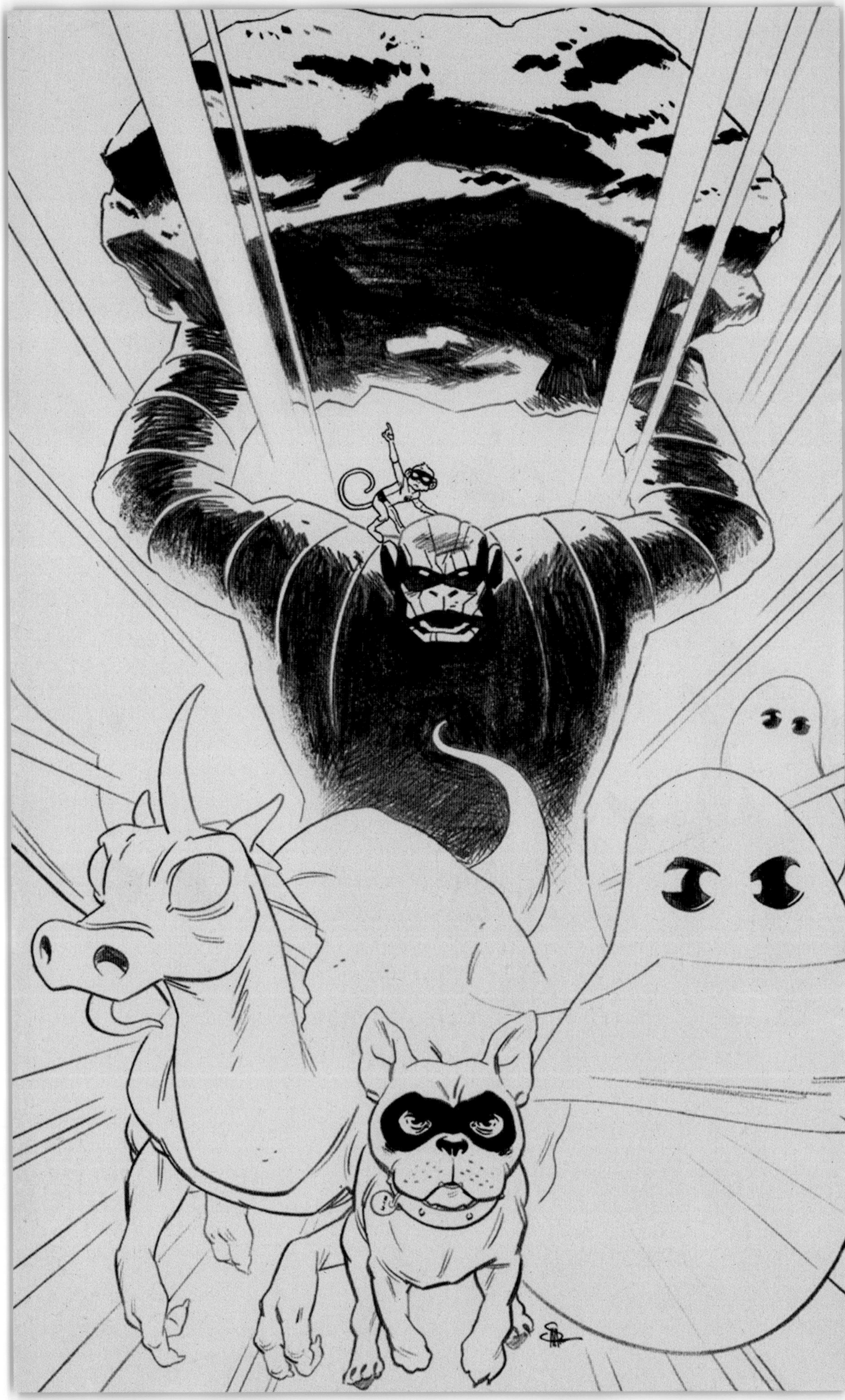

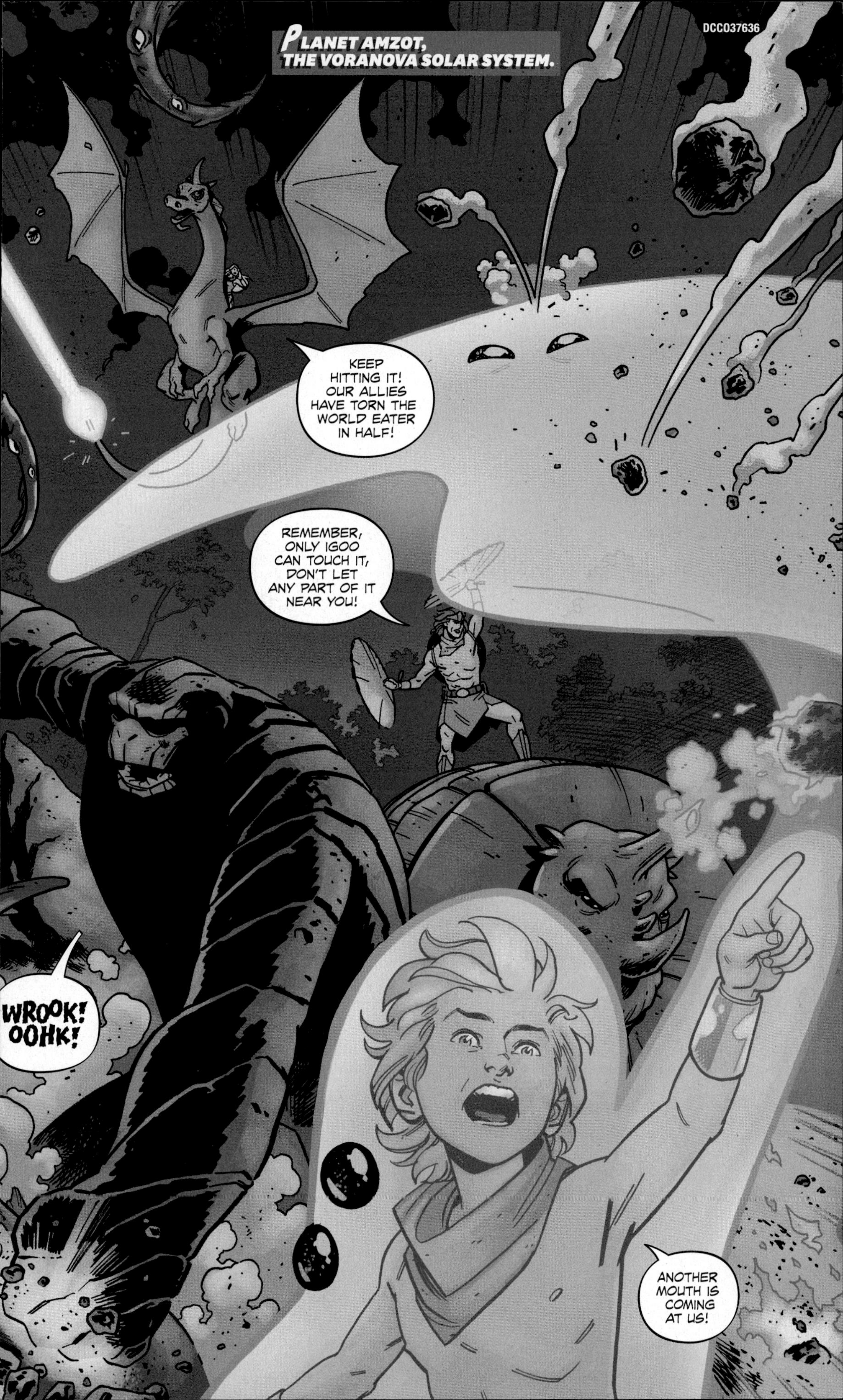
DCC037636
PLANET AMZOT, THE VORANOVA SOLAR SYSTEM.
KEEP HITTING IT! OUR ALLIES HAVE TORN THE WORLD EATER IN HALF!
REMEMBER, ONLY IGOO CAN TOUCH IT, DON'T LET ANY PART OF IT NEAR YOU!
WROOK! OOHK!
ANOTHER MOUTH IS COMING AT US!

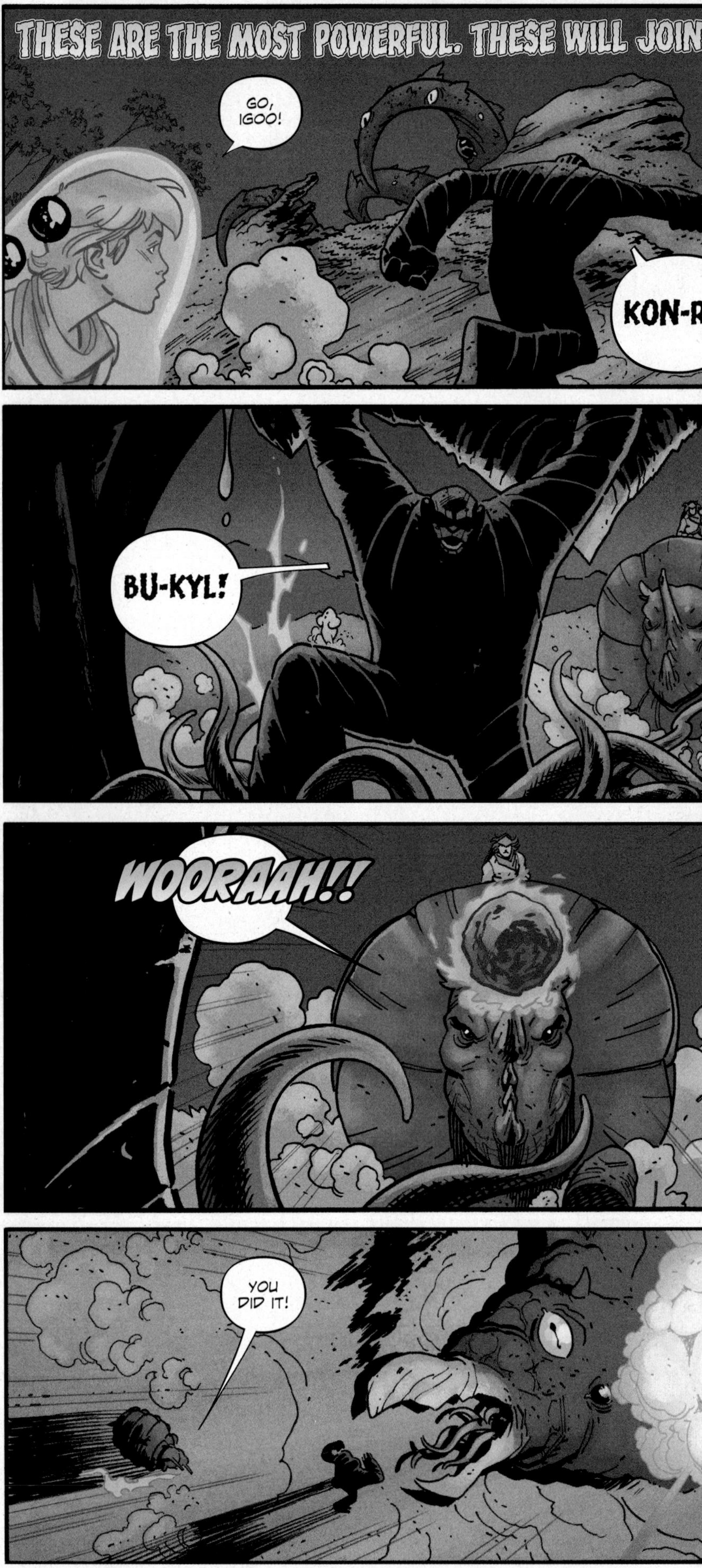
THESE ARE THE MOST POWERFUL. THESE WILL JOIN
GO, IGOO!
KON-R
BU-KYL!
WOORAAH!!
YOU DID IT!

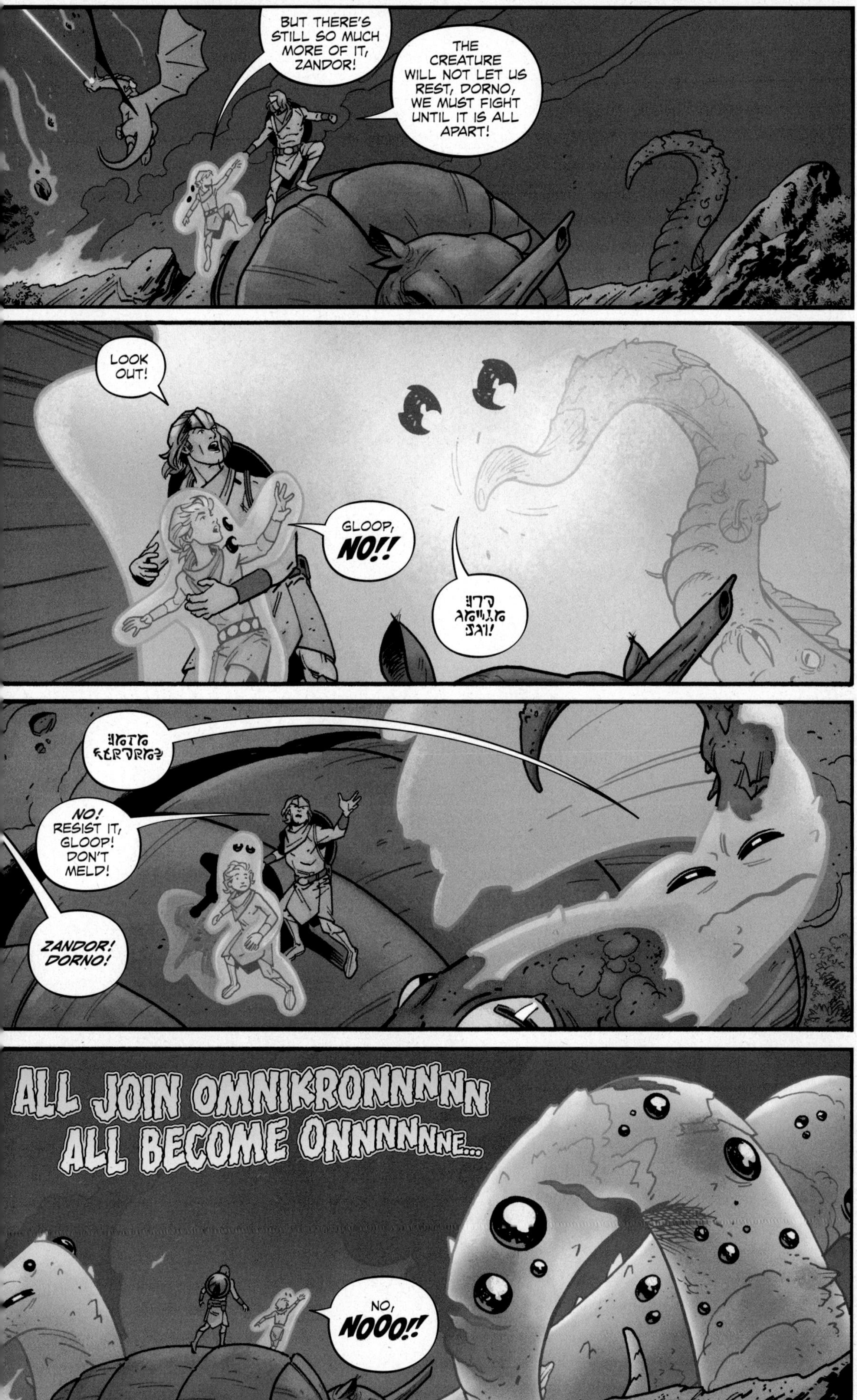
BUT THERE'S STILL SO MUCH MORE OF IT, ZANDOR!
THE CREATURE WILL NOT LET US REST, DORNO, WE MUST FIGHT UNTIL IT IS ALL APART!
LOOK OUT!
GLOOP, NO!!
NO! RESIST IT, GLOOP! DON'T MELD!
ZANDOR! DORNO!
ALL JOIN OMNIKRONNNNNN ALL BECOME ONNNNNNE...
NO, NOOO!!

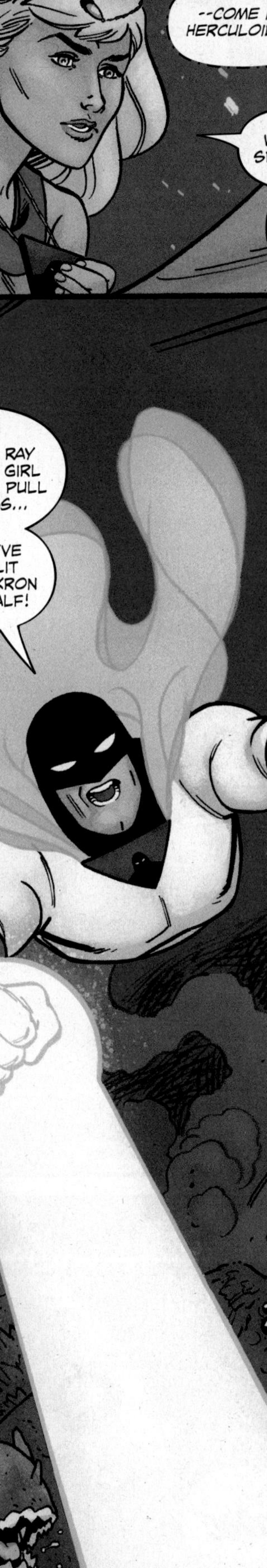
--COME
HERCULOI
RAY GIRL PULL S...
VE LIT KRON ALF!

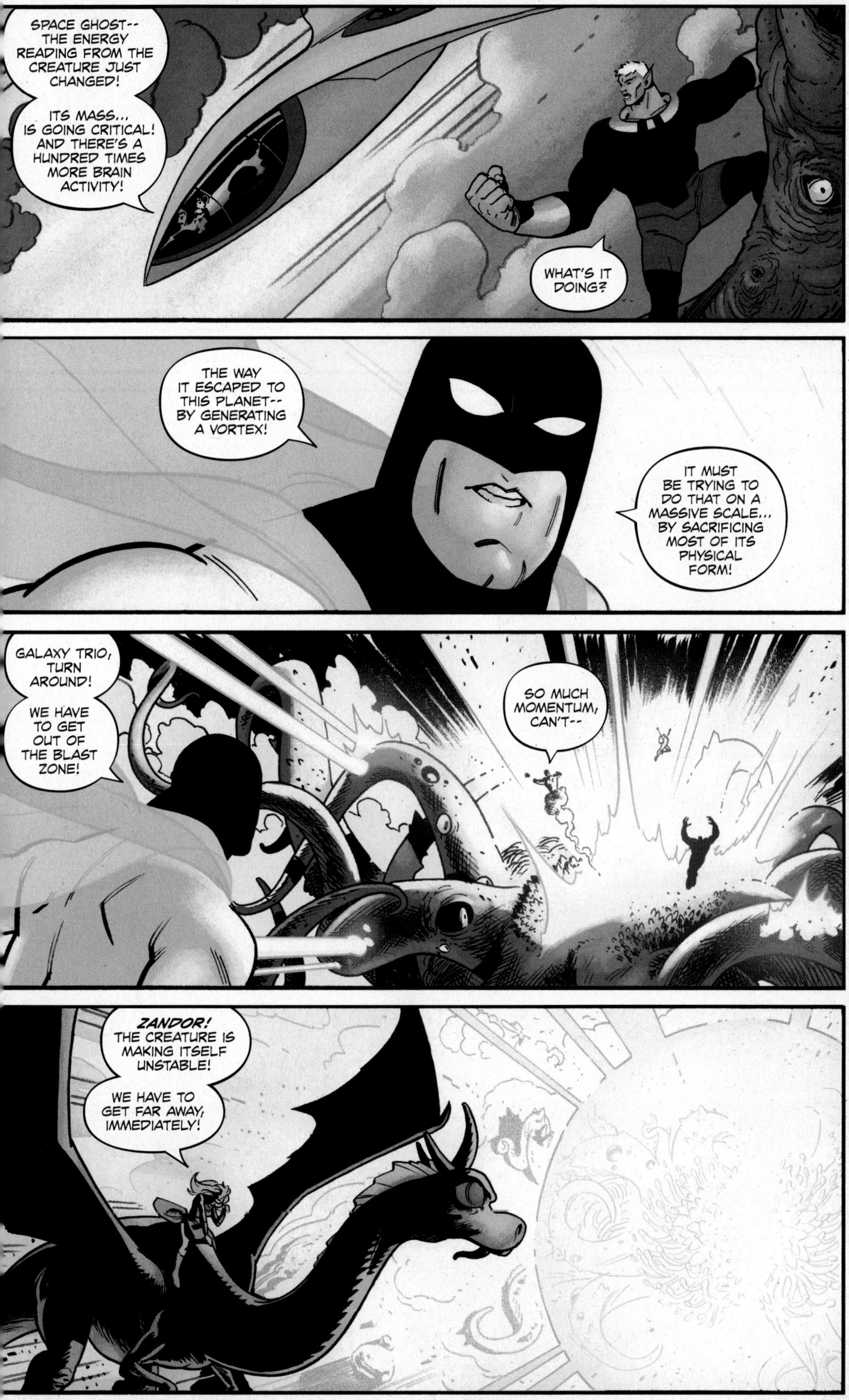
SPACE GHOST-- THE ENERGY READING FROM THE CREATURE JUST CHANGED!
ITS MASS... IS GOING CRITICAL! AND THERE'S A HUNDRED TIMES MORE BRAIN ACTIVITY!
WHAT'S IT DOING?
THE WAY IT ESCAPED TO THIS PLANET-- BY GENERATING A VORTEX!
IT MUST BE TRYING TO DO THAT ON A MASSIVE SCALE... BY SACRIFICING MOST OF ITS PHYSICAL FORM!
GALAXY TRIO, TURN AROUND!
WE HAVE TO GET OUT OF THE BLAST ZONE!
SO MUCH MOMENTUM, CAN'T--
ZANDOR! THE CREATURE IS MAKING ITSELF UNSTABLE!
WE HAVE TO GET FAR AWAY, IMMEDIATELY!

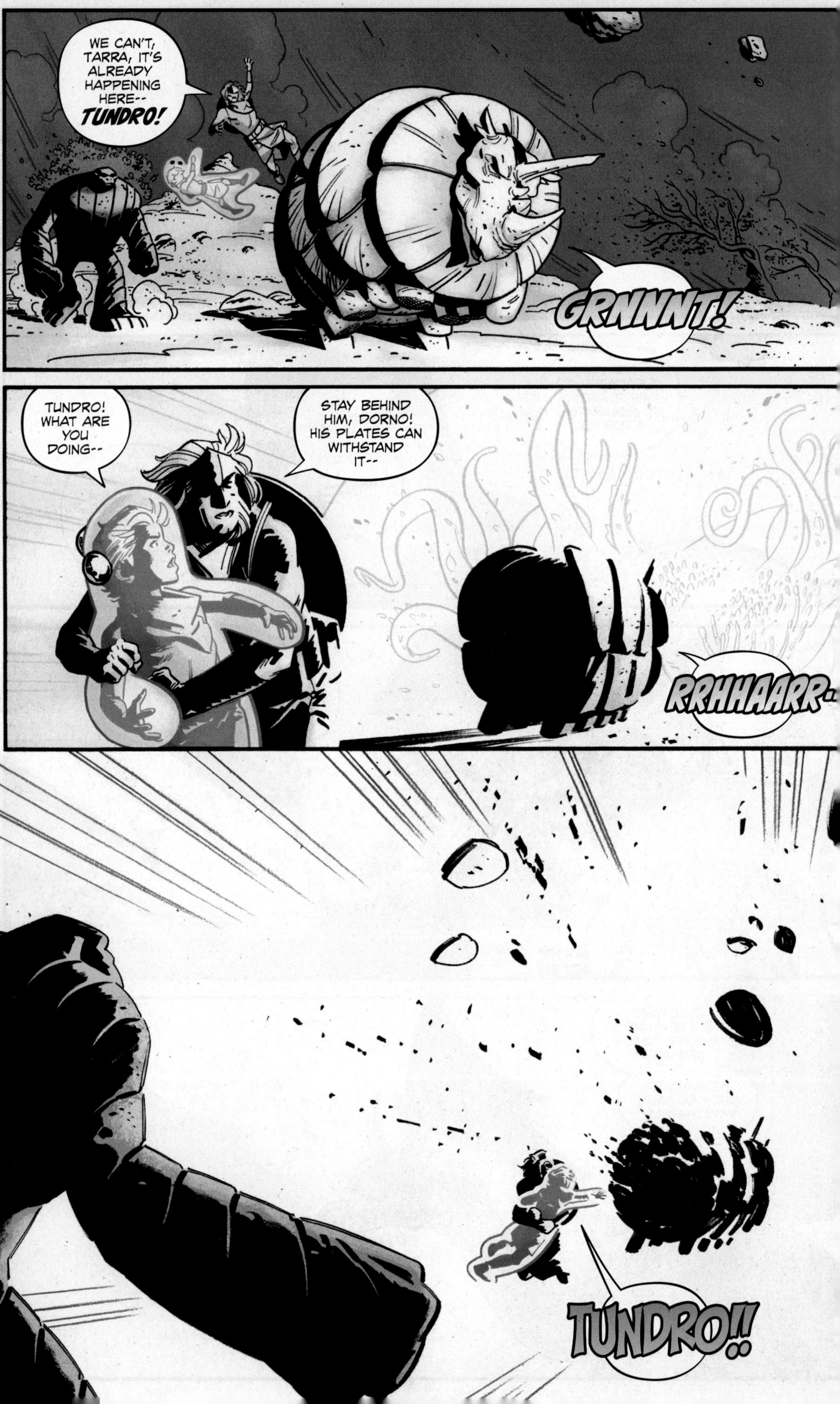

WE CAN'T, TARRA, IT'S ALREADY HAPPENING HERE-- TUNDRO!
GRNNNT!
TUNDRO! WHAT ARE YOU DOING--
STAY BEHIND HIM, DORNO! HIS PLATES CAN WITHSTAND IT--
RRHHAARR-
TUNDRO!!

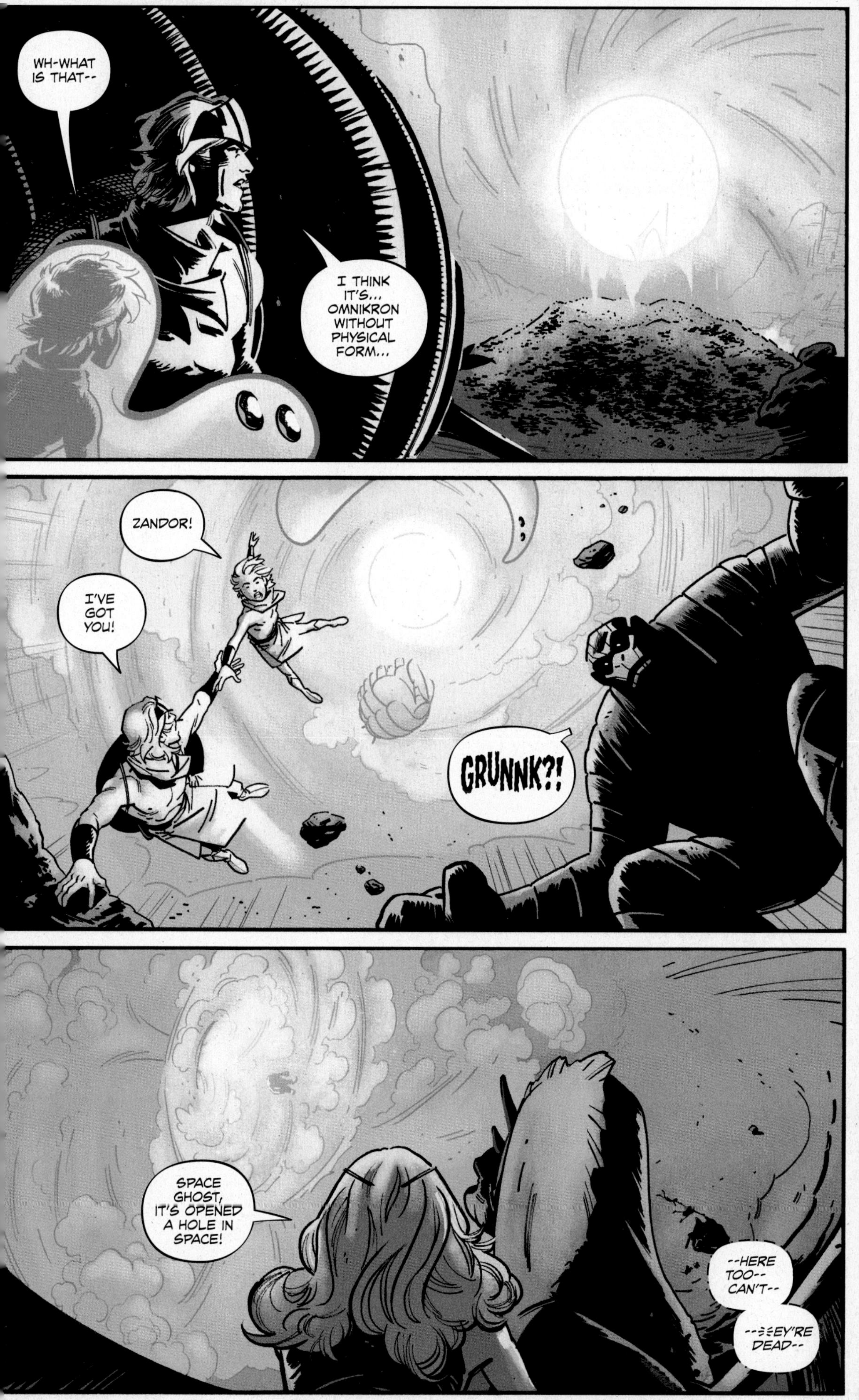
WH-WHAT IS THAT--
I THINK IT'S... OMNIKRON WITHOUT PHYSICAL FORM...
ZANDOR!
I'VE GOT YOU!
GRUNNK?!
SPACE GHOST, IT'S OPENED A HOLE IN SPACE!
--HERE TOO-- CAN'T--
--EY'RE DEAD--

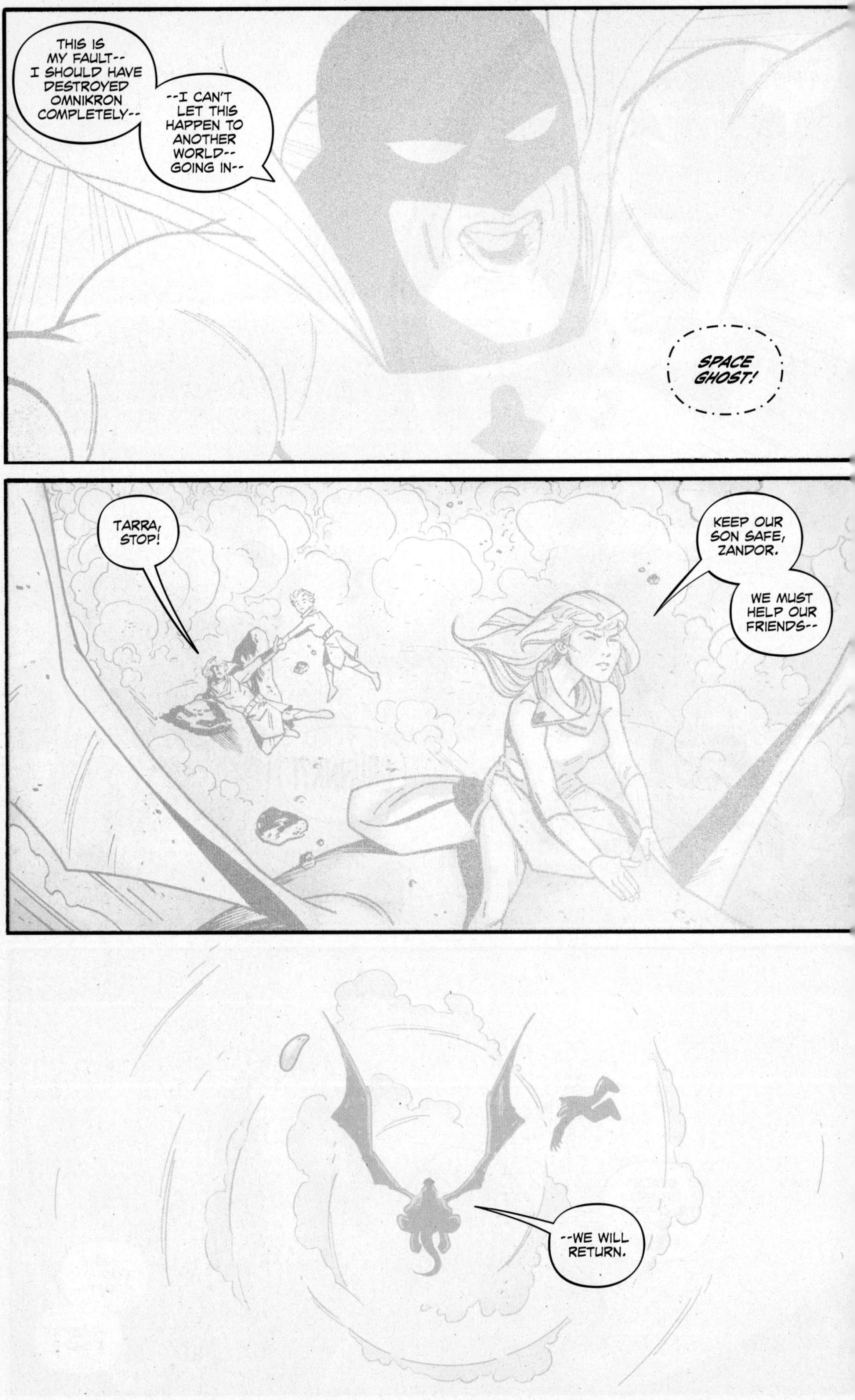

THIS IS MY FAULT-- I SHOULD HAVE DESTROYED OMNIKRON COMPLETELY--
--I CAN'T LET THIS HAPPEN TO ANOTHER WORLD-- GOING IN--
SPACE GHOST!
TARRA, STOP!
KEEP OUR SON SAFE, ZANDOR.
WE MUST HELP OUR FRIENDS--
--WE WILL RETURN.

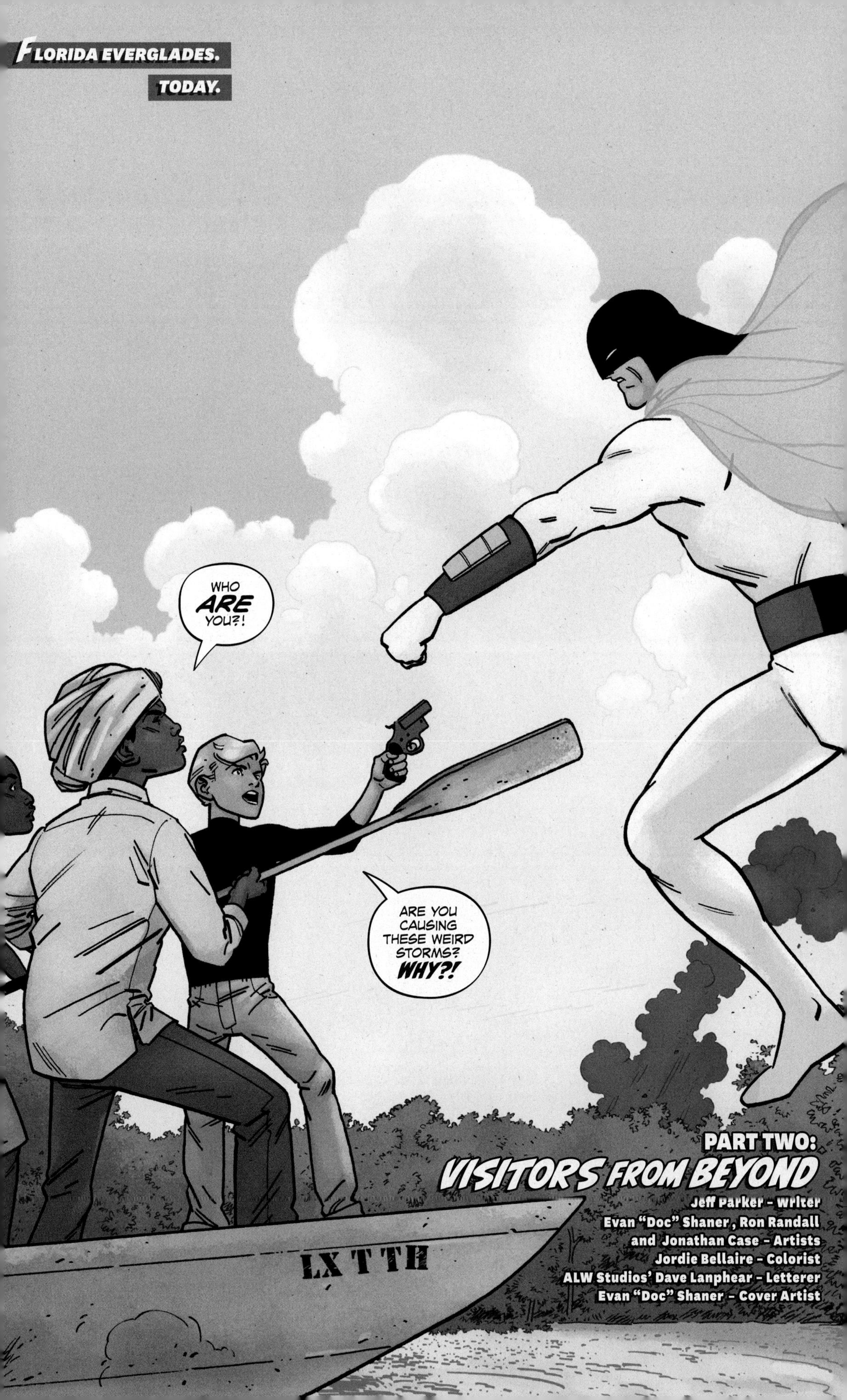
FLORIDA EVERGLADES.
TODAY.
WHO ARE YOU?!
ARE YOU CAUSING THESE WEIRD STORMS? WHY?!
PART TWO:
VISITORS FROM BEYOND
Jeff Parker - Writer
Evan "Doc" Shaner, Ron Randall
and Jonathan Case - Artists
Jordie Bellaire - Colorist
ALW Studios' Dave Lanphear - Letterer
Evan "Doc" Shaner - Cover Artist

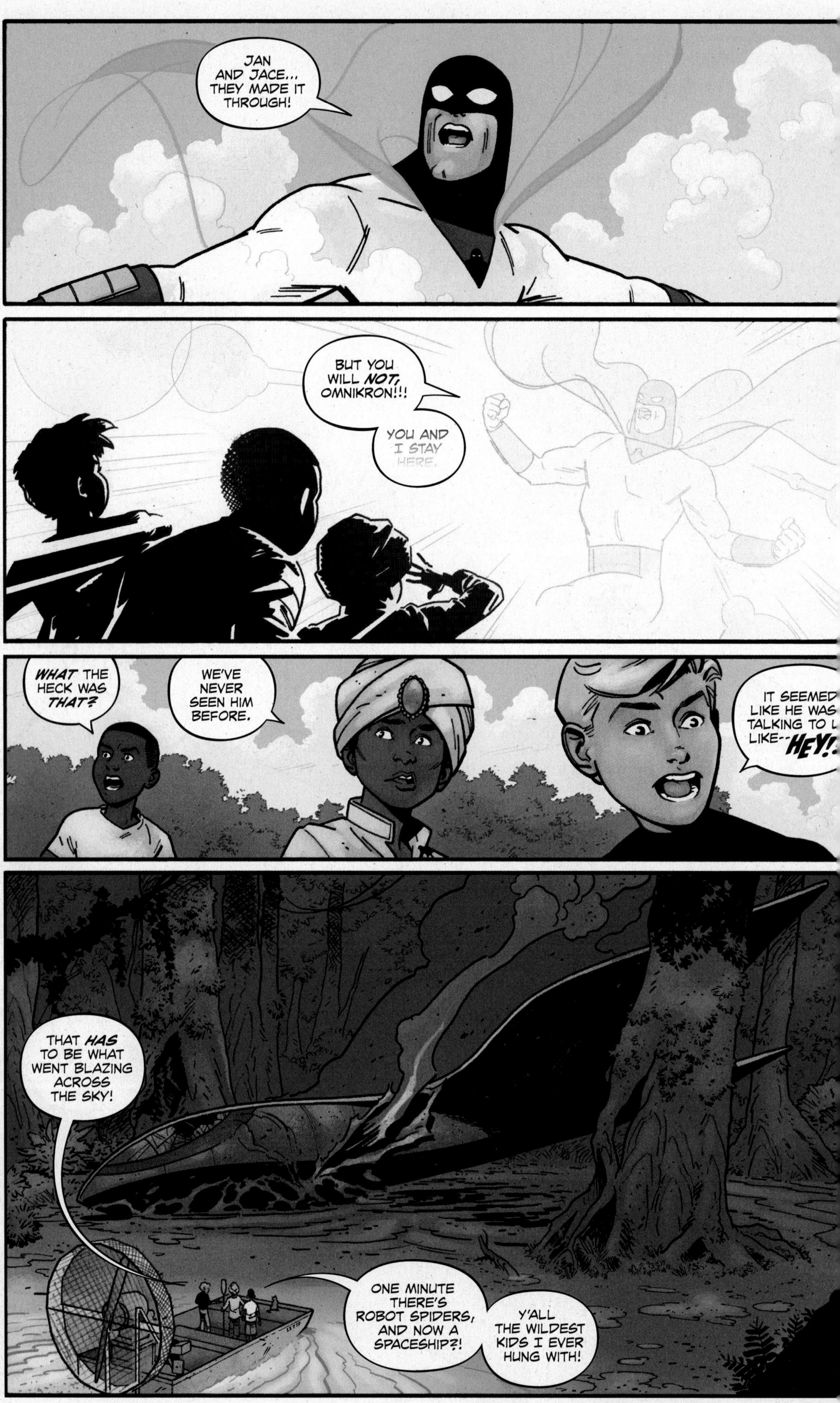

JAN AND JACE... THEY MADE IT THROUGH!
BUT YOU WILL NOT, OMNIKRON!!!
YOU AND I STAY HERE.
WHAT THE HECK WAS THAT?
WE'VE NEVER SEEN HIM BEFORE.
IT SEEMED LIKE HE WAS TALKING TO LIKE--HEY!
THAT HAS TO BE WHAT WENT BLAZING ACROSS THE SKY!
ONE MINUTE THERE'S ROBOT SPIDERS, AND NOW A SPACESHIP?!
Y'ALL THE WILDEST KIDS I EVER HUNG WITH!

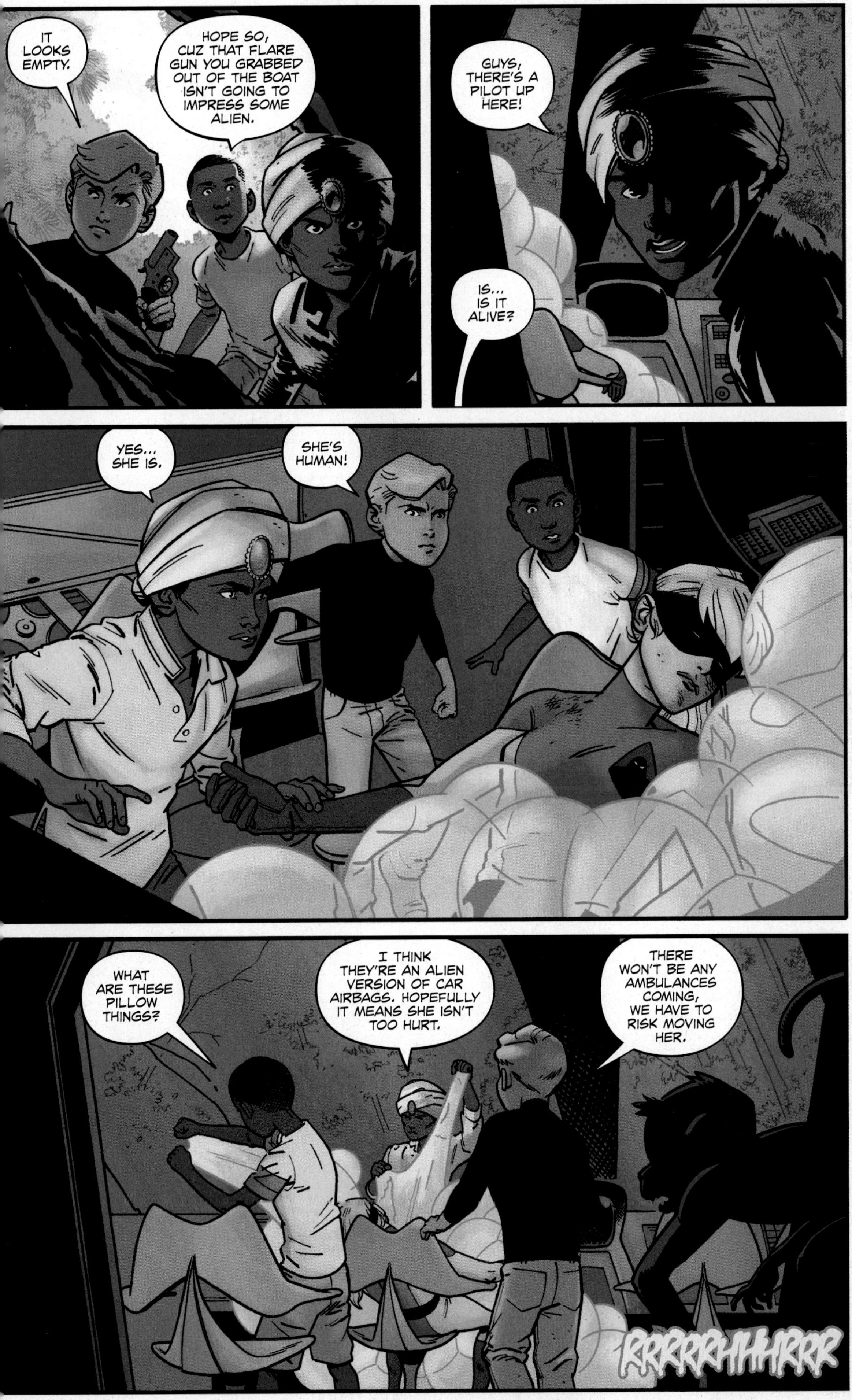
IT LOOKS EMPTY.
HOPE SO, CUZ THAT FLARE GUN YOU GRABBED OUT OF THE BOAT ISN'T GOING TO IMPRESS SOME ALIEN.
GUYS, THERE'S A PILOT UP HERE!
IS... IS IT ALIVE?
YES... SHE IS.
SHE'S HUMAN!
WHAT ARE THESE PILLOW THINGS?
I THINK THEY'RE AN ALIEN VERSION OF CAR AIRBAGS. HOPEFULLY IT MEANS SHE ISN'T TOO HURT.
THERE WON'T BE ANY AMBULANCES COMING, WE HAVE TO RISK MOVING HER.
RRRRRHHHRRR

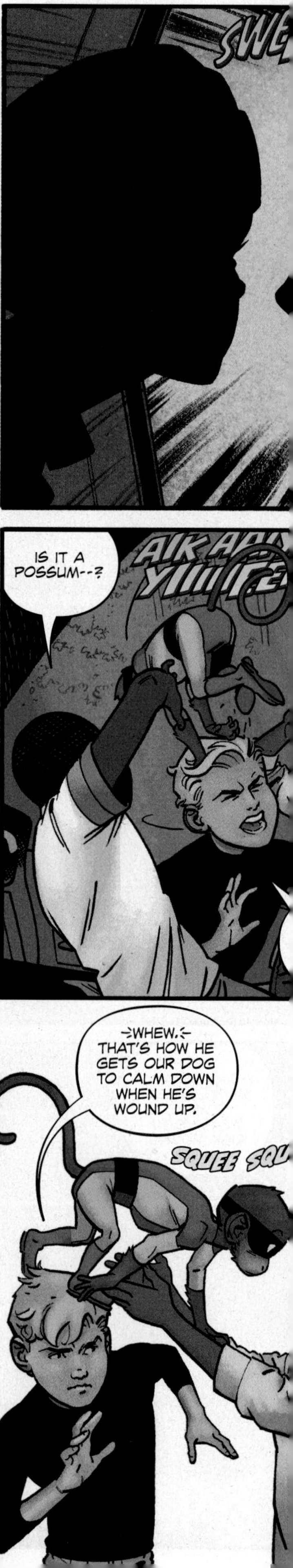
SWE
IS IT A POSSUM--?
WHEW. THAT'S HOW HE GETS OUR DOG TO CALM DOWN WHEN HE'S WOUND UP.
SQUEE SQU

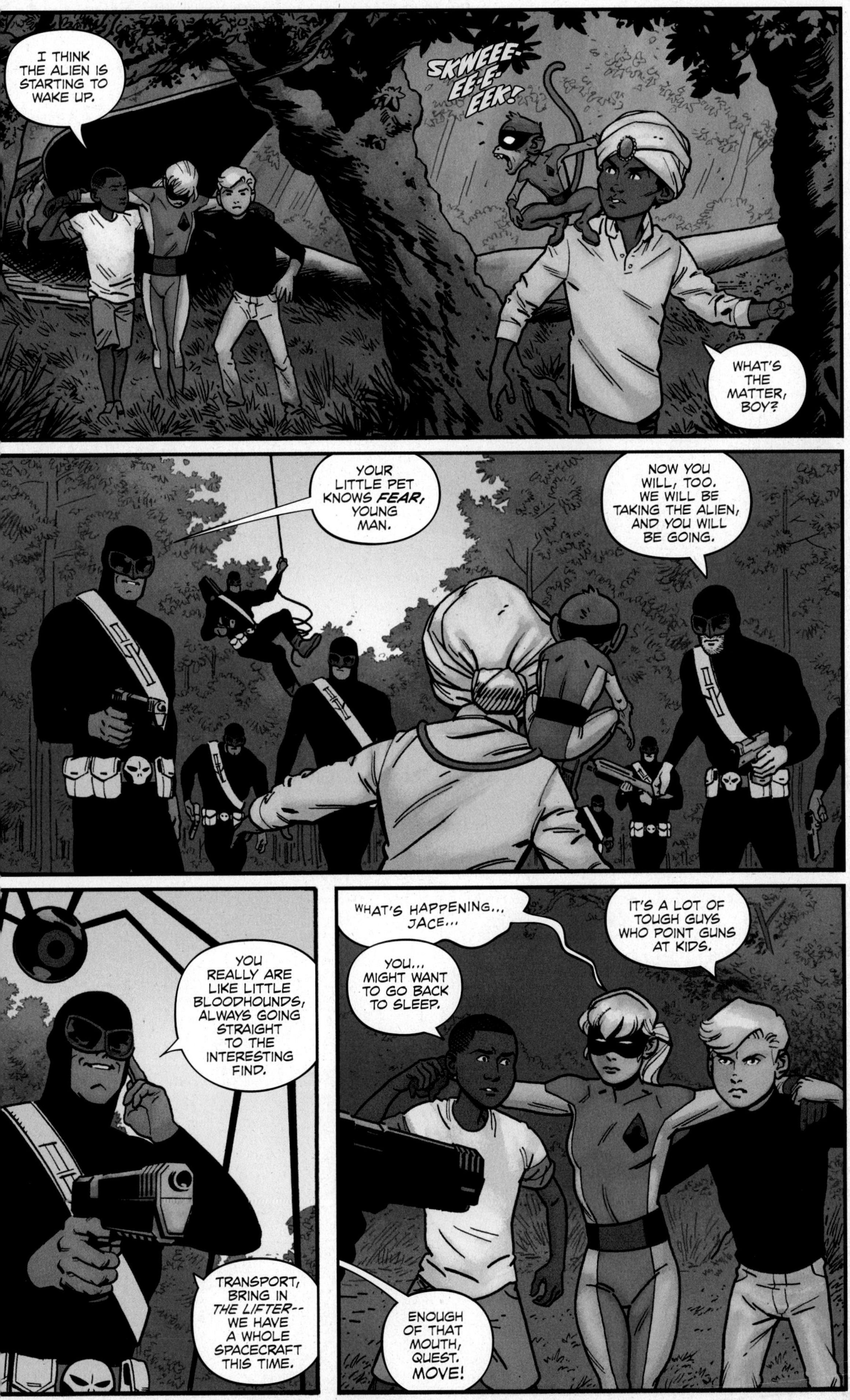
I THINK THE ALIEN IS STARTING TO WAKE UP.
SKWEEE-EE-E-EEK!
WHAT'S THE MATTER, BOY?
YOUR LITTLE PET KNOWS *FEAR*, YOUNG MAN.
NOW YOU WILL, TOO. WE WILL BE TAKING THE ALIEN, AND YOU WILL BE GOING.
YOU REALLY ARE LIKE LITTLE BLOODHOUNDS, ALWAYS GOING STRAIGHT TO THE INTERESTING FIND.
TRANSPORT, BRING IN *THE LIFTER*-- WE HAVE A WHOLE SPACECRAFT THIS TIME.
WHAT'S HAPPENING... JACE...
IT'S A LOT OF TOUGH GUYS WHO POINT GUNS AT KIDS.
YOU... MIGHT WANT TO GO BACK TO SLEEP.
ENOUGH OF THAT MOUTH, QUEST. MOVE!

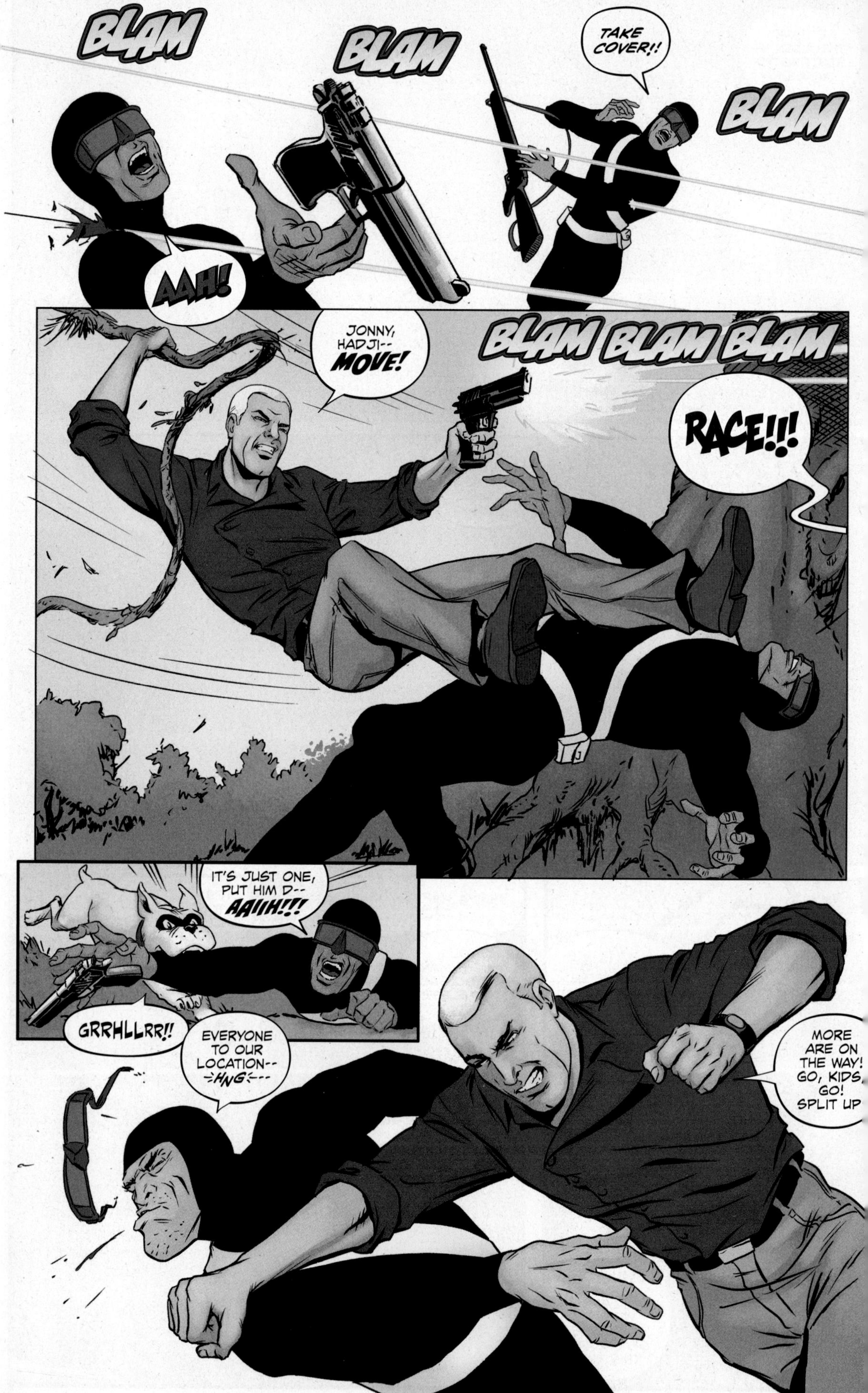
BLAM
BLAM
TAKE COVER!!
BLAM
AAH!
JONNY, HADJI-- MOVE!
BLAM BLAM BLAM
RACE!!!
IT'S JUST ONE, PUT HIM D-- AAIIH!!!
GRRHLLRR!!
EVERYONE TO OUR LOCATION-- HNG---
MORE ARE ON THE WAY! GO, KIDS, GO! SPLIT UP

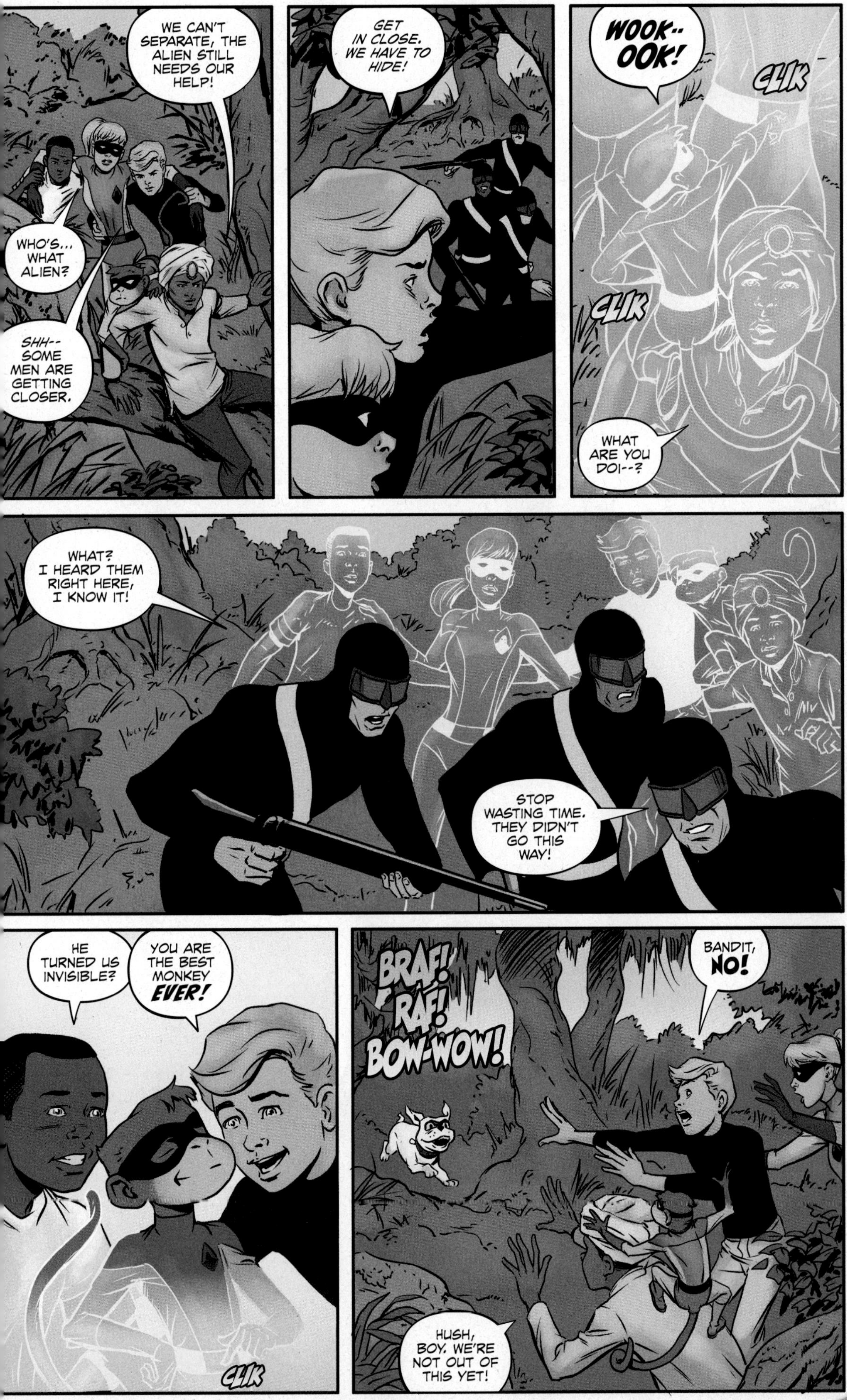

WE CAN'T SEPARATE, THE ALIEN STILL NEEDS OUR HELP!
WHO'S... WHAT ALIEN?
SHH-- SOME MEN ARE GETTING CLOSER.
GET IN CLOSE. WE HAVE TO HIDE!
WOOK.. OOK!
CLIK
CLIK
WHAT ARE YOU DOI--?
WHAT? I HEARD THEM RIGHT HERE, I KNOW IT!
STOP WASTING TIME. THEY DIDN'T GO THIS WAY!
HE TURNED US INVISIBLE?
YOU ARE THE BEST MONKEY EVER!
CLIK
BRAF! RAF! BOW-WOW!
BANDIT, NO!
HUSH, BOY. WE'RE NOT OUT OF THIS YET!

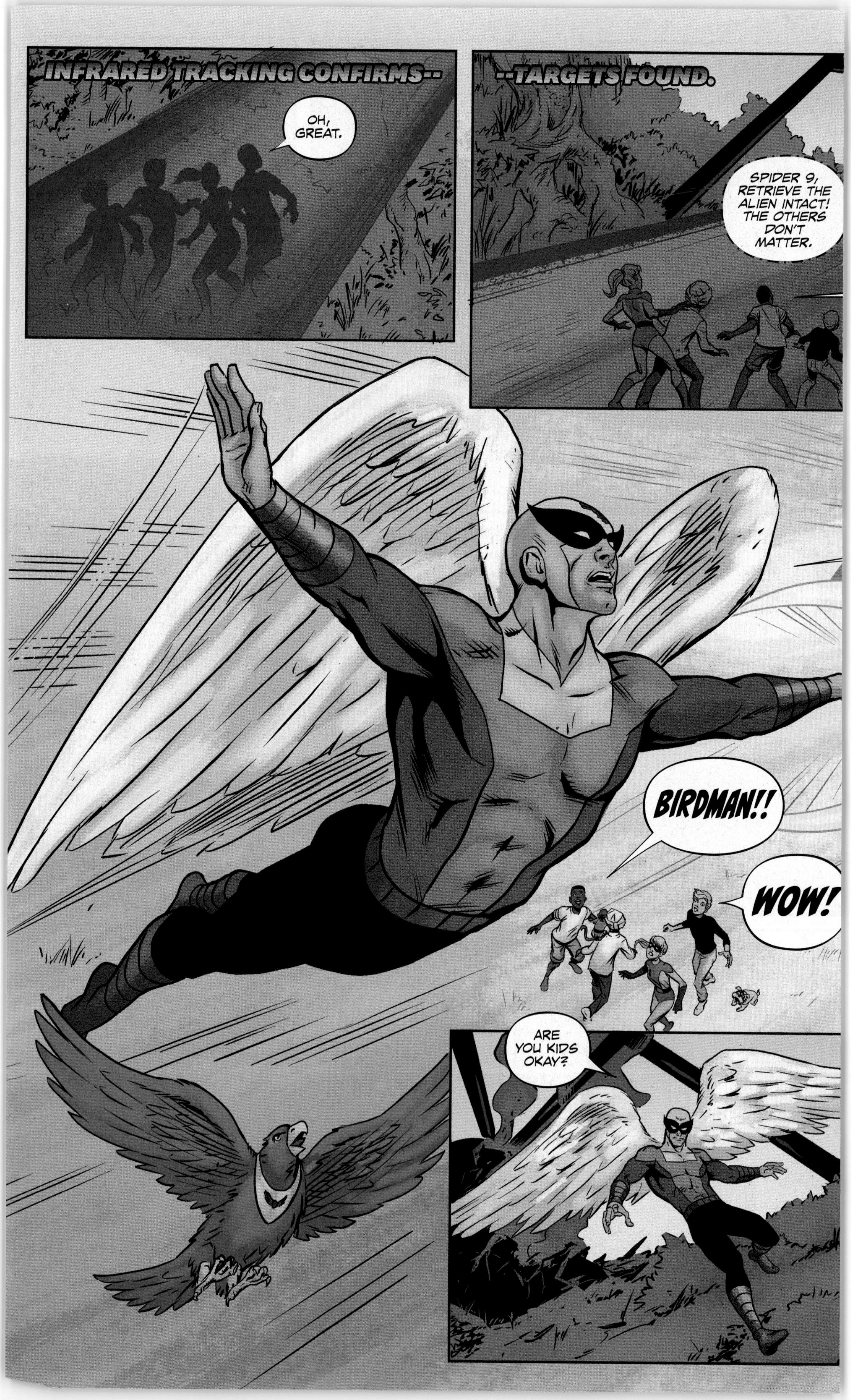
INFRARED TRACKING CONFIRMS--
OH, GREAT.
--TARGETS FOUND.
SPIDER 9, RETRIEVE THE ALIEN INTACT! THE OTHERS DON'T MATTER.
BIRDMAN!!
WOW!
ARE YOU KIDS OKAY?

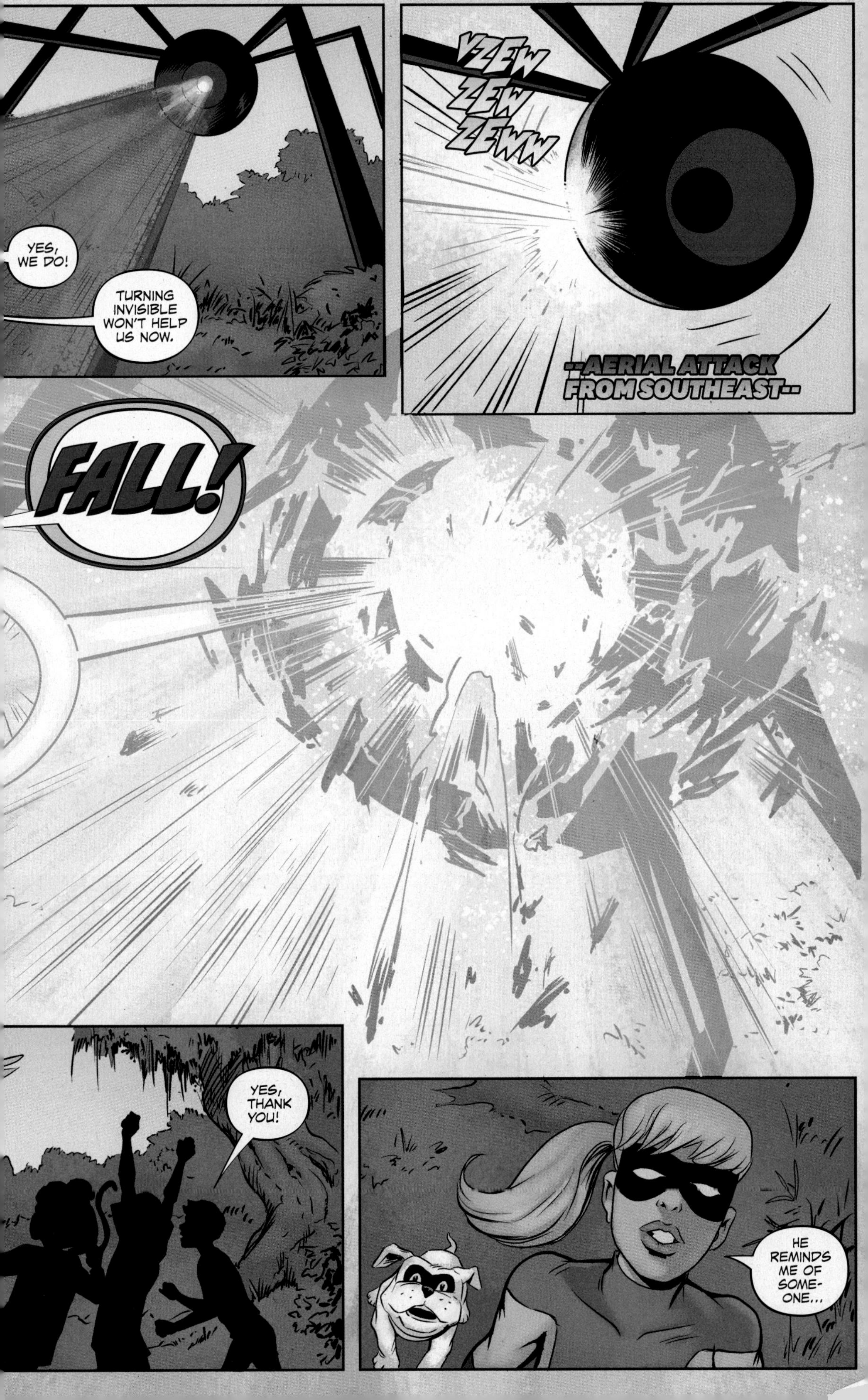
YES, WE DO!
TURNING INVISIBLE WON'T HELP US NOW.
VZEW ZEW ZEWW
--AERIAL ATTACK FROM SOUTHEAST--
FALL!
YES, THANK YOU!
HE REMINDS ME OF SOME- ONE...

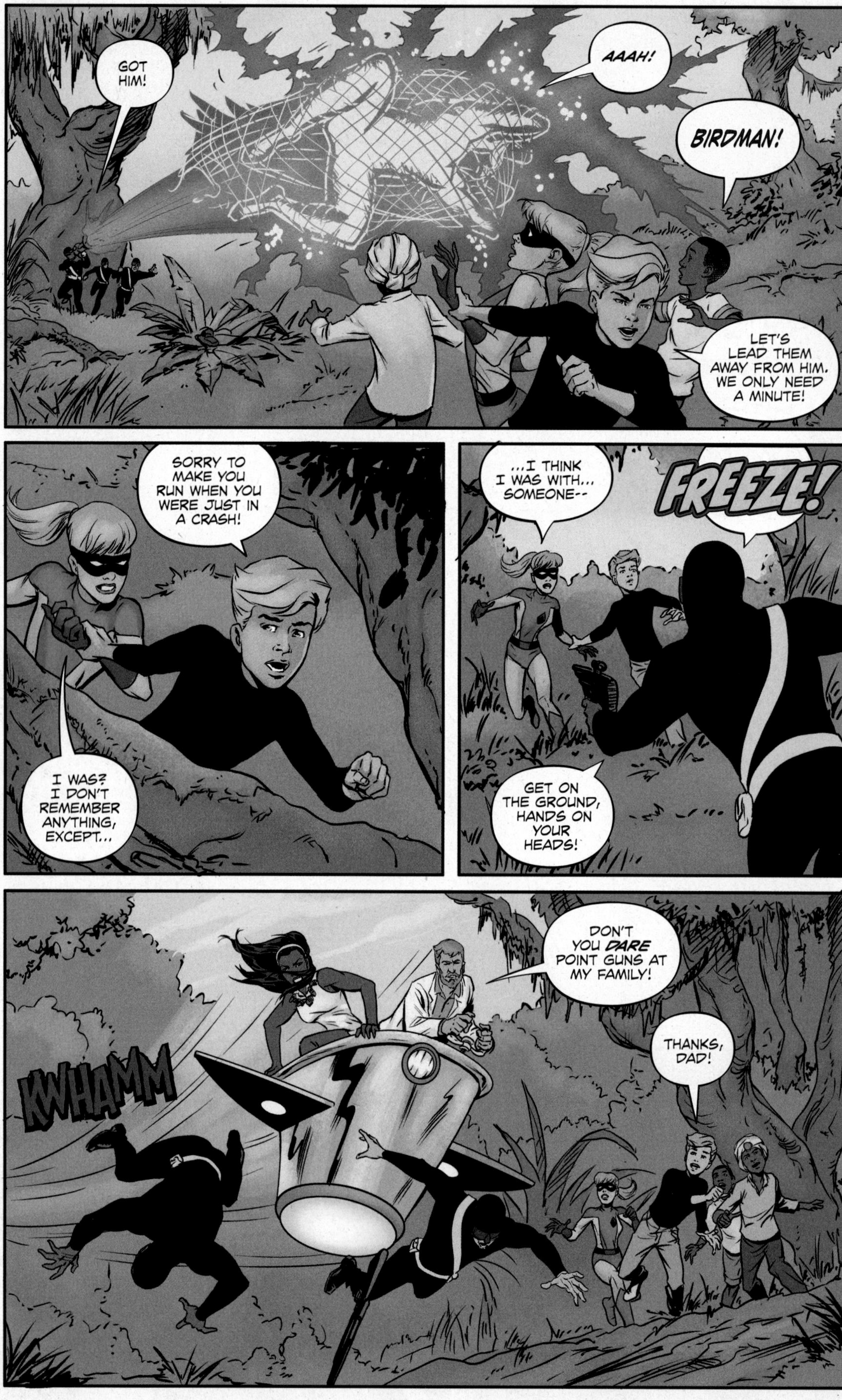
GOT HIM!
AAAH!
BIRDMAN!
LET'S LEAD THEM AWAY FROM HIM. WE ONLY NEED A MINUTE!
SORRY TO MAKE YOU RUN WHEN YOU WERE JUST IN A CRASH!
I WAS? I DON'T REMEMBER ANYTHING, EXCEPT...
...I THINK I WAS WITH... SOMEONE--
FREEZE!
GET ON THE GROUND, HANDS ON YOUR HEADS!
KWHAMM
DON'T YOU DARE POINT GUNS AT MY FAMILY!
THANKS, DAD!

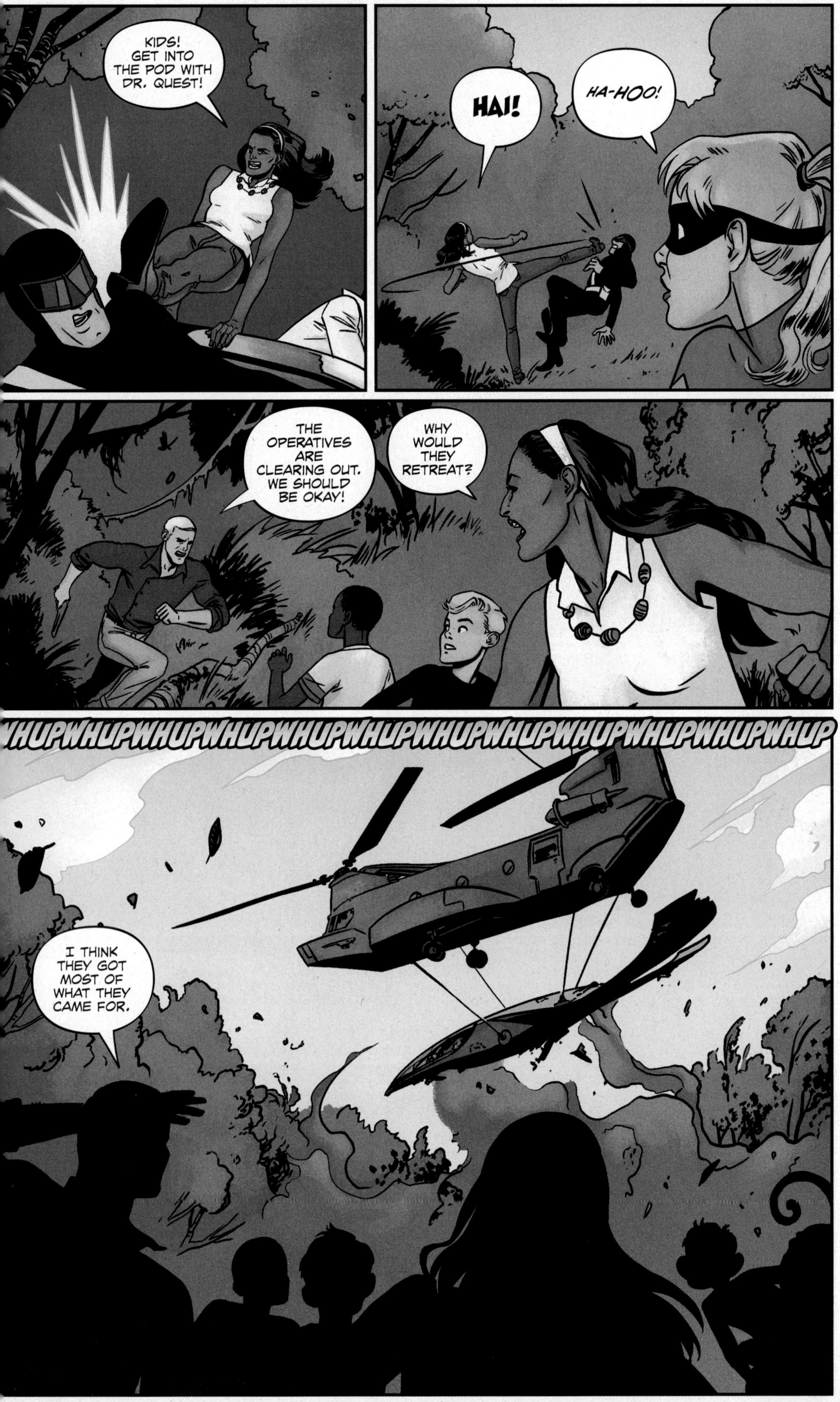

KIDS! GET INTO THE POD WITH DR. QUEST!
HAJ!
HA-HOO!
THE OPERATIVES ARE CLEARING OUT. WE SHOULD BE OKAY!
WHY WOULD THEY RETREAT?
WHUPWHUPWHUPWHUPWHUPWHUPWHUPWHUPWHUPWHUPWHUP
I THINK THEY GOT MOST OF WHAT THEY CAME FOR.

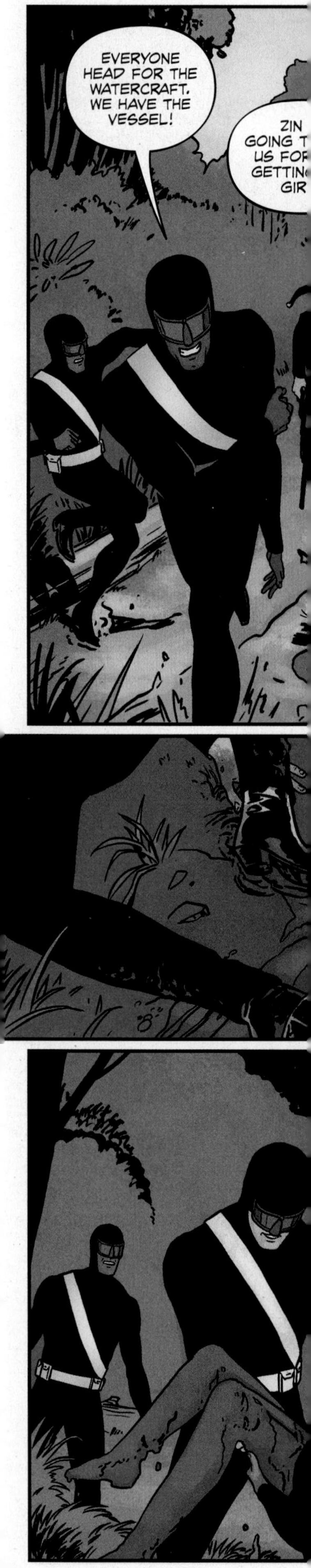
EVERYONE HEAD FOR THE WATERCRAFT. WE HAVE THE VESSEL!

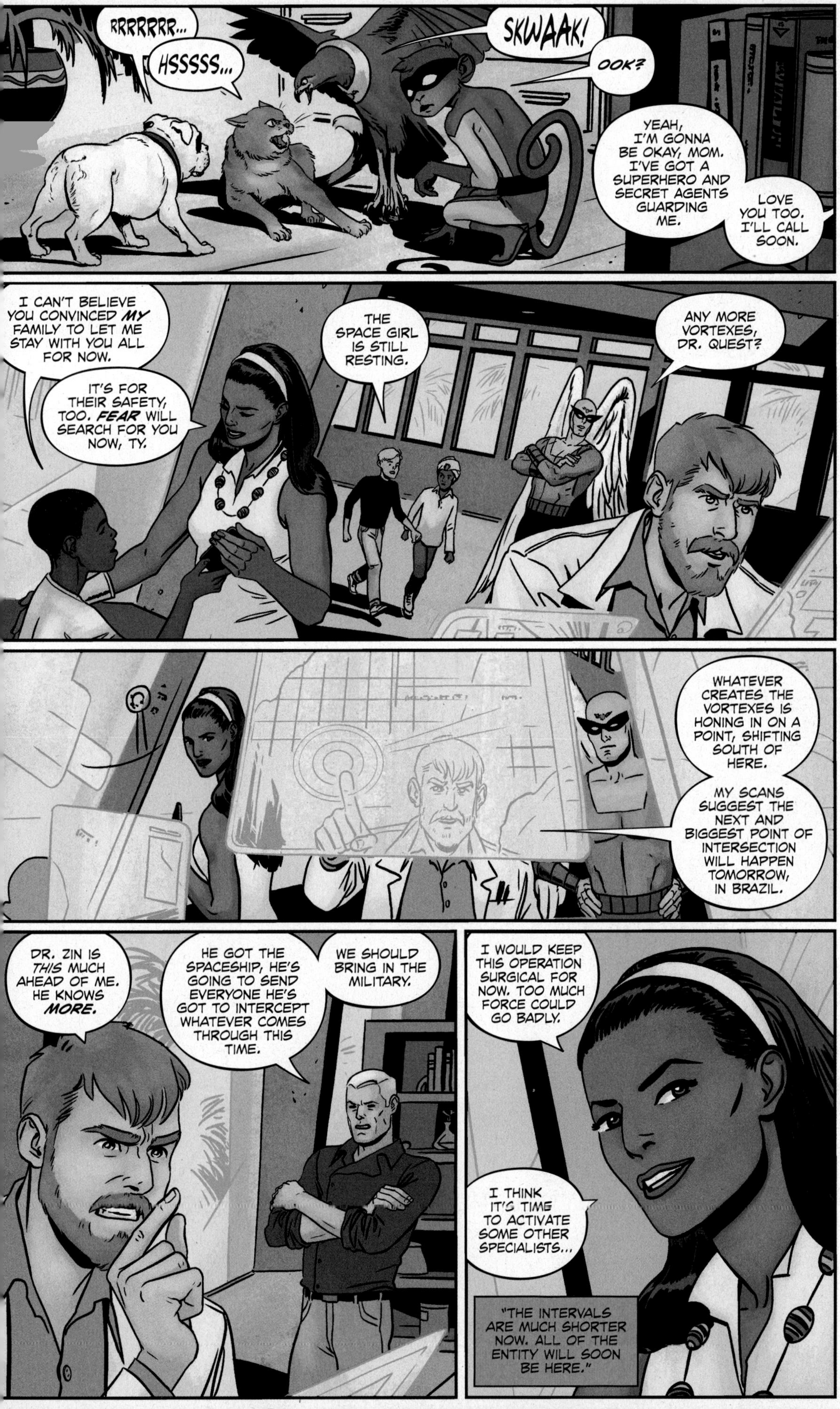
RRRRRRR...
HSSSSS...
SKWAAK!
OOK?
YEAH, I'M GONNA BE OKAY, MOM. I'VE GOT A SUPERHERO AND SECRET AGENTS GUARDING ME.
LOVE YOU TOO. I'LL CALL SOON.
I CAN'T BELIEVE YOU CONVINCED MY FAMILY TO LET ME STAY WITH YOU ALL FOR NOW.
IT'S FOR THEIR SAFETY, TOO. FEAR WILL SEARCH FOR YOU NOW, TY.
THE SPACE GIRL IS STILL RESTING.
ANY MORE VORTEXES, DR. QUEST?
WHATEVER CREATES THE VORTEXES IS HONING IN ON A POINT, SHIFTING SOUTH OF HERE.
MY SCANS SUGGEST THE NEXT AND BIGGEST POINT OF INTERSECTION WILL HAPPEN TOMORROW, IN BRAZIL.
DR. ZIN IS THIS MUCH AHEAD OF ME. HE KNOWS MORE.
HE GOT THE SPACESHIP, HE'S GOING TO SEND EVERYONE HE'S GOT TO INTERCEPT WHATEVER COMES THROUGH THIS TIME.
WE SHOULD BRING IN THE MILITARY.
I WOULD KEEP THIS OPERATION SURGICAL FOR NOW. TOO MUCH FORCE COULD GO BADLY.
I THINK IT'S TIME TO ACTIVATE SOME OTHER SPECIALISTS...
"THE INTERVALS ARE MUCH SHORTER NOW. ALL OF THE ENTITY WILL SOON BE HERE."

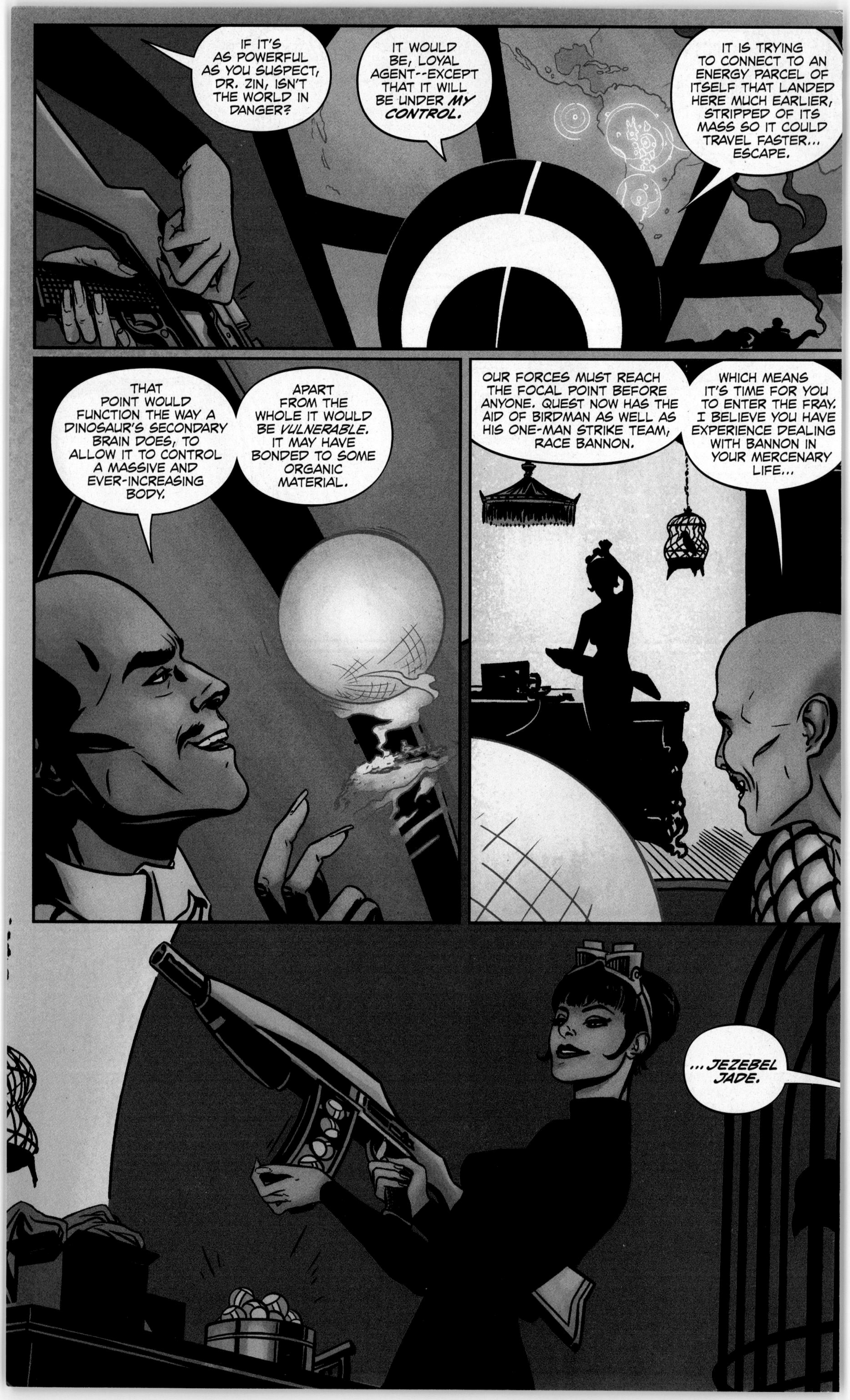
IF IT'S AS POWERFUL AS YOU SUSPECT, DR. ZIN, ISN'T THE WORLD IN DANGER?
IT WOULD BE, LOYAL AGENT--EXCEPT THAT IT WILL BE UNDER MY CONTROL.
IT IS TRYING TO CONNECT TO AN ENERGY PARCEL OF ITSELF THAT LANDED HERE MUCH EARLIER, STRIPPED OF ITS MASS SO IT COULD TRAVEL FASTER... ESCAPE.
THAT POINT WOULD FUNCTION THE WAY A DINOSAUR'S SECONDARY BRAIN DOES, TO ALLOW IT TO CONTROL A MASSIVE AND EVER-INCREASING BODY.
APART FROM THE WHOLE IT WOULD BE VULNERABLE. IT MAY HAVE BONDED TO SOME ORGANIC MATERIAL.
OUR FORCES MUST REACH THE FOCAL POINT BEFORE ANYONE. QUEST NOW HAS THE AID OF BIRDMAN AS WELL AS HIS ONE-MAN STRIKE TEAM, RACE BANNON.
WHICH MEANS IT'S TIME FOR YOU TO ENTER THE FRAY. I BELIEVE YOU HAVE EXPERIENCE DEALING WITH BANNON IN YOUR MERCENARY LIFE...
...JEZEBEL JADE.

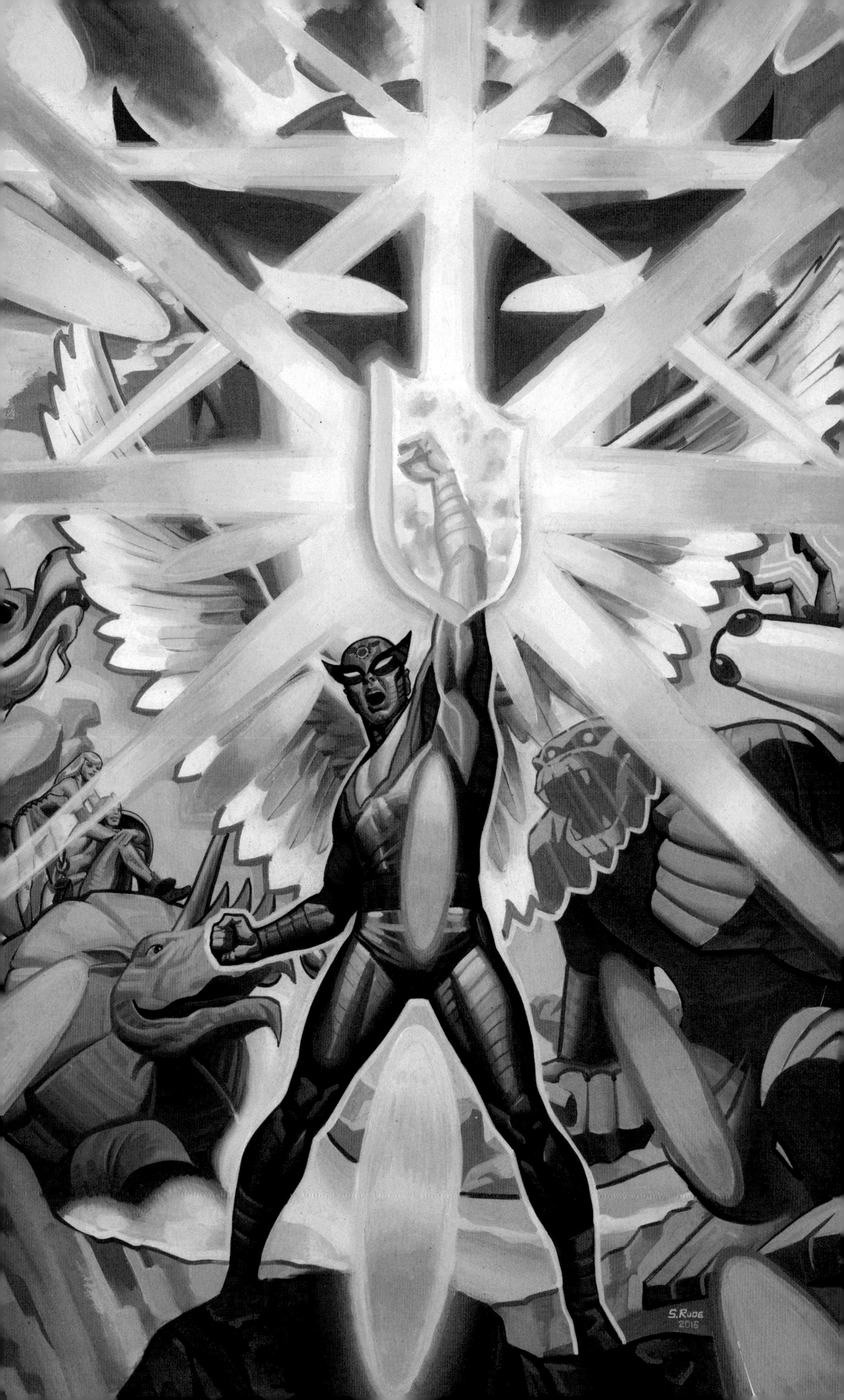
S.RUDE
2016

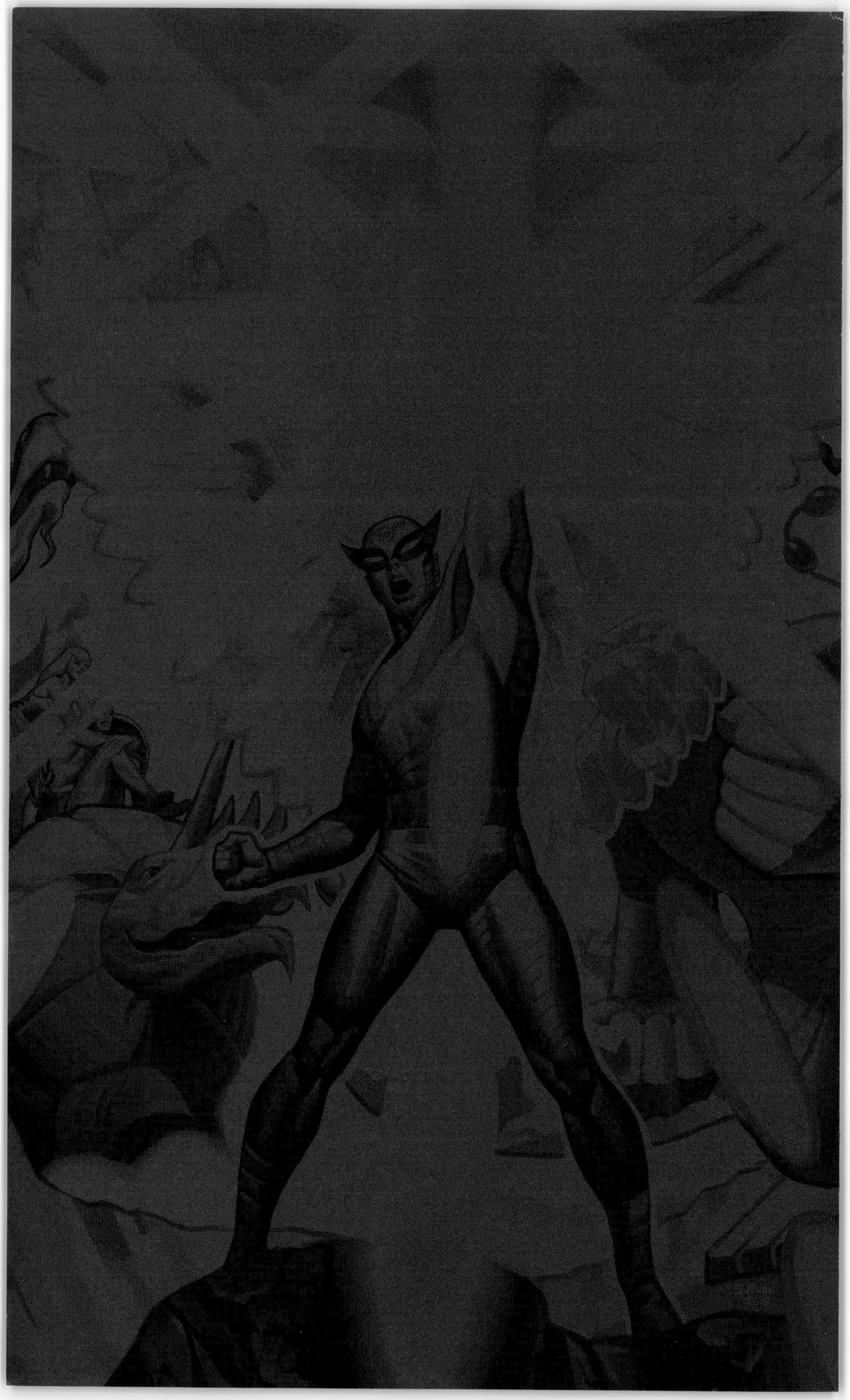

DCC037637

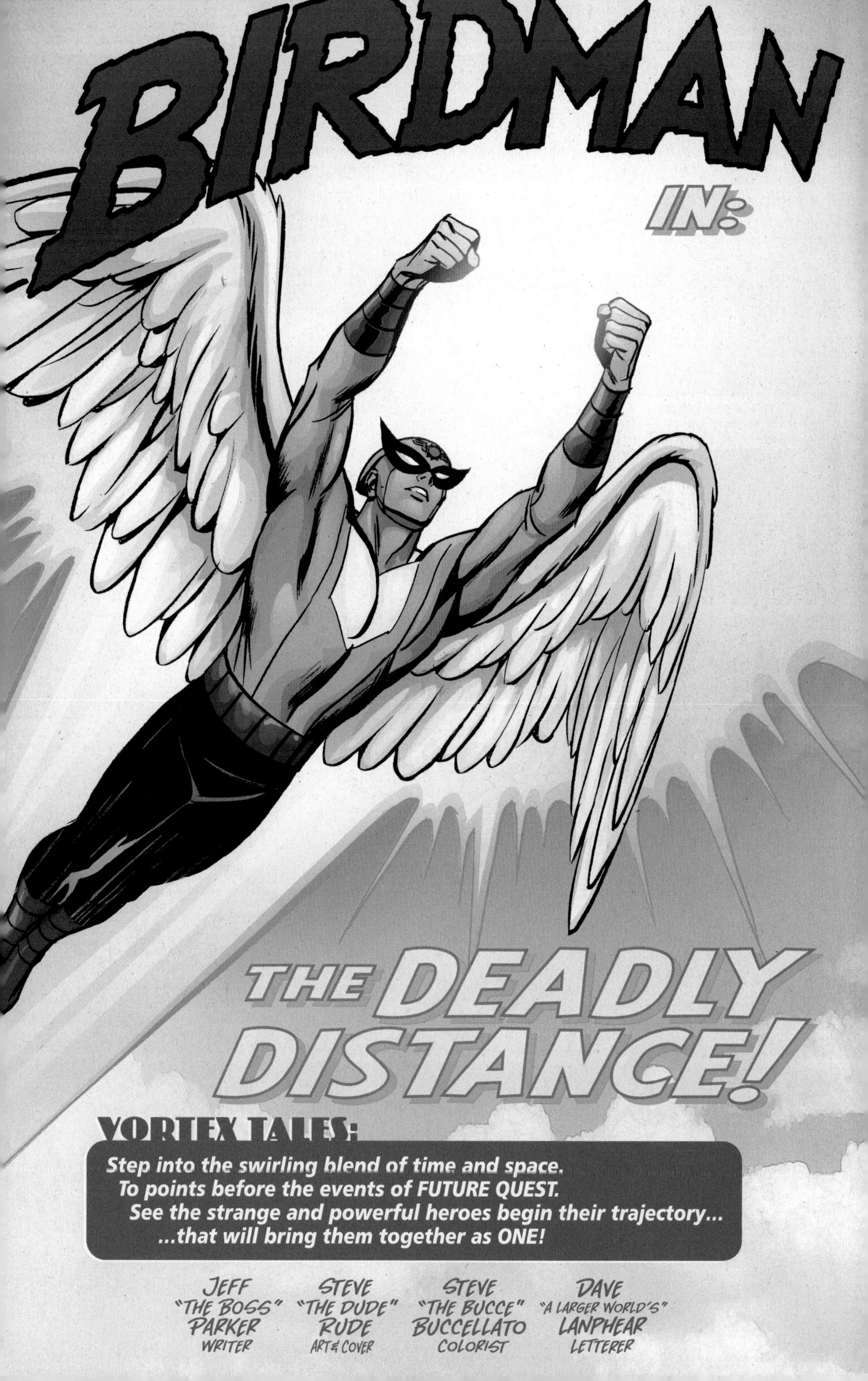

BIRDMAN
IN:
THE DEADLY DISTANCE!
VORTEX TALES:
Step into the swirling blend of time and space.
To points before the events of FUTURE QUEST.
See the strange and powerful heroes begin their trajectory...
...that will bring them together as ONE!
JEFF "THE BOSS" PARKER WRITER
STEVE "THE DUDE" RUDE ART & COVER
STEVE "THE BUCCE" BUCCELLATO COLORIST
DAVE "A LARGER WORLD'S" LANPHEAR LETTERER

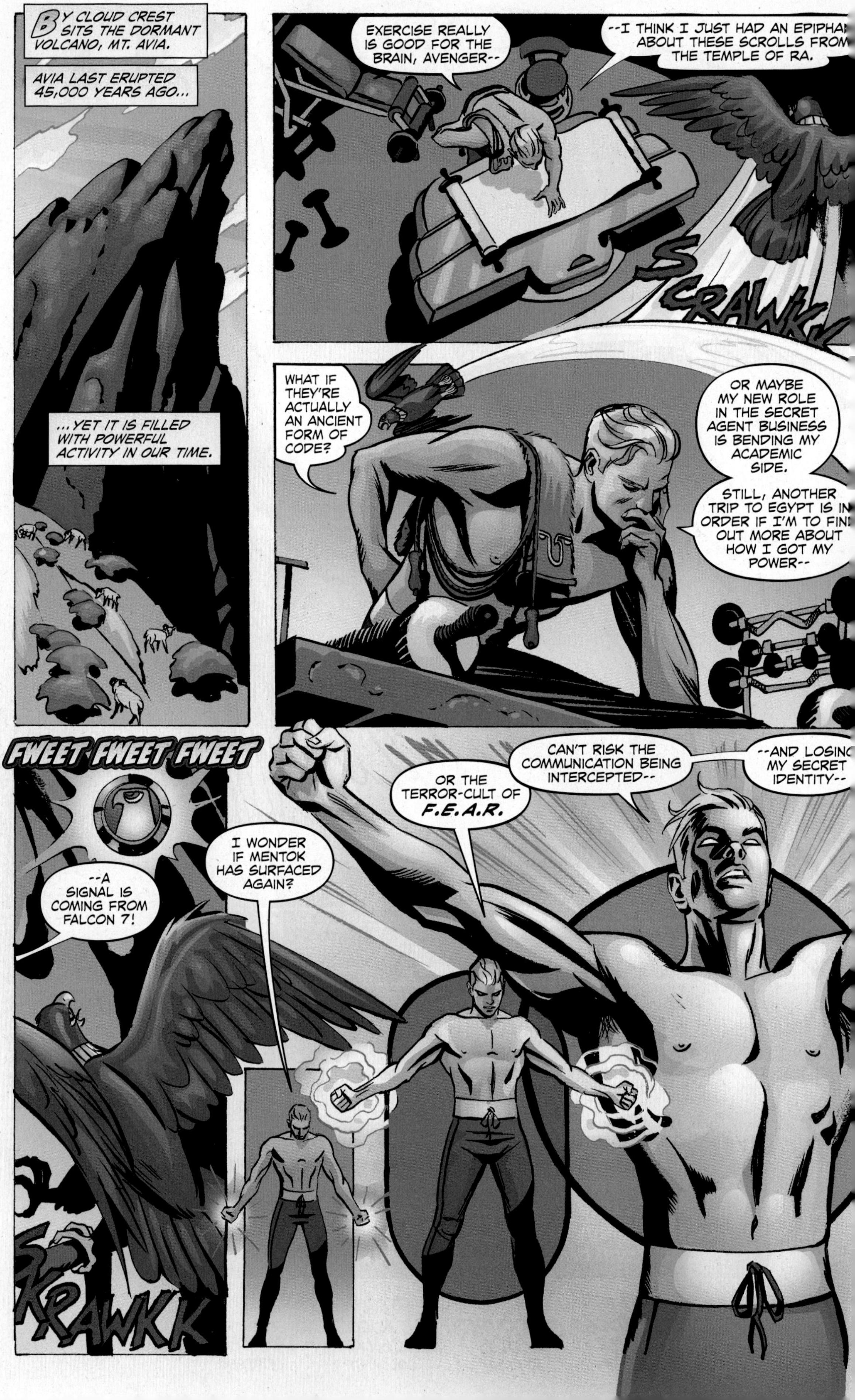
BY CLOUD CREST SITS THE DORMANT VOLCANO, MT. AVIA.
AVIA LAST ERUPTED 45,000 YEARS AGO...
...YET IT IS FILLED WITH POWERFUL ACTIVITY IN OUR TIME.
EXERCISE REALLY IS GOOD FOR THE BRAIN, AVENGER--
--I THINK I JUST HAD AN EPIPHA ABOUT THESE SCROLLS FROM THE TEMPLE OF RA.
SCRAWKK
WHAT IF THEY'RE ACTUALLY AN ANCIENT FORM OF CODE?
OR MAYBE MY NEW ROLE IN THE SECRET AGENT BUSINESS IS BENDING MY ACADEMIC SIDE.
STILL, ANOTHER TRIP TO EGYPT IS IN ORDER IF I'M TO FIND OUT MORE ABOUT HOW I GOT MY POWER--
FWEET FWEET FWEET
--A SIGNAL IS COMING FROM FALCON 7!
SKRAWKK
I WONDER IF MENTOK HAS SURFACED AGAIN?
OR THE TERROR-CULT OF F.E.A.R.
CAN'T RISK THE COMMUNICATION BEING INTERCEPTED--
--AND LOSING MY SECRET IDENTITY--

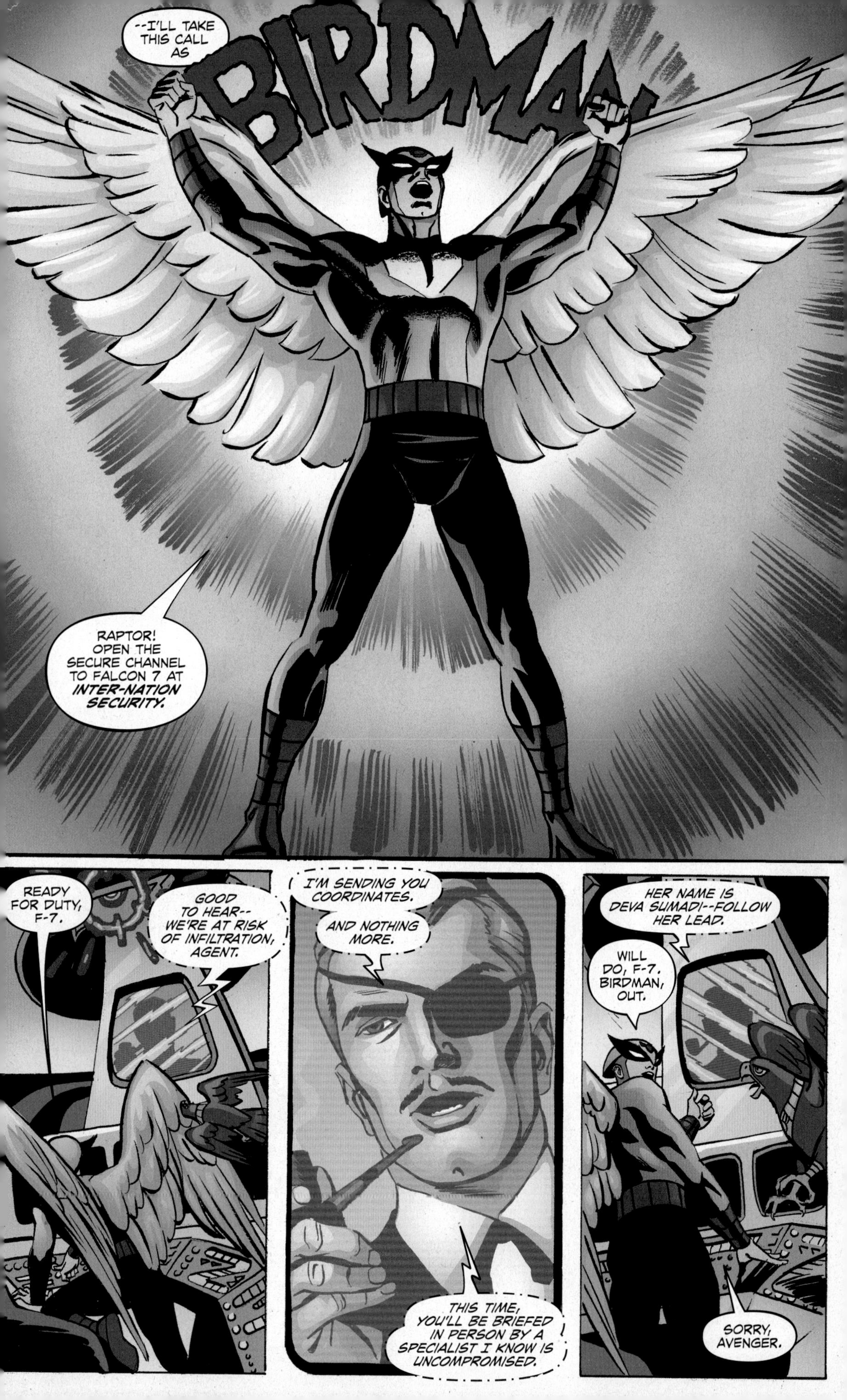

--I'LL TAKE THIS CALL AS
BIRDMAN
RAPTOR! OPEN THE SECURE CHANNEL TO FALCON 7 AT *INTER-NATION SECURITY.*
READY FOR DUTY, F-7.
GOOD TO HEAR-- WE'RE AT RISK OF INFILTRATION, AGENT.
I'M SENDING YOU COORDINATES.
AND NOTHING MORE.
THIS TIME, YOU'LL BE BRIEFED IN PERSON BY A SPECIALIST I KNOW IS UNCOMPROMISED.
HER NAME IS DEVA SUMADI--FOLLOW HER LEAD.
WILL DO, F-7. BIRDMAN, OUT.
SORRY, AVENGER.

I PROMISE I'LL TAKE YOU NEXT TIME.

SKRAAAWK!

S.W. UTAH.

I SHOULD HAVE ASKED FOR A PASS PHRASE.

STILL, THERE'S ONLY ONE PERSON, RIGHT ON THE LOCATION.

HI, MISS SUMADI-- UM--

SORRY, MR. RANDALL-- REFLEX.

THINGS HAVE GOTTEN MUCH MORE DANGEROUS LATELY WITH *F.E.A.R.*

A SCIENTIST NAMED ZIN HAS JOINED THEM AND UPPED THEIR GAME.

SO IF I SEEM ON EDGE...

...IT'S JUST THAT I AM.

GOTCHA. NOW WHAT ARE THEY DOING WAY OUT HERE?

WAITING FOR *SOMETHING* TO ARRIVE, DOWN IN THE CANYON.

YOU'LL NEED TO DEMATERIALIZE YOUR HARD-LIGHT WINGS TO FIT THROUGH THIS PASS, RAY.

YOU SEEM TO KNOW A LOT ABOUT ME, BUT I ONLY KNOW YOUR--

SHHH.

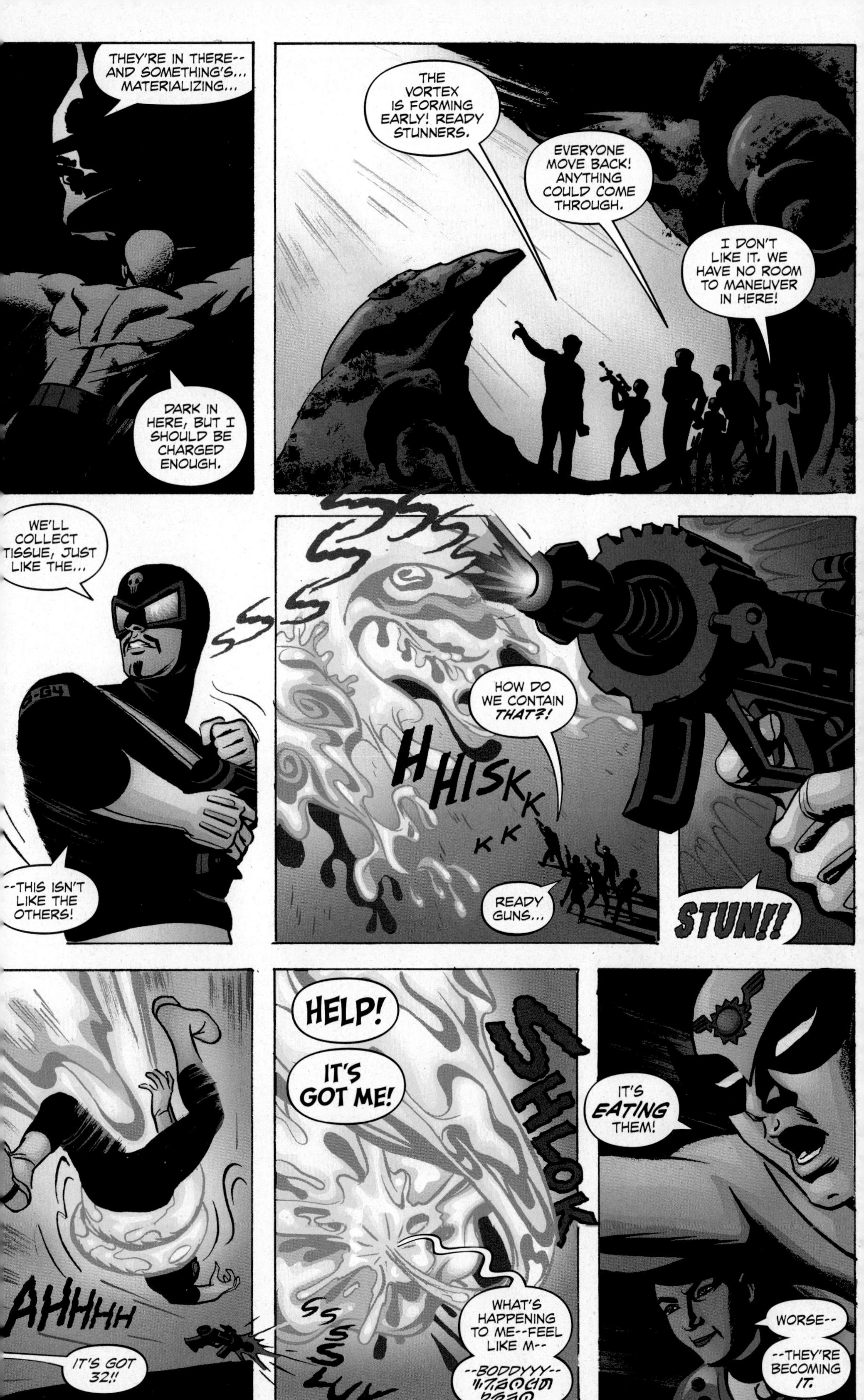

THEY'RE IN THERE--AND SOMETHING'S... MATERIALIZING...
DARK IN HERE, BUT I SHOULD BE CHARGED ENOUGH.
THE VORTEX IS FORMING EARLY! READY STUNNERS.
EVERYONE MOVE BACK! ANYTHING COULD COME THROUGH.
I DON'T LIKE IT. WE HAVE NO ROOM TO MANEUVER IN HERE!
WE'LL COLLECT TISSUE, JUST LIKE THE...
SSSS
--THIS ISN'T LIKE THE OTHERS!
SSSSSS
HOW DO WE CONTAIN *THAT?!*
HHISKKKK
READY GUNS...
STUN!!
AHHHH
IT'S GOT 32!!
HELP!
IT'S GOT ME!
SHLOOK
WHAT'S HAPPENING TO ME--FEEL LIKE M--
--BODDYYY--
SSSSLUK
IT'S *EATING* THEM!
WORSE--
--THEY'RE BECOMING *IT.*

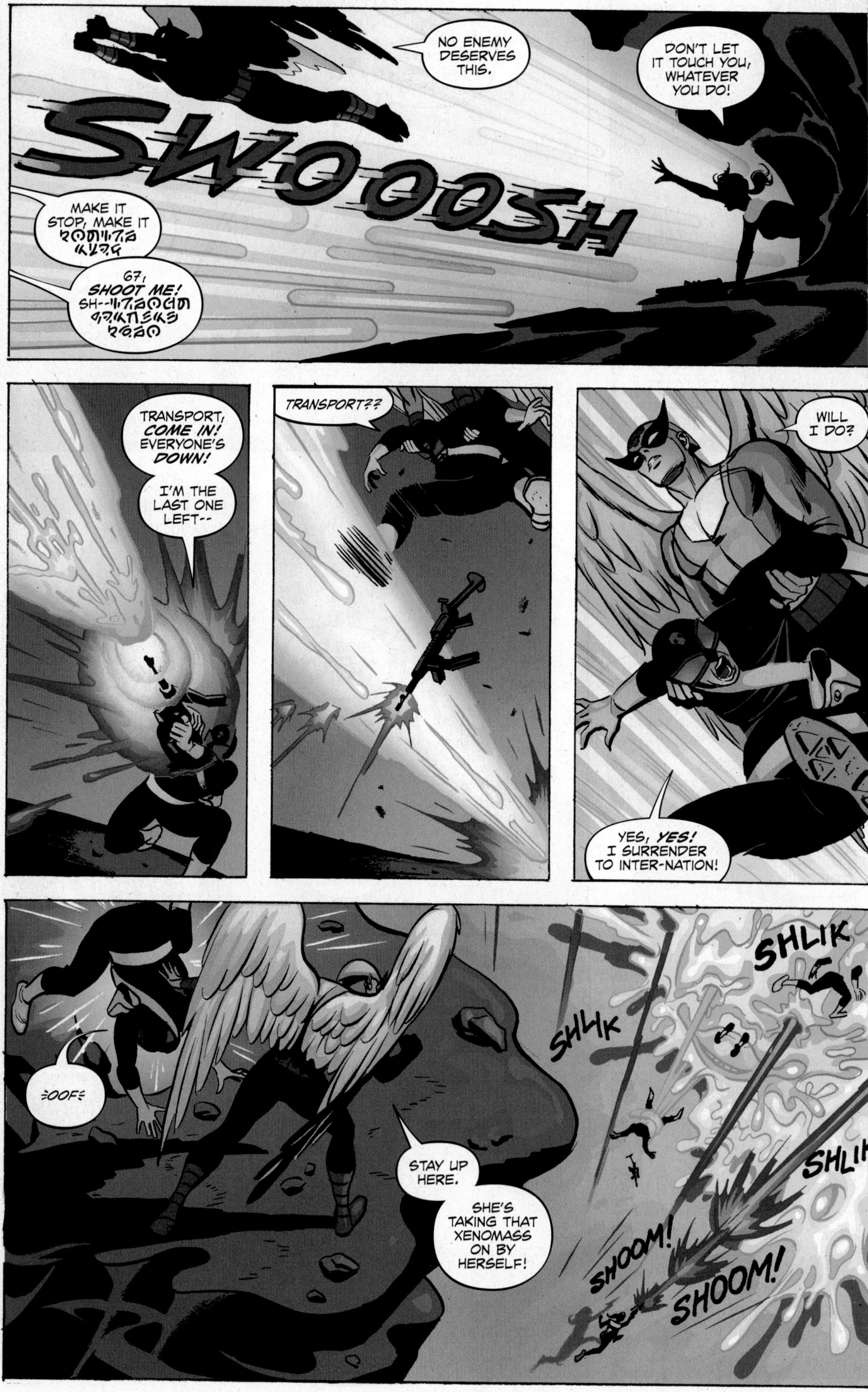

NO ENEMY DESERVES THIS.
DON'T LET IT TOUCH YOU, WHATEVER YOU DO!
SWOOOSH
MAKE IT STOP, MAKE IT
67, SHOOT ME! SH--
TRANSPORT, COME IN! EVERYONE'S DOWN!
I'M THE LAST ONE LEFT--
TRANSPORT??
WILL I DO?
YES, YES! I SURRENDER TO INTER-NATION!
OOF
STAY UP HERE.
SHE'S TAKING THAT XENOMASS ON BY HERSELF!
SHLIK
SHLIK
SHLIK
SHOOM!
SHOOM!

BLAM
BLAM
BLAM
BLAM
BLAM
BLAM
BLAM

AT LEAST SLOW DOWN--

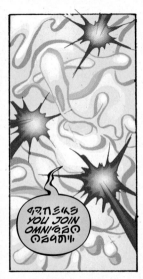

YOU JOIN OMNI

--FEEL IT-- IN MY HEAD--

ALL LIFE ALL TIME

SHOULD'VE USED--LAST ROUNDS--

--FOR MYSELF--

SHIELD!

I DON'T KNOW HOW LONG I CAN HOLD IT OFF-- I CAN'T CONVERT SOLAR ENERGY IN HERE!

GO BACK OUT THE WAY WE CAME, HURRY!

NOT GOING ANYWHERE, FLIER.

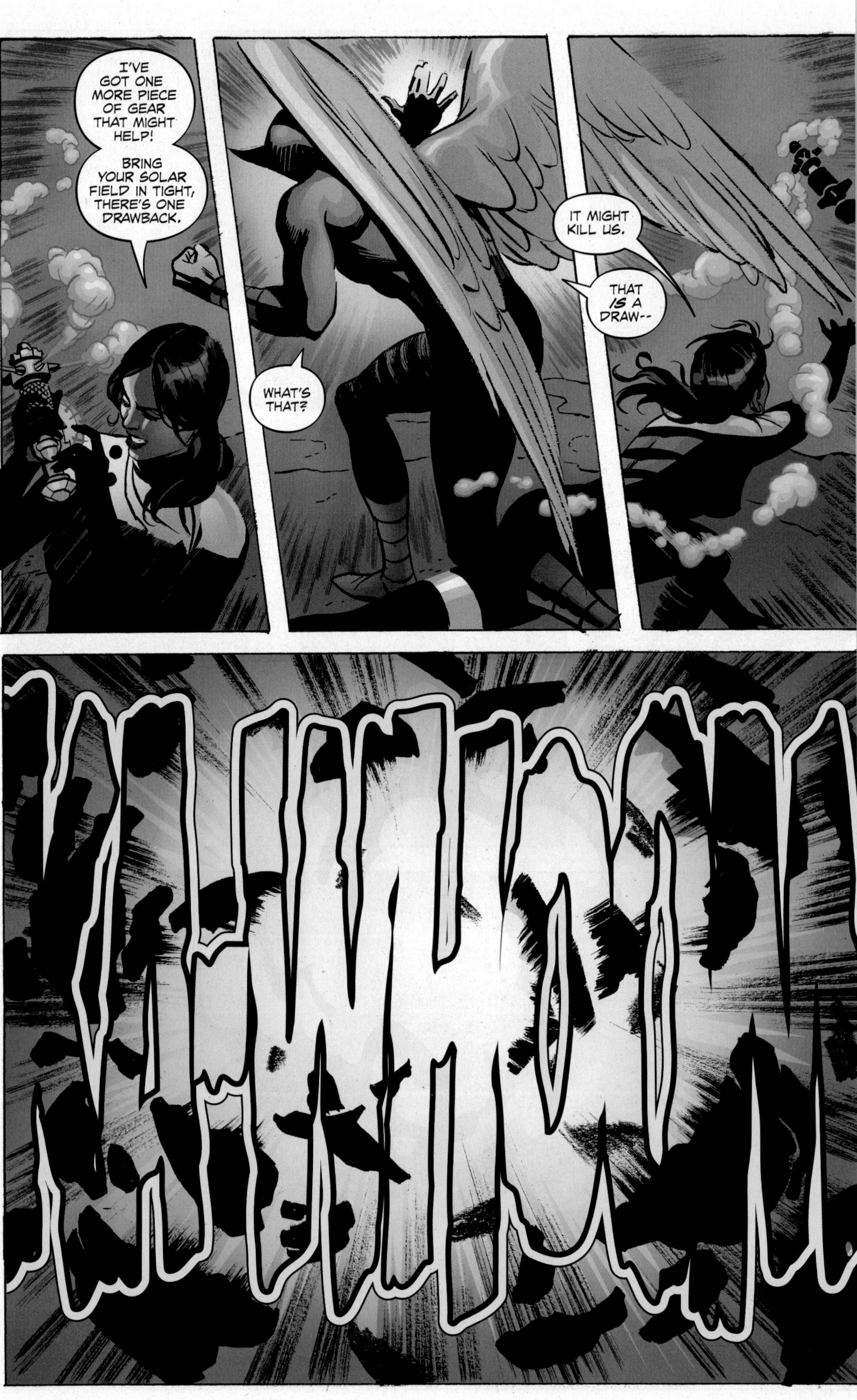
I'VE GOT ONE MORE PIECE OF GEAR THAT MIGHT HELP!
BRING YOUR SOLAR FIELD IN TIGHT, THERE'S ONE DRAWBACK.
WHAT'S THAT?
IT MIGHT KILL US.
THAT *IS* A DRAW--

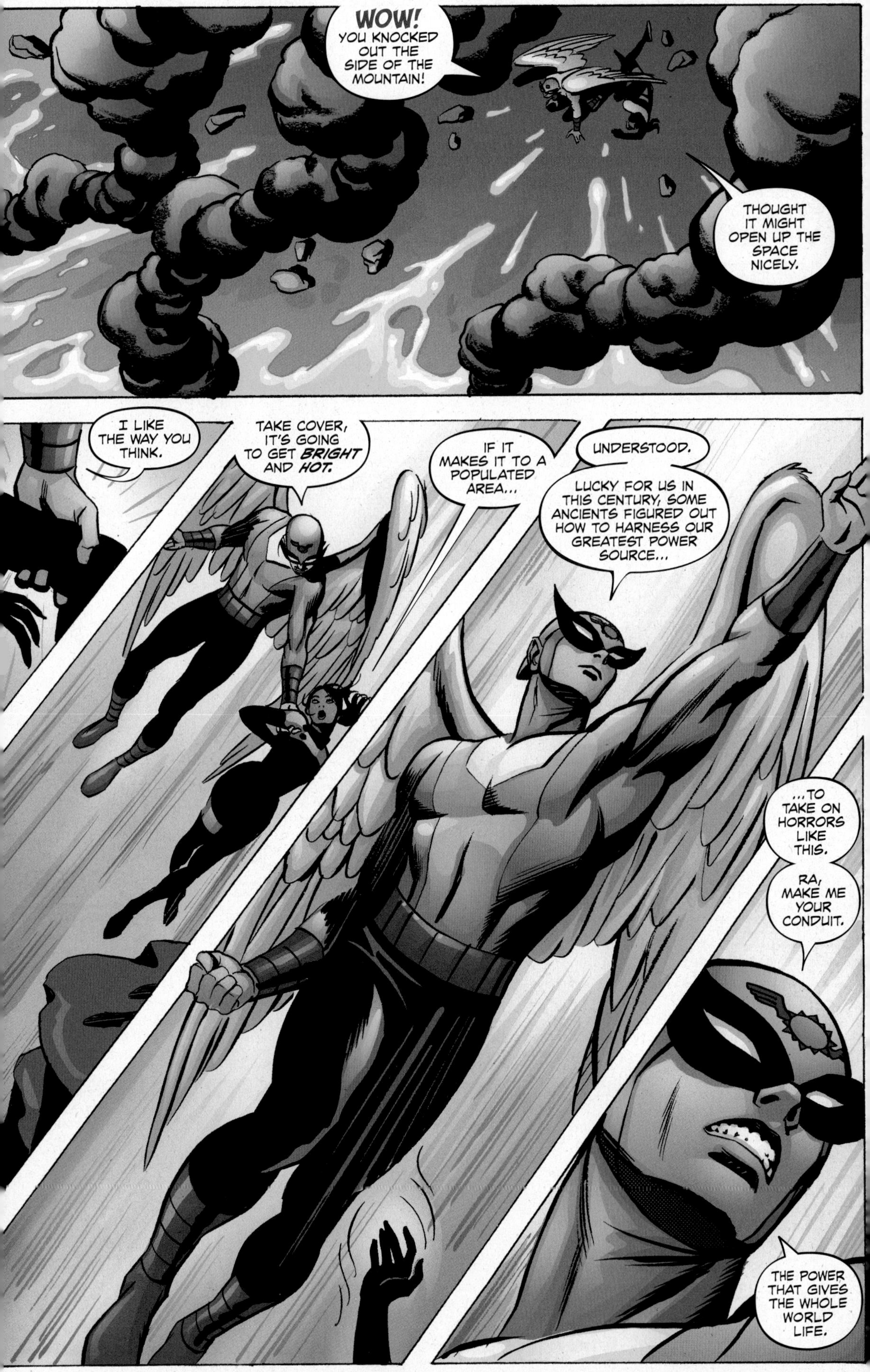
WOW! YOU KNOCKED OUT THE SIDE OF THE MOUNTAIN!
THOUGHT IT MIGHT OPEN UP THE SPACE NICELY.
I LIKE THE WAY YOU THINK.
TAKE COVER, IT'S GOING TO GET BRIGHT AND HOT.
IF IT MAKES IT TO A POPULATED AREA...
UNDERSTOOD.
LUCKY FOR US IN THIS CENTURY, SOME ANCIENTS FIGURED OUT HOW TO HARNESS OUR GREATEST POWER SOURCE...
...TO TAKE ON HORRORS LIKE THIS.
RA, MAKE ME YOUR CONDUIT.
THE POWER THAT GIVES THE WHOLE WORLD LIFE.

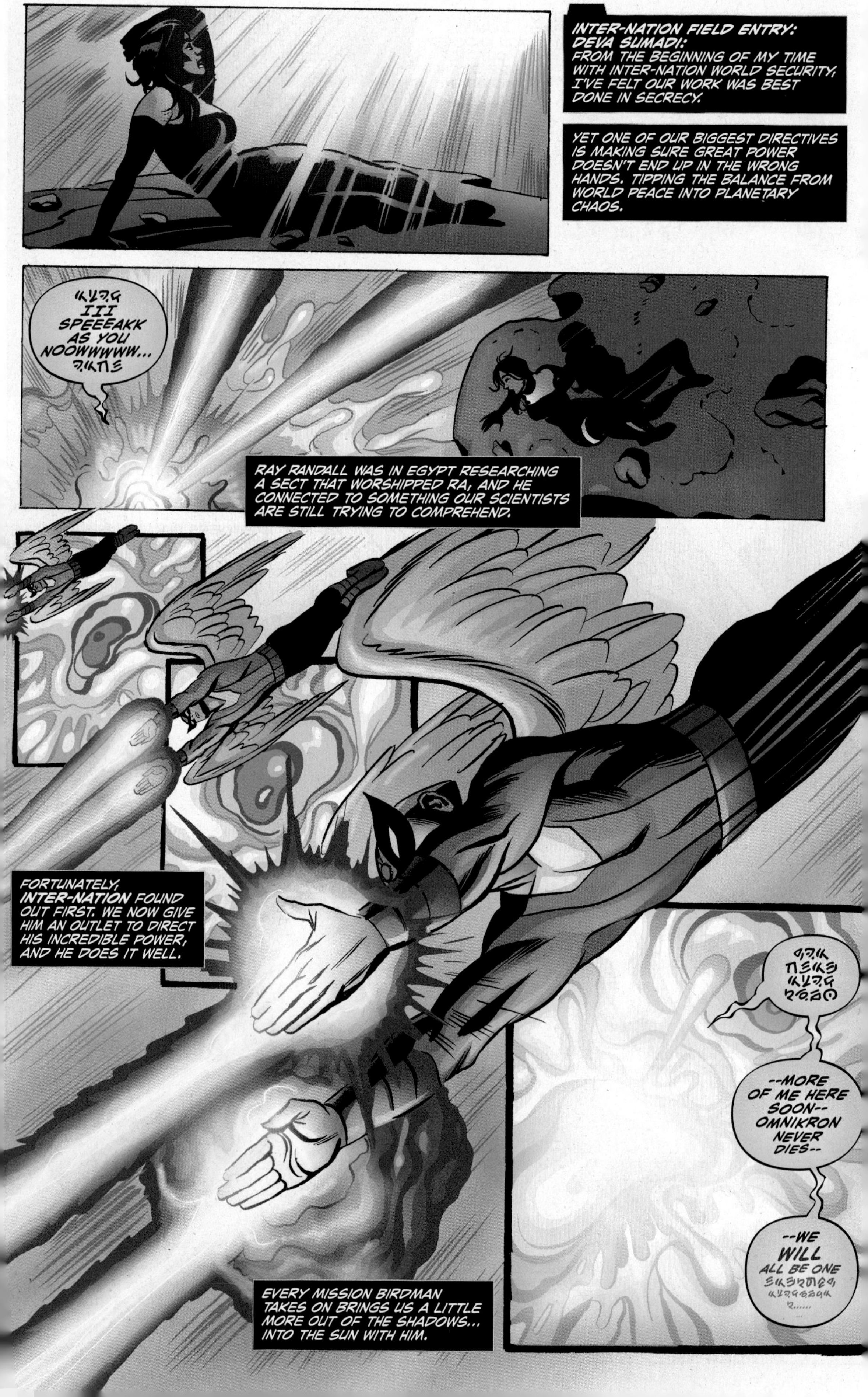
INTER-NATION FIELD ENTRY: DEVA SUMADI:
FROM THE BEGINNING OF MY TIME WITH INTER-NATION WORLD SECURITY, I'VE FELT OUR WORK WAS BEST DONE IN SECRECY.
YET ONE OF OUR BIGGEST DIRECTIVES IS MAKING SURE GREAT POWER DOESN'T END UP IN THE WRONG HANDS. TIPPING THE BALANCE FROM WORLD PEACE INTO PLANETARY CHAOS.
III SPEEEAKK AS YOU NOOWWWWW...
RAY RANDALL WAS IN EGYPT RESEARCHING A SECT THAT WORSHIPPED RA, AND HE CONNECTED TO SOMETHING OUR SCIENTISTS ARE STILL TRYING TO COMPREHEND.
FORTUNATELY, INTER-NATION FOUND OUT FIRST. WE NOW GIVE HIM AN OUTLET TO DIRECT HIS INCREDIBLE POWER, AND HE DOES IT WELL.
--MORE OF ME HERE SOON-- OMNIKRON NEVER DIES--
--WE WILL ALL BE ONE
EVERY MISSION BIRDMAN TAKES ON BRINGS US A LITTLE MORE OUT OF THE SHADOWS... INTO THE SUN WITH HIM.

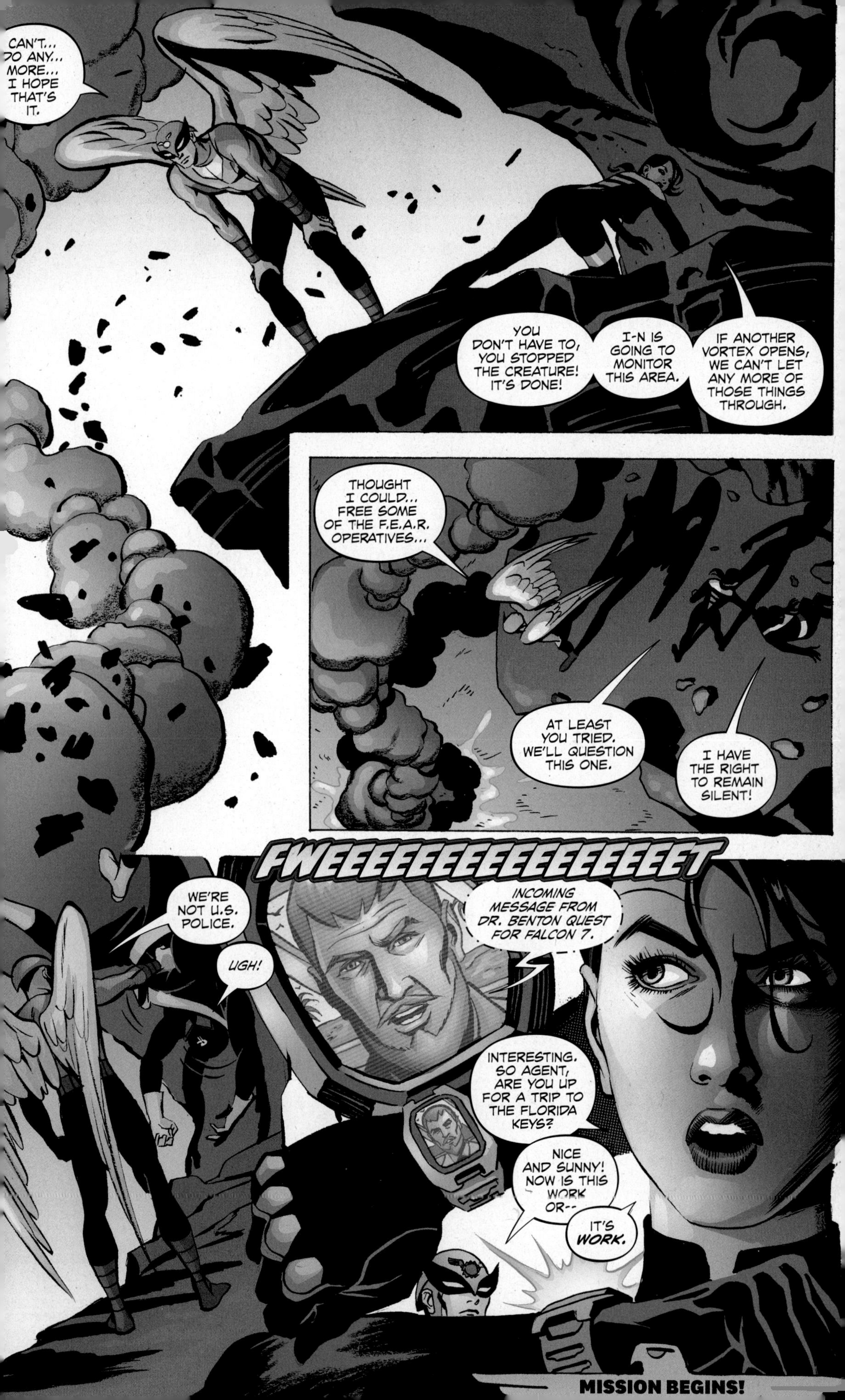
CAN'T... DO ANY... MORE... I HOPE THAT'S IT.
YOU DON'T HAVE TO, YOU STOPPED THE CREATURE! IT'S DONE!
I-N IS GOING TO MONITOR THIS AREA.
IF ANOTHER VORTEX OPENS, WE CAN'T LET ANY MORE OF THOSE THINGS THROUGH.
THOUGHT I COULD... FREE SOME OF THE F.E.A.R. OPERATIVES...
AT LEAST YOU TRIED. WE'LL QUESTION THIS ONE.
I HAVE THE RIGHT TO REMAIN SILENT!
FWEEEEEEEEEEEEEEEEET
WE'RE NOT U.S. POLICE.
UGH!
INCOMING MESSAGE FROM DR. BENTON QUEST FOR FALCON 7.
INTERESTING. SO AGENT, ARE YOU UP FOR A TRIP TO THE FLORIDA KEYS?
NICE AND SUNNY! NOW IS THIS WORK OR--
IT'S WORK.
MISSION BEGINS!

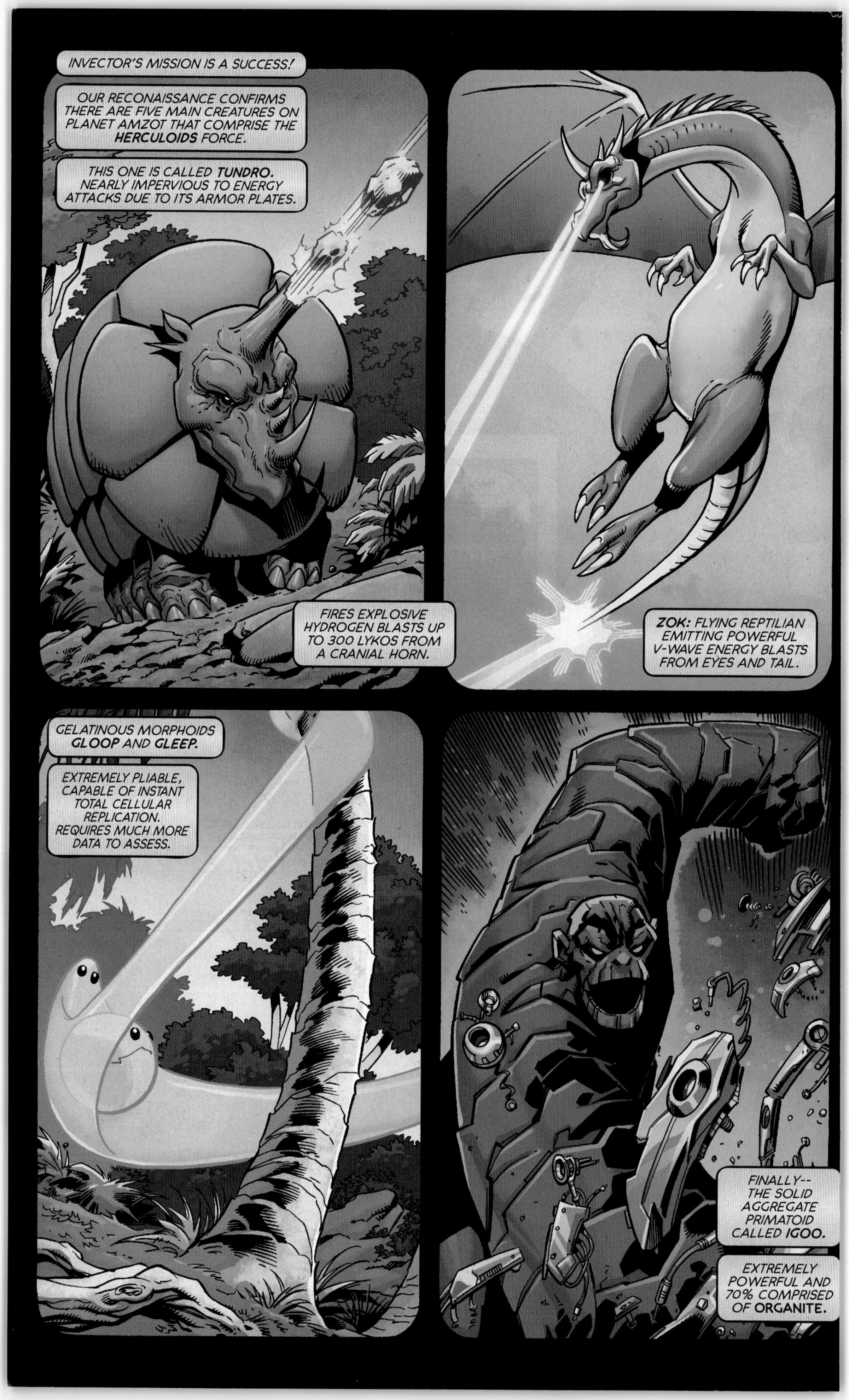
INVECTOR'S MISSION IS A SUCCESS!
OUR RECONAISSANCE CONFIRMS THERE ARE FIVE MAIN CREATURES ON PLANET AMZOT THAT COMPRISE THE HERCULOIDS FORCE.
THIS ONE IS CALLED TUNDRO. NEARLY IMPERVIOUS TO ENERGY ATTACKS DUE TO ITS ARMOR PLATES.
FIRES EXPLOSIVE HYDROGEN BLASTS UP TO 300 LYKOS FROM A CRANIAL HORN.
ZOK: FLYING REPTILIAN EMITTING POWERFUL V-WAVE ENERGY BLASTS FROM EYES AND TAIL.
GELATINOUS MORPHOIDS GLOOP AND GLEEP.
EXTREMELY PLIABLE, CAPABLE OF INSTANT TOTAL CELLULAR REPLICATION. REQUIRES MUCH MORE DATA TO ASSESS.
FINALLY-- THE SOLID AGGREGATE PRIMATOID CALLED IGOO.
EXTREMELY POWERFUL AND 70% COMPRISED OF ORGANITE.

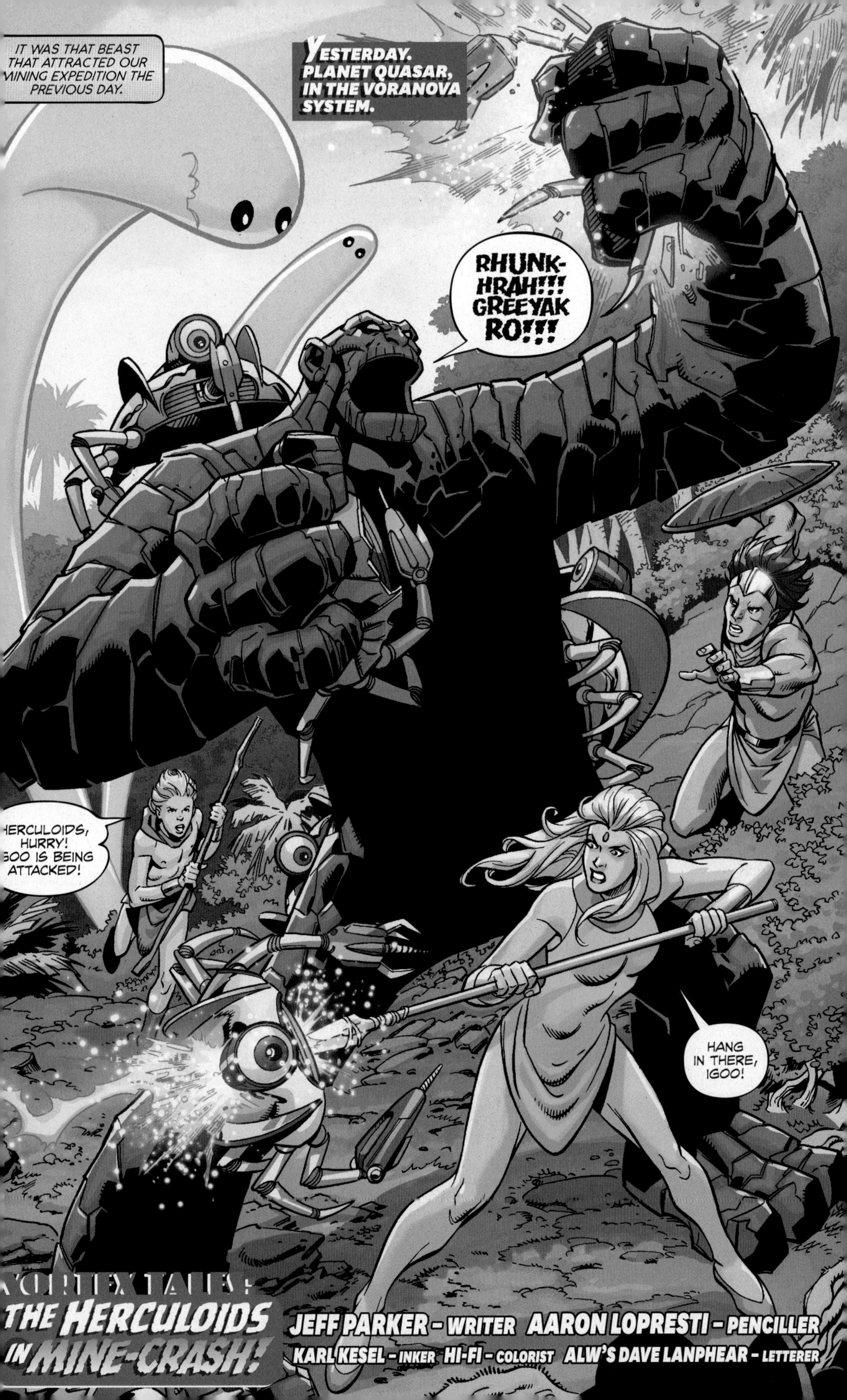
IT WAS THAT BEAST THAT ATTRACTED OUR MINING EXPEDITION THE PREVIOUS DAY.
YESTERDAY. PLANET QUASAR, IN THE VORANOVA SYSTEM.
RHUNK-HRAH!!! GREEYAK RO!!!
HERCULOIDS, HURRY! IGOO IS BEING ATTACKED!
HANG IN THERE, IGOO!
VORTEX TALES:
THE HERCULOIDS IN MINE-CRASH!
JEFF PARKER - WRITER AARON LOPRESTI - PENCILLER
KARL KESEL - INKER HI-FI - COLORIST ALW'S DAVE LANPHEAR - LETTERER

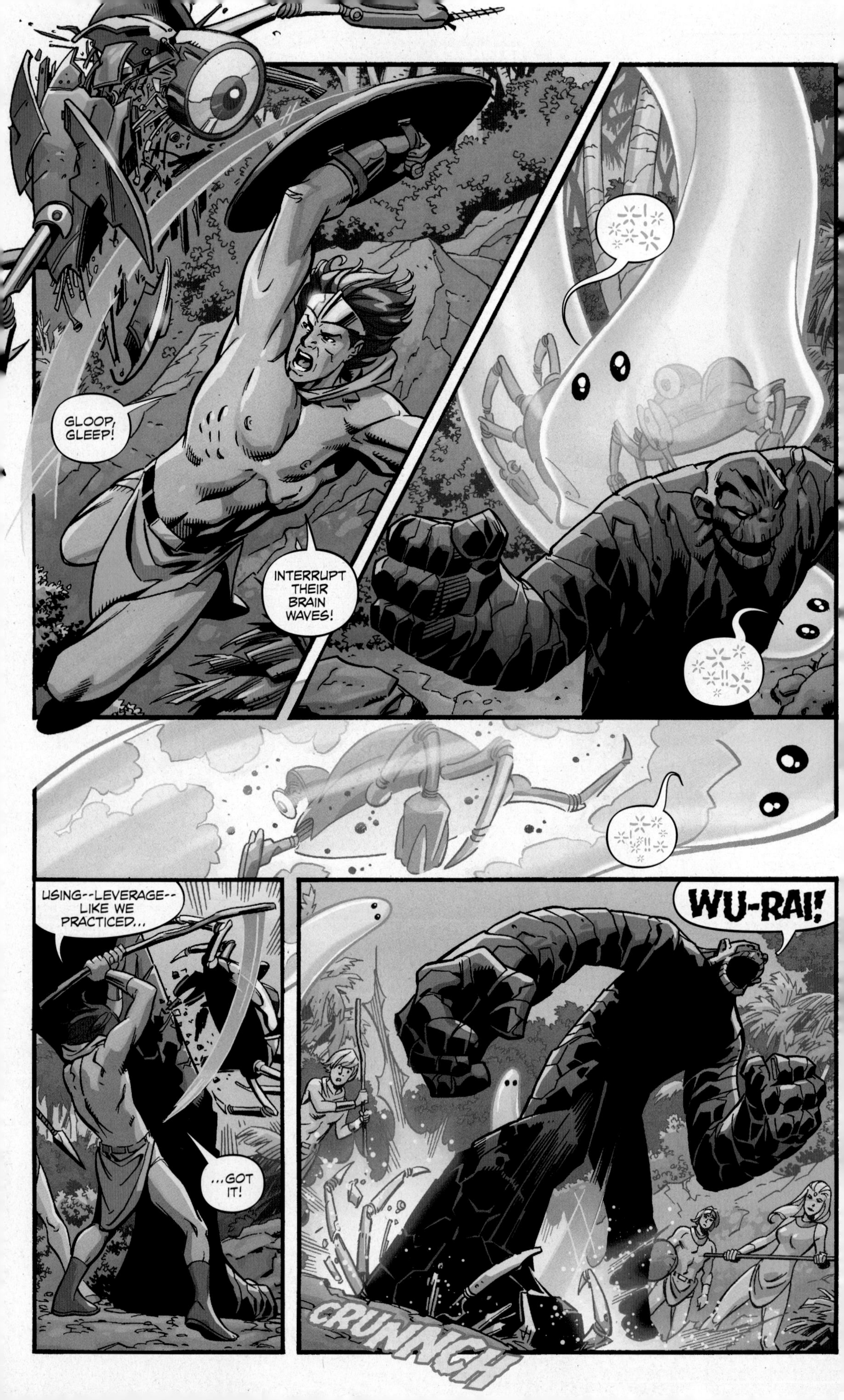
GLOOP, GLEEP!
INTERRUPT THEIR BRAIN WAVES!
USING--LEVERAGE--LIKE WE PRACTICED...
...GOT IT!
WU-RAI!
CRUNNCH

IT'S OKAY, TUNDRO, ZOK. THE THREAT IS OVER FOR NOW.

≋SNORT≋

WHAT ARE THESE ROBOTS, WHAT WERE THEY TRYING TO DO TO IGOO?

THESE ARE MINING ROBOTS, DORNO. THEY MUST HAVE BEEN RELEASED BY AN INTERPLANETARY SHIP.

THEY'LL BE BACK TOMORROW, THEY NEED THE SOLAR ENERGY OF DAY.

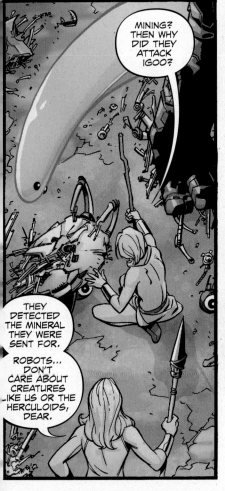

MINING? THEN WHY DID THEY ATTACK IGOO?

THEY DETECTED THE MINERAL THEY WERE SENT FOR.

ROBOTS... DON'T CARE ABOUT CREATURES LIKE US OR THE HERCULOIDS, DEAR.

I DON'T GET IT, WHY THEY WOULD TRY TO DRILL INTO IGOO...

...OR WHERE THEY EVEN COME FROM.

YOU NEED TO KNOW THE HISTORY. LET'S GATHER FOOD AND BUILD A FIRE.

AND I'LL TELL YOU OF THE ROBOT UPRISING.

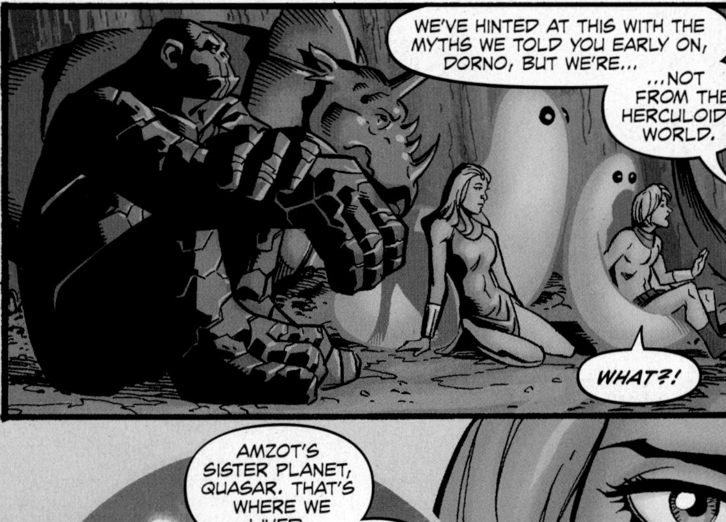
WE'VE HINTED AT THIS WITH THE MYTHS WE TOLD YOU EARLY ON, DORNO, BUT WE'RE...
...NOT FROM THE HERCULOID WORLD.
WHAT?!
AMZOT'S SISTER PLANET, QUASAR. THAT'S WHERE WE

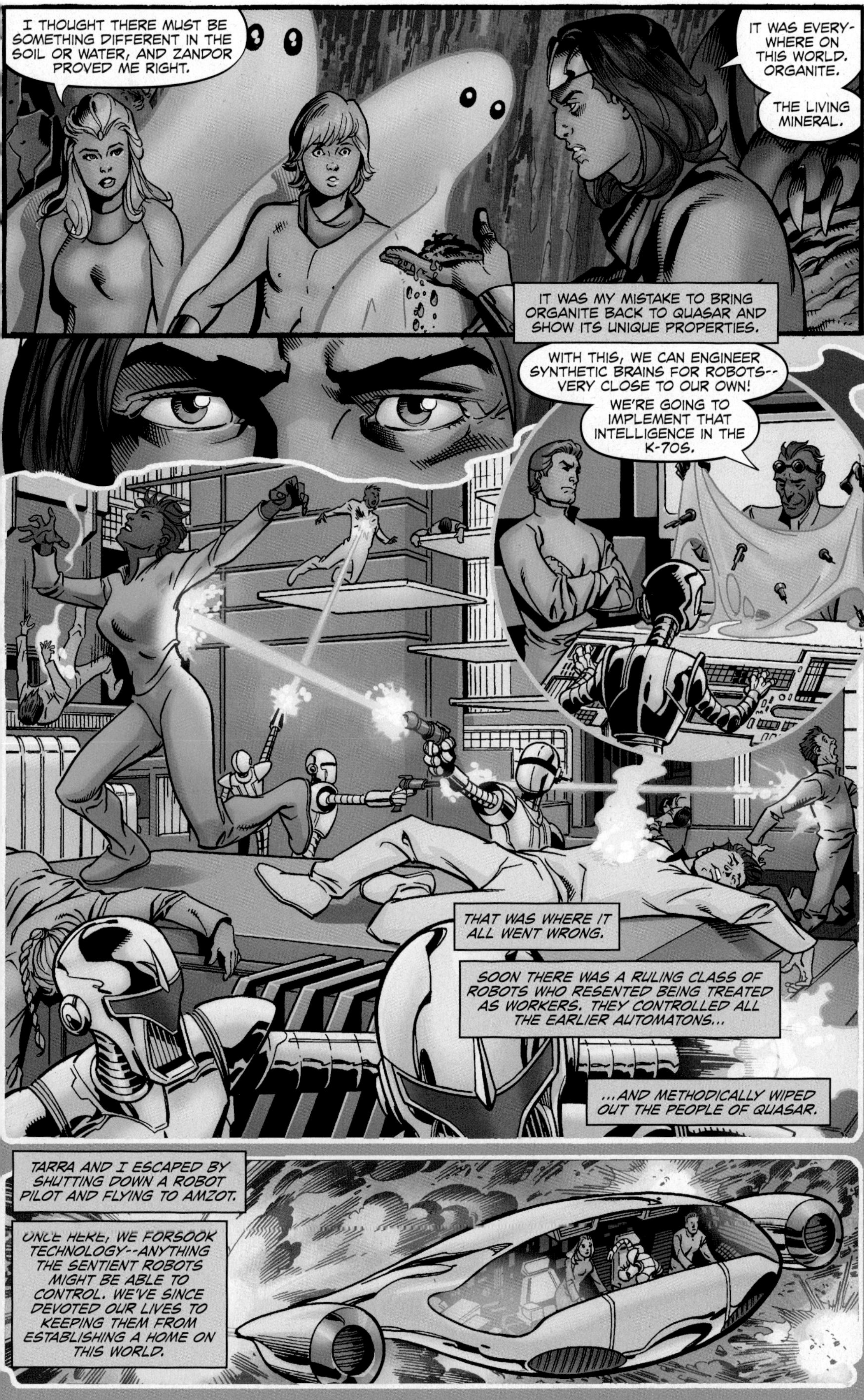

I THOUGHT THERE MUST BE SOMETHING DIFFERENT IN THE SOIL OR WATER, AND ZANDOR PROVED ME RIGHT.
IT WAS EVERY-WHERE ON THIS WORLD. ORGANITE.
THE LIVING MINERAL.
IT WAS MY MISTAKE TO BRING ORGANITE BACK TO QUASAR AND SHOW ITS UNIQUE PROPERTIES.
WITH THIS, WE CAN ENGINEER SYNTHETIC BRAINS FOR ROBOTS--VERY CLOSE TO OUR OWN!
WE'RE GOING TO IMPLEMENT THAT INTELLIGENCE IN THE K-70S.
THAT WAS WHERE IT ALL WENT WRONG.
SOON THERE WAS A RULING CLASS OF ROBOTS WHO RESENTED BEING TREATED AS WORKERS. THEY CONTROLLED ALL THE EARLIER AUTOMATONS...
...AND METHODICALLY WIPED OUT THE PEOPLE OF QUASAR.
TARRA AND I ESCAPED BY SHUTTING DOWN A ROBOT PILOT AND FLYING TO AMZOT.
ONCE HERE, WE FORSOOK TECHNOLOGY--ANYTHING THE SENTIENT ROBOTS MIGHT BE ABLE TO CONTROL. WE'VE SINCE DEVOTED OUR LIVES TO KEEPING THEM FROM ESTABLISHING A HOME ON THIS WORLD.

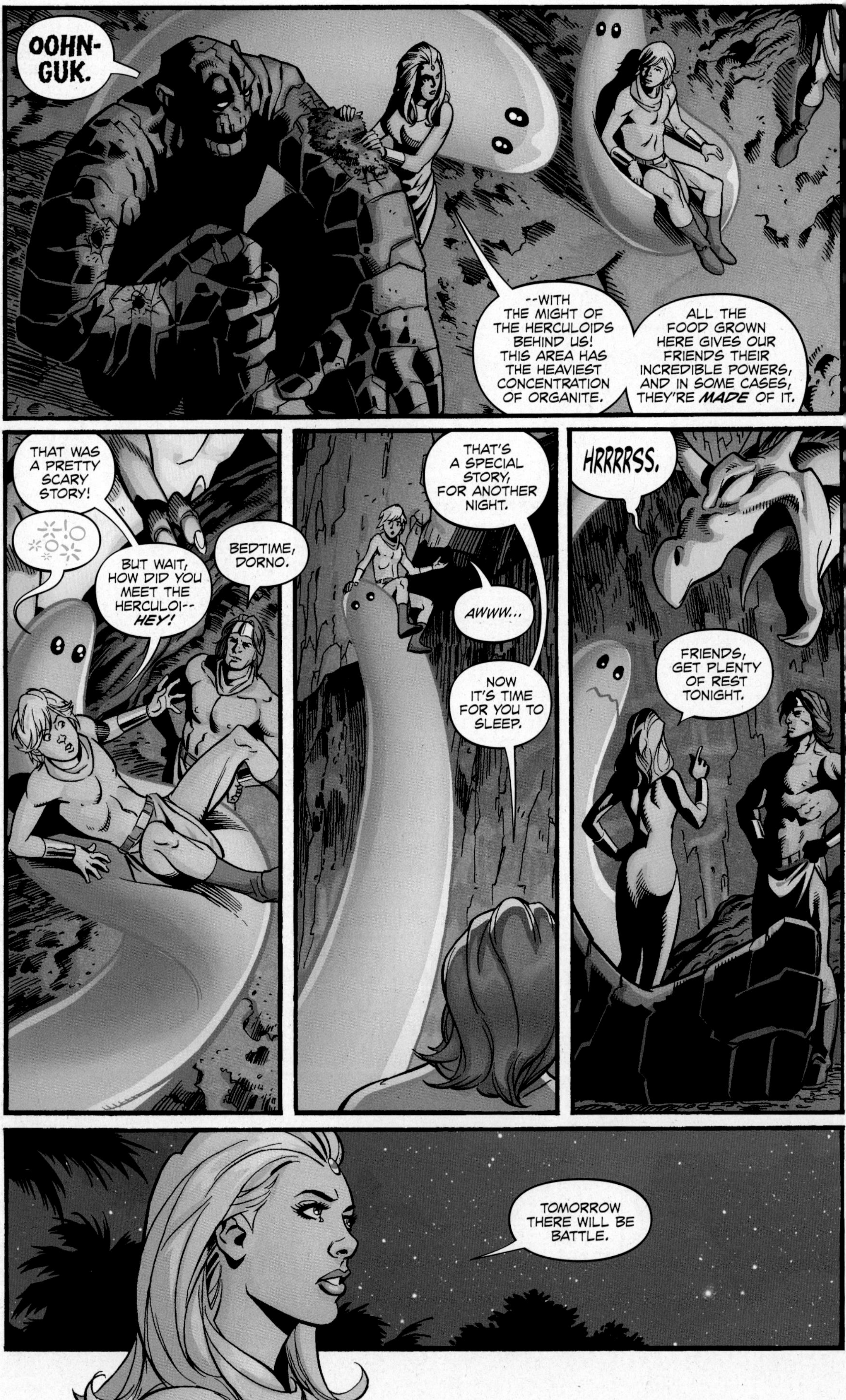
OOHN-
GUK.
--WITH THE MIGHT OF THE HERCULOIDS BEHIND US! THIS AREA HAS THE HEAVIEST CONCENTRATION OF ORGANITE.
ALL THE FOOD GROWN HERE GIVES OUR FRIENDS THEIR INCREDIBLE POWERS, AND IN SOME CASES, THEY'RE *MADE* OF IT.
THAT WAS A PRETTY SCARY STORY!
BUT WAIT, HOW DID YOU MEET THE HERCULOI--*HEY!*
BEDTIME, DORNO.
THAT'S A SPECIAL STORY, FOR ANOTHER NIGHT.
AWWW...
NOW IT'S TIME FOR YOU TO SLEEP.
HRRRRSS.
FRIENDS, GET PLENTY OF REST TONIGHT.
TOMORROW THERE WILL BE BATTLE.

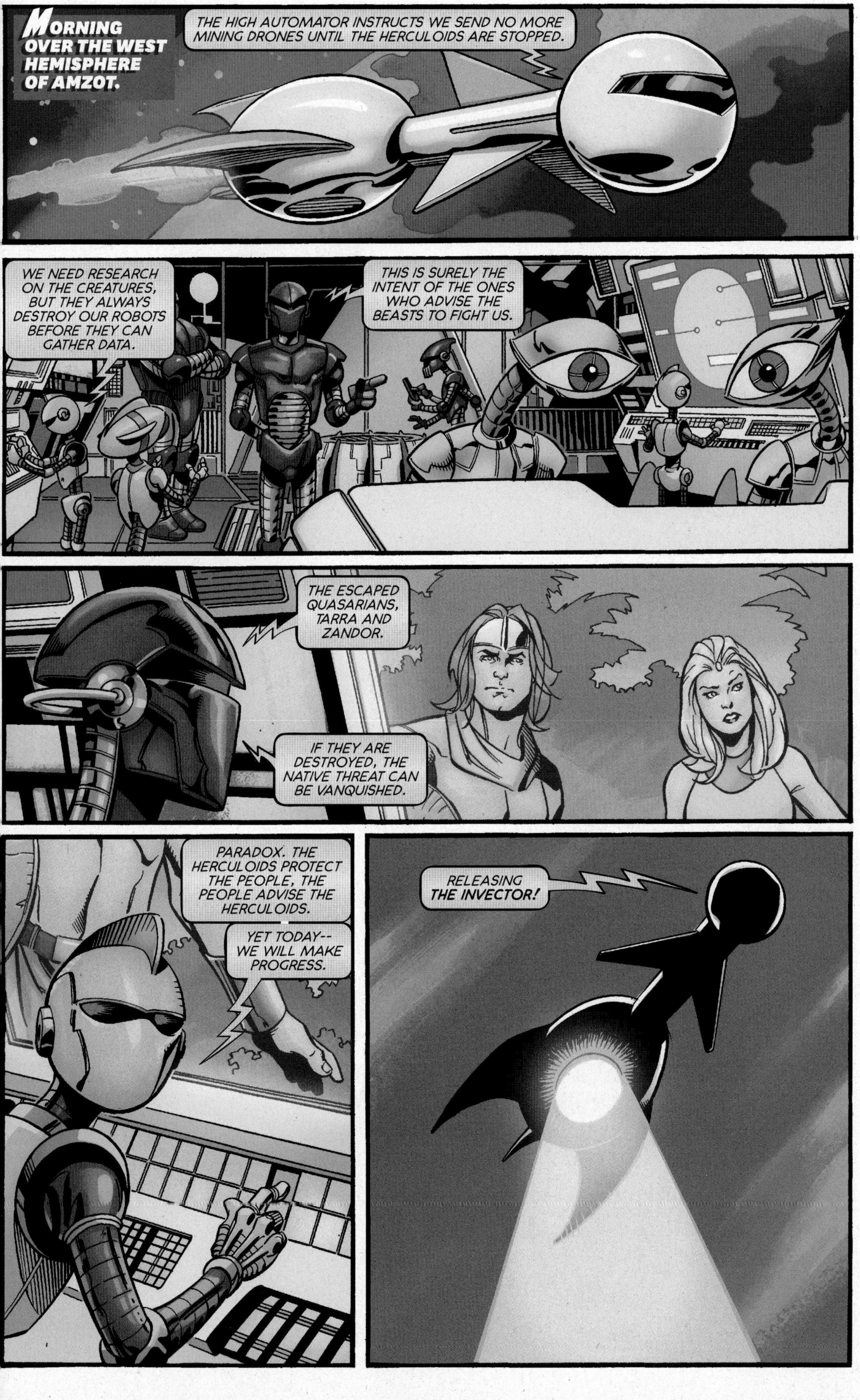
MORNING OVER THE WEST HEMISPHERE OF AMZOT.
THE HIGH AUTOMATOR INSTRUCTS WE SEND NO MORE MINING DRONES UNTIL THE HERCULOIDS ARE STOPPED.
WE NEED RESEARCH ON THE CREATURES, BUT THEY ALWAYS DESTROY OUR ROBOTS BEFORE THEY CAN GATHER DATA.
THIS IS SURELY THE INTENT OF THE ONES WHO ADVISE THE BEASTS TO FIGHT US.
THE ESCAPED QUASARIANS, TARRA AND ZANDOR.
IF THEY ARE DESTROYED, THE NATIVE THREAT CAN BE VANQUISHED.
PARADOX. THE HERCULOIDS PROTECT THE PEOPLE, THE PEOPLE ADVISE THE HERCULOIDS.
YET TODAY-- WE WILL MAKE PROGRESS.
RELEASING THE INVECTOR!

REAAA

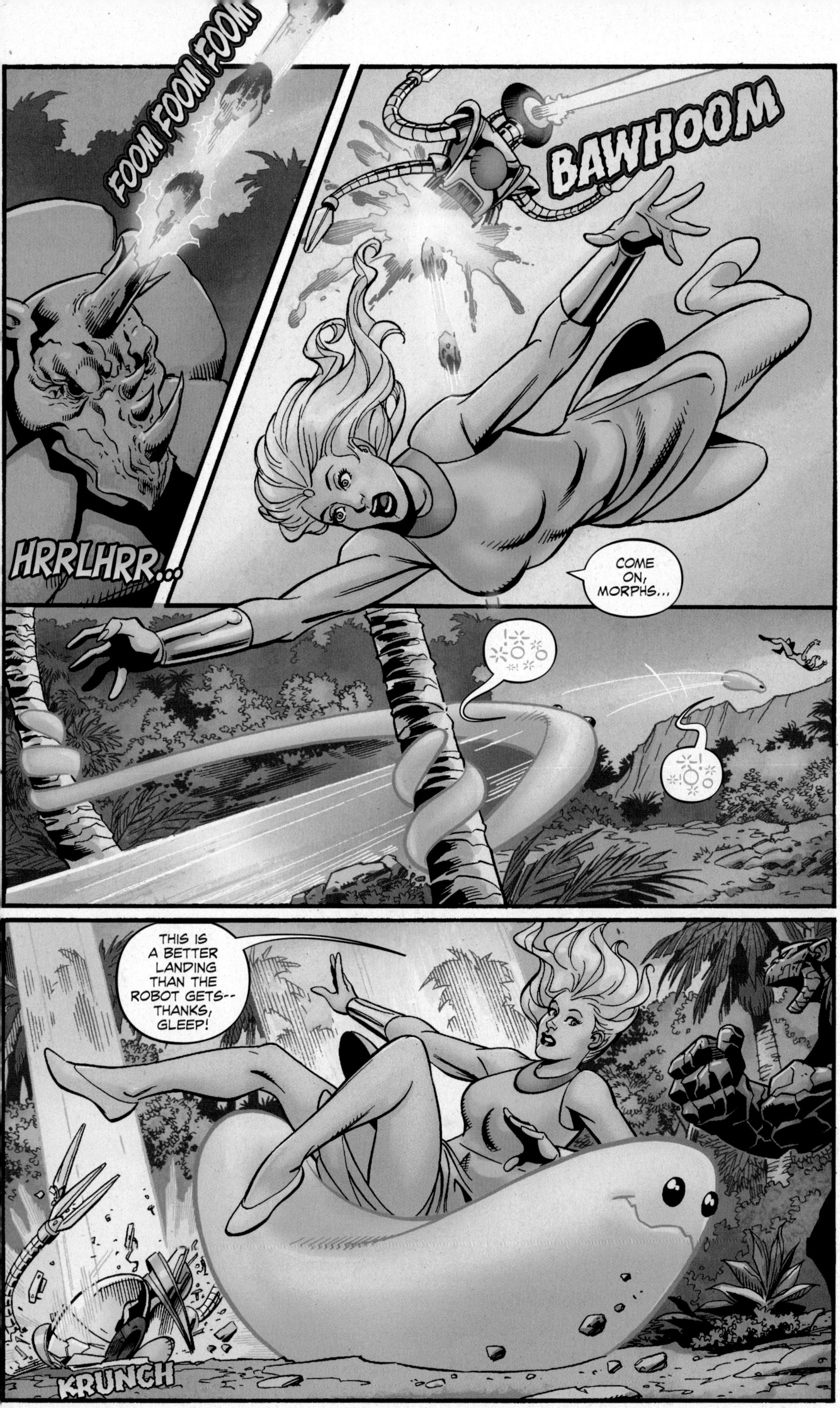
FOOM FOOM FOOM
BAWHOOM
HRRLHRR...
COME ON, MORPHS...
THIS IS A BETTER LANDING THAN THE ROBOT GETS-- THANKS, GLEEP!
KRUNCH

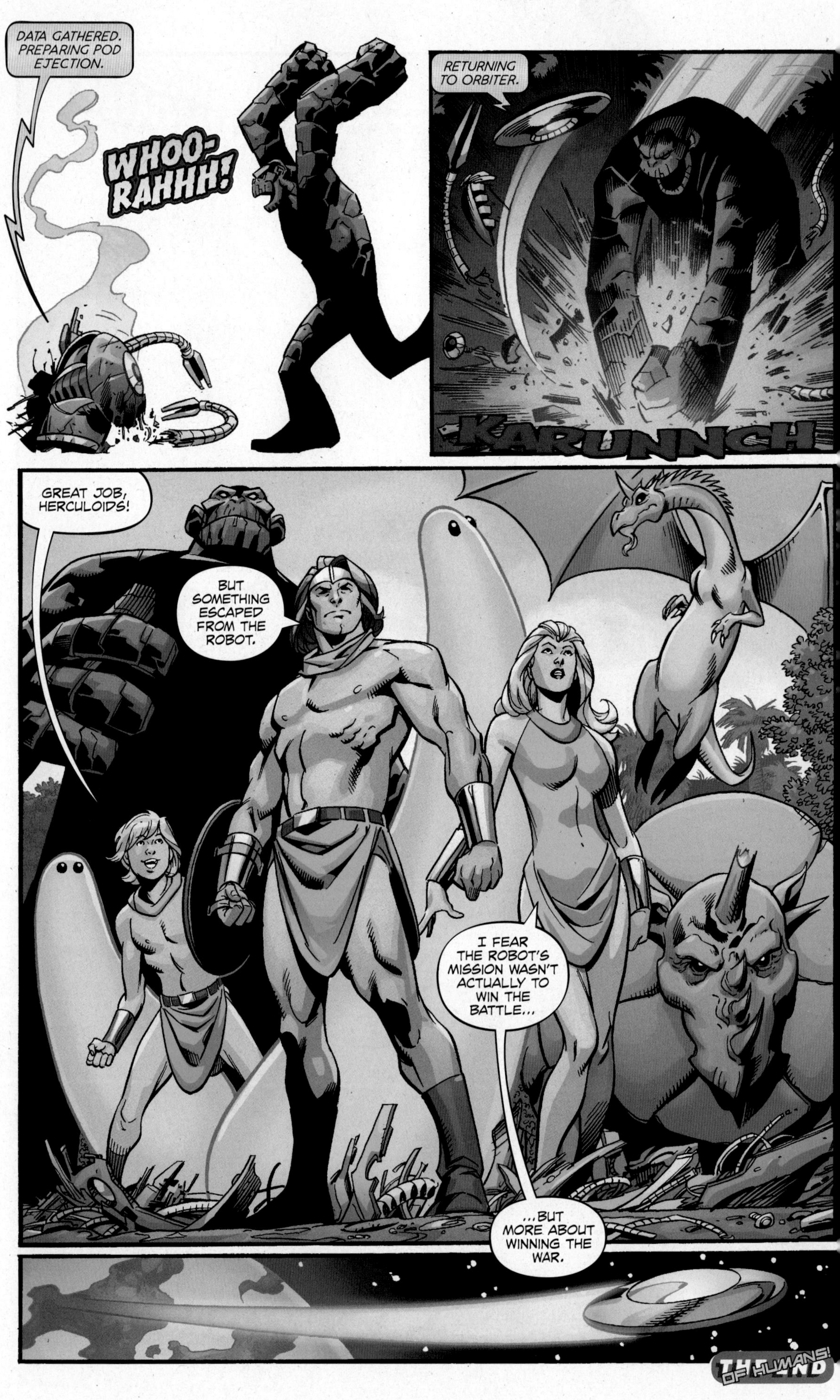

DATA GATHERED. PREPARING POD EJECTION.
WHOO-RAHHH!
RETURNING TO ORBITER.
KARUNNCH
GREAT JOB, HERCULOIDS!
BUT SOMETHING ESCAPED FROM THE ROBOT.
I FEAR THE ROBOT'S MISSION WASN'T ACTUALLY TO WIN THE BATTLE...
...BUT MORE ABOUT WINNING THE WAR.
THE END OF HUMANS!

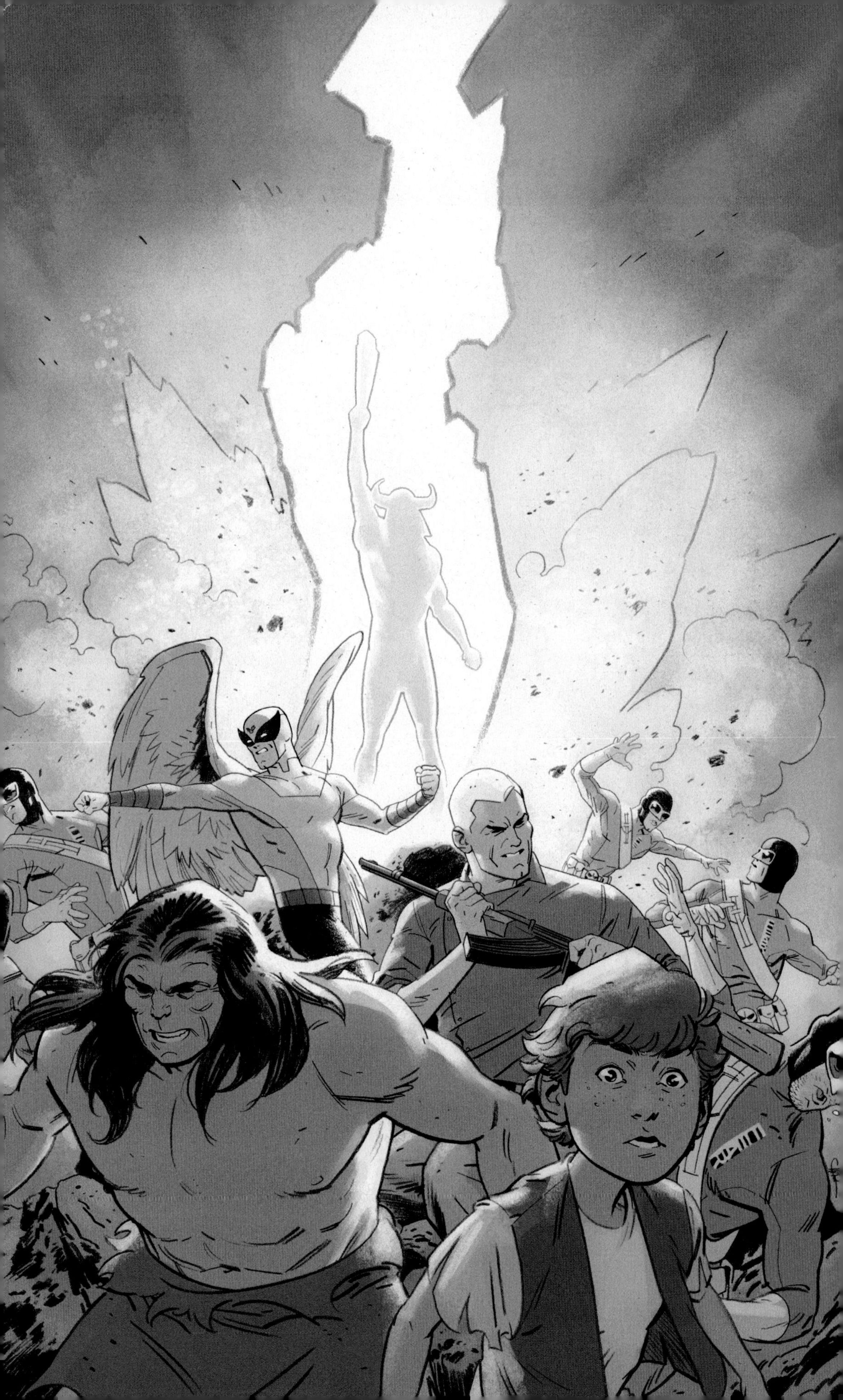

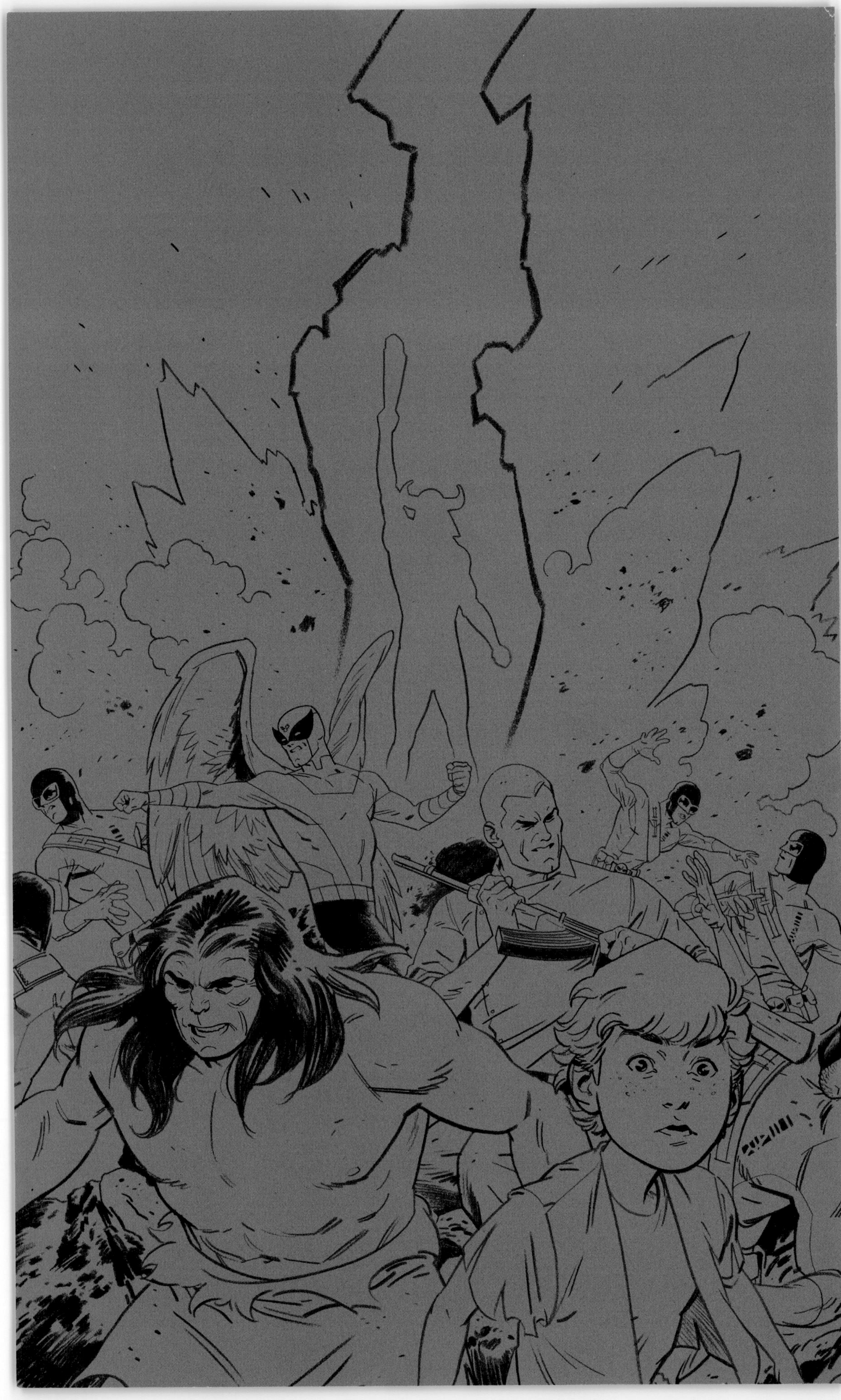

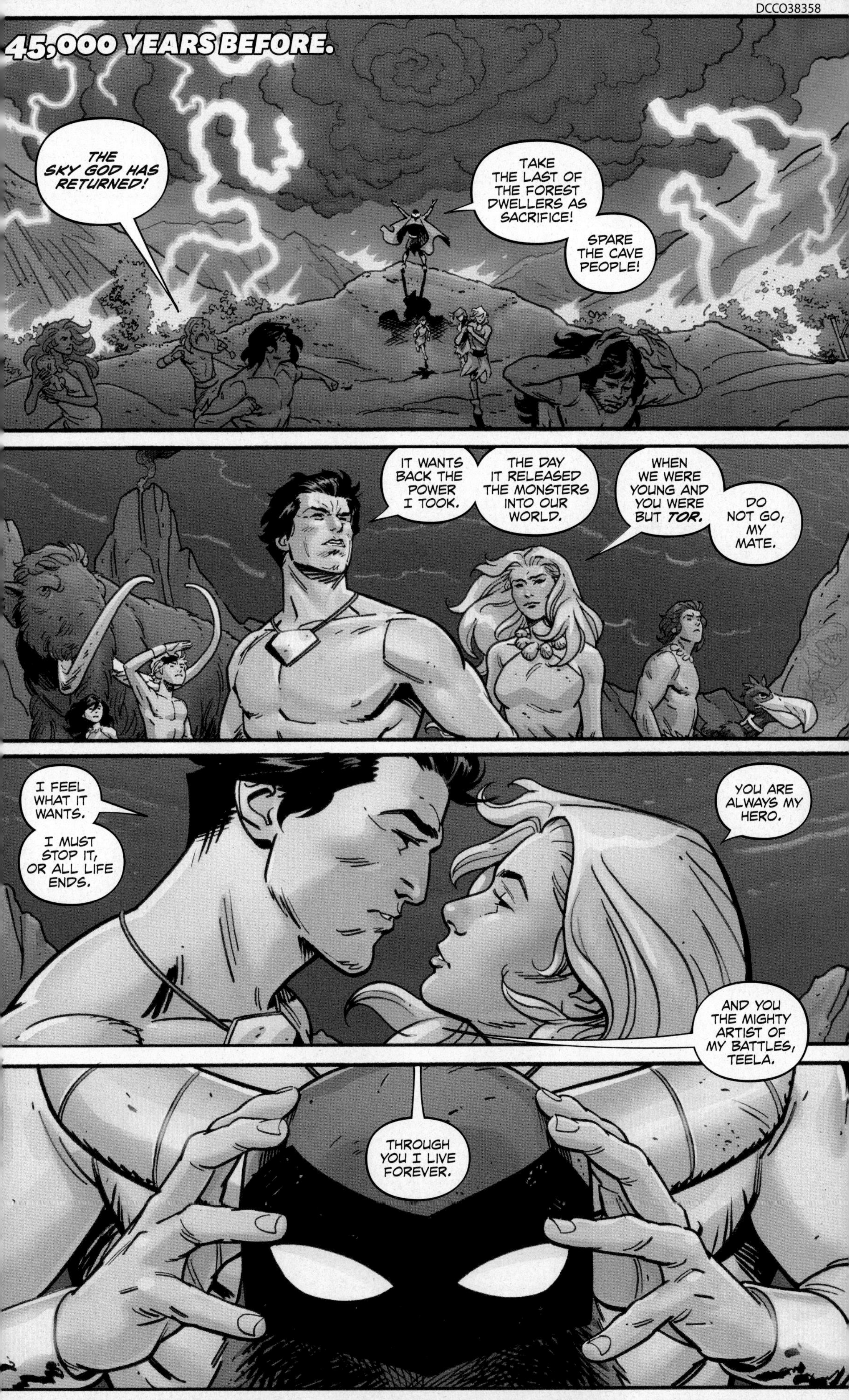
45,000 YEARS BEFORE.
THE SKY GOD HAS RETURNED!
TAKE THE LAST OF THE FOREST DWELLERS AS SACRIFICE!
SPARE THE CAVE PEOPLE!
IT WANTS BACK THE POWER I TOOK.
THE DAY IT RELEASED THE MONSTERS INTO OUR WORLD.
WHEN WE WERE YOUNG AND YOU WERE BUT TOR.
DO NOT GO, MY MATE.
I FEEL WHAT IT WANTS.
I MUST STOP IT, OR ALL LIFE ENDS.
YOU ARE ALWAYS MY HERO.
AND YOU THE MIGHTY ARTIST OF MY BATTLES, TEELA.
THROUGH YOU I LIVE FOREVER.

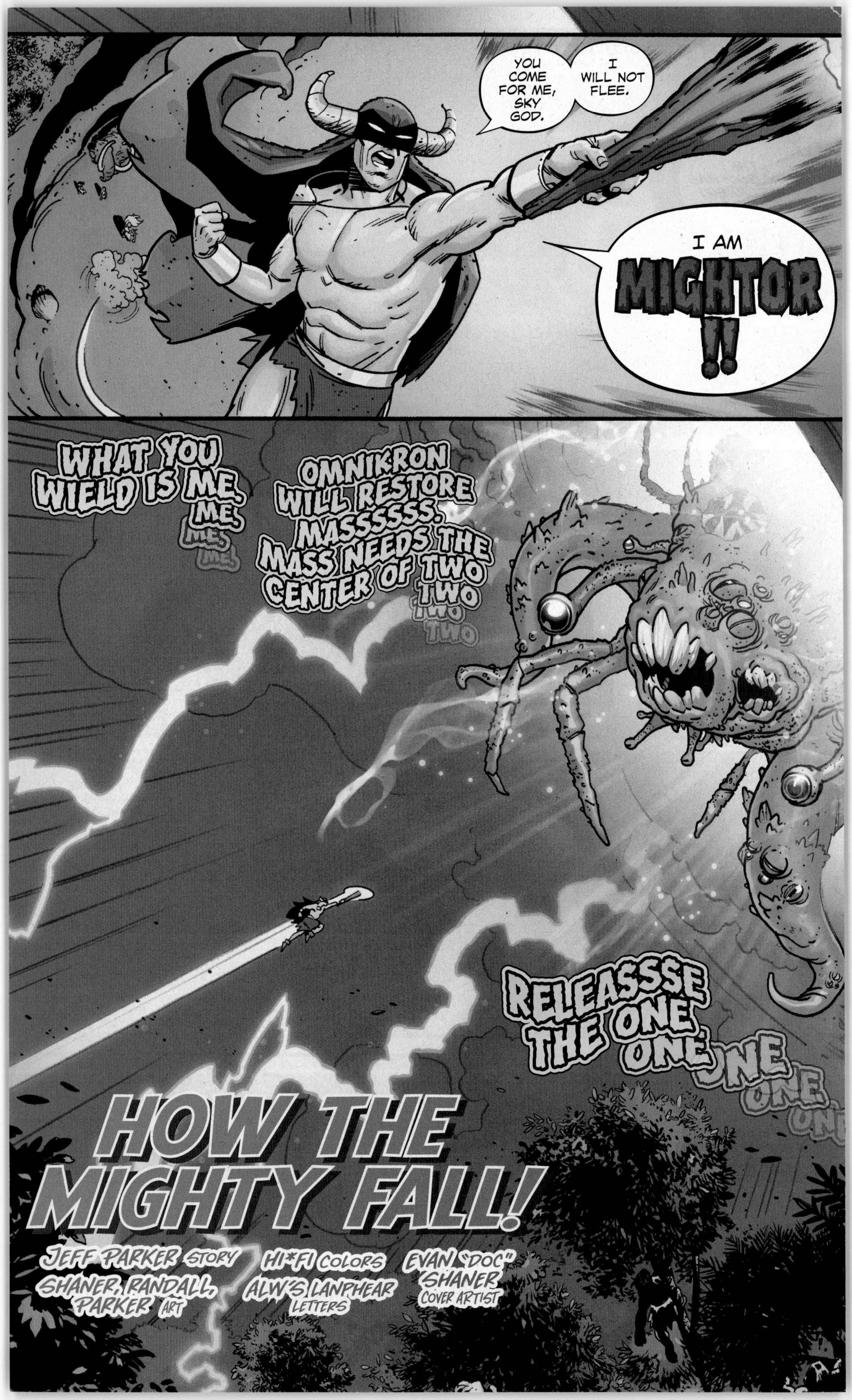
YOU COME FOR ME, SKY GOD.
I WILL NOT FLEE.
I AM MIGHTOR !!
WHAT YOU WIELD IS ME. ME. ME. ME.
OMNIKRON WILL RESTORE MASSSSSS. MASS NEEDS THE CENTER OF TWO TWO TWO TWO
RELEASSSE THE ONE ONE ONE ONE
HOW THE MIGHTY FALL!
JEFF PARKER STORY
SHANER, RANDALL, PARKER ART
HI*FI COLORS
ALW'S LANPHEAR LETTERS
EVAN "DOC" SHANER COVER ARTIST

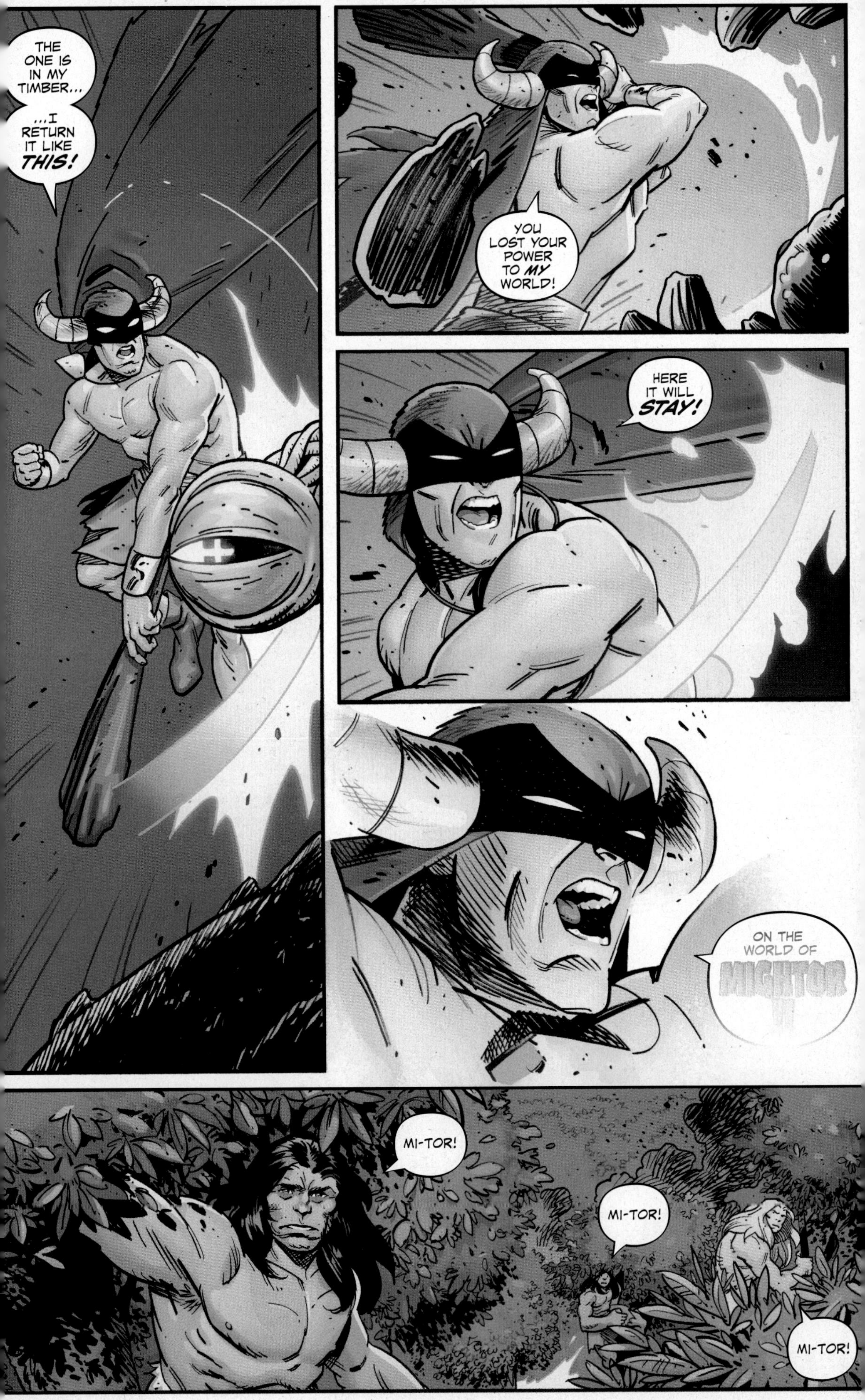
THE ONE IS IN MY TIMBER...
...I RETURN IT LIKE *THIS!*
YOU LOST YOUR POWER TO *MY* WORLD!
HERE IT WILL *STAY!*
ON THE WORLD OF MIGHTOR
MI-TOR!
MI-TOR!
MI-TOR!

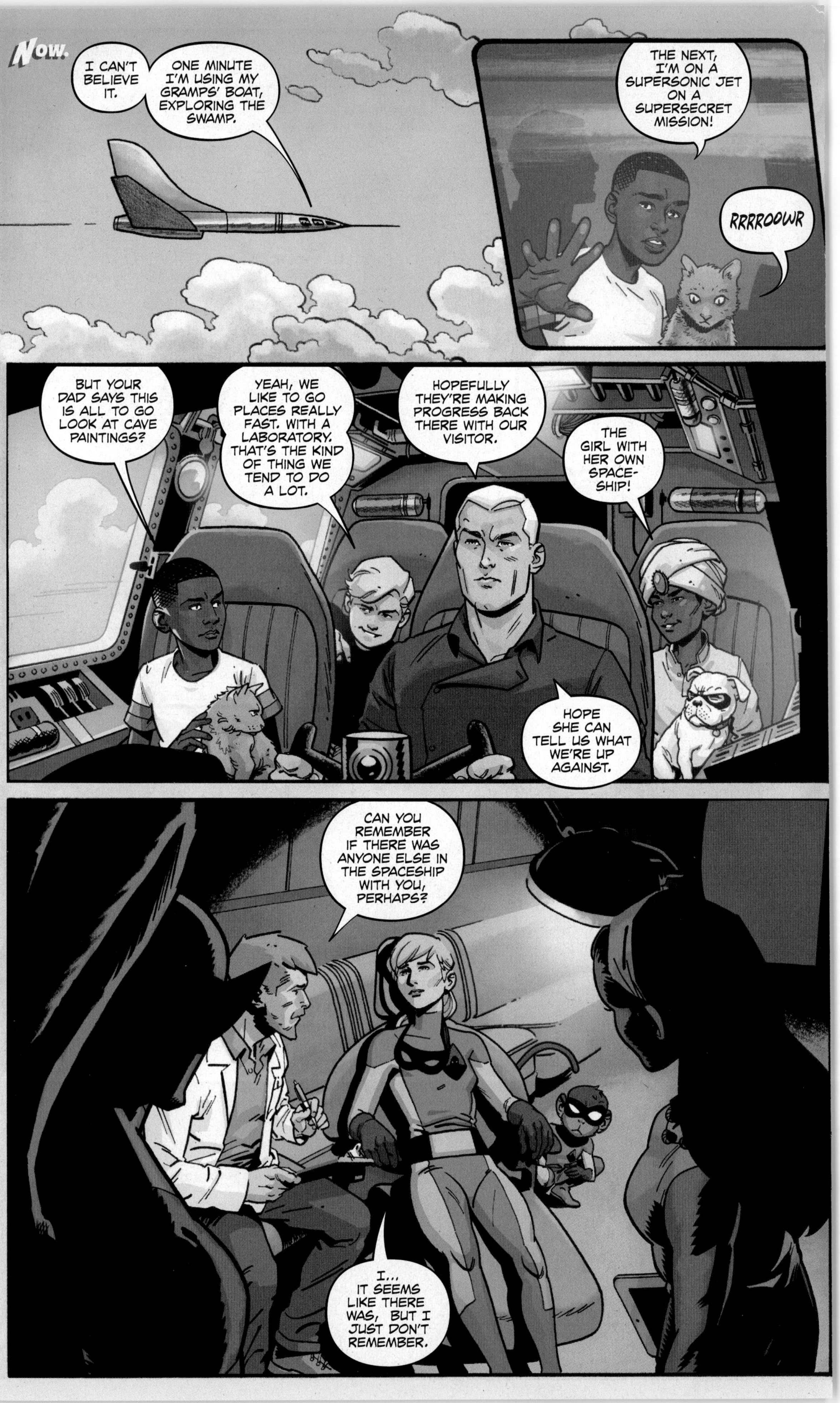
NOW.
I CAN'T BELIEVE IT.
ONE MINUTE I'M USING MY GRAMPS' BOAT, EXPLORING THE SWAMP.
THE NEXT, I'M ON A SUPERSONIC JET ON A SUPERSECRET MISSION!
RRRROOWR
BUT YOUR DAD SAYS THIS IS ALL TO GO LOOK AT CAVE PAINTINGS?
YEAH, WE LIKE TO GO PLACES REALLY FAST. WITH A LABORATORY. THAT'S THE KIND OF THING WE TEND TO DO A LOT.
HOPEFULLY THEY'RE MAKING PROGRESS BACK THERE WITH OUR VISITOR.
THE GIRL WITH HER OWN SPACE-SHIP!
HOPE SHE CAN TELL US WHAT WE'RE UP AGAINST.
CAN YOU REMEMBER IF THERE WAS ANYONE ELSE IN THE SPACESHIP WITH YOU, PERHAPS?
I... IT SEEMS LIKE THERE WAS, BUT I JUST DON'T REMEMBER.

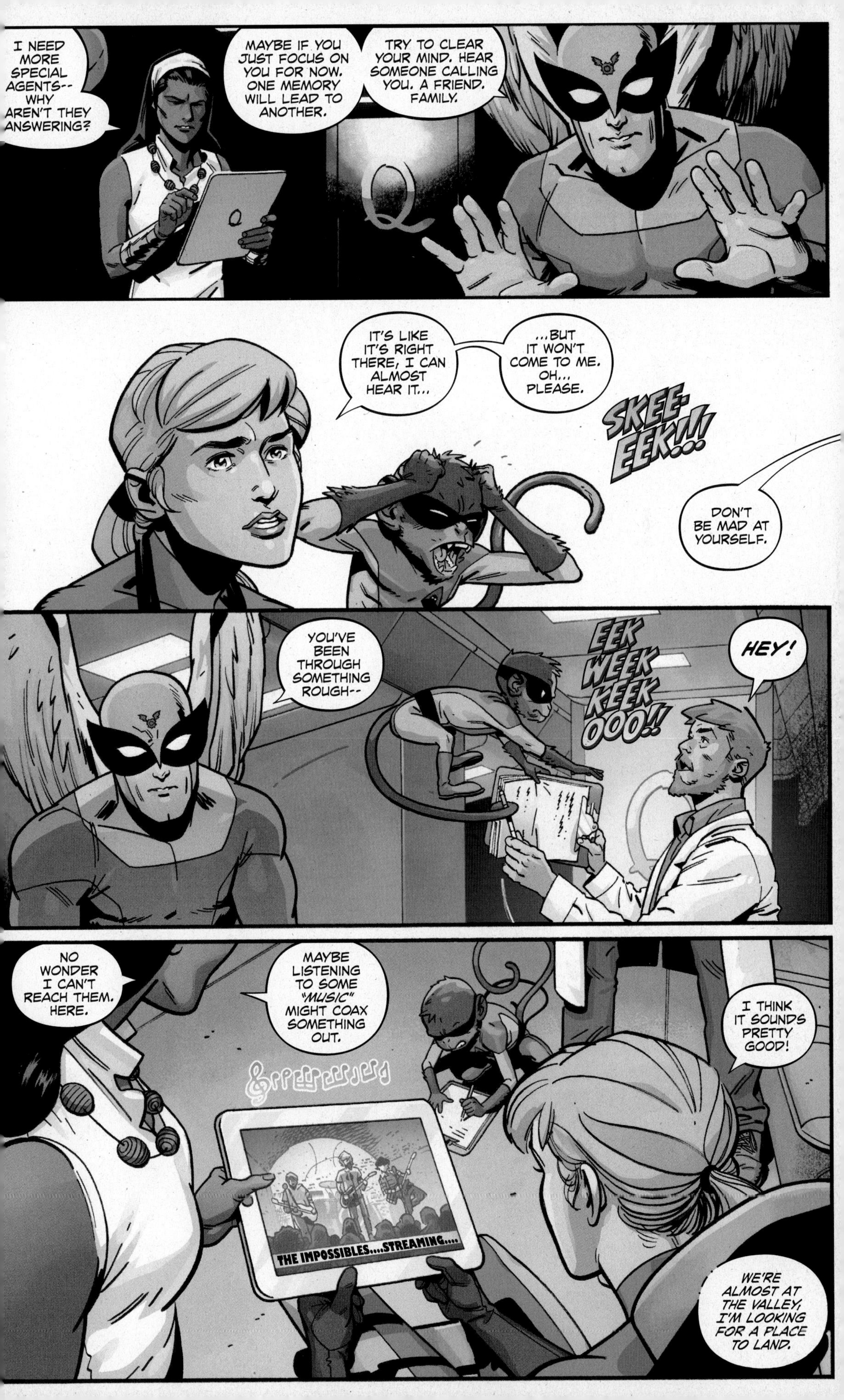
I NEED MORE SPECIAL AGENTS--WHY AREN'T THEY ANSWERING?
MAYBE IF YOU JUST FOCUS ON YOU FOR NOW. ONE MEMORY WILL LEAD TO ANOTHER.
TRY TO CLEAR YOUR MIND. HEAR SOMEONE CALLING YOU. A FRIEND. FAMILY.
IT'S LIKE IT'S RIGHT THERE, I CAN ALMOST HEAR IT...
...BUT IT WON'T COME TO ME. OH... PLEASE.
SKEE-EEK!!!
DON'T BE MAD AT YOURSELF.
YOU'VE BEEN THROUGH SOMETHING ROUGH--
EEK WEEK KEEK OOO!!
HEY!
NO WONDER I CAN'T REACH THEM. HERE.
MAYBE LISTENING TO SOME "MUSIC" MIGHT COAX SOMETHING OUT.
I THINK IT SOUNDS PRETTY GOOD!
THE IMPOSSIBLES....STREAMING....
WE'RE ALMOST AT THE VALLEY, I'M LOOKING FOR A PLACE TO LAND.

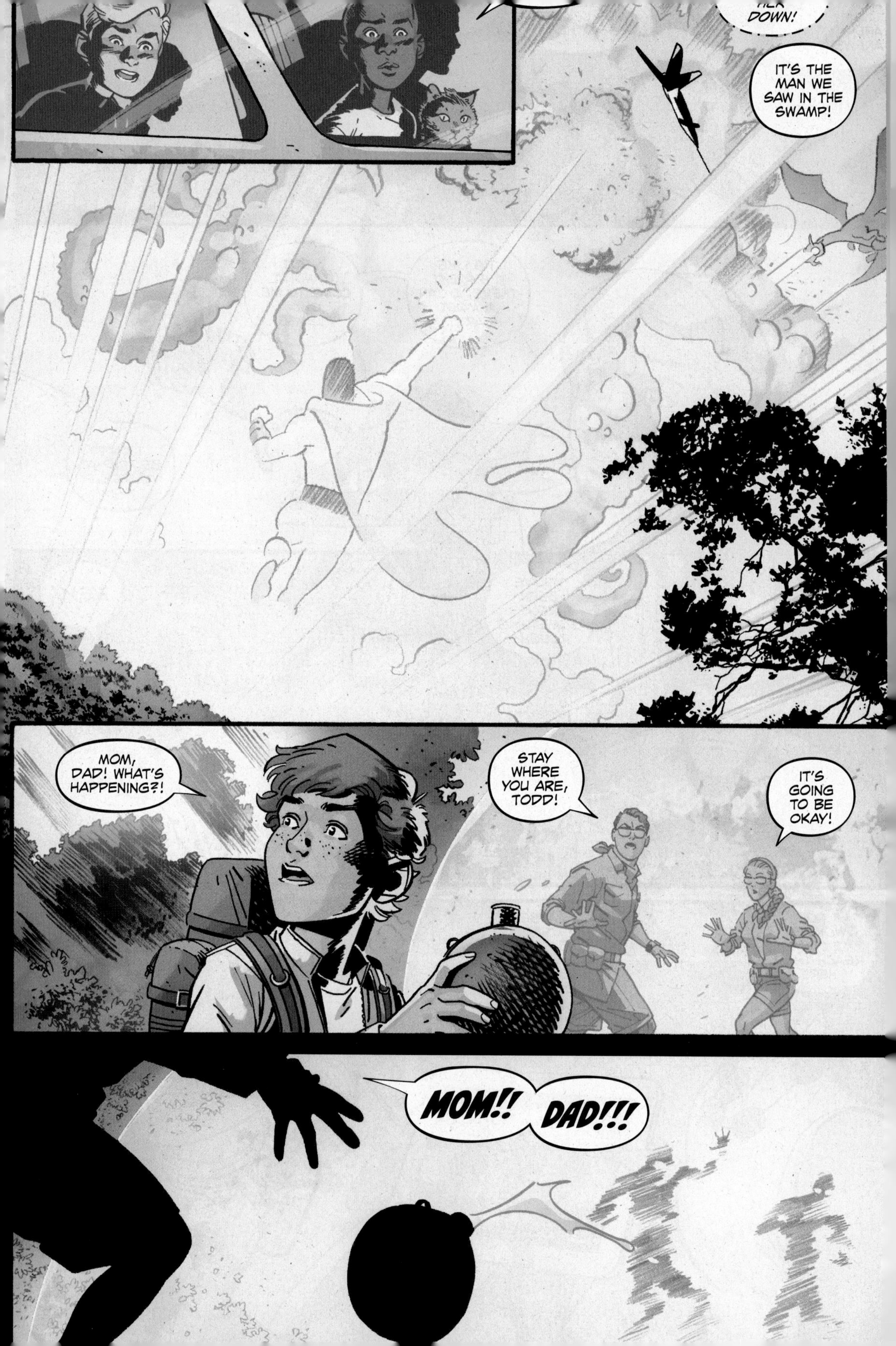
DOWN!
IT'S THE MAN WE SAW IN THE SWAMP!
MOM, DAD! WHAT'S HAPPENING?!
STAY WHERE YOU ARE, TODD!
IT'S GOING TO BE OKAY!
MOM!!
DAD!!!

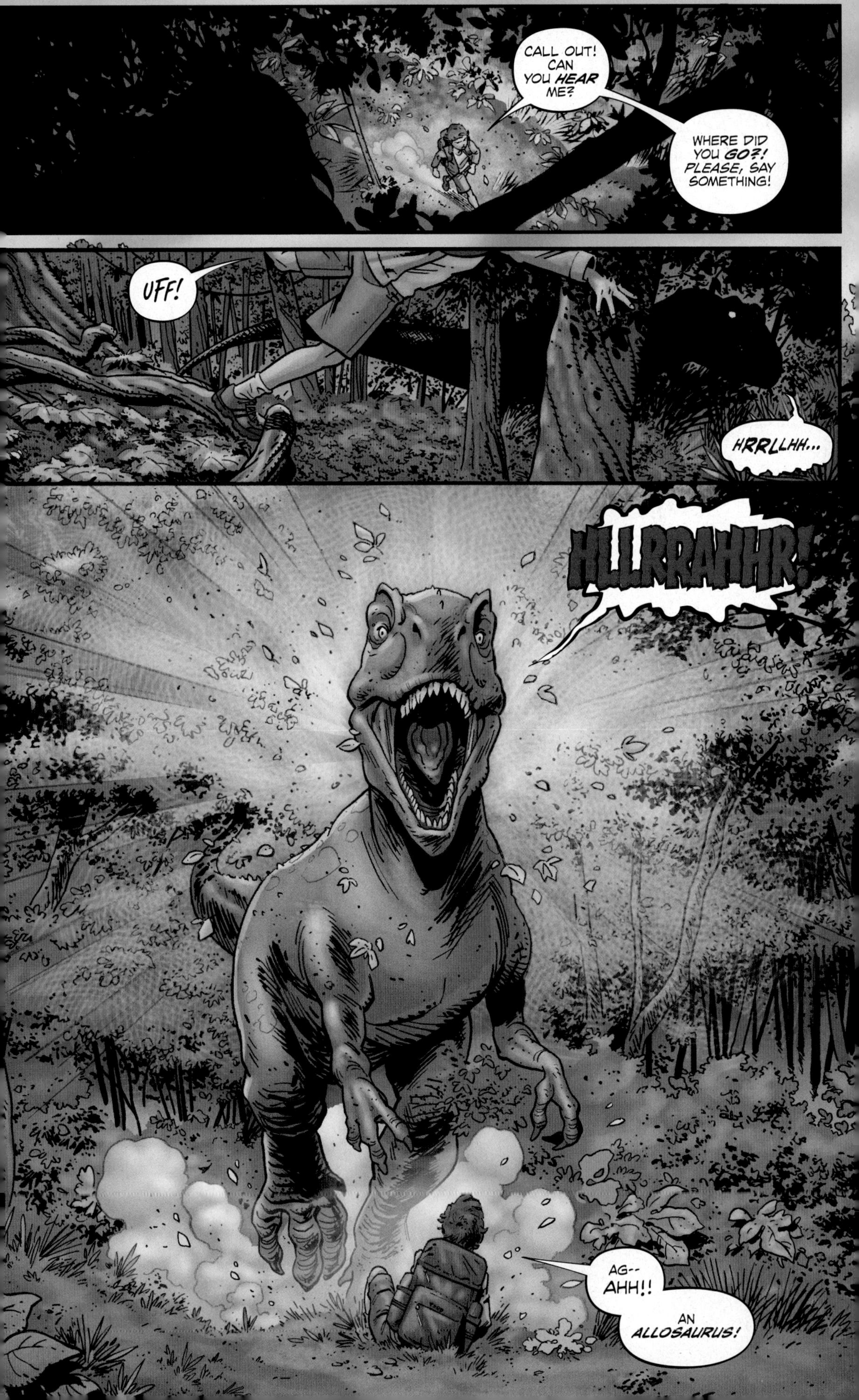
CALL OUT! CAN YOU HEAR ME?
WHERE DID YOU GO?! PLEASE, SAY SOMETHING!
UFF!
HRRLLHH...
HLLRRAHHR!
AG-- AHH!!
AN ALLOSAURUS!

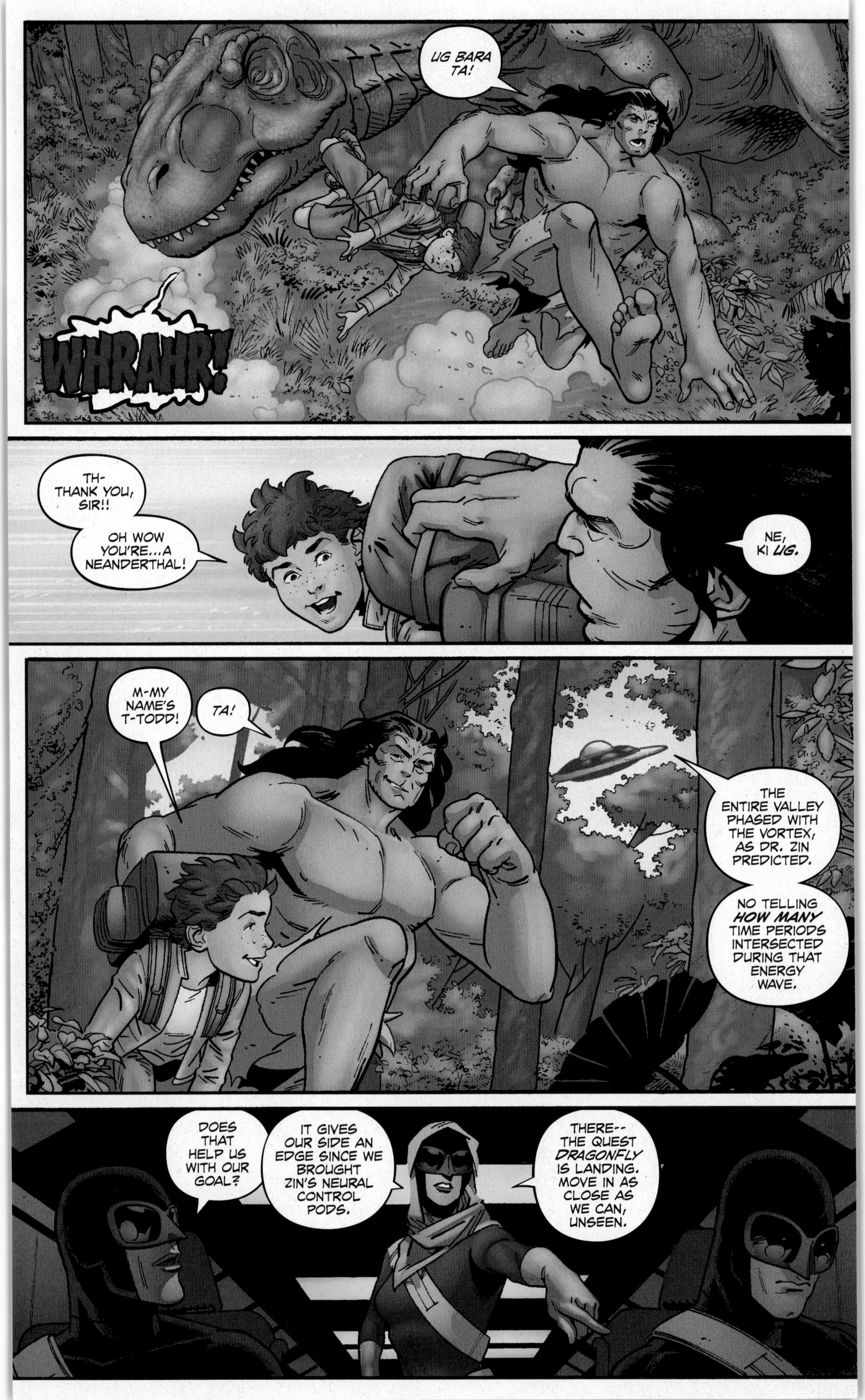

UG BARA TA!
WHRAHR!
TH-THANK YOU, SIR!!
OH WOW YOU'RE...A NEANDERTHAL!
NE, KI *UG.*
M-MY NAME'S T-TODD!
TA!
THE ENTIRE VALLEY PHASED WITH THE VORTEX, AS DR. ZIN PREDICTED.
NO TELLING *HOW MANY* TIME PERIODS INTERSECTED DURING THAT ENERGY WAVE.
DOES THAT HELP US WITH OUR GOAL?
IT GIVES OUR SIDE AN EDGE SINCE WE BROUGHT ZIN'S NEURAL CONTROL PODS.
THERE--THE QUEST *DRAGONFLY* IS LANDING. MOVE IN AS CLOSE AS WE CAN, UNSEEN.

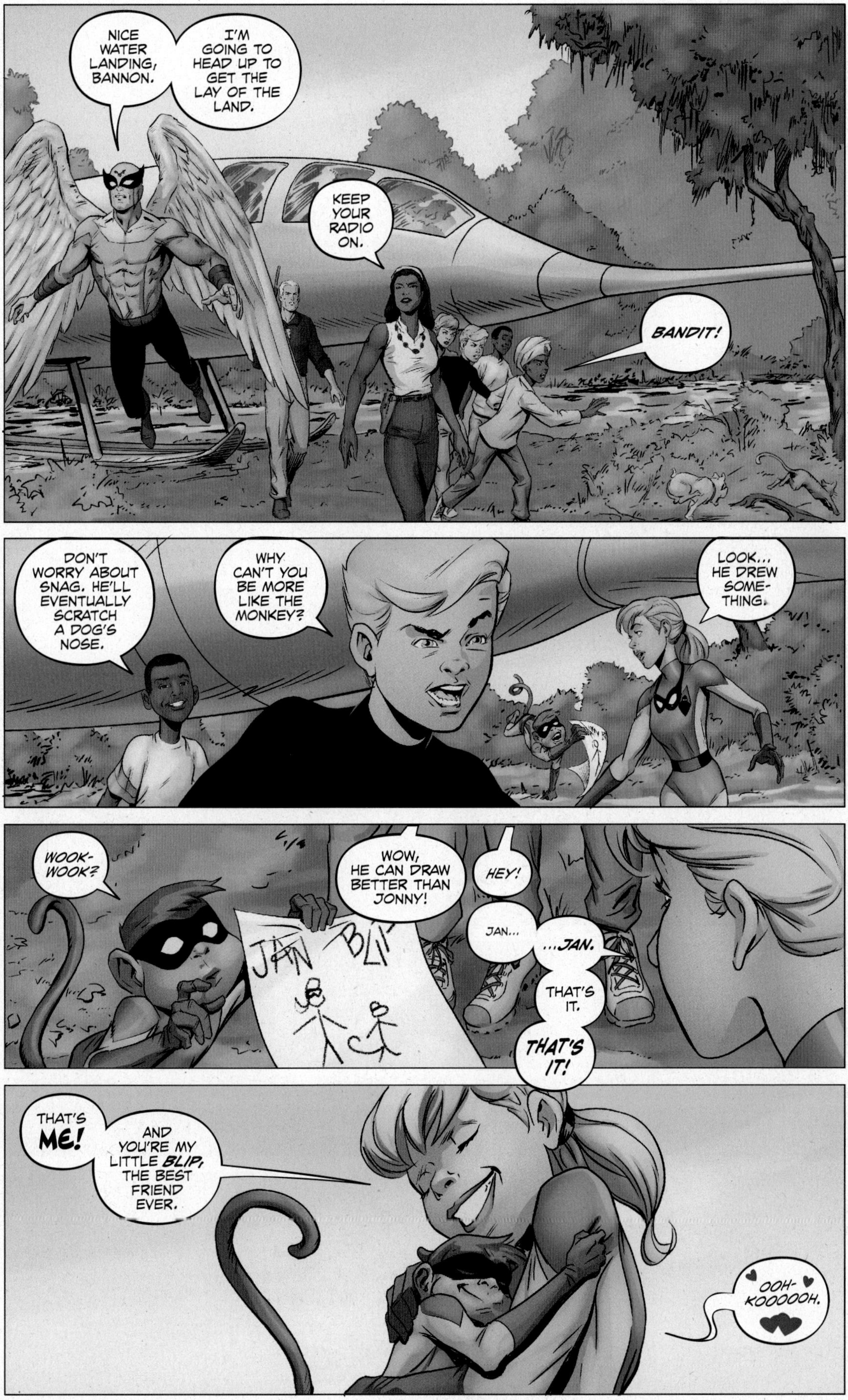
NICE WATER LANDING, BANNON.
I'M GOING TO HEAD UP TO GET THE LAY OF THE LAND.
KEEP YOUR RADIO ON.
BANDIT!
DON'T WORRY ABOUT SNAG. HE'LL EVENTUALLY SCRATCH A DOG'S NOSE.
WHY CAN'T YOU BE MORE LIKE THE MONKEY?
LOOK... HE DREW SOME-THING.
WOOK-WOOK?
JAN
BLIP
WOW, HE CAN DRAW BETTER THAN JONNY!
HEY!
JAN...
...JAN.
THAT'S IT.
THAT'S IT!
THAT'S ME!
AND YOU'RE MY LITTLE BLIP, THE BEST FRIEND EVER.
OOH-KOOOOOH.

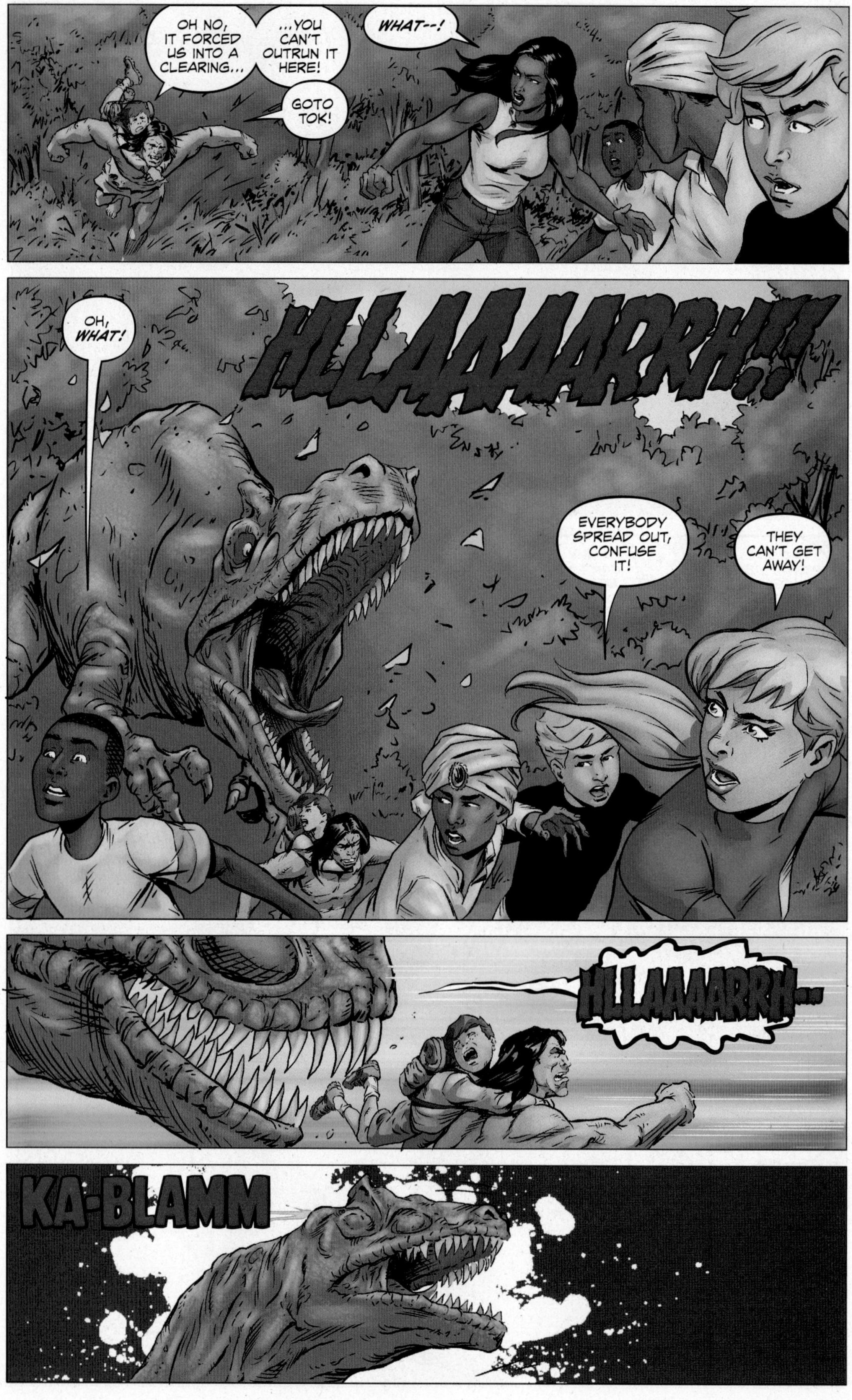
OH NO, IT FORCED US INTO A CLEARING...
...YOU CAN'T OUTRUN IT HERE!
GOTO TOK!
WHAT--!
OH, WHAT!
HLLAAAAARRH!!!
EVERYBODY SPREAD OUT, CONFUSE IT!
THEY CAN'T GET AWAY!
HLLAAAARRH--
KA-BLAMM

WHEW.

ARE YOU OKAY?

YES!

THANKS TO YOU GUYS AND MY NEW FRIEND, UG!

BI KOLA, TA.

YOU'RE THE MESSICK'S SON! TODD?

YES SIR, THEY SAID WE'D HAVE FRIENDS VISITING TODAY.

BUT AFTER THAT WEIRD STORM, WE GOT SEPARATED-- I CAN'T FIND THEM!

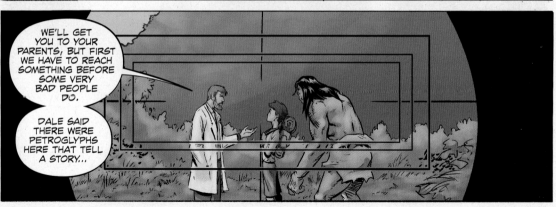

WE'LL GET YOU TO YOUR PARENTS, BUT FIRST WE HAVE TO REACH SOMETHING BEFORE SOME VERY BAD PEOPLE DO.

DALE SAID THERE WERE PETROGLYPHS HERE THAT TELL A STORY...

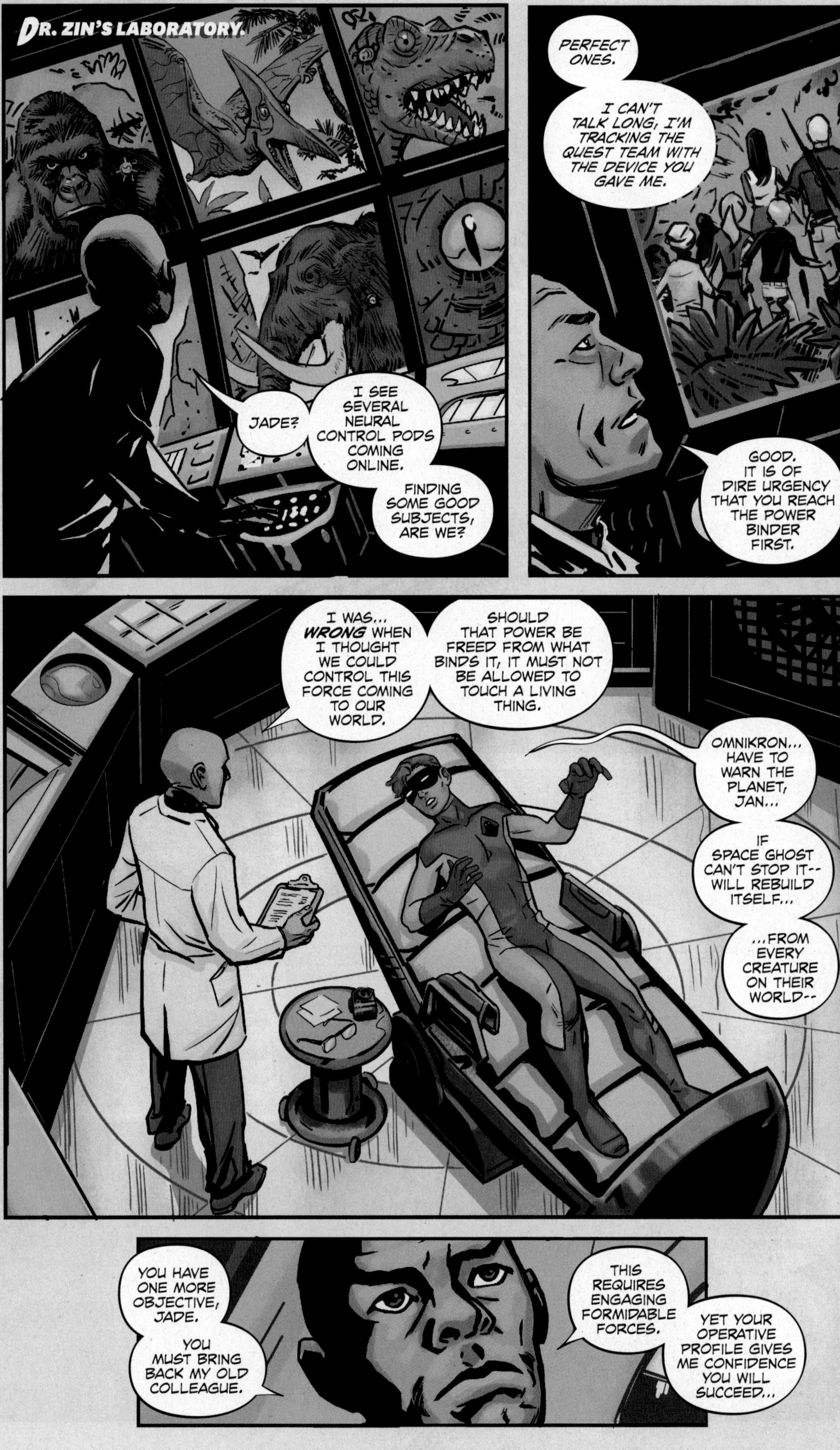
DR. ZIN'S LABORATORY.
JADE?
I SEE SEVERAL NEURAL CONTROL PODS COMING ONLINE.
FINDING SOME GOOD SUBJECTS, ARE WE?
PERFECT ONES.
I CAN'T TALK LONG, I'M TRACKING THE QUEST TEAM WITH THE DEVICE YOU GAVE ME.
GOOD. IT IS OF DIRE URGENCY THAT YOU REACH THE POWER BINDER FIRST.
I WAS... WRONG WHEN I THOUGHT WE COULD CONTROL THIS FORCE COMING TO OUR WORLD.
SHOULD THAT POWER BE FREED FROM WHAT BINDS IT, IT MUST NOT BE ALLOWED TO TOUCH A LIVING THING.
OMNIKRON... HAVE TO WARN THE PLANET, JAN...
IF SPACE GHOST CAN'T STOP IT-- WILL REBUILD ITSELF...
...FROM EVERY CREATURE ON THEIR WORLD--
YOU HAVE ONE MORE OBJECTIVE, JADE.
YOU MUST BRING BACK MY OLD COLLEAGUE.
THIS REQUIRES ENGAGING FORMIDABLE FORCES.
YET YOUR OPERATIVE PROFILE GIVES ME CONFIDENCE YOU WILL SUCCEED...

F.E.A.R. OPERATIVE FILE:

JADE X:
TRUE NAME UNKNOWN

ALIASES:
JANE AYDEN
JD BALLOU
"JEZEBEL" JADE

Mercenary operating primarily in Seychelles, Maldives and Bay of Bengal, but owns forged passports for most countries.

SKILLS:
Pilots most crafts.
Sharpshooter familiar with all modern armaments.
Martial Arts—
a mesh of judo and Krav Maga.
Languages—
conversant in Mandarin, Cantonese, French, Italian, English, Portuguese, Spanish, Russian, Greek, Romani.

POSSIBLE BACKGROUND:
Likely of Eurasian family though all records destroyed; anecdotal history of grifting/confidence schemes since early youth.

MOTIVATION:
Does not respond well to intimidation, provides excellent service when higher fees are offered. Will never formally join F.E.A.R. organization, do not waste time asking. Only works freelance on per-job basis.

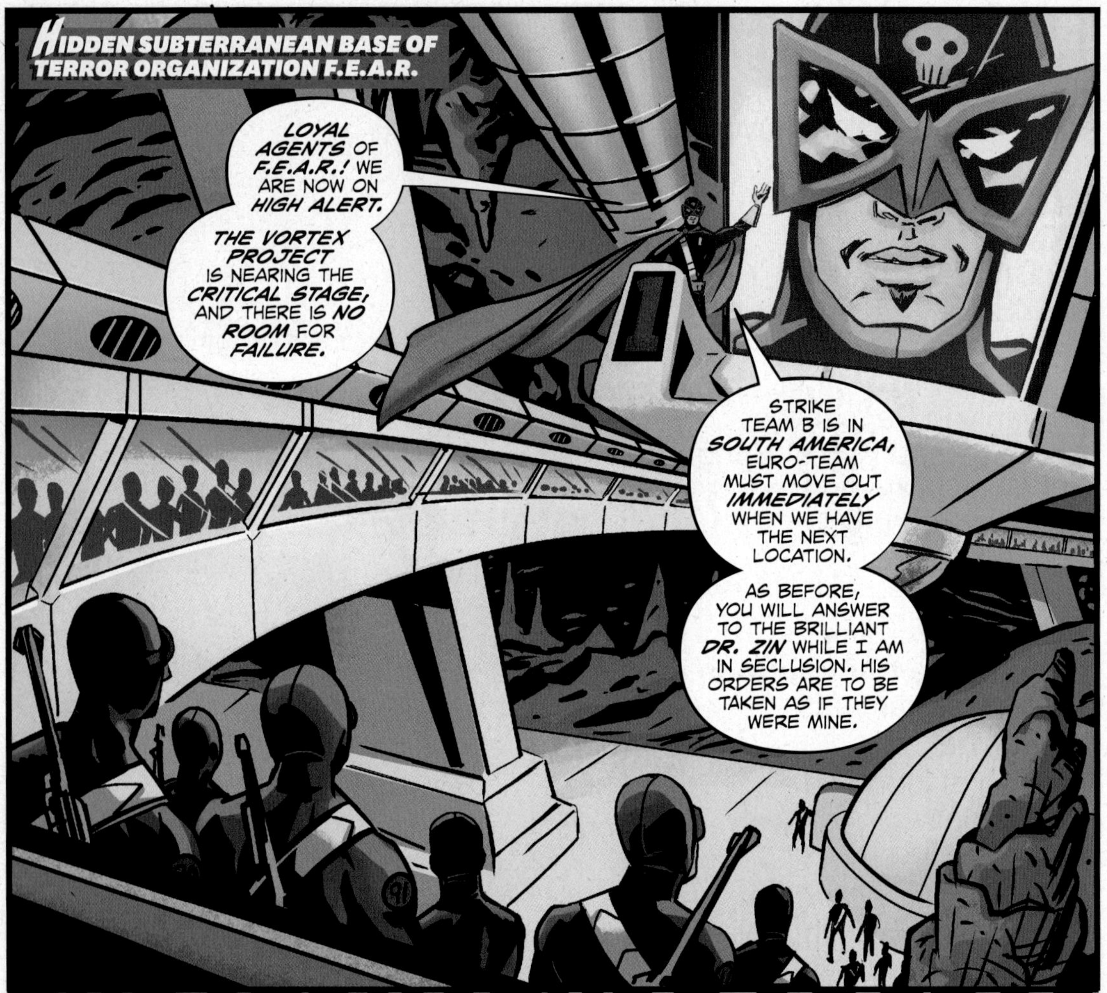
HIDDEN SUBTERRANEAN BASE OF TERROR ORGANIZATION F.E.A.R.
LOYAL AGENTS OF F.E.A.R.! WE ARE NOW ON HIGH ALERT.
THE VORTEX PROJECT IS NEARING THE CRITICAL STAGE, AND THERE IS NO ROOM FOR FAILURE.
STRIKE TEAM B IS IN SOUTH AMERICA, EURO-TEAM MUST MOVE OUT IMMEDIATELY WHEN WE HAVE THE NEXT LOCATION.
AS BEFORE, YOU WILL ANSWER TO THE BRILLIANT DR. ZIN WHILE I AM IN SECLUSION. HIS ORDERS ARE TO BE TAKEN AS IF THEY WERE MINE.

THE STRUCTURE OF FEAR

Jeff Parker story & art / **Hi*Fi** colors / **ALWS' Dave Lanphear** letters

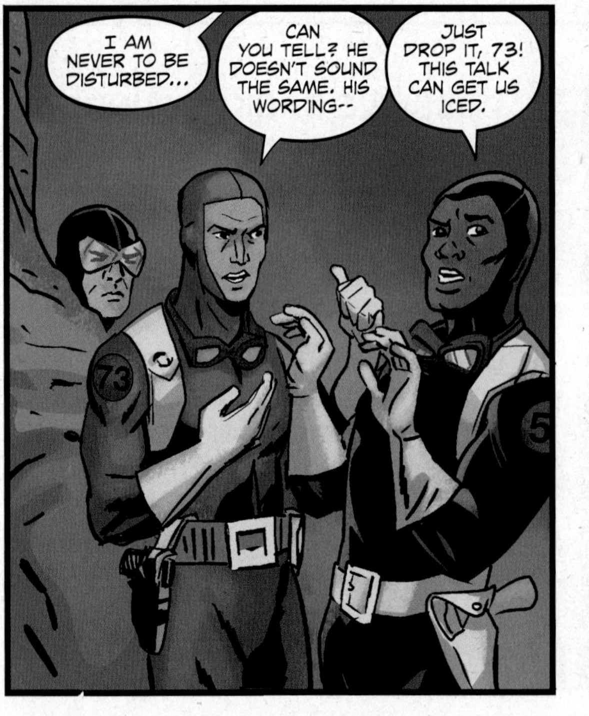
I AM NEVER TO BE DISTURBED...
CAN YOU TELL? HE DOESN'T SOUND THE SAME. HIS WORDING--
JUST DROP IT, 73! THIS TALK CAN GET US ICED.
73

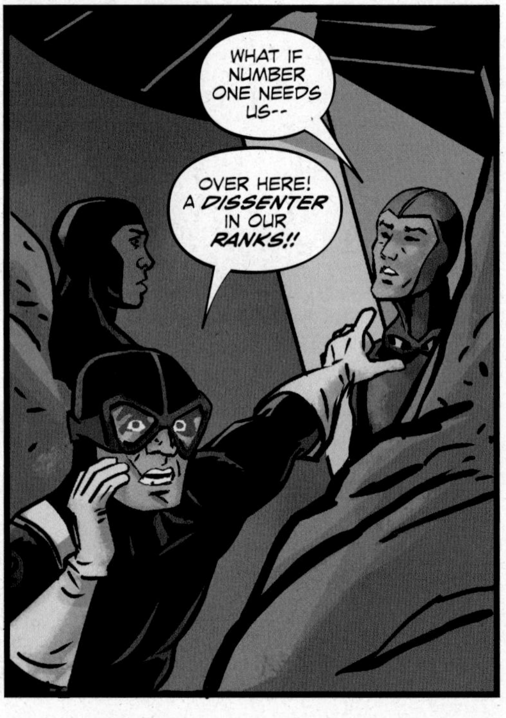
WHAT IF NUMBER ONE NEEDS US--
OVER HERE! A DISSENTER IN OUR RANKS!!

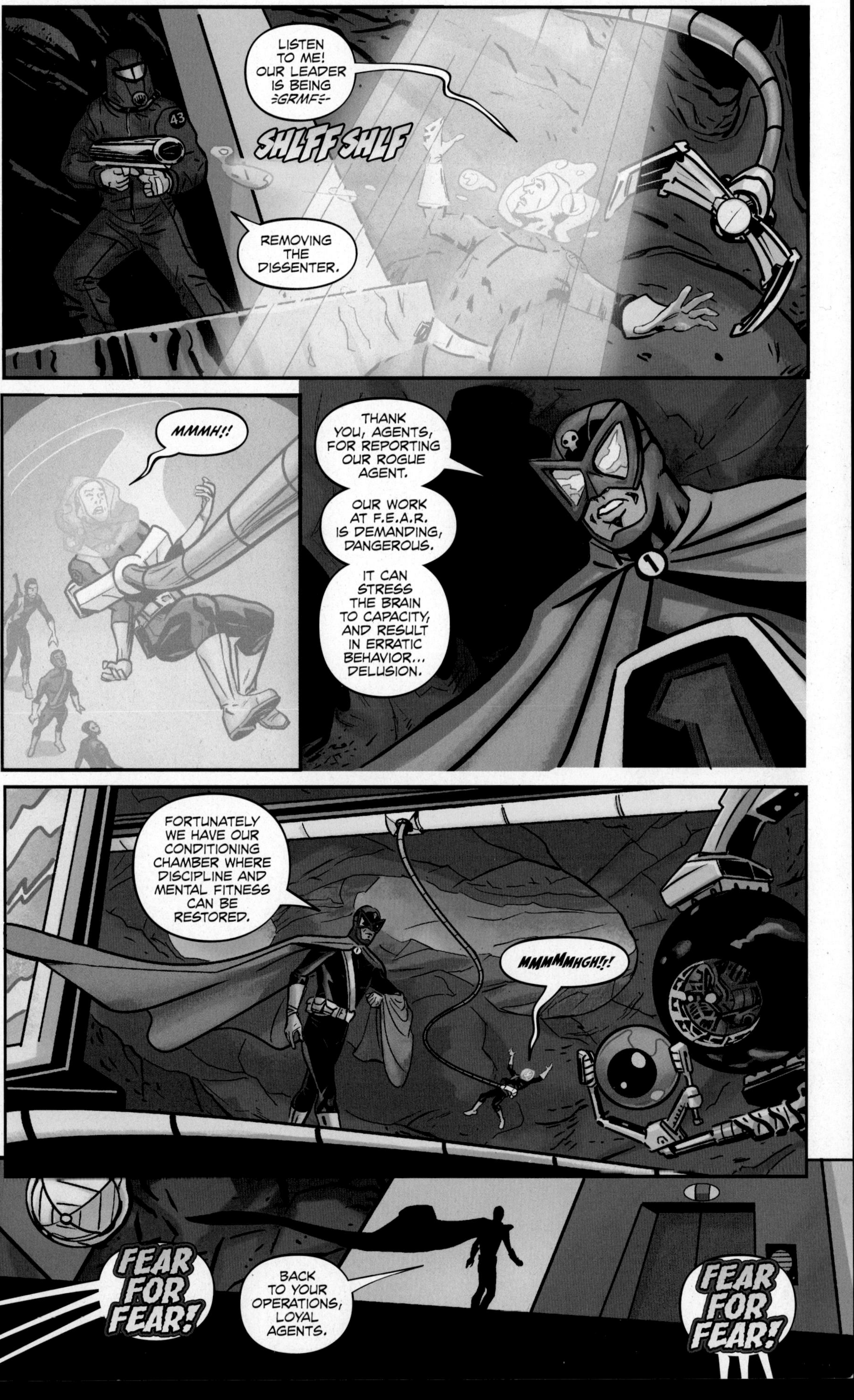
LISTEN TO ME! OUR LEADER IS BEING -GRMF-
SHLFF SHLF
REMOVING THE DISSENTER.
MMMH!!
THANK YOU, AGENTS, FOR REPORTING OUR ROGUE AGENT.
OUR WORK AT F.E.A.R. IS DEMANDING, DANGEROUS.
IT CAN STRESS THE BRAIN TO CAPACITY, AND RESULT IN ERRATIC BEHAVIOR... DELUSION.
FORTUNATELY WE HAVE OUR CONDITIONING CHAMBER WHERE DISCIPLINE AND MENTAL FITNESS CAN BE RESTORED.
MMMMMHGH!!!
FEAR FOR FEAR!
BACK TO YOUR OPERATIONS, LOYAL AGENTS.
FEAR FOR FEAR!

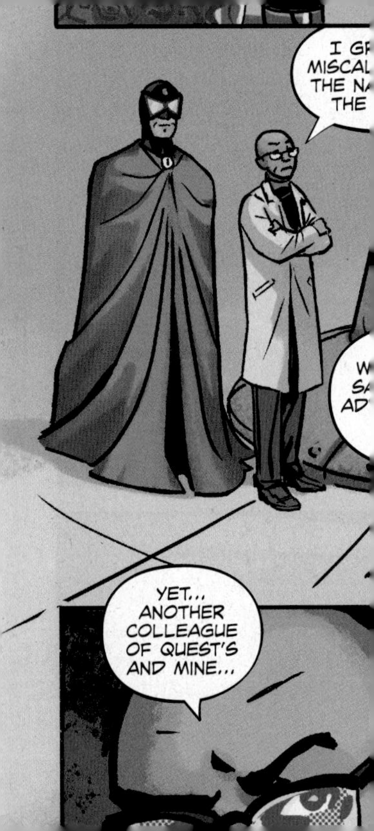
YET... ANOTHER COLLEAGUE OF QUEST'S AND MINE...

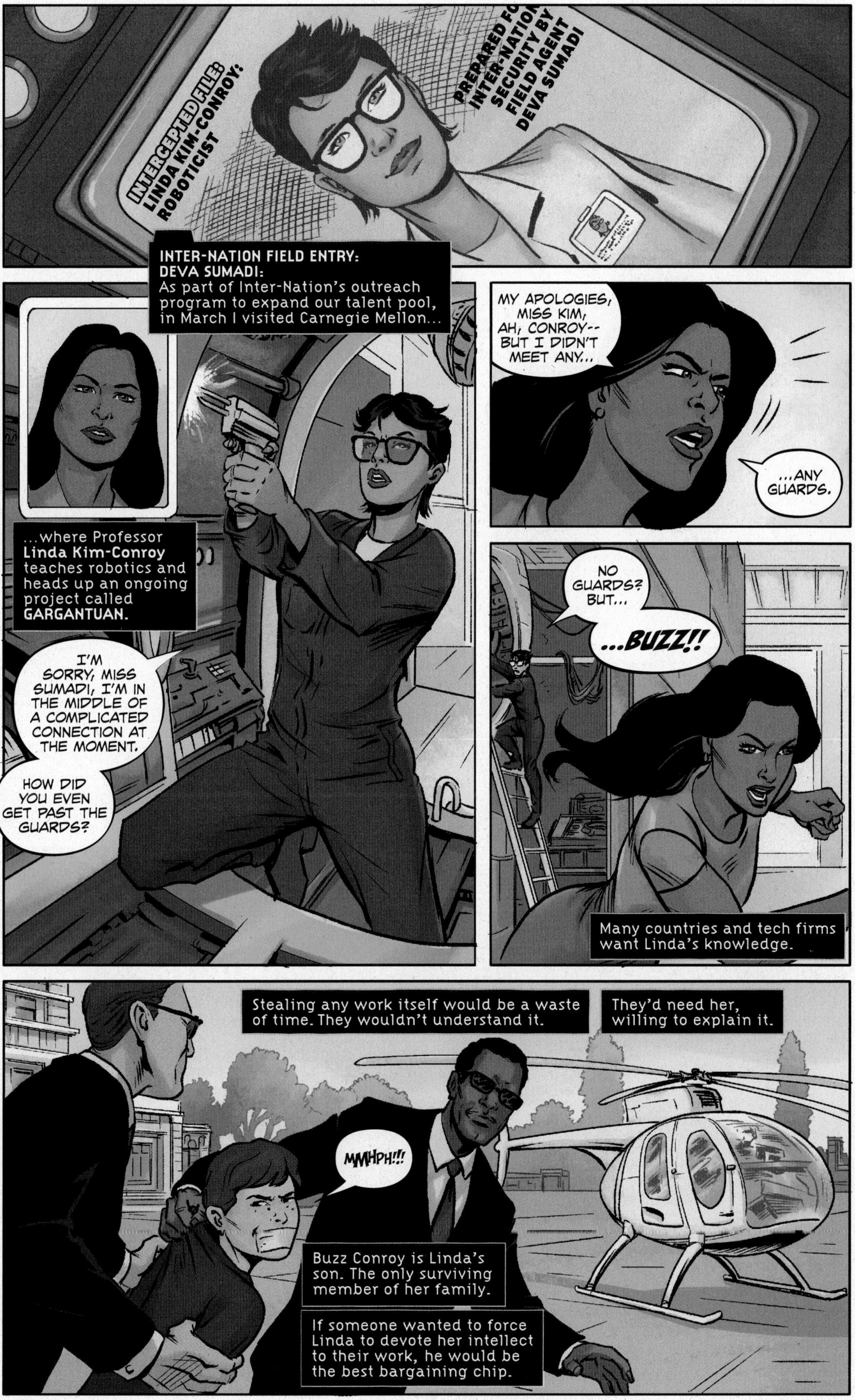
INTERCEPTED FILE: LINDA KIM-CONROY: ROBOTICIST
PREPARED FOR INTER-NATION SECURITY BY FIELD AGENT DEVA SUMADI
INTER-NATION FIELD ENTRY: DEVA SUMADI: As part of Inter-Nation's outreach program to expand our talent pool, in March I visited Carnegie Mellon...
...where Professor Linda Kim-Conroy teaches robotics and heads up an ongoing project called GARGANTUAN.
I'M SORRY, MISS SUMADI, I'M IN THE MIDDLE OF A COMPLICATED CONNECTION AT THE MOMENT.
HOW DID YOU EVEN GET PAST THE GUARDS?
MY APOLOGIES, MISS KIM, AH, CONROY-- BUT I DIDN'T MEET ANY...
...ANY GUARDS.
NO GUARDS? BUT...
...BUZZ!!
Many countries and tech firms want Linda's knowledge.
Stealing any work itself would be a waste of time. They wouldn't understand it.
They'd need her, willing to explain it.
MMHPH!!!
Buzz Conroy is Linda's son. The only surviving member of her family.
If someone wanted to force Linda to devote her intellect to their work, he would be the best bargaining chip.

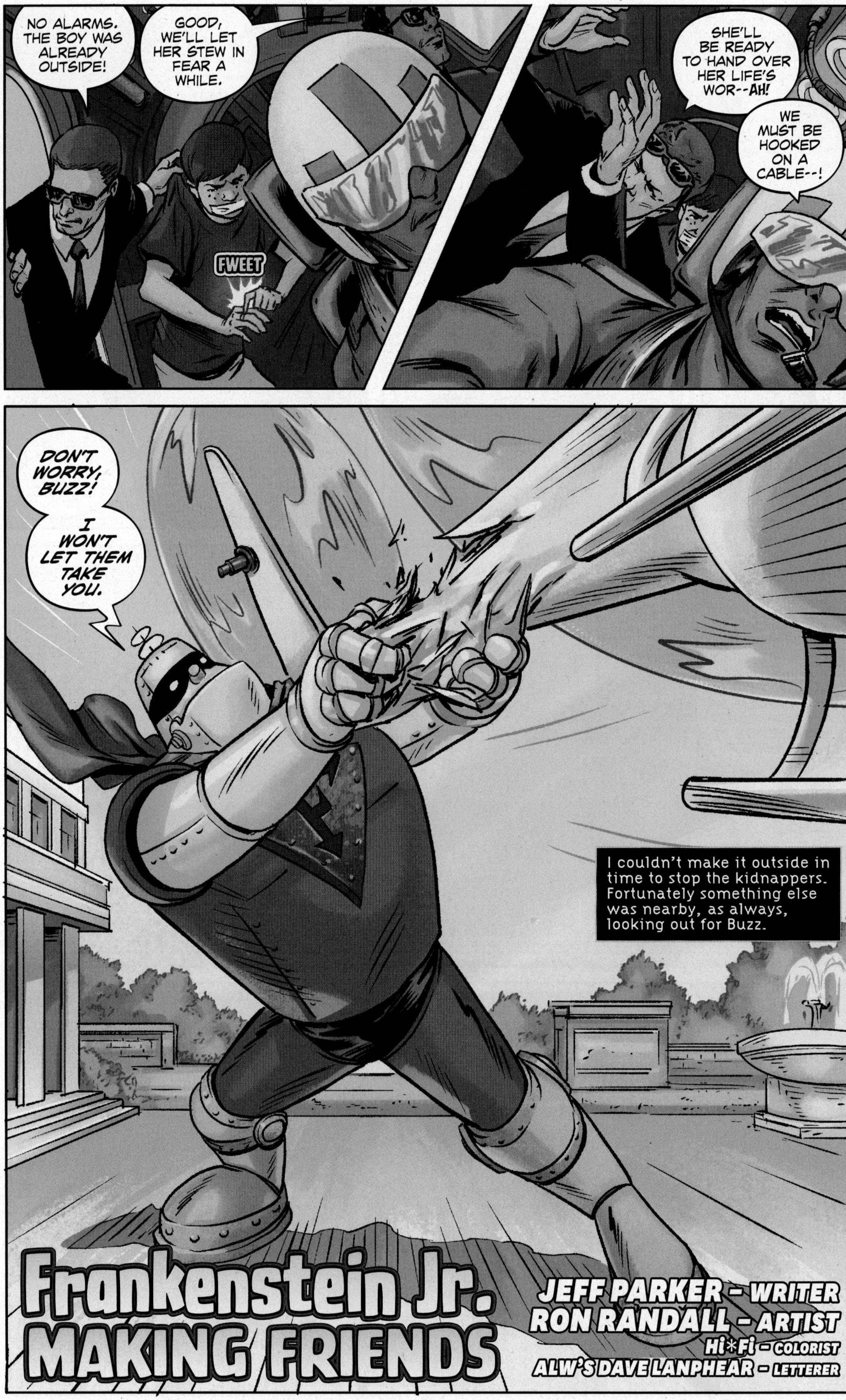
NO ALARMS. THE BOY WAS ALREADY OUTSIDE!
GOOD, WE'LL LET HER STEW IN FEAR A WHILE.
FWEET
SHE'LL BE READY TO HAND OVER HER LIFE'S WOR--AH!
WE MUST BE HOOKED ON A CABLE--!
DON'T WORRY, BUZZ!
I WON'T LET THEM TAKE YOU.
I couldn't make it outside in time to stop the kidnappers. Fortunately something else was nearby, as always, looking out for Buzz.
Frankenstein Jr.
MAKING FRIENDS
JEFF PARKER - WRITER
RON RANDALL - ARTIST
Hi*Fi - COLORIST
ALW'S DAVE LANPHEAR - LETTERER

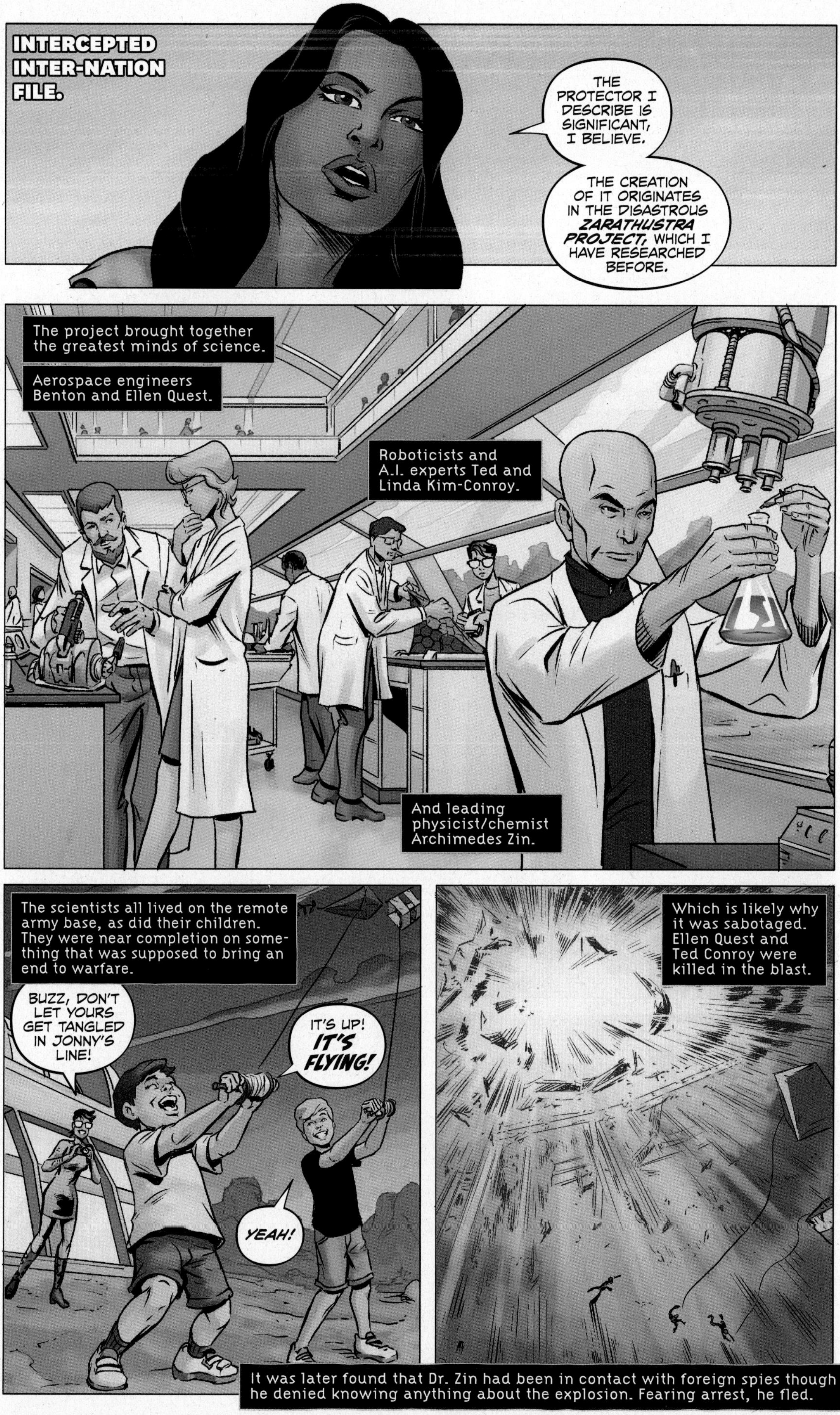
INTERCEPTED INTER-NATION FILE.
THE PROTECTOR I DESCRIBE IS SIGNIFICANT, I BELIEVE.
THE CREATION OF IT ORIGINATES IN THE DISASTROUS *ZARATHUSTRA PROJECT,* WHICH I HAVE RESEARCHED BEFORE.
The project brought together the greatest minds of science.
Aerospace engineers Benton and Ellen Quest.
Roboticists and A.I. experts Ted and Linda Kim-Conroy.
And leading physicist/chemist Archimedes Zin.
The scientists all lived on the remote army base, as did their children. They were near completion on something that was supposed to bring an end to warfare.
BUZZ, DON'T LET YOURS GET TANGLED IN JONNY'S LINE!
IT'S UP! *IT'S FLYING!*
YEAH!
Which is likely why it was sabotaged. Ellen Quest and Ted Conroy were killed in the blast.
It was later found that Dr. Zin had been in contact with foreign spies though he denied knowing anything about the explosion. Fearing arrest, he fled.

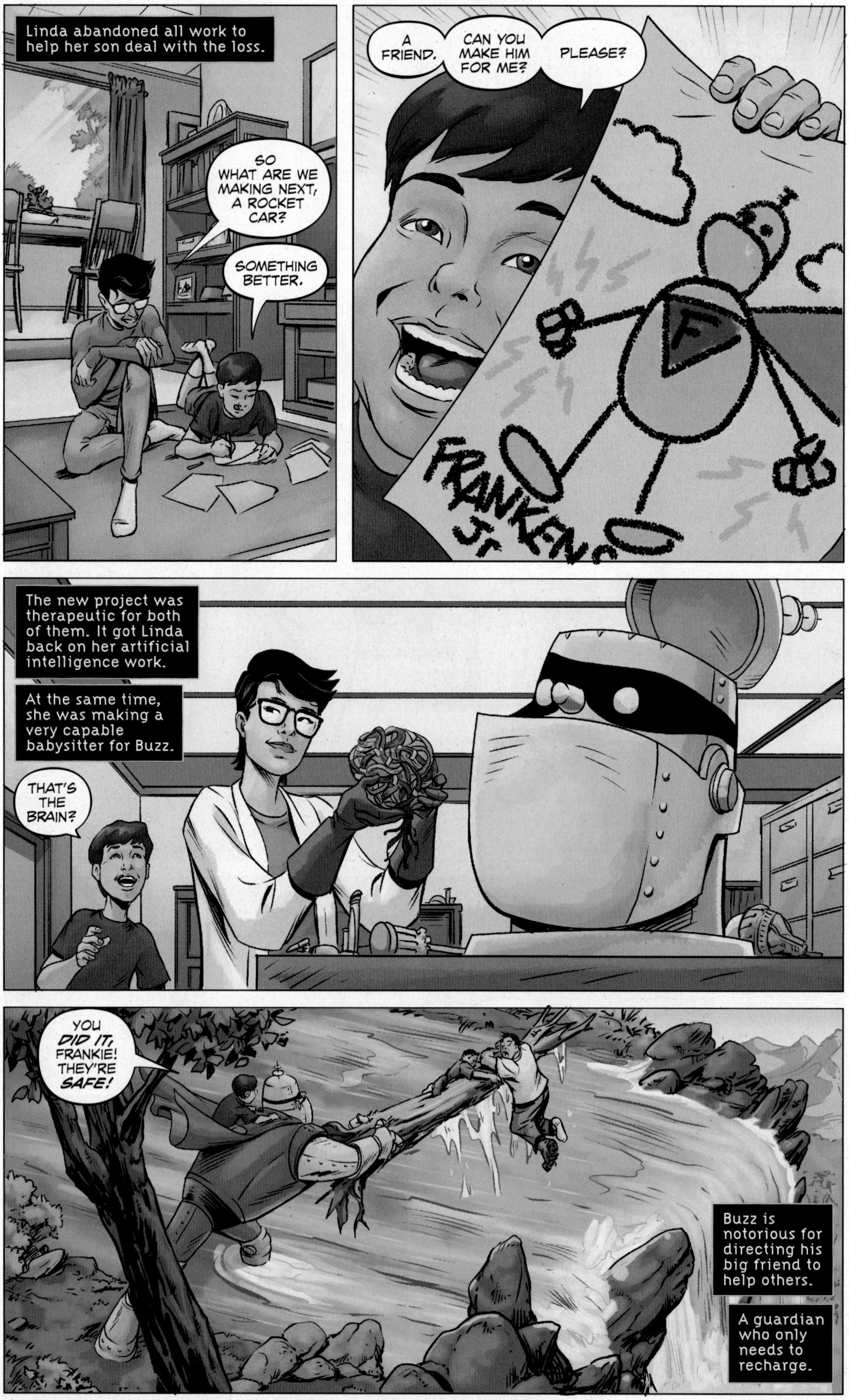

Linda abandoned all work to help her son deal with the loss.
SO WHAT ARE WE MAKING NEXT, A ROCKET CAR?
SOMETHING BETTER.
A FRIEND.
CAN YOU MAKE HIM FOR ME?
PLEASE?
FRANKENS
Jr
The new project was therapeutic for both of them. It got Linda back on her artificial intelligence work.
At the same time, she was making a very capable babysitter for Buzz.
THAT'S THE BRAIN?
YOU *DID IT,* FRANKIE! THEY'RE *SAFE!*
Buzz is notorious for directing his big friend to help others.
A guardian who only needs to recharge.

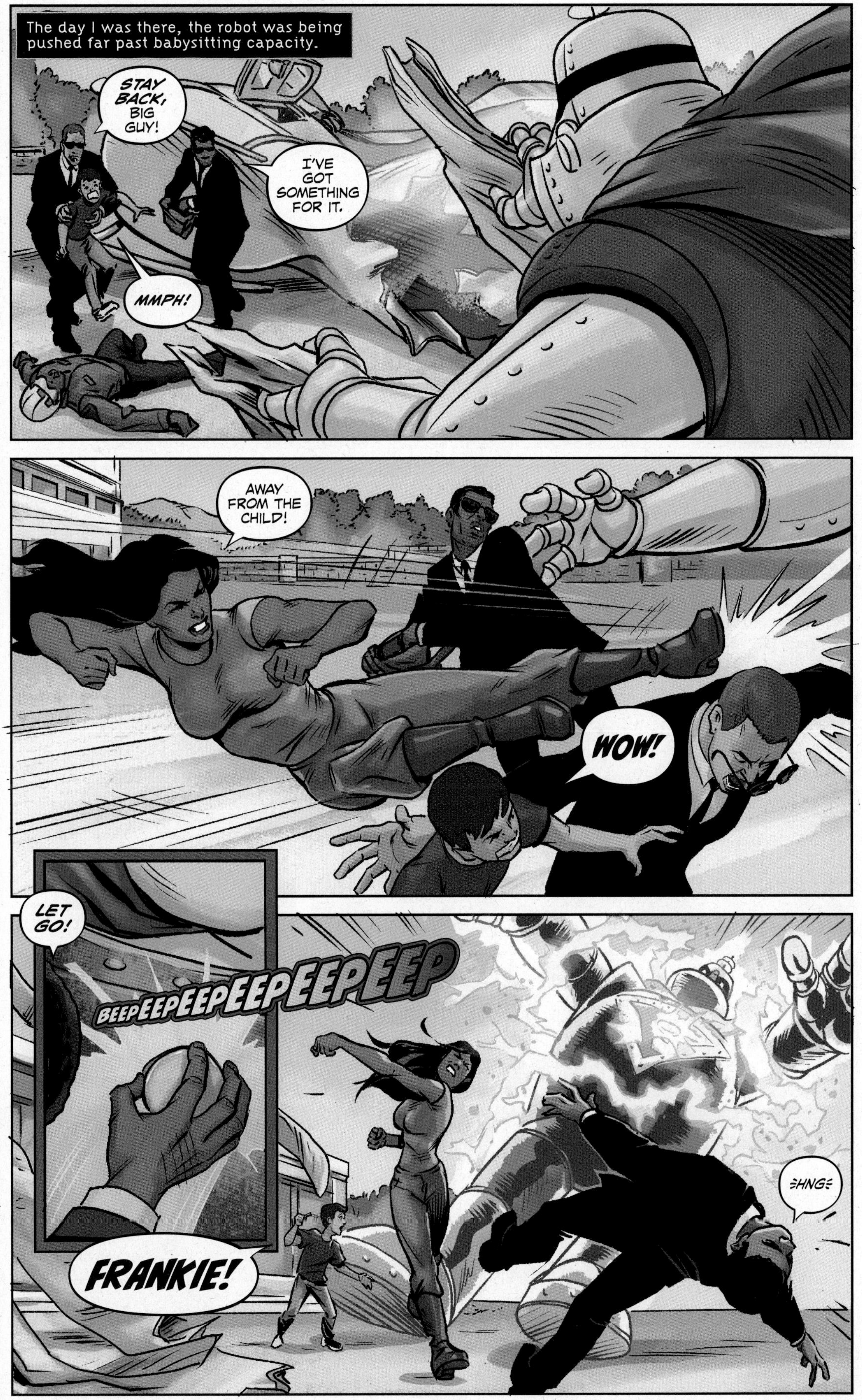
The day I was there, the robot was being pushed far past babysitting capacity.
STAY BACK, BIG GUY!
I'VE GOT SOMETHING FOR IT.
MMPH!
AWAY FROM THE CHILD!
WOW!
LET GO!
BEEPEEPEEPEEPEEPEEP
FRANKIE!
HNG

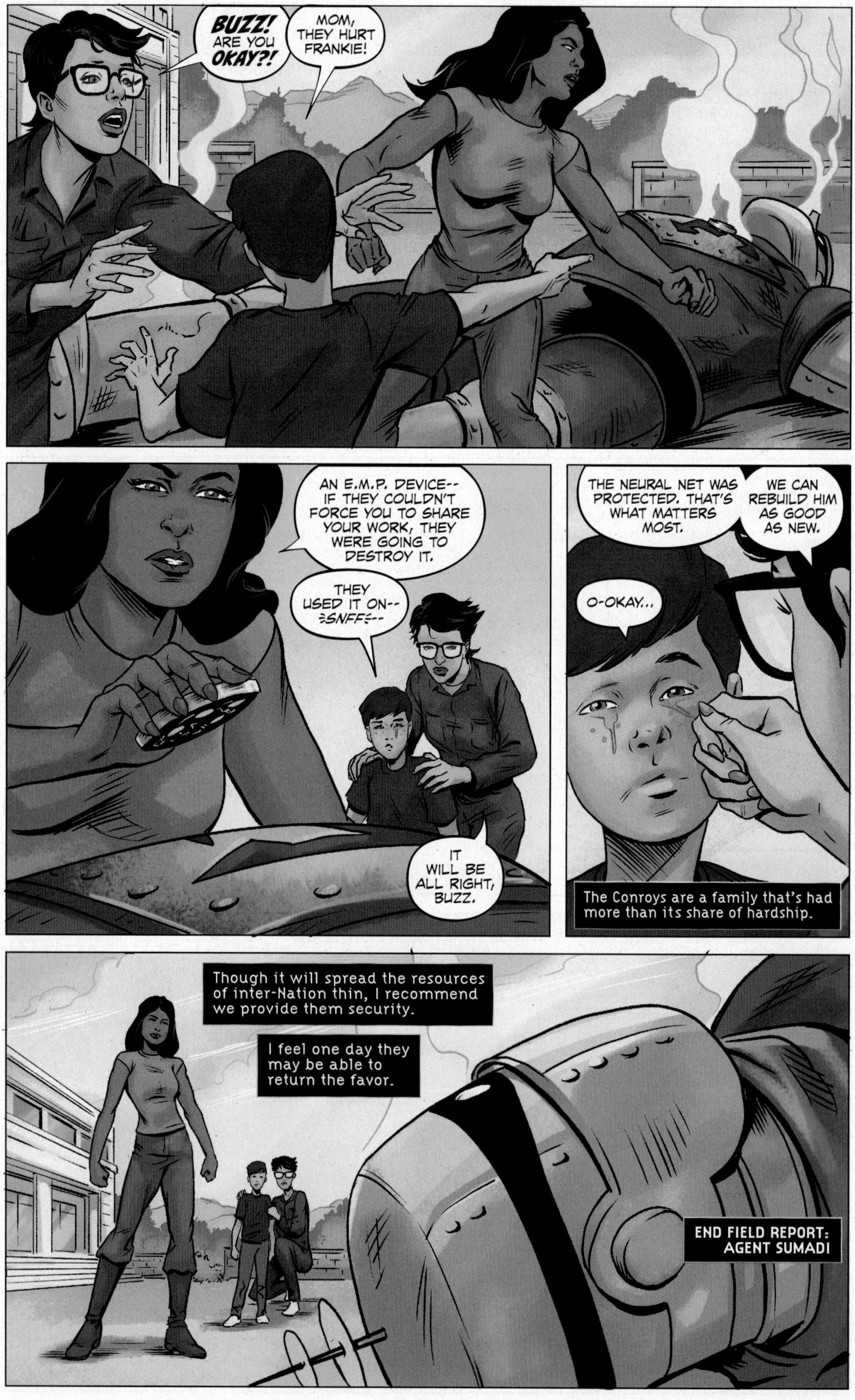
BUZZ! ARE YOU OKAY?!
MOM, THEY HURT FRANKIE!
AN E.M.P. DEVICE-- IF THEY COULDN'T FORCE YOU TO SHARE YOUR WORK, THEY WERE GOING TO DESTROY IT.
THEY USED IT ON-- *SNFF*--
IT WILL BE ALL RIGHT, BUZZ.
THE NEURAL NET WAS PROTECTED. THAT'S WHAT MATTERS MOST.
WE CAN REBUILD HIM AS GOOD AS NEW.
O-OKAY...
The Conroys are a family that's had more than its share of hardship.
Though it will spread the resources of inter-Nation thin, I recommend we provide them security.
I feel one day they may be able to return the favor.
END FIELD REPORT: AGENT SUMADI

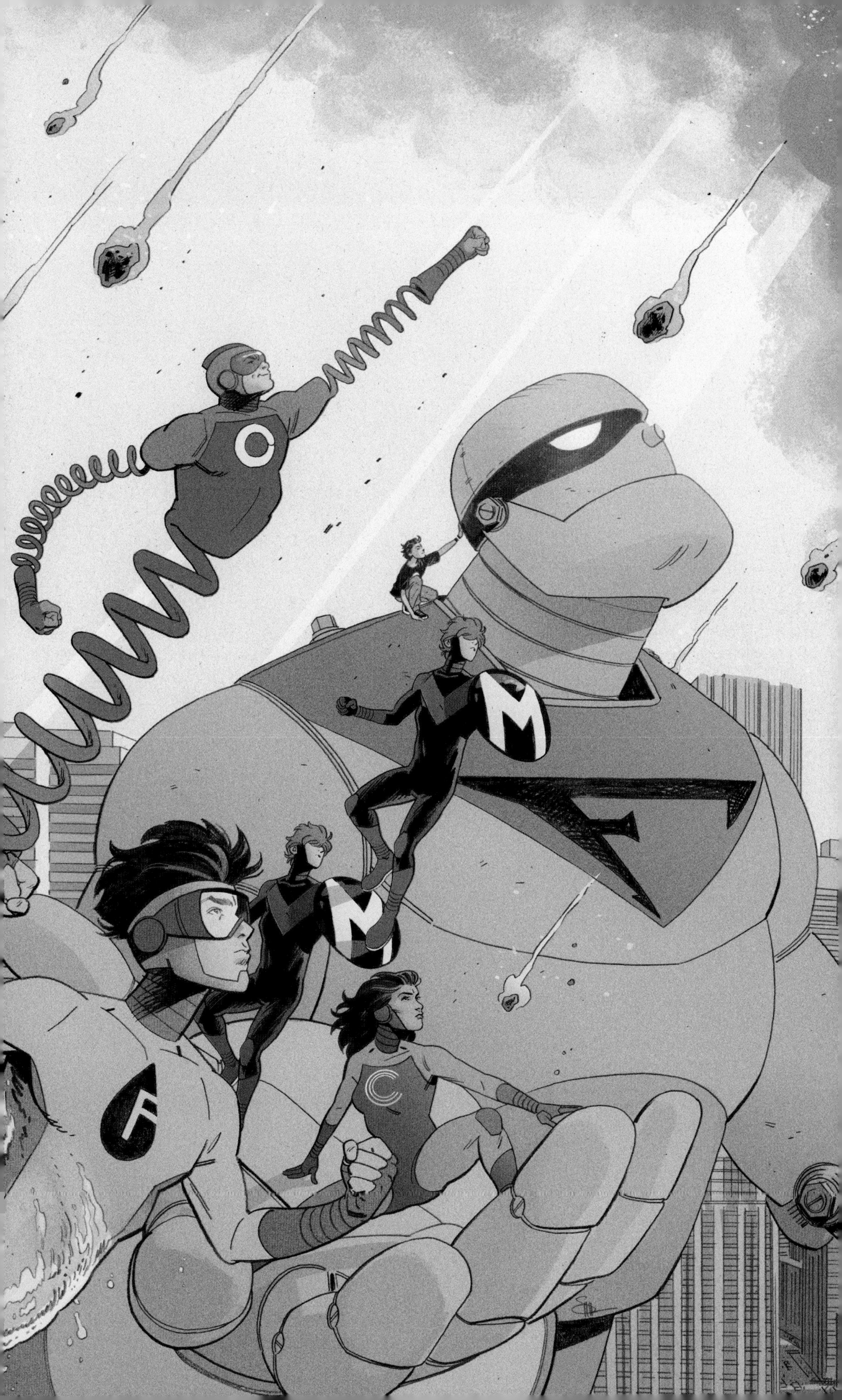

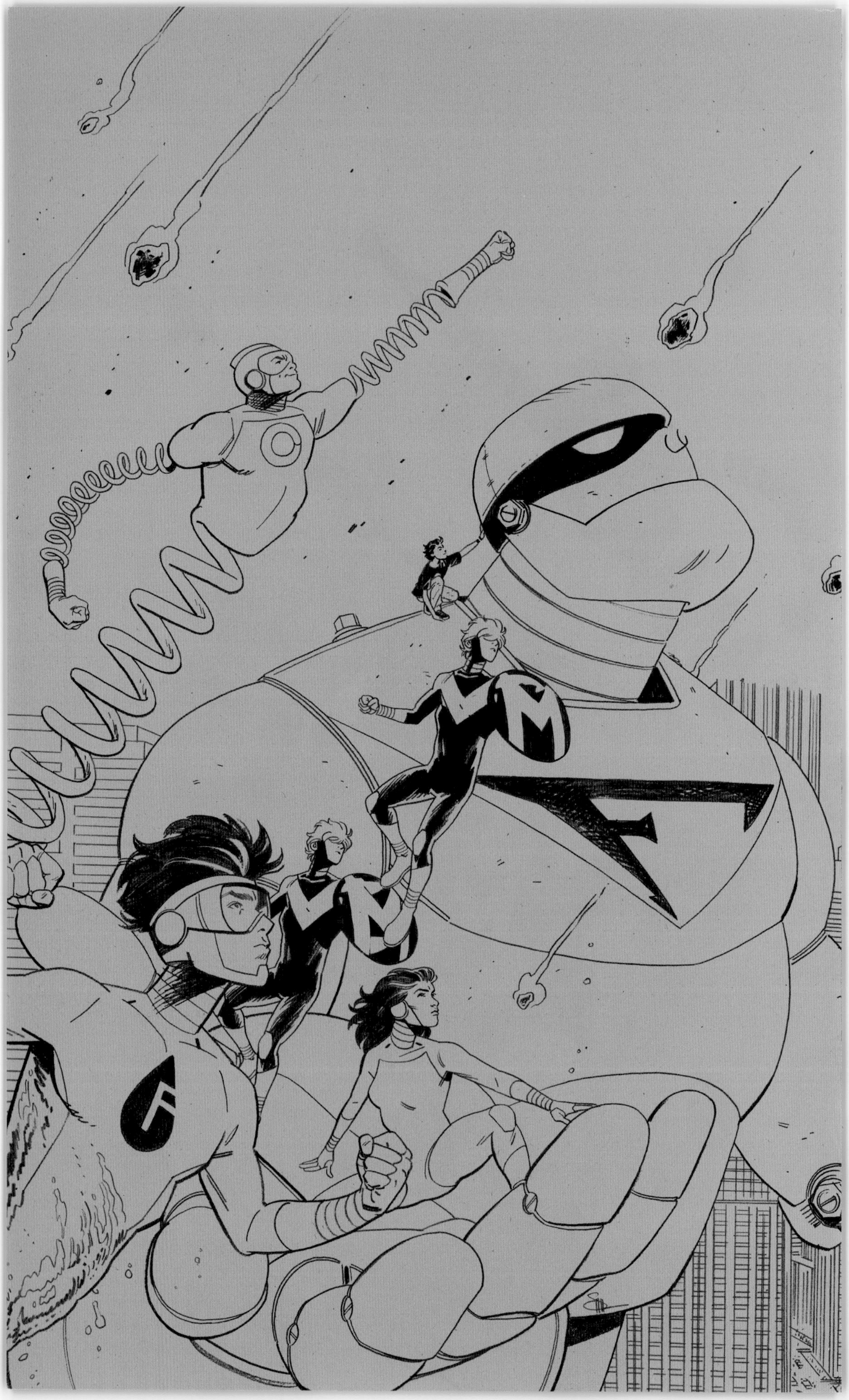

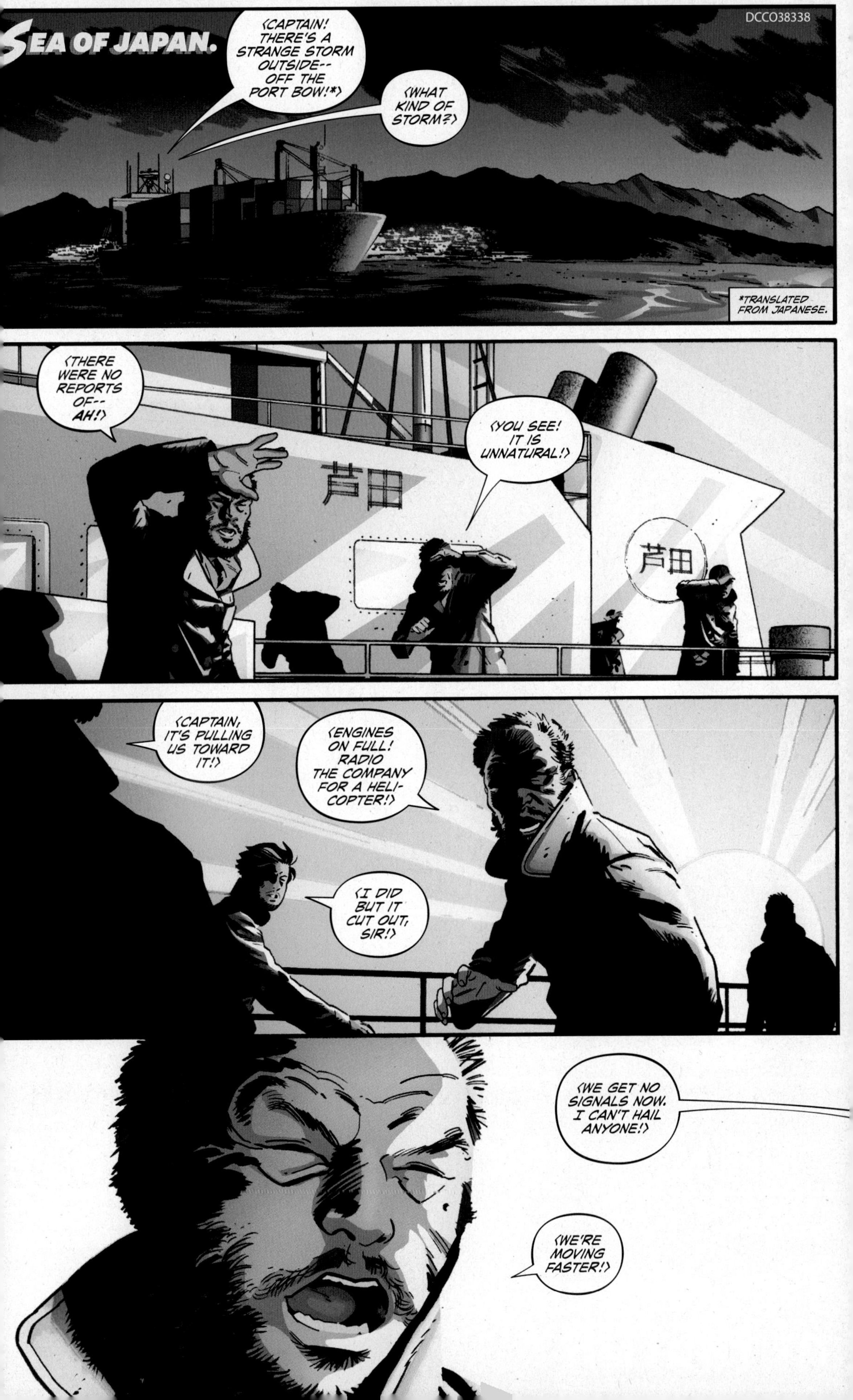
DCCO38338
SEA OF JAPAN.
‹CAPTAIN! THERE'S A STRANGE STORM OUTSIDE-- OFF THE PORT BOW!*›
‹WHAT KIND OF STORM?›
*TRANSLATED FROM JAPANESE.
‹THERE WERE NO REPORTS OF-- AH!›
‹YOU SEE! IT IS UNNATURAL!›
芦田
芦田
‹CAPTAIN, IT'S PULLING US TOWARD IT!›
‹ENGINES ON FULL! RADIO THE COMPANY FOR A HELI-COPTER!›
‹I DID BUT IT CUT OUT, SIR!›
‹WE GET NO SIGNALS NOW. I CAN'T HAIL ANYONE!›
‹WE'RE MOVING FASTER!›

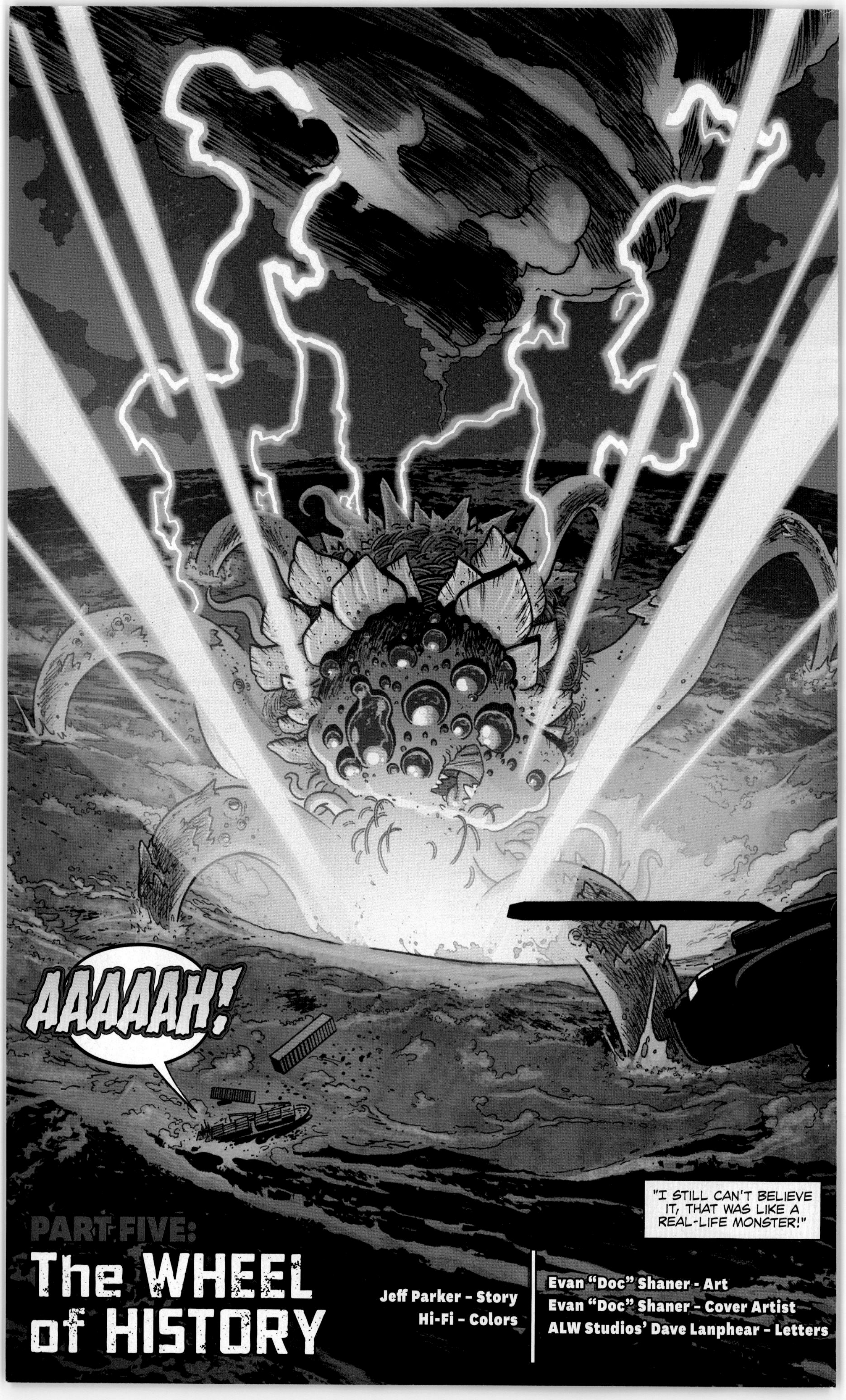
AAAAAH!
"I STILL CAN'T BELIEVE IT, THAT WAS LIKE A REAL-LIFE MONSTER!"
PART FIVE:
The WHEEL of HISTORY
Jeff Parker - Story
Hi-Fi - Colors
Evan "Doc" Shaner - Art
Evan "Doc" Shaner - Cover Artist
ALW Studios' Dave Lanphear - Letters

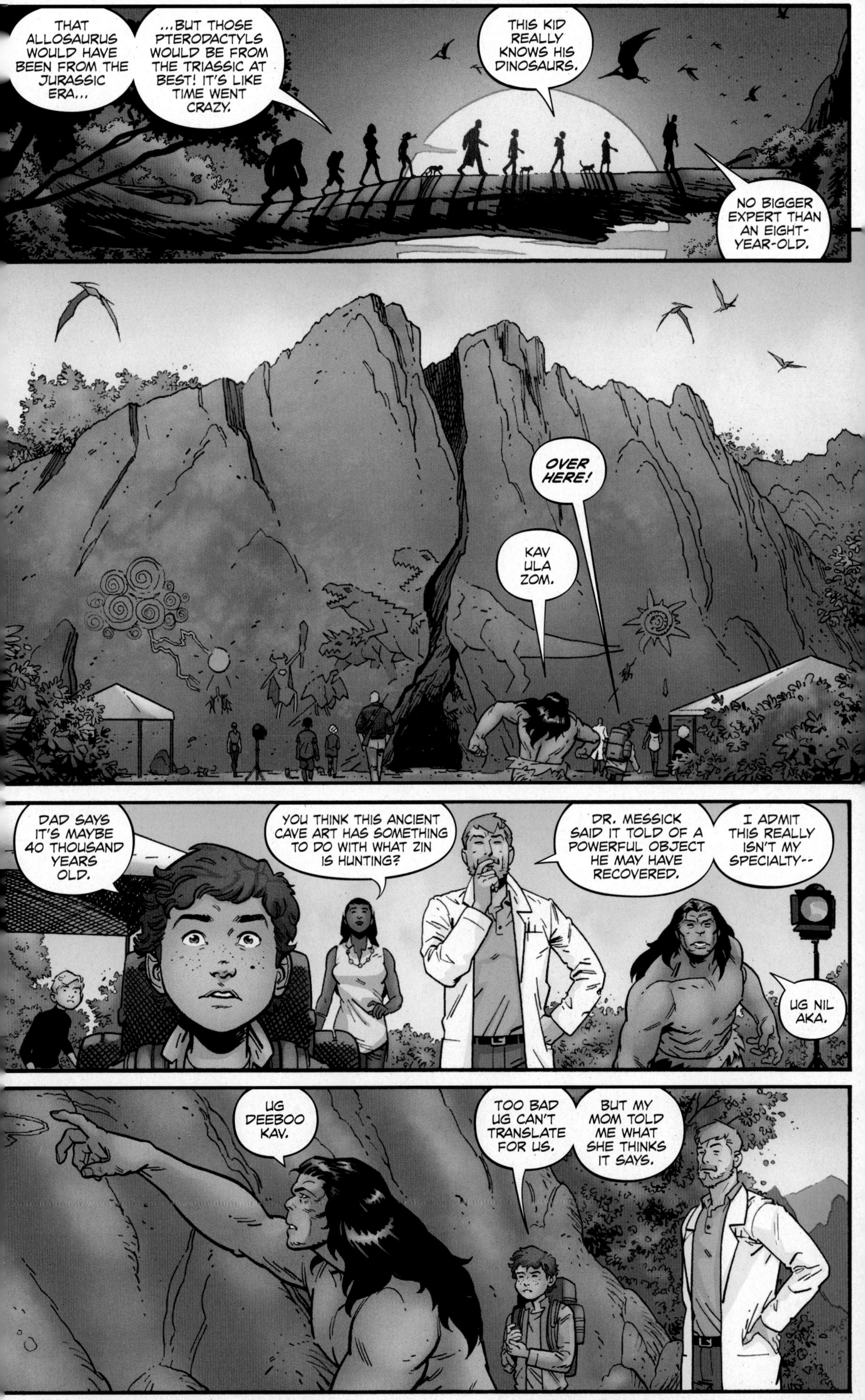
THAT ALLOSAURUS WOULD HAVE BEEN FROM THE JURASSIC ERA...
...BUT THOSE PTERODACTYLS WOULD BE FROM THE TRIASSIC AT BEST! IT'S LIKE TIME WENT CRAZY.
THIS KID REALLY KNOWS HIS DINOSAURS.
NO BIGGER EXPERT THAN AN EIGHT-YEAR-OLD.
OVER HERE!
KAV ULA ZOM.
DAD SAYS IT'S MAYBE 40 THOUSAND YEARS OLD.
YOU THINK THIS ANCIENT CAVE ART HAS SOMETHING TO DO WITH WHAT ZIN IS HUNTING?
DR. MESSICK SAID IT TOLD OF A POWERFUL OBJECT HE MAY HAVE RECOVERED.
I ADMIT THIS REALLY ISN'T MY SPECIALTY--
UG NIL AKA.
UG DEEBOO KAV.
TOO BAD UG CAN'T TRANSLATE FOR US.
BUT MY MOM TOLD ME WHAT SHE THINKS IT SAYS.

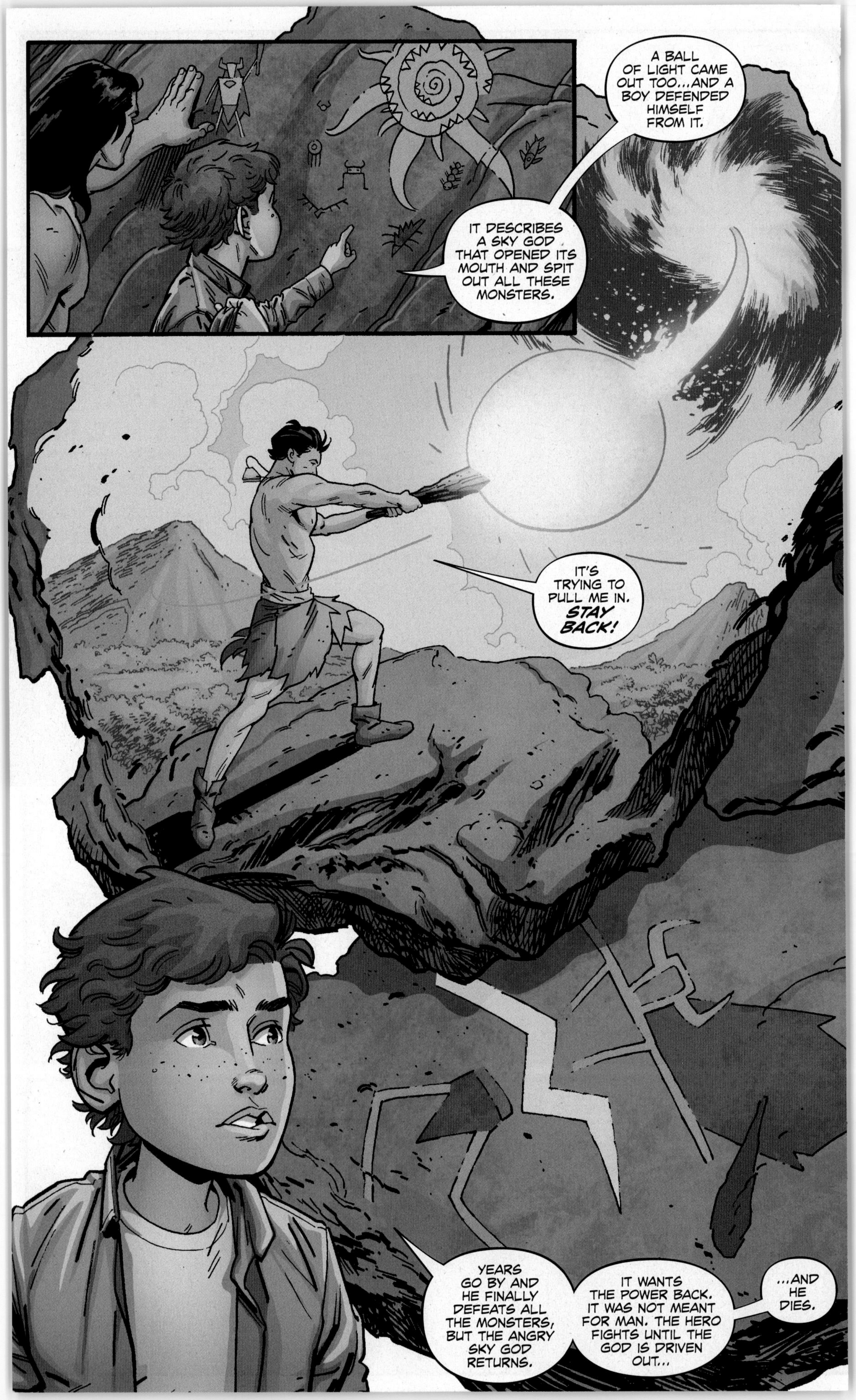
IT DESCRIBES A SKY GOD THAT OPENED ITS MOUTH AND SPIT OUT ALL THESE MONSTERS.
A BALL OF LIGHT CAME OUT TOO...AND A BOY DEFENDED HIMSELF FROM IT.
IT'S TRYING TO PULL ME IN. STAY BACK!
YEARS GO BY AND HE FINALLY DEFEATS ALL THE MONSTERS, BUT THE ANGRY SKY GOD RETURNS.
IT WANTS THE POWER BACK. IT WAS NOT MEANT FOR MAN. THE HERO FIGHTS UNTIL THE GOD IS DRIVEN OUT...
...AND HE DIES.

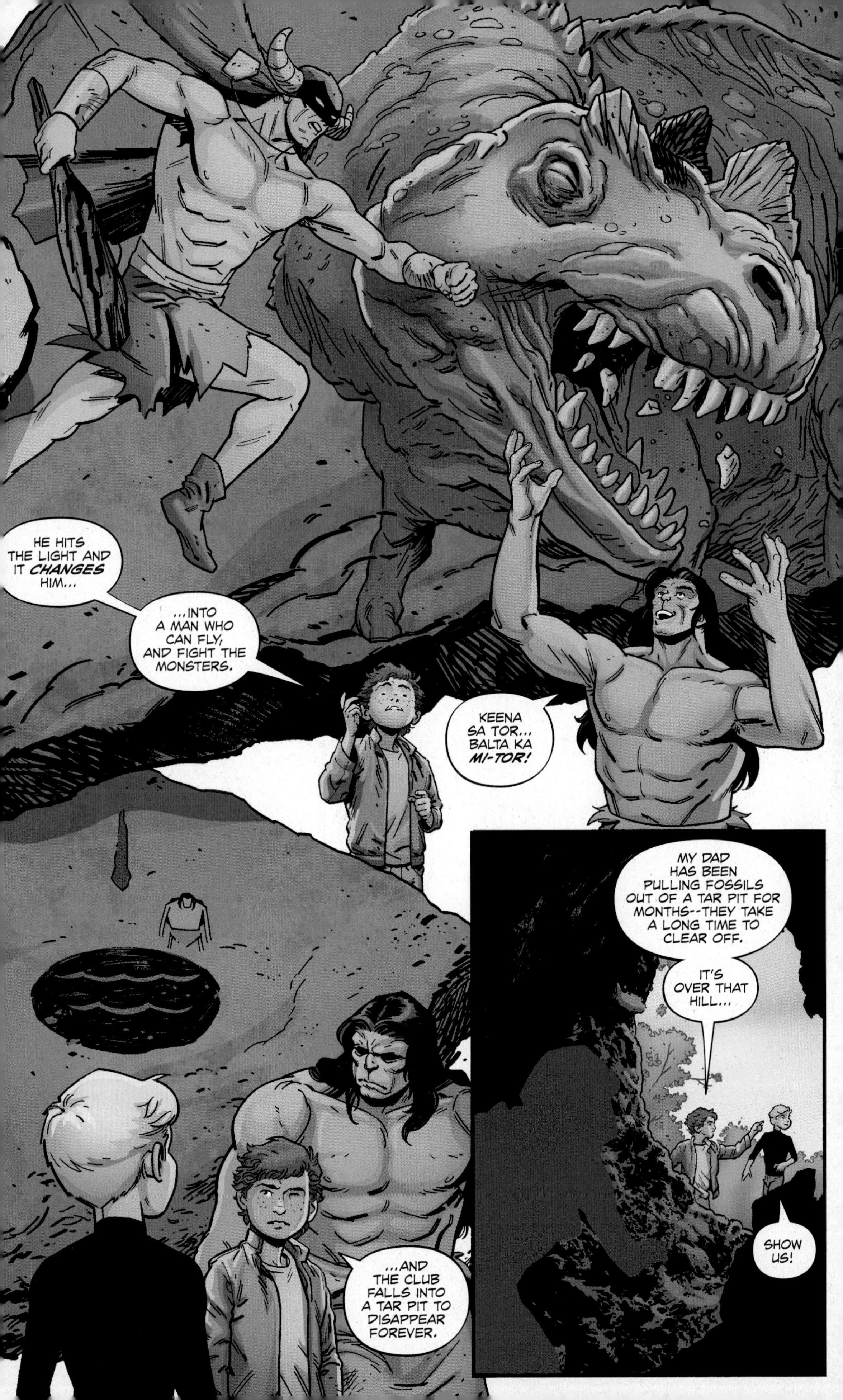

HE HITS THE LIGHT AND IT *CHANGES* HIM...
...INTO A MAN WHO CAN FLY, AND FIGHT THE MONSTERS.
KEENA SA TOR... BALTA KA *MI-TOR!*
...AND THE CLUB FALLS INTO A TAR PIT TO DISAPPEAR FOREVER.
MY DAD HAS BEEN PULLING FOSSILS OUT OF A TAR PIT FOR MONTHS--THEY TAKE A LONG TIME TO CLEAR OFF.
IT'S OVER THAT HILL...
SHOW US!

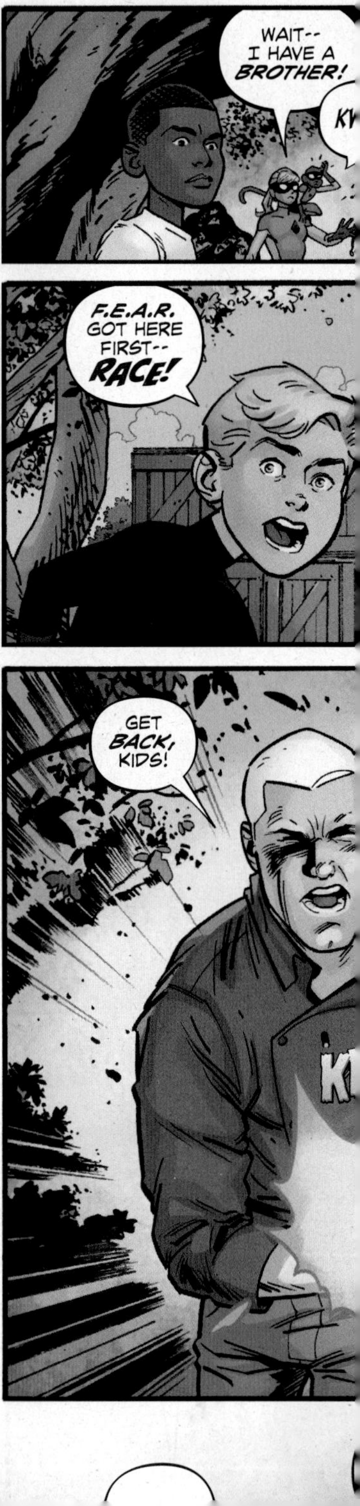
WAIT-- I HAVE A BROTHER!
F.E.A.R. GOT HERE FIRST-- RACE!
GET BACK, KIDS!

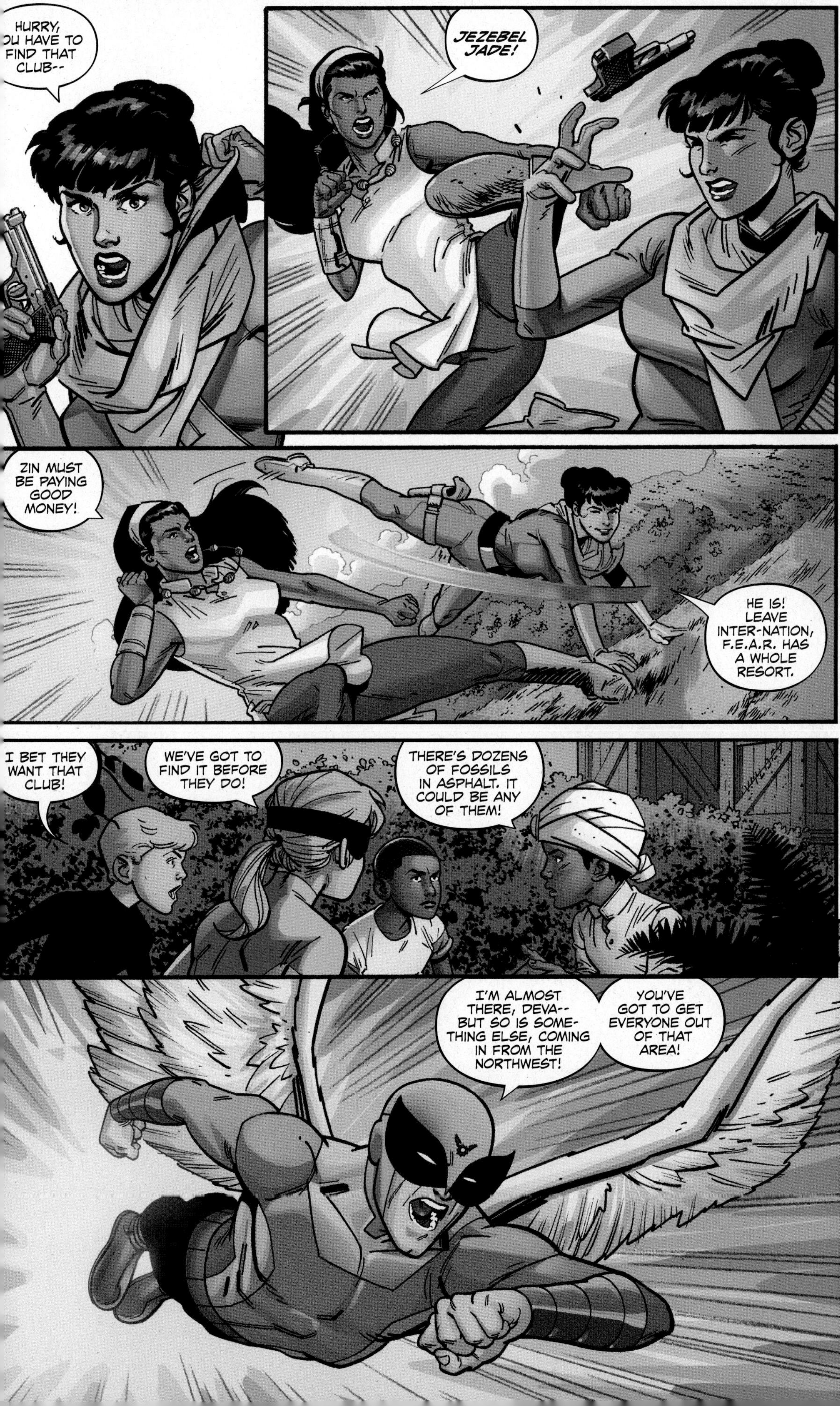

HURRY, OU HAVE TO FIND THAT CLUB--
JEZEBEL JADE!
ZIN MUST BE PAYING GOOD MONEY!
HE IS! LEAVE INTER-NATION, F.E.A.R. HAS A WHOLE RESORT.
I BET THEY WANT THAT CLUB!
WE'VE GOT TO FIND IT BEFORE THEY DO!
THERE'S DOZENS OF FOSSILS IN ASPHALT. IT COULD BE ANY OF THEM!
I'M ALMOST THERE, DEVA-- BUT SO IS SOME-THING ELSE, COMING IN FROM THE NORTHWEST!
YOU'VE GOT TO GET EVERYONE OUT OF THAT AREA!

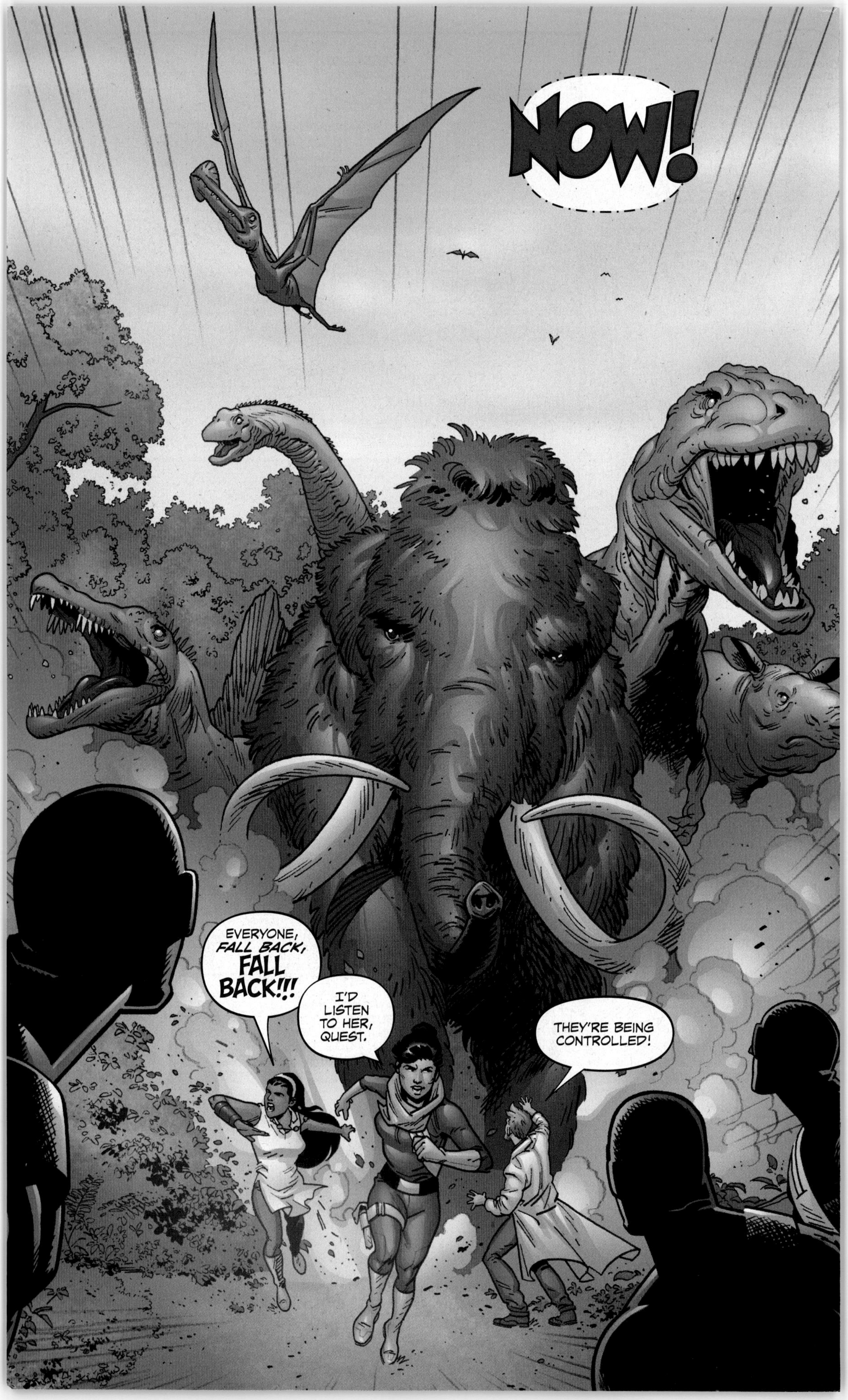
NOW!
EVERYONE, FALL BACK, FALL BACK!!!
I'D LISTEN TO HER, QUEST.
THEY'RE BEING CONTROLLED!

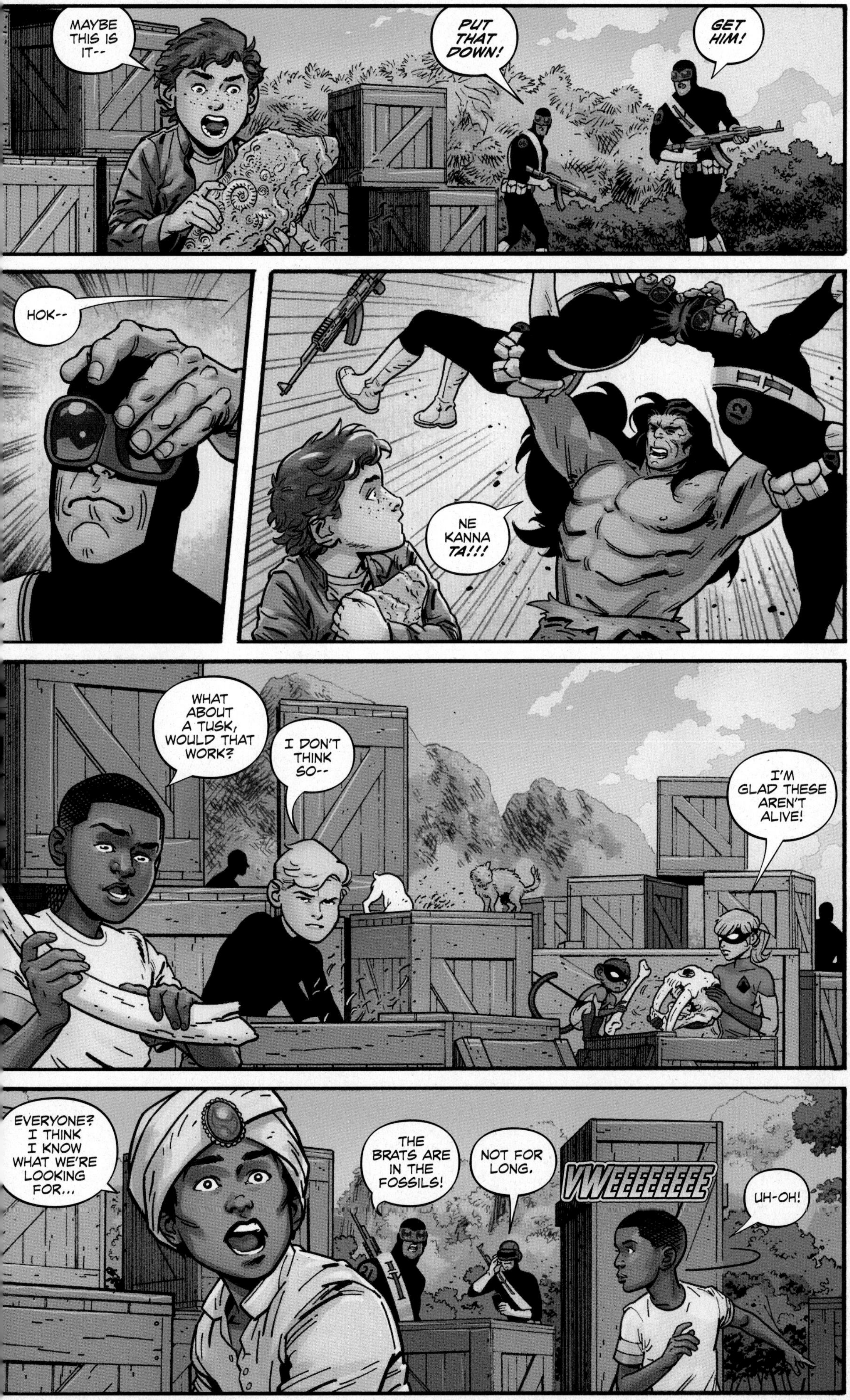

MAYBE THIS IS IT--
PUT THAT DOWN!
GET HIM!
HOK--
NE KANNA TA!!!
WHAT ABOUT A TUSK, WOULD THAT WORK?
I DON'T THINK SO--
I'M GLAD THESE AREN'T ALIVE!
EVERYONE? I THINK I KNOW WHAT WE'RE LOOKING FOR...
THE BRATS ARE IN THE FOSSILS!
NOT FOR LONG.
VWEEEEEEEE
UH-OH!

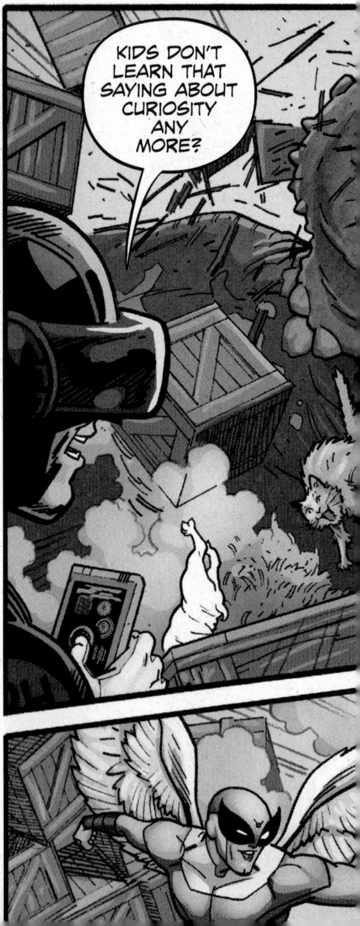
KIDS DON'T LEARN THAT SAYING ABOUT CURIOSITY ANY MORE?

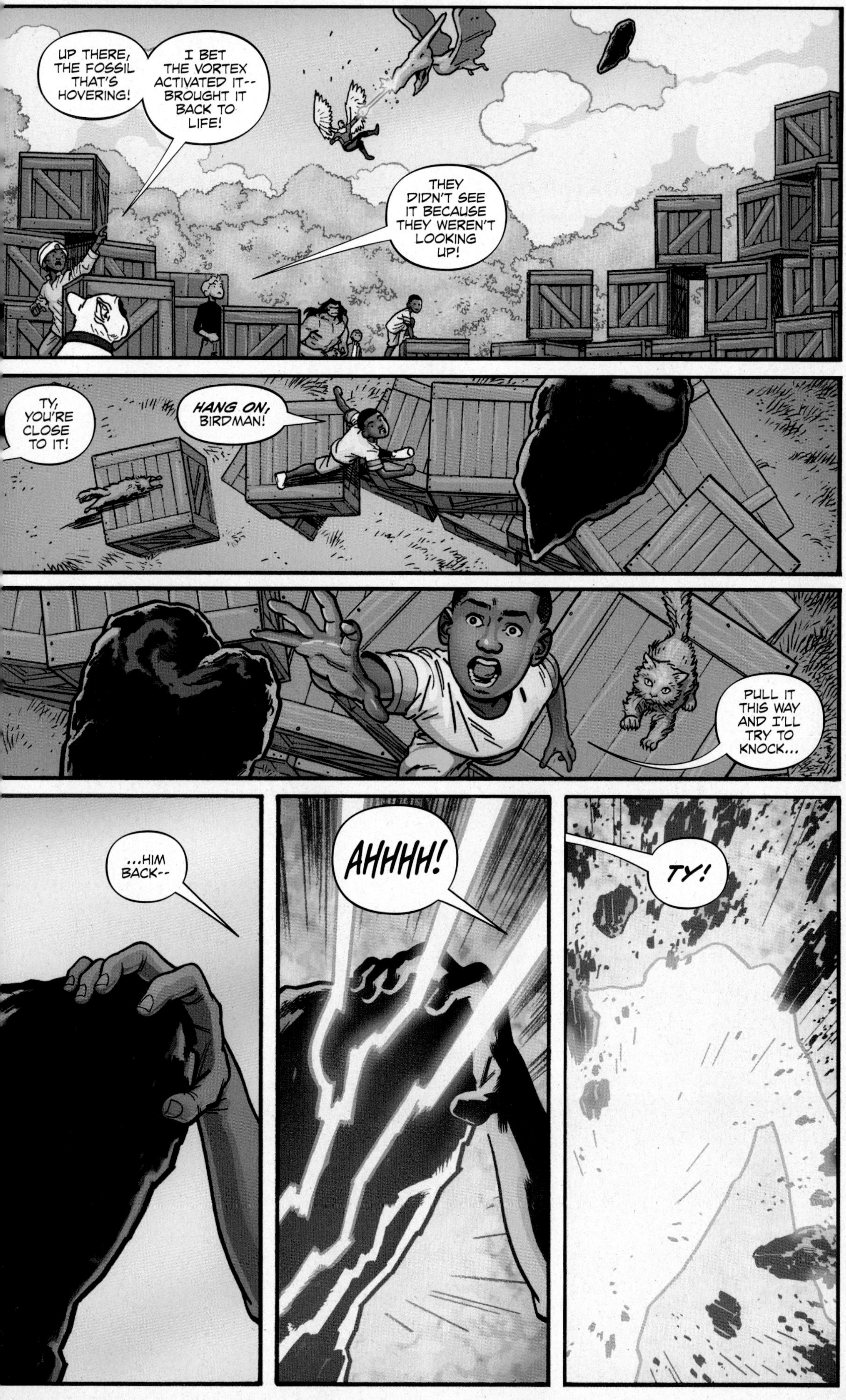
UP THERE, THE FOSSIL THAT'S HOVERING!
I BET THE VORTEX ACTIVATED IT--BROUGHT IT BACK TO LIFE!
THEY DIDN'T SEE IT BECAUSE THEY WEREN'T LOOKING UP!
TY, YOU'RE CLOSE TO IT!
HANG ON, BIRDMAN!
PULL IT THIS WAY AND I'LL TRY TO KNOCK...
...HIM BACK--
AHHHH!
TY!

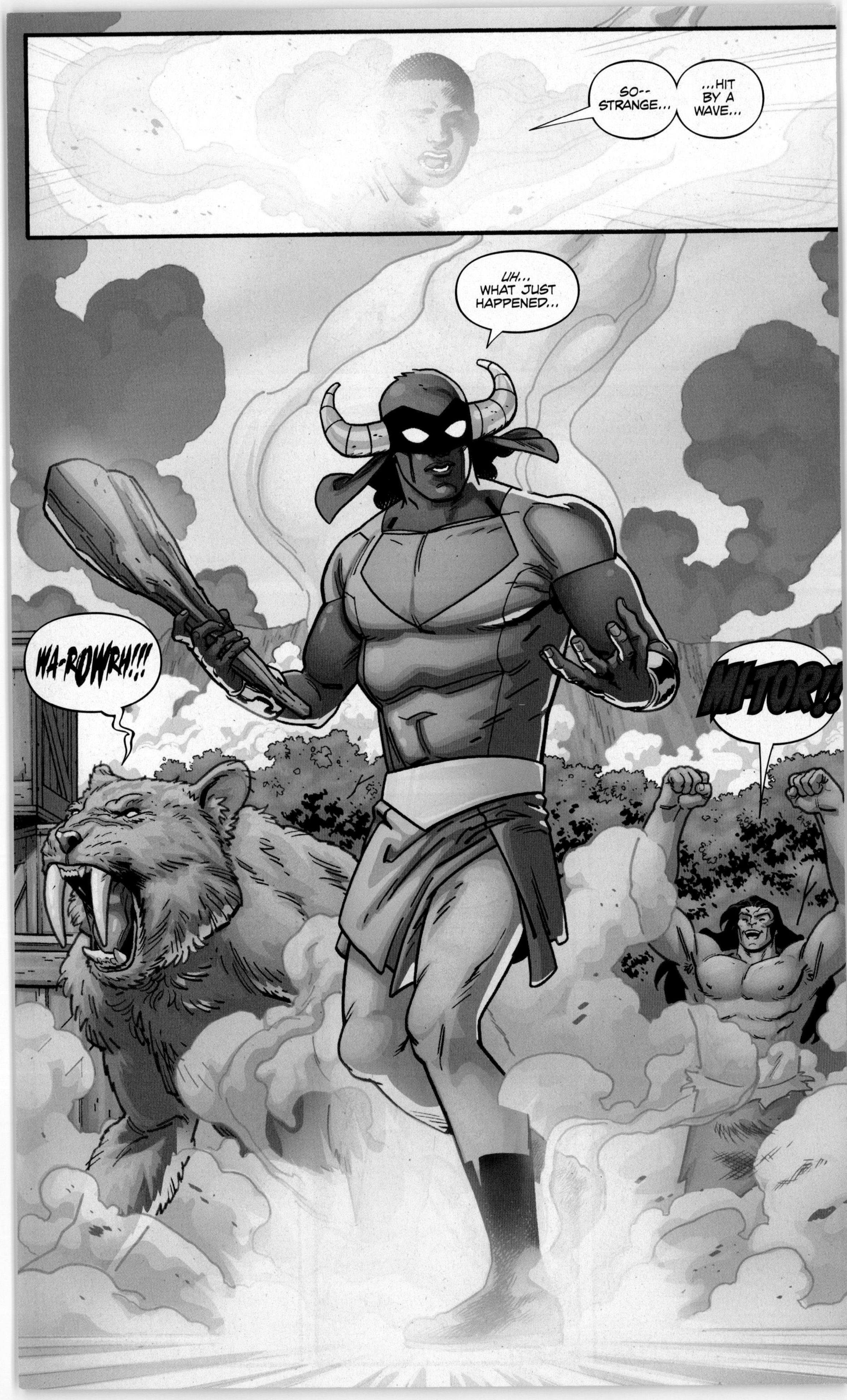
SO-- STRANGE...
...HIT BY A WAVE...
UH... WHAT JUST HAPPENED...
WA-ROWRH!!!
MI-TOR!!

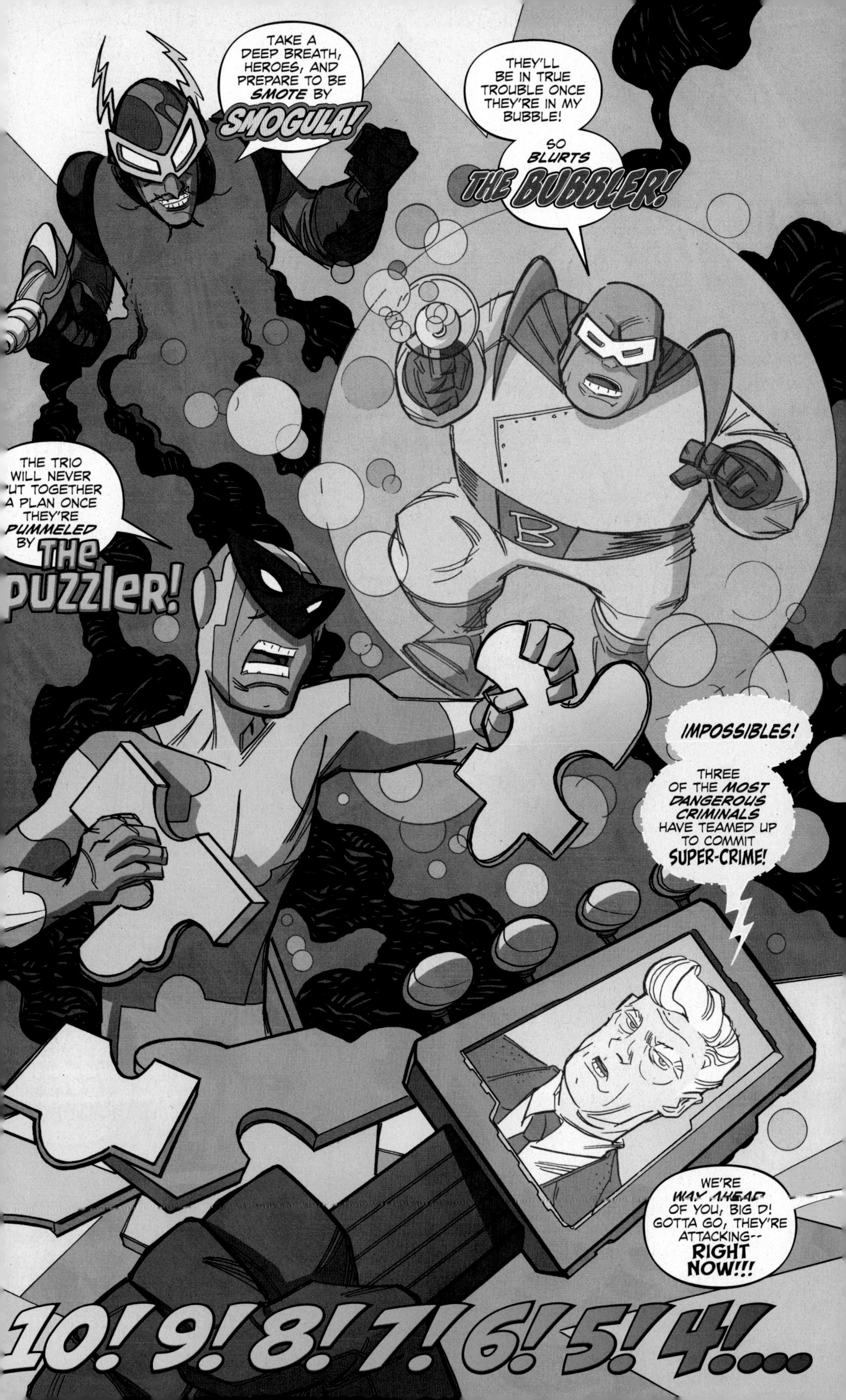

TAKE A DEEP BREATH, HEROES, AND PREPARE TO BE SMOTE BY SMOGULA!
THEY'LL BE IN TRUE TROUBLE ONCE THEY'RE IN MY BUBBLE!
SO BLURTS THE BUBBLER!
THE TRIO WILL NEVER 'UT TOGETHER A PLAN ONCE THEY'RE PUMMELED BY THE PUZZLER!
IMPOSSIBLES!
THREE OF THE MOST DANGEROUS CRIMINALS HAVE TEAMED UP TO COMMIT SUPER-CRIME!
WE'RE WAY AHEAD OF YOU, BIG D! GOTTA GO, THEY'RE ATTACKING-- RIGHT NOW!!!
10! 9! 8! 7! 6! 5! 4!...

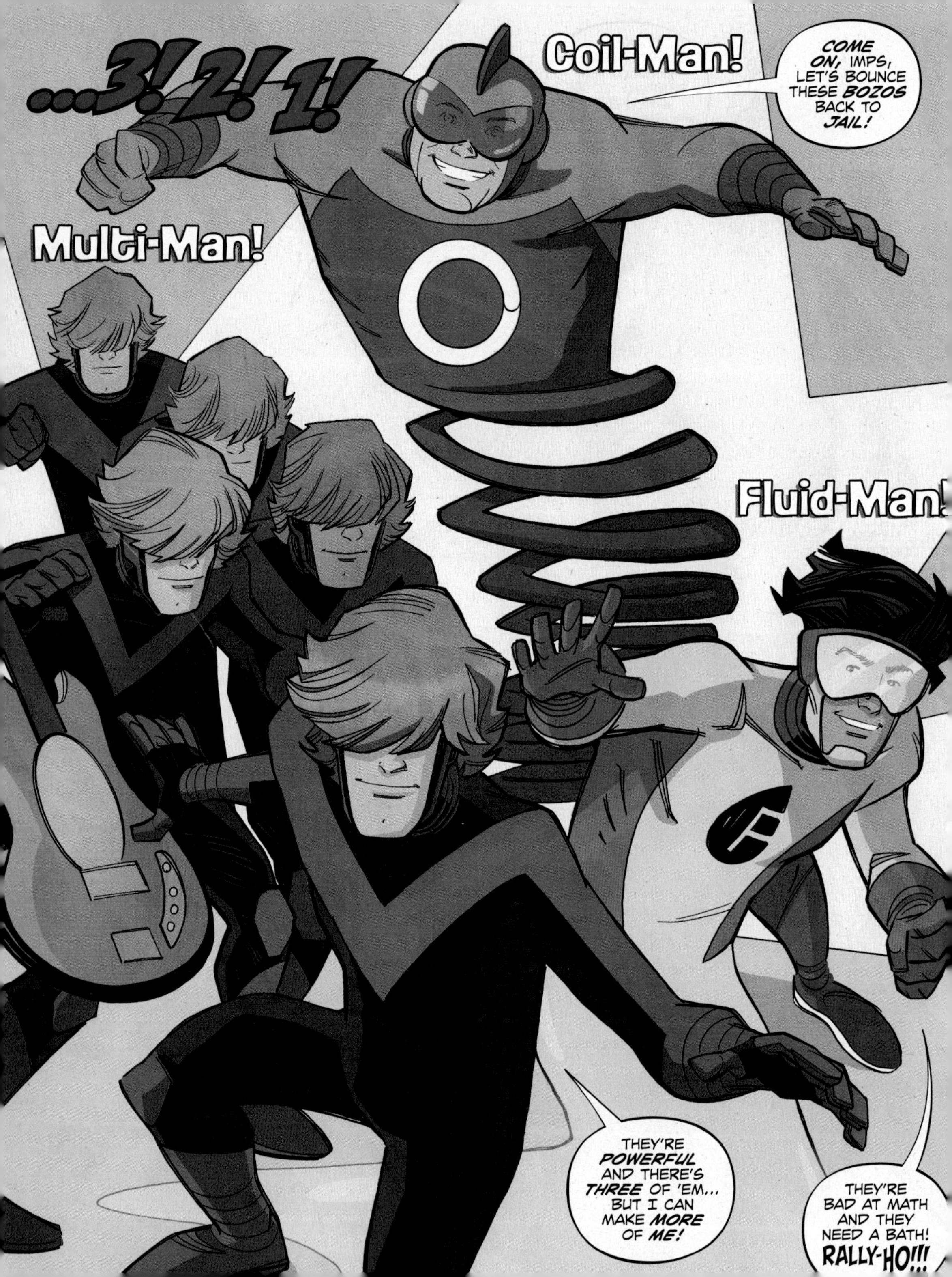
...3! 2! 1!
Coil-Man!
COME ON, IMPS, LET'S BOUNCE THESE BOZOS BACK TO JAIL!
Multi-Man!
Fluid-Man!
THEY'RE POWERFUL AND THERE'S THREE OF 'EM... BUT I CAN MAKE MORE OF ME!
THEY'RE BAD AT MATH AND THEY NEED A BATH! RALLY-HO!!!

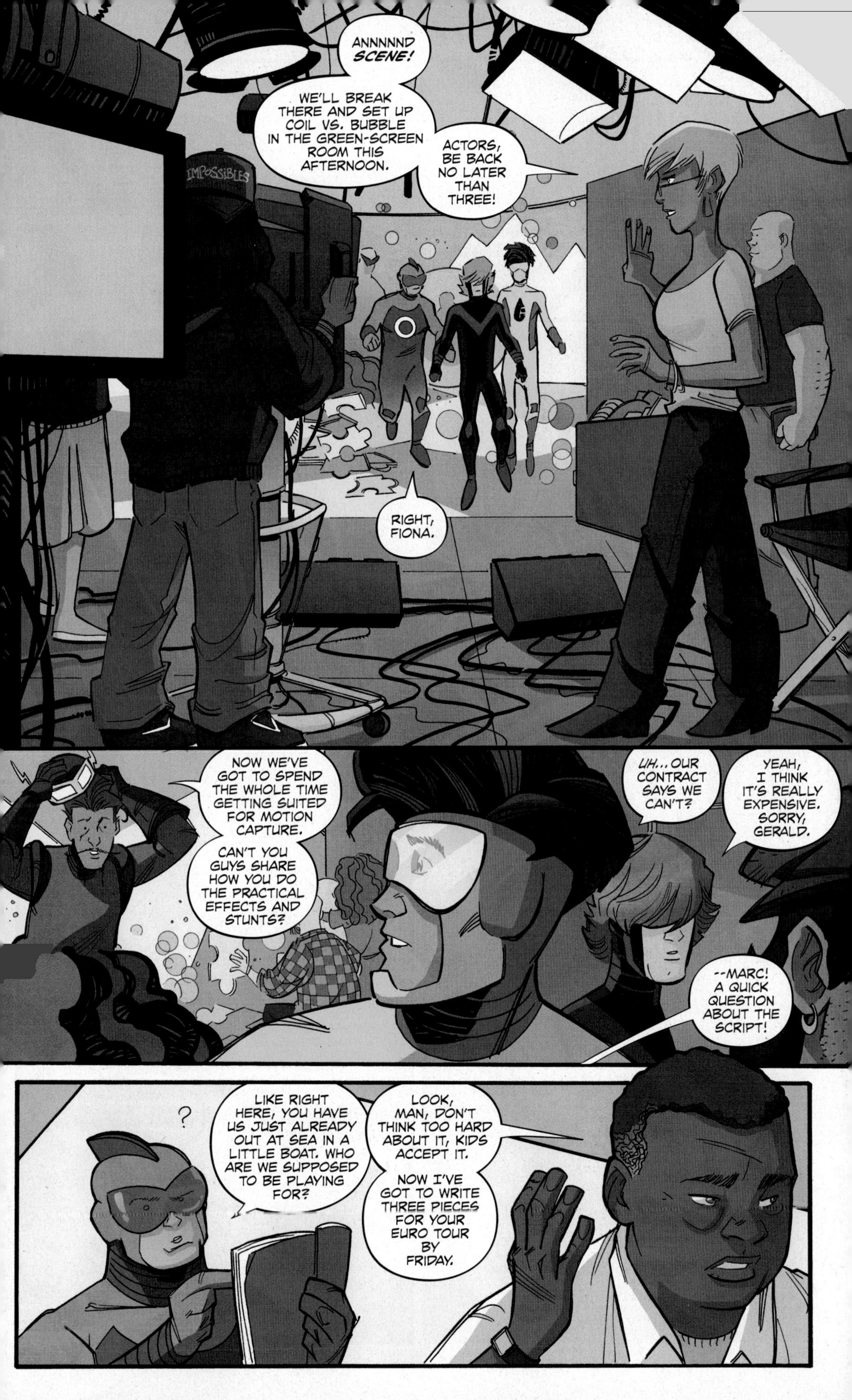
ANNNNND *SCENE!*
WE'LL BREAK THERE AND SET UP COIL VS. BUBBLE IN THE GREEN-SCREEN ROOM THIS AFTERNOON.
ACTORS, BE BACK NO LATER THAN THREE!
IMPOSSIBLES
RIGHT, FIONA.
NOW WE'VE GOT TO SPEND THE WHOLE TIME GETTING SUITED FOR MOTION CAPTURE.
CAN'T YOU GUYS SHARE HOW YOU DO THE PRACTICAL EFFECTS AND STUNTS?
UH... OUR CONTRACT SAYS WE CAN'T?
YEAH, I THINK IT'S REALLY EXPENSIVE. SORRY, GERALD.
--MARC! A QUICK QUESTION ABOUT THE SCRIPT!
?
LIKE RIGHT HERE, YOU HAVE US JUST ALREADY OUT AT SEA IN A LITTLE BOAT. WHO ARE WE SUPPOSED TO BE PLAYING FOR?
LOOK, MAN, DON'T THINK TOO HARD ABOUT IT, KIDS ACCEPT IT.
NOW I'VE GOT TO WRITE THREE PIECES FOR YOUR EURO TOUR BY FRIDAY.

CAN YOU AT LEAST GIVE US ANOTHER PHRASE BESIDES RALLY-HO?!

C'MON, COIL, GOT SOME GOOD NEWS!

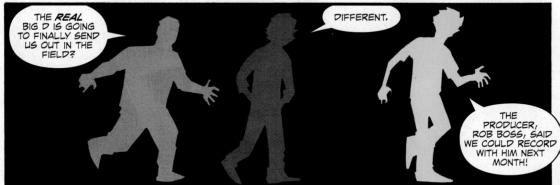

THE *REAL* BIG D IS GOING TO FINALLY SEND US OUT IN THE FIELD?

DIFFERENT.

THE PRODUCER, ROB BOSS, SAID WE COULD RECORD WITH HIM NEXT MONTH!

WHOA-HO! WE COULD GET REAL AIRPLAY WITH BOSS!

YEAH, I'M STILL NOT SURE. THE KID'S MARKET IS WAY LESS VICIOUS....

YEAH, BUT EVERY YEAR A CHUNK OF OUR AUDIENCE OUT-GROWS US AND THEN TURNS ON US SO HARD.

IT'S KINDA PAINFUL REALLY-- WHA-*HEY!*

SUPER-FAN ALERT!

NO WAIT, I'M HERE FOR THE INTERVIEW! DIDN'T MY EDITOR SEND A REMINDER FOR TODAY?

I'M *ESME SANTOS*, FROM *TIMEATRON ONLINE*.

BIG D SAID NOT TO DO ANY LIVE INTERVIEWS!

WELL SHE HASN'T CALLED IN WEEKS, AND THIS IS *TIMEATRON!*

THAT'S REAL MUSIC NEWS! THIS WILL REALLY HELP US GET TAKEN SERIOUSLY!

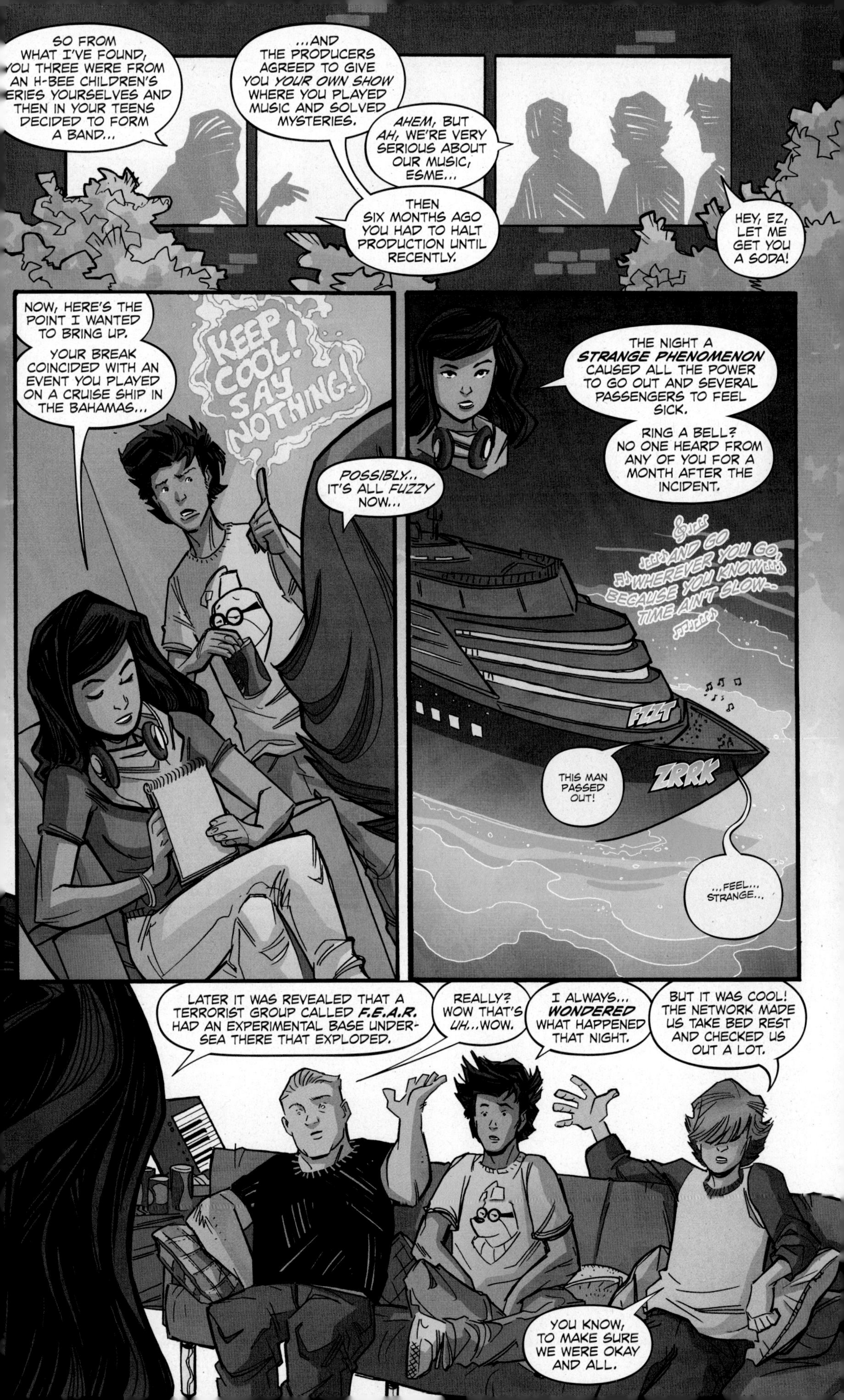

SO FROM WHAT I'VE FOUND, OU THREE WERE FROM AN H-BEE CHILDREN'S ERIES YOURSELVES AND THEN IN YOUR TEENS DECIDED TO FORM A BAND...
...AND THE PRODUCERS AGREED TO GIVE YOU *YOUR OWN SHOW* WHERE YOU PLAYED MUSIC AND SOLVED MYSTERIES.
AHEM, BUT *AH*, WE'RE VERY SERIOUS ABOUT OUR MUSIC, ESME...
THEN SIX MONTHS AGO YOU HAD TO HALT PRODUCTION UNTIL RECENTLY.
HEY, EZ, LET ME GET YOU A SODA!
NOW, HERE'S THE POINT I WANTED TO BRING UP.
YOUR BREAK COINCIDED WITH AN EVENT YOU PLAYED ON A CRUISE SHIP IN THE BAHAMAS...
KEEP COOL! SAY NOTHING!
POSSIBLY... IT'S ALL *FUZZY* NOW...
THE NIGHT A ***STRANGE PHENOMENON*** CAUSED ALL THE POWER TO GO OUT AND SEVERAL PASSENGERS TO FEEL SICK.
RING A BELL? NO ONE HEARD FROM ANY OF YOU FOR A MONTH AFTER THE INCIDENT.
AND GO WHEREVER YOU GO, BECAUSE YOU KNOW TIME AIN'T SLOW--
FZZT
ZRRK
THIS MAN PASSED OUT!
...FEEL... STRANGE...
LATER IT WAS REVEALED THAT A TERRORIST GROUP CALLED ***F.E.A.R.*** HAD AN EXPERIMENTAL BASE UNDER-SEA THERE THAT EXPLODED.
REALLY? WOW THAT'S *UH*...WOW.
I ALWAYS... ***WONDERED*** WHAT HAPPENED THAT NIGHT.
BUT IT WAS COOL! THE NETWORK MADE US TAKE BED REST AND CHECKED US OUT A LOT.
YOU KNOW, TO MAKE SURE WE WERE OKAY AND ALL.

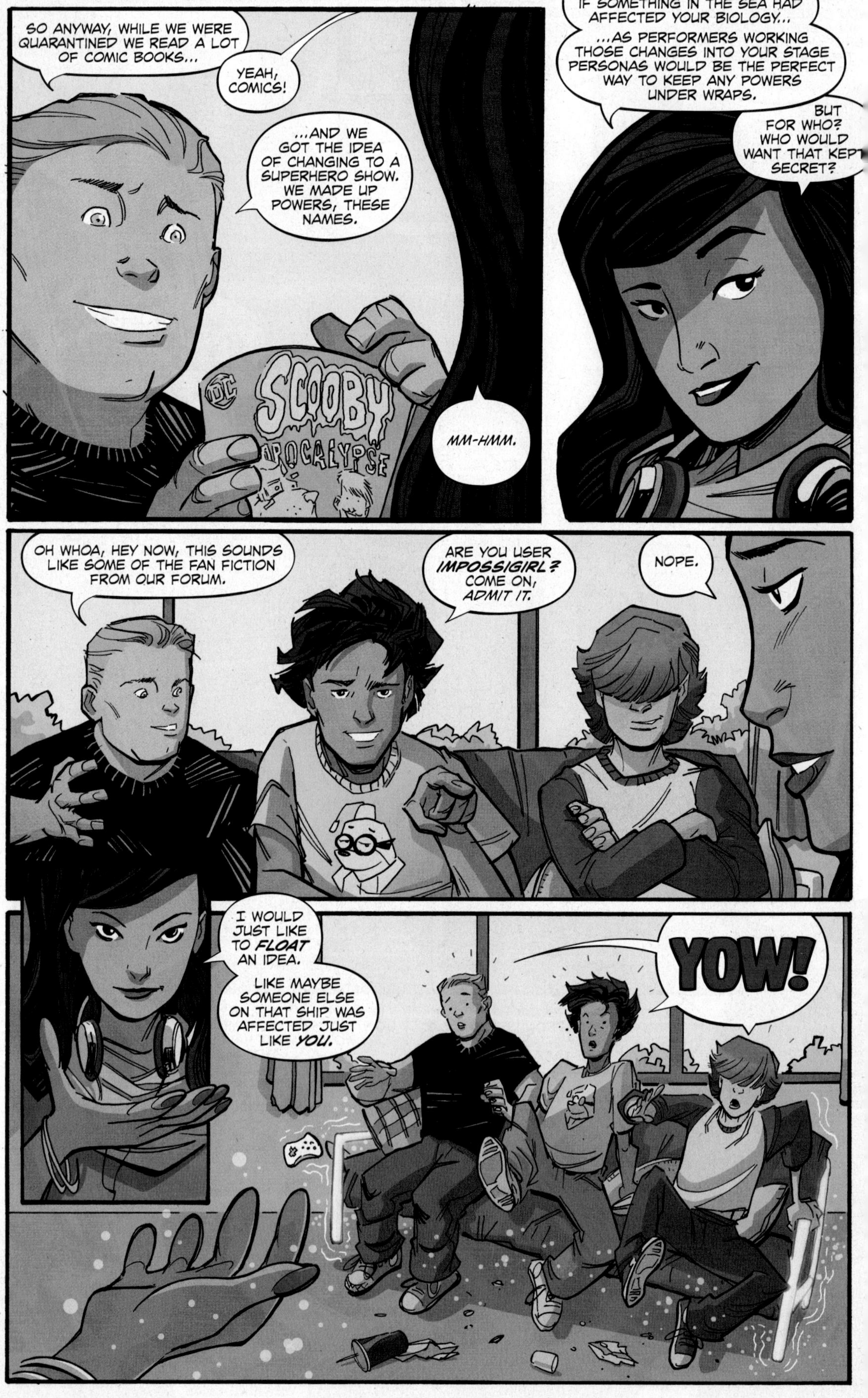
SO ANYWAY, WHILE WE WERE QUARANTINED WE READ A LOT OF COMIC BOOKS...
YEAH, COMICS!
...AND WE GOT THE IDEA OF CHANGING TO A SUPERHERO SHOW. WE MADE UP POWERS, THESE NAMES.
SCOOBY APOCALYPSE
MM-HMM.
IT'S INTERESTING BECAUSE... IF SOMETHING IN THE SEA HAD AFFECTED YOUR BIOLOGY...
...AS PERFORMERS WORKING THOSE CHANGES INTO YOUR STAGE PERSONAS WOULD BE THE PERFECT WAY TO KEEP ANY POWERS UNDER WRAPS.
BUT FOR WHO? WHO WOULD WANT THAT KEPT SECRET?
OH WHOA, HEY NOW, THIS SOUNDS LIKE SOME OF THE FAN FICTION FROM OUR FORUM.
ARE YOU USER *IMPOSSIGIRL?* COME ON, *ADMIT IT.*
NOPE.
I WOULD JUST LIKE TO *FLOAT* AN IDEA.
LIKE MAYBE SOMEONE ELSE ON THAT SHIP WAS AFFECTED JUST LIKE *YOU.*
YOW!

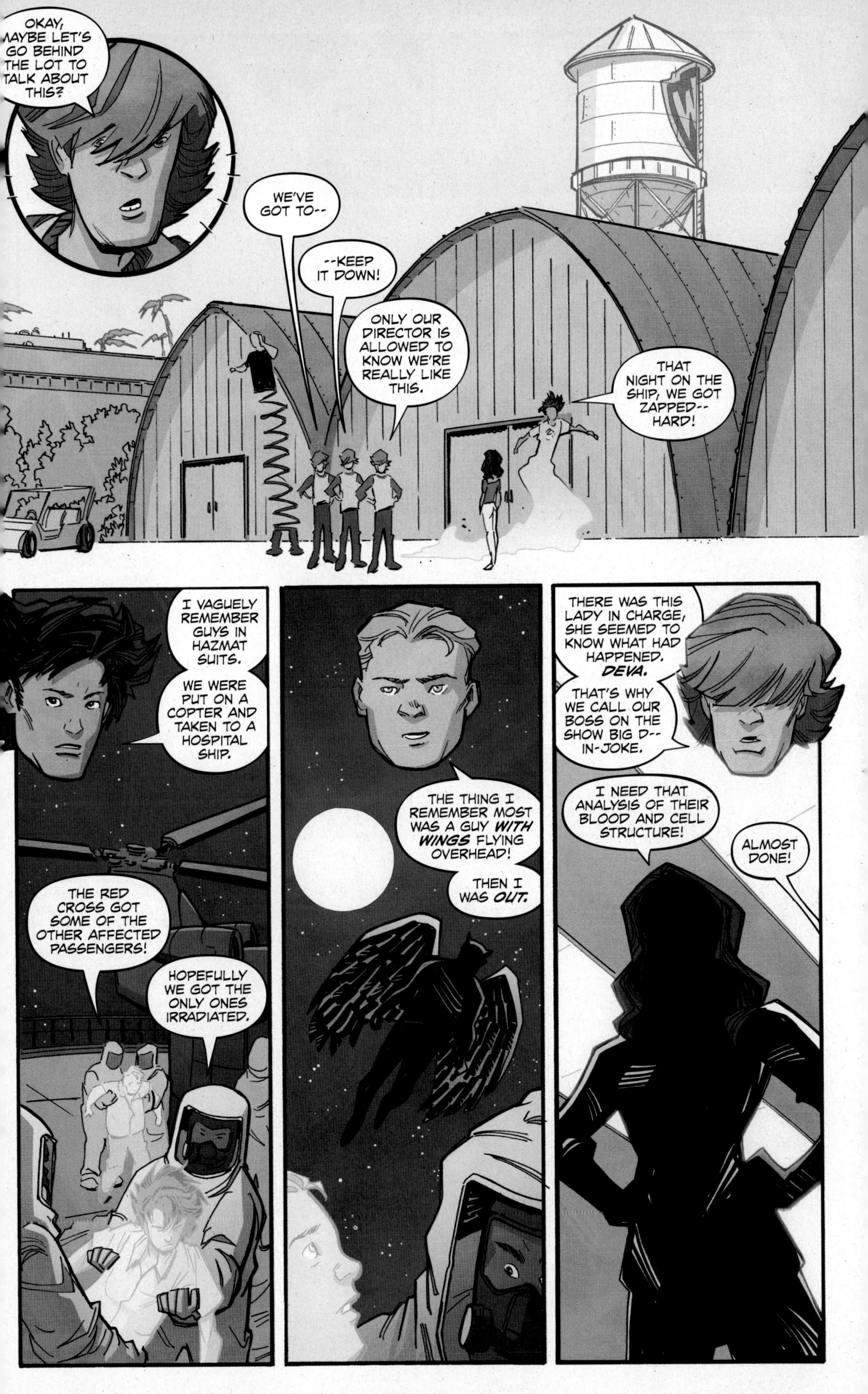
OKAY, MAYBE LET'S GO BEHIND THE LOT TO TALK ABOUT THIS?
WE'VE GOT TO--
--KEEP IT DOWN!
ONLY OUR DIRECTOR IS ALLOWED TO KNOW WE'RE REALLY LIKE THIS.
THAT NIGHT ON THE SHIP, WE GOT ZAPPED--HARD!
I VAGUELY REMEMBER GUYS IN HAZMAT SUITS.
WE WERE PUT ON A COPTER AND TAKEN TO A HOSPITAL SHIP.
THE RED CROSS GOT SOME OF THE OTHER AFFECTED PASSENGERS!
HOPEFULLY WE GOT THE ONLY ONES IRRADIATED.
THE THING I REMEMBER MOST WAS A GUY WITH WINGS FLYING OVERHEAD!
THEN I WAS OUT.
THERE WAS THIS LADY IN CHARGE, SHE SEEMED TO KNOW WHAT HAD HAPPENED. DEVA.
THAT'S WHY WE CALL OUR BOSS ON THE SHOW BIG D--IN-JOKE.
I NEED THAT ANALYSIS OF THEIR BLOOD AND CELL STRUCTURE!
ALMOST DONE!

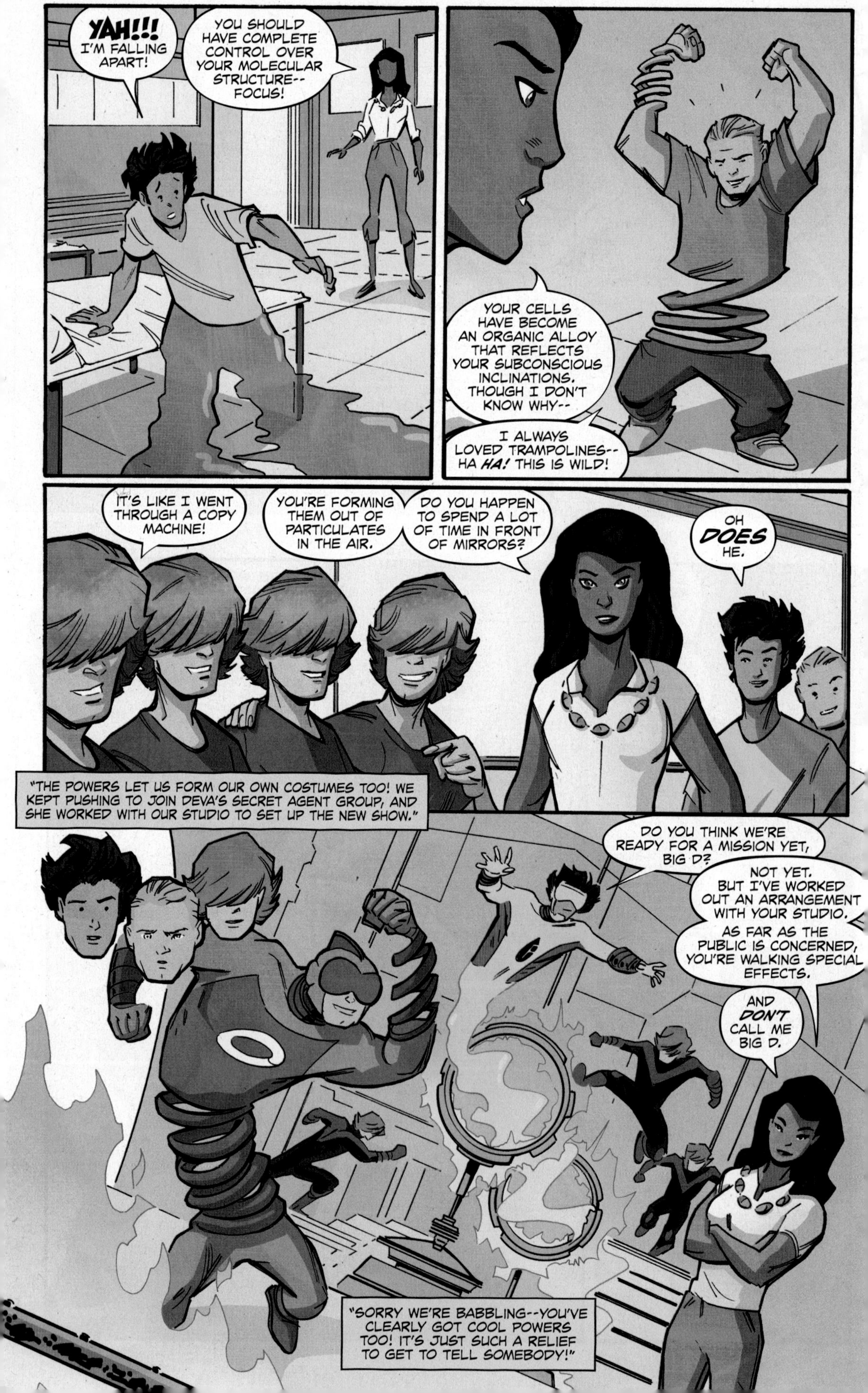
YAH!!! I'M FALLING APART!
YOU SHOULD HAVE COMPLETE CONTROL OVER YOUR MOLECULAR STRUCTURE--FOCUS!
YOUR CELLS HAVE BECOME AN ORGANIC ALLOY THAT REFLECTS YOUR SUBCONSCIOUS INCLINATIONS. THOUGH I DON'T KNOW WHY--
I ALWAYS LOVED TRAMPOLINES--HA HA! THIS IS WILD!
IT'S LIKE I WENT THROUGH A COPY MACHINE!
YOU'RE FORMING THEM OUT OF PARTICULATES IN THE AIR.
DO YOU HAPPEN TO SPEND A LOT OF TIME IN FRONT OF MIRRORS?
OH DOES HE.
"THE POWERS LET US FORM OUR OWN COSTUMES TOO! WE KEPT PUSHING TO JOIN DEVA'S SECRET AGENT GROUP, AND SHE WORKED WITH OUR STUDIO TO SET UP THE NEW SHOW."
DO YOU THINK WE'RE READY FOR A MISSION YET, BIG D?
NOT YET. BUT I'VE WORKED OUT AN ARRANGEMENT WITH YOUR STUDIO.
AS FAR AS THE PUBLIC IS CONCERNED, YOU'RE WALKING SPECIAL EFFECTS.
AND DON'T CALL ME BIG D.
"SORRY WE'RE BABBLING--YOU'VE CLEARLY GOT COOL POWERS TOO! IT'S JUST SUCH A RELIEF TO GET TO TELL SOMEBODY!"

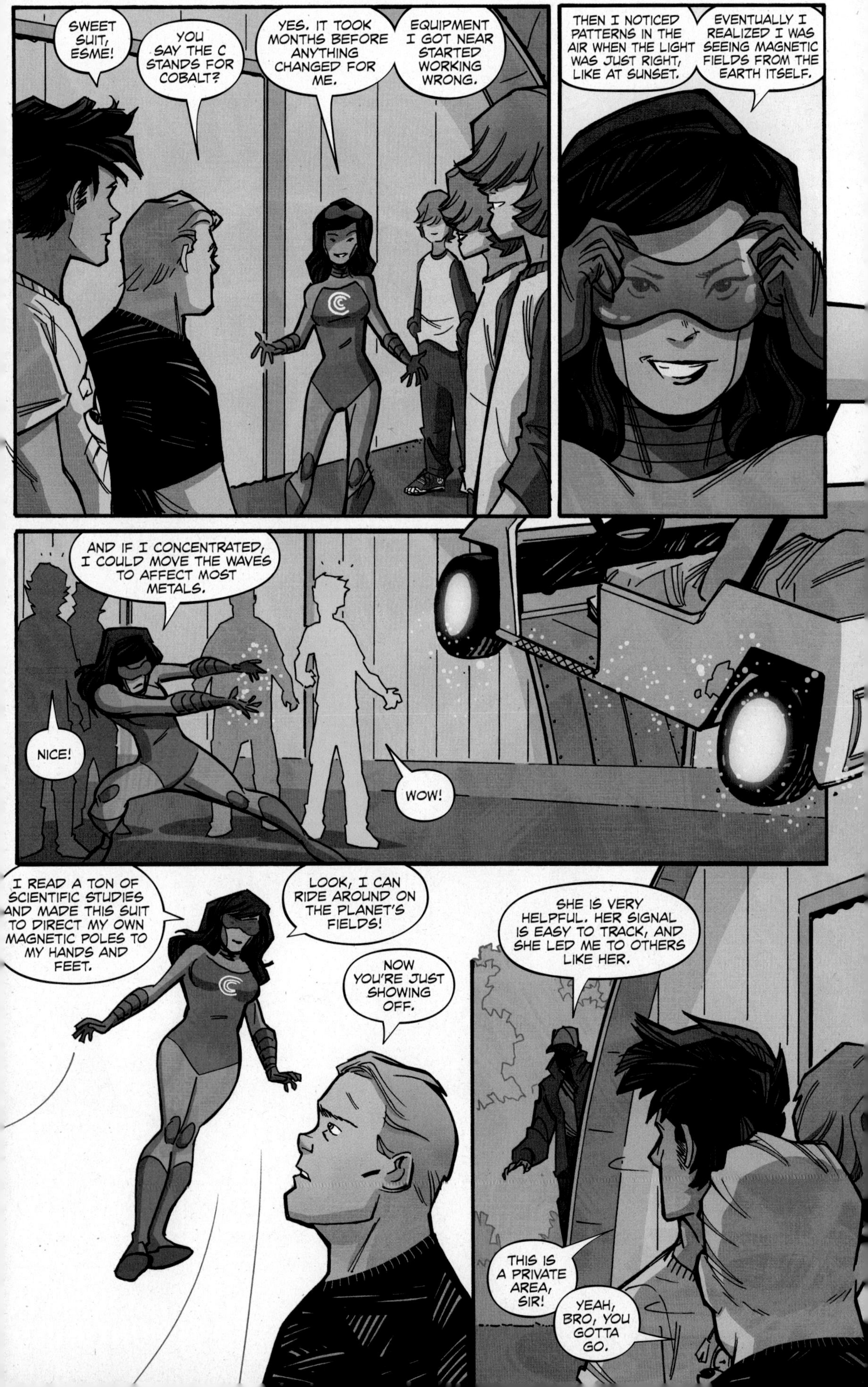
SWEET SUIT, ESME!
YOU SAY THE C STANDS FOR COBALT?
YES. IT TOOK MONTHS BEFORE ANYTHING CHANGED FOR ME.
EQUIPMENT I GOT NEAR STARTED WORKING WRONG.
THEN I NOTICED PATTERNS IN THE AIR WHEN THE LIGHT WAS JUST RIGHT, LIKE AT SUNSET.
EVENTUALLY I REALIZED I WAS SEEING MAGNETIC FIELDS FROM THE EARTH ITSELF.
AND IF I CONCENTRATED, I COULD MOVE THE WAVES TO AFFECT MOST METALS.
NICE!
WOW!
I READ A TON OF SCIENTIFIC STUDIES AND MADE THIS SUIT TO DIRECT MY OWN MAGNETIC POLES TO MY HANDS AND FEET.
LOOK, I CAN RIDE AROUND ON THE PLANET'S FIELDS!
NOW YOU'RE JUST SHOWING OFF.
SHE IS VERY HELPFUL. HER SIGNAL IS EASY TO TRACK, AND SHE LED ME TO OTHERS LIKE HER.
THIS IS A PRIVATE AREA, SIR!
YEAH, BRO, YOU GOTTA GO.

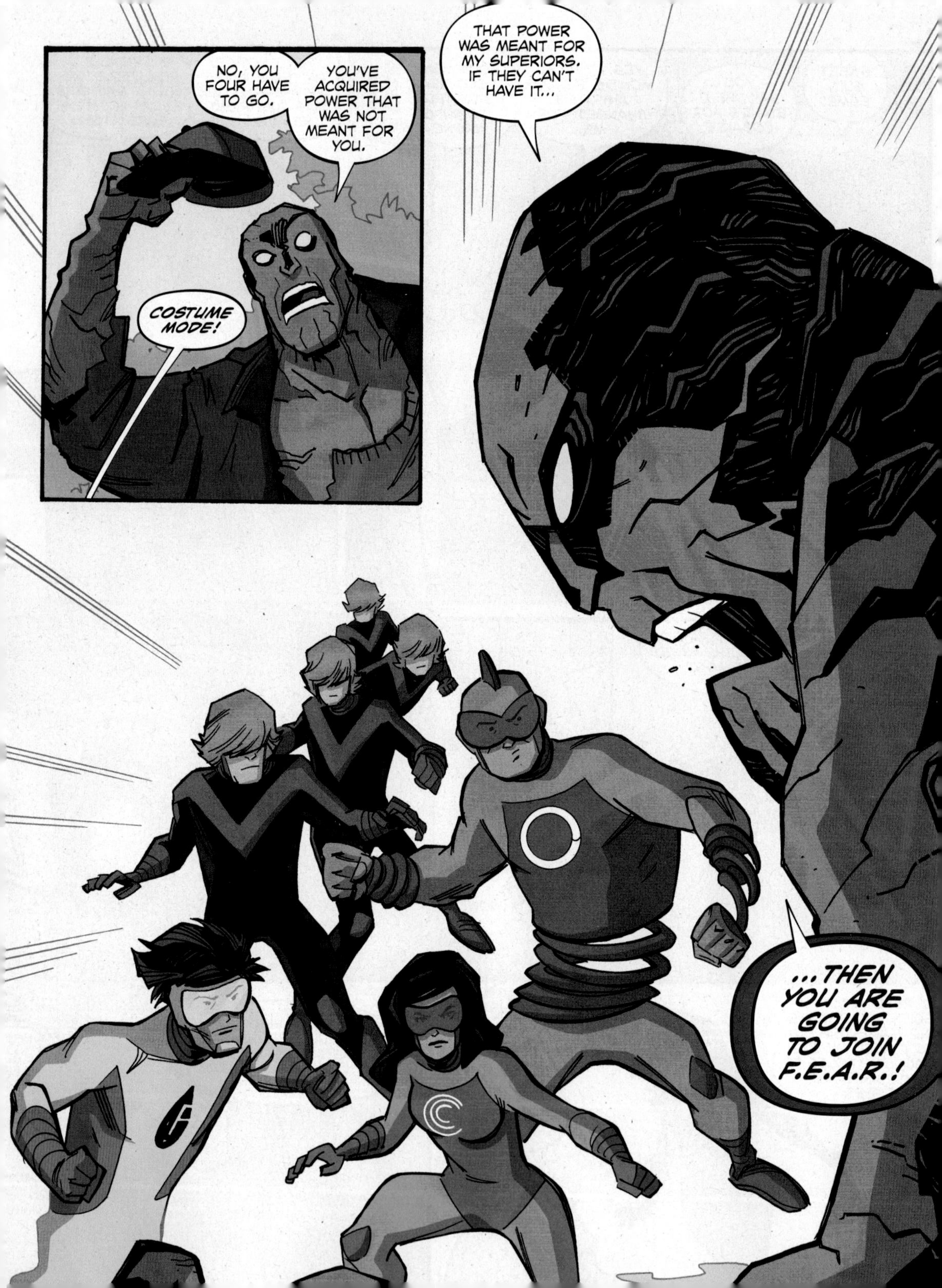
NO, YOU FOUR HAVE TO GO.
YOU'VE ACQUIRED POWER THAT WAS NOT MEANT FOR YOU.
COSTUME MODE!
THAT POWER WAS MEANT FOR MY SUPERIORS. IF THEY CAN'T HAVE IT...
...THEN YOU ARE GOING TO JOIN F.E.A.R.!

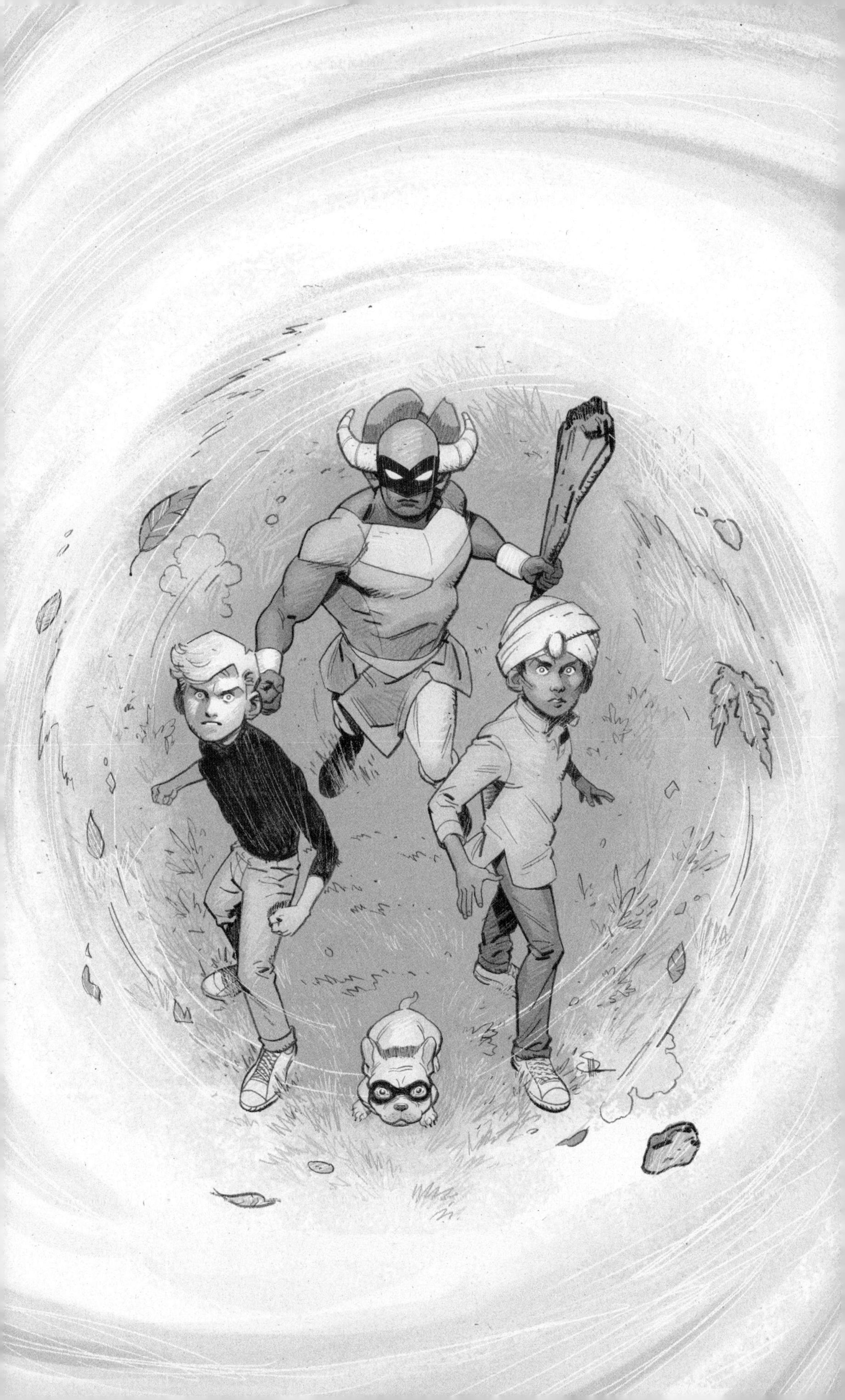

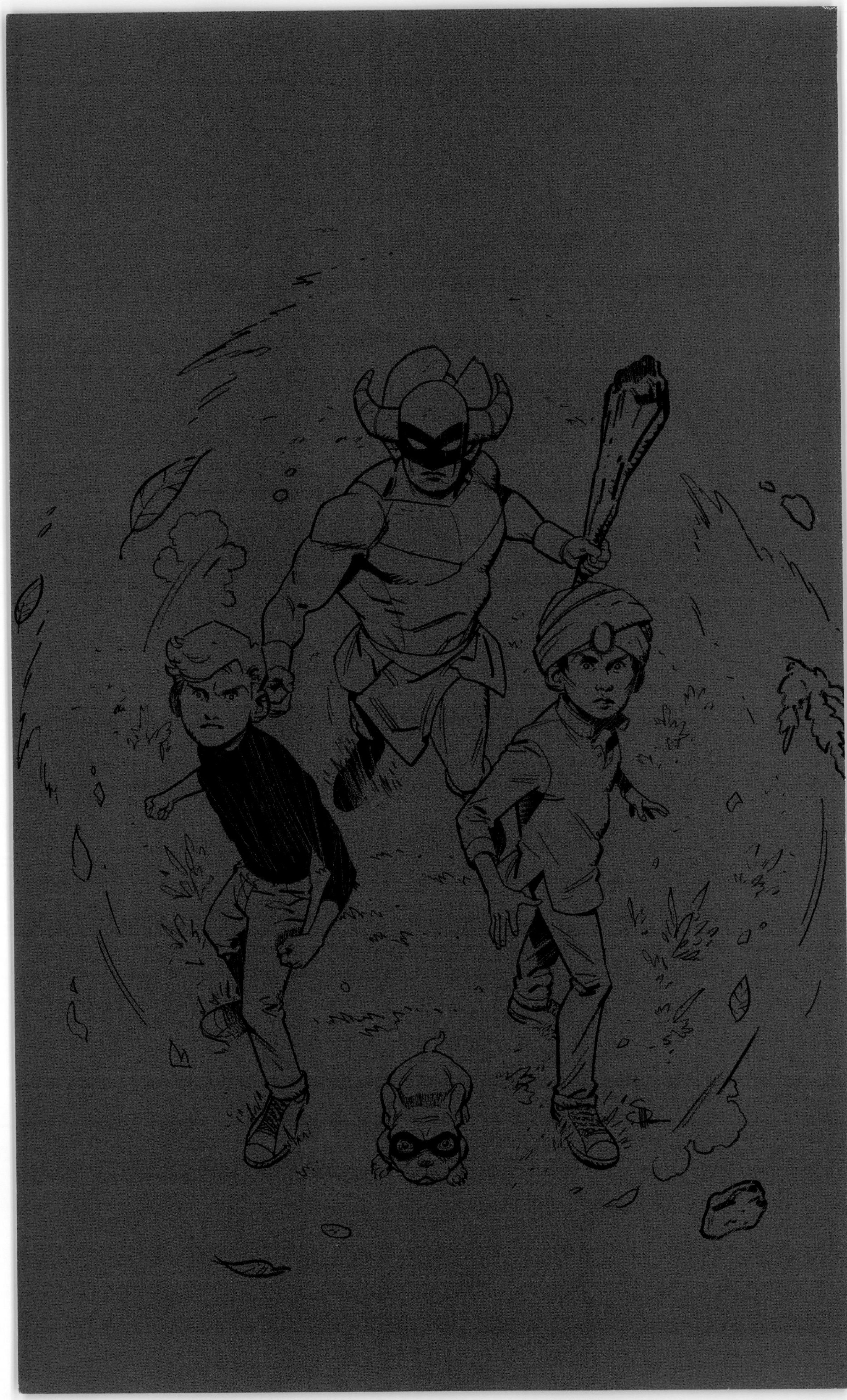

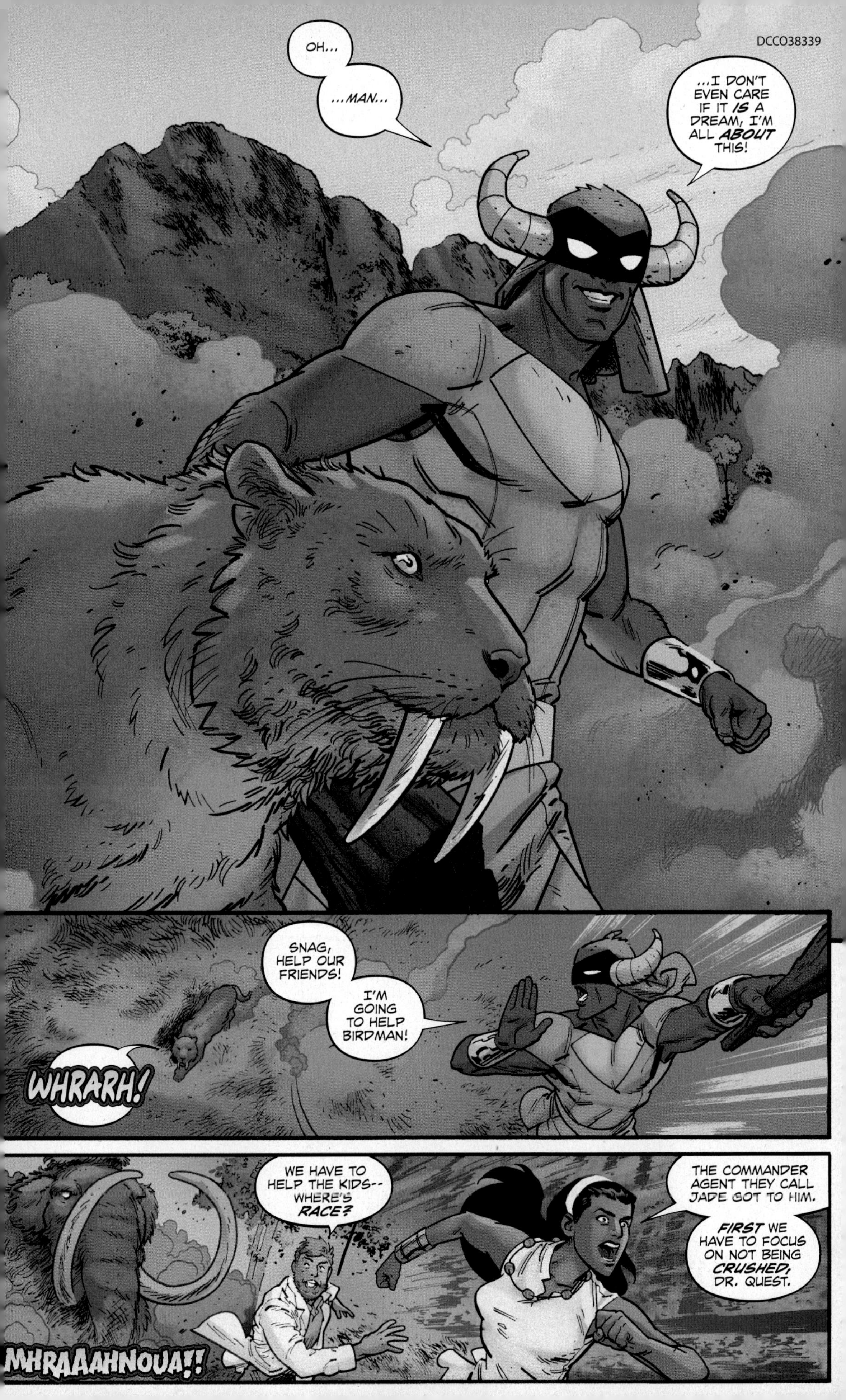
DCCO38339
OH...
...MAN...
...I DON'T EVEN CARE IF IT IS A DREAM, I'M ALL ABOUT THIS!
SNAG, HELP OUR FRIENDS!
I'M GOING TO HELP BIRDMAN!
WHRARH!
WE HAVE TO HELP THE KIDS-- WHERE'S RACE?
THE COMMANDER AGENT THEY CALL JADE GOT TO HIM.
FIRST WE HAVE TO FOCUS ON NOT BEING CRUSHED, DR. QUEST.
MHRAAAHNOUA!!

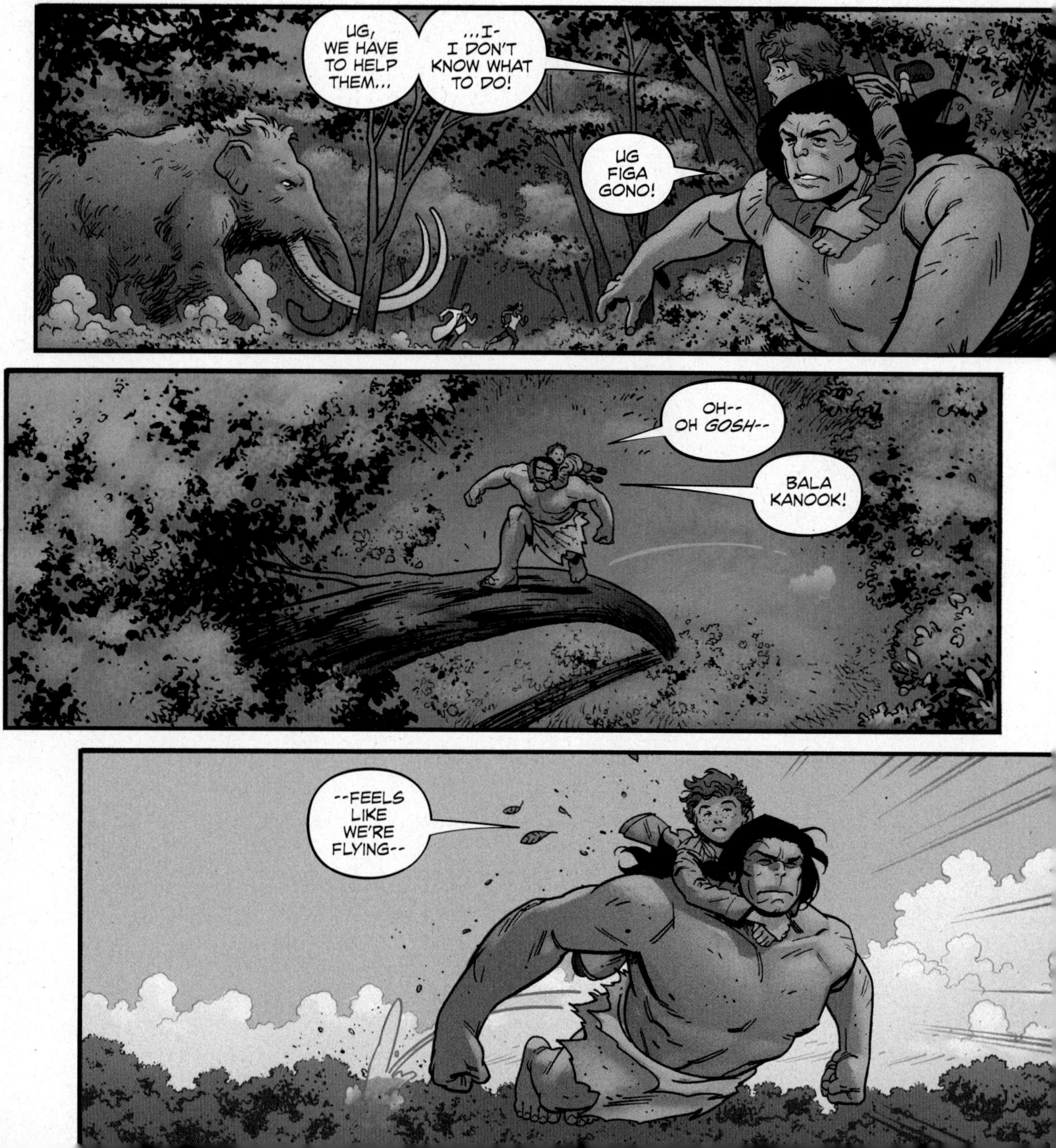
UG, WE HAVE TO HELP THEM...
...I- I DON'T KNOW WHAT TO DO!
UG FIGA GONO!
OH-- OH GOSH--
BALA KANOOK!
--FEELS LIKE WE'RE FLYING--

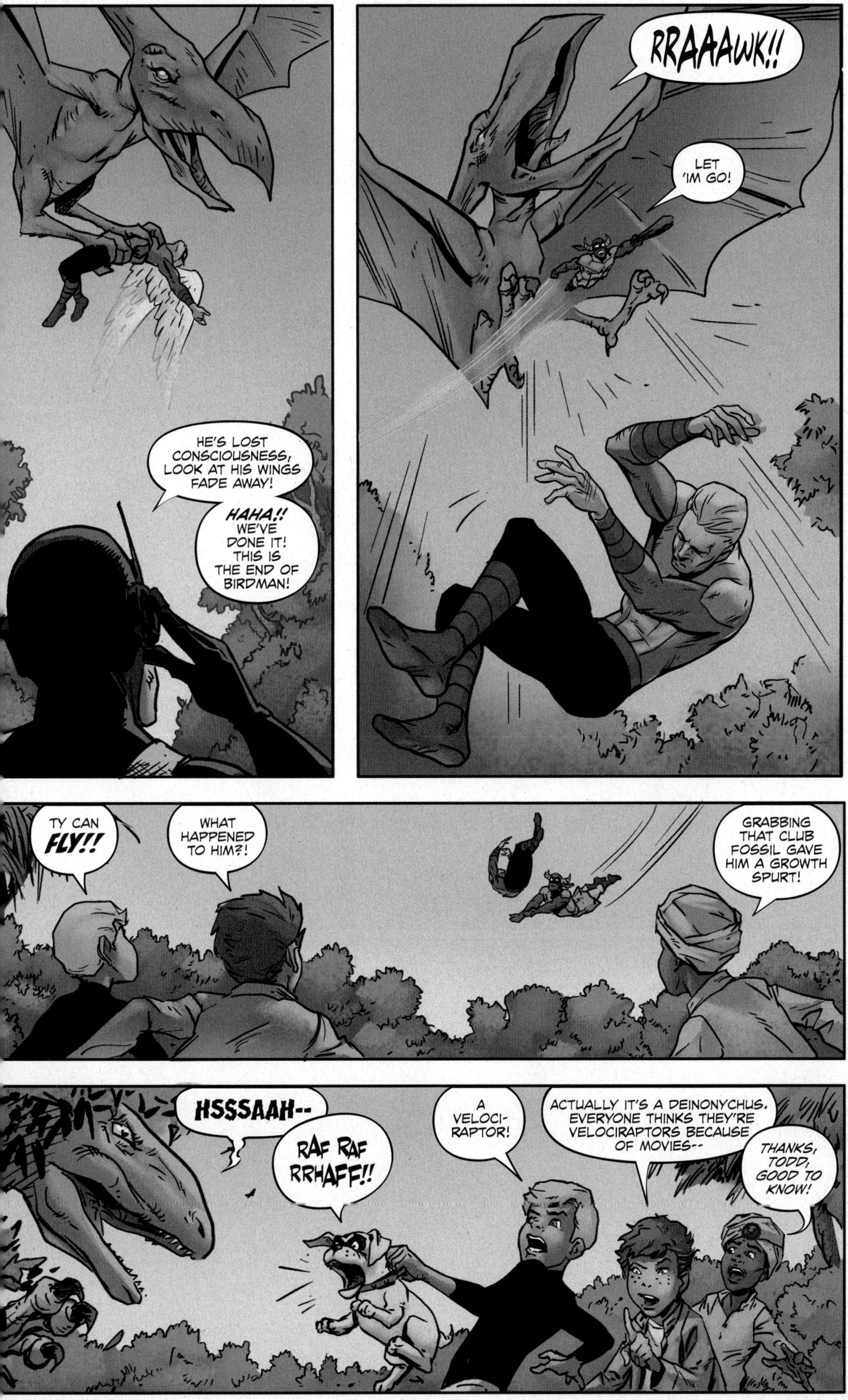
RRAAAWK!!
LET 'IM GO!
HE'S LOST CONSCIOUSNESS, LOOK AT HIS WINGS FADE AWAY!
HAHA!! WE'VE DONE IT! THIS IS THE END OF BIRDMAN!
TY CAN FLY!!
WHAT HAPPENED TO HIM?!
GRABBING THAT CLUB FOSSIL GAVE HIM A GROWTH SPURT!
HSSSAAH--
RAF RAF RRHAFF!!
A VELOCI-RAPTOR!
ACTUALLY IT'S A DEINONYCHUS. EVERYONE THINKS THEY'RE VELOCIRAPTORS BECAUSE OF MOVIES--
THANKS, TODD, GOOD TO KNOW!

GET
BACK!

HRRSAK!

HRON

TOLD YO
SNAG WA
SCRAPPE

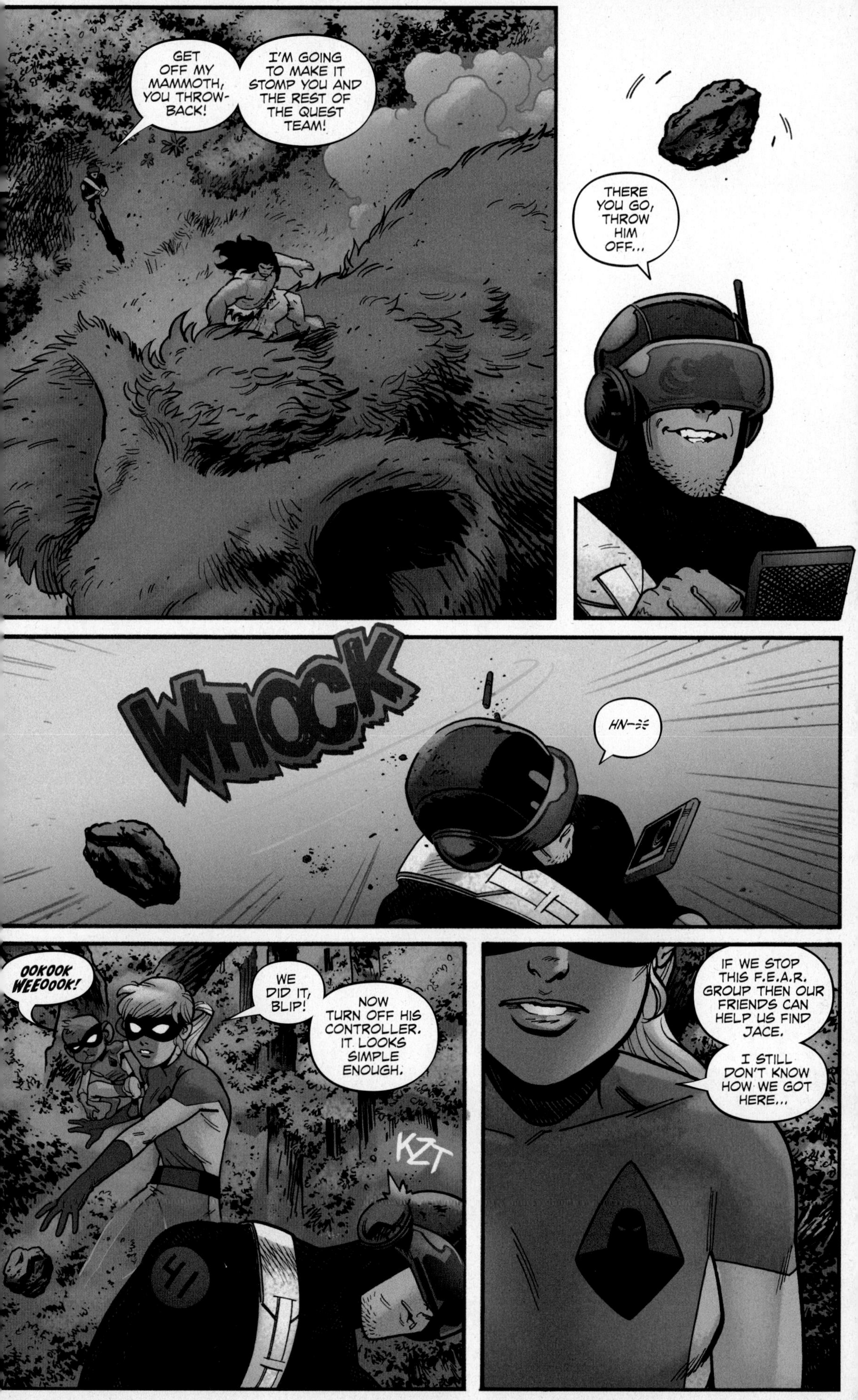
GET OFF MY MAMMOTH, YOU THROW-BACK!
I'M GOING TO MAKE IT STOMP YOU AND THE REST OF THE QUEST TEAM!
THERE YOU GO, THROW HIM OFF...
WHOCK
HN--
OOKOOK WEEOOOK!
WE DID IT, BLIP!
NOW TURN OFF HIS CONTROLLER. IT LOOKS SIMPLE ENOUGH.
KZT
IF WE STOP THIS F.E.A.R. GROUP THEN OUR FRIENDS CAN HELP US FIND JACE.
I STILL DON'T KNOW HOW WE GOT HERE...

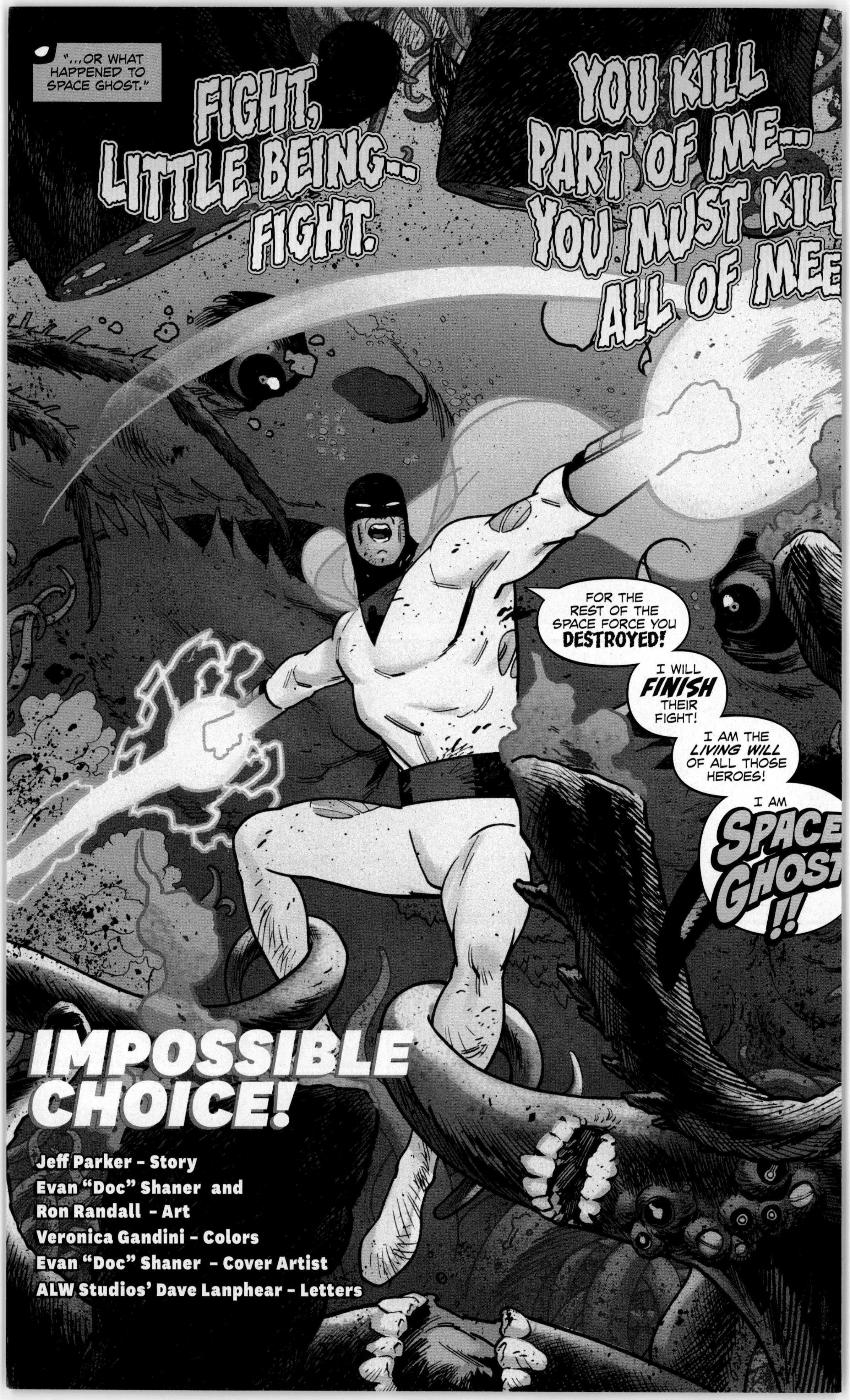

"...OR WHAT HAPPENED TO SPACE GHOST."
FIGHT, LITTLE BEING-- FIGHT.
YOU KILL PART OF ME-- YOU MUST KILL ALL OF MEE
FOR THE REST OF THE SPACE FORCE YOU DESTROYED!
I WILL FINISH THEIR FIGHT!
I AM THE LIVING WILL OF ALL THOSE HEROES!
I AM SPACE GHOST!!
IMPOSSIBLE CHOICE!
Jeff Parker - Story
Evan "Doc" Shaner and Ron Randall - Art
Veronica Gandini - Colors
Evan "Doc" Shaner - Cover Artist
ALW Studios' Dave Lanphear - Letters

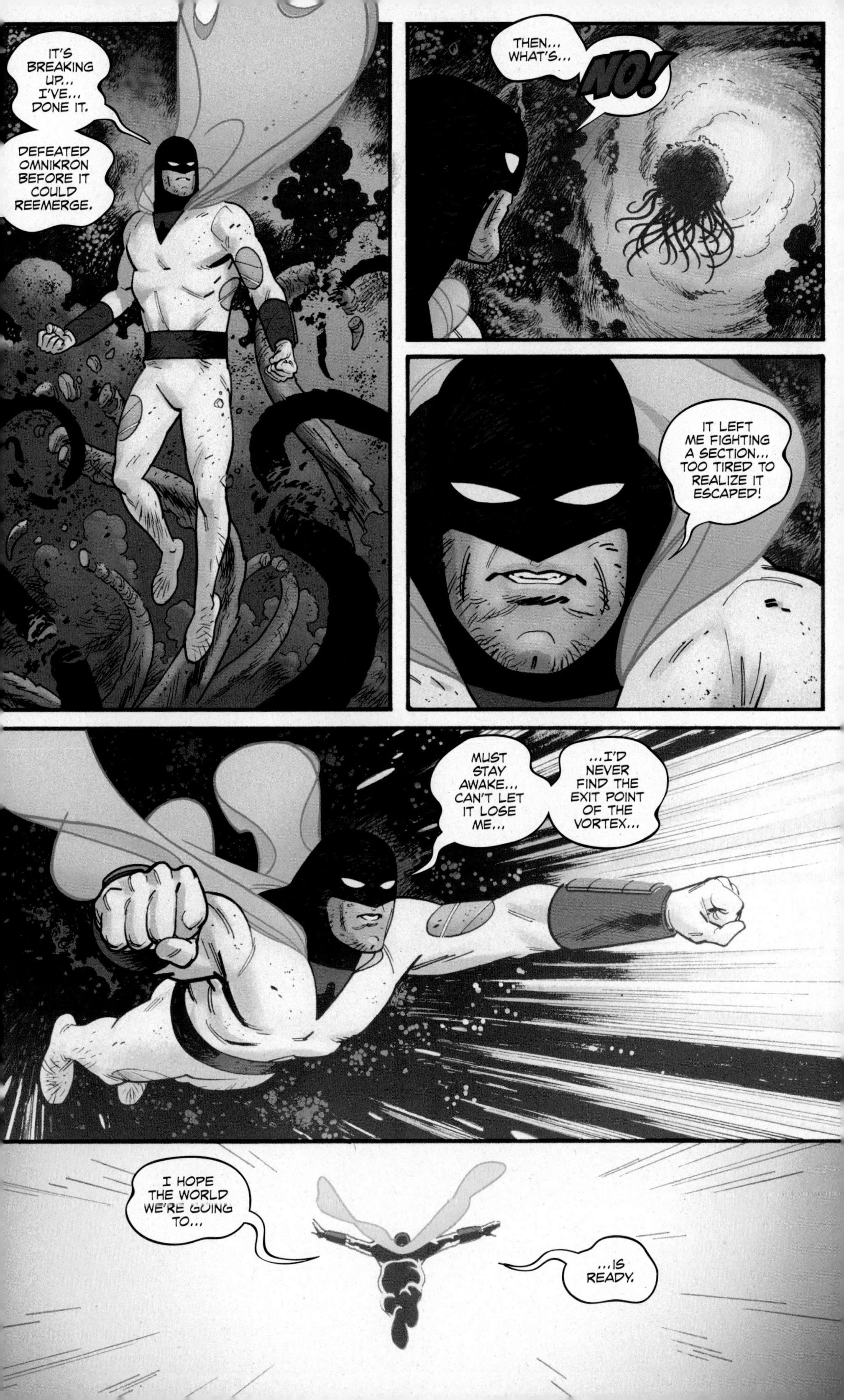
IT'S BREAKING UP... I'VE... DONE IT.
DEFEATED OMNIKRON BEFORE IT COULD REEMERGE.
THEN... WHAT'S...
NO!
IT LEFT ME FIGHTING A SECTION... TOO TIRED TO REALIZE IT ESCAPED!
MUST STAY AWAKE... CAN'T LET IT LOSE ME...
...I'D NEVER FIND THE EXIT POINT OF THE VORTEX...
I HOPE THE WORLD WE'RE GOING TO...
...IS READY.

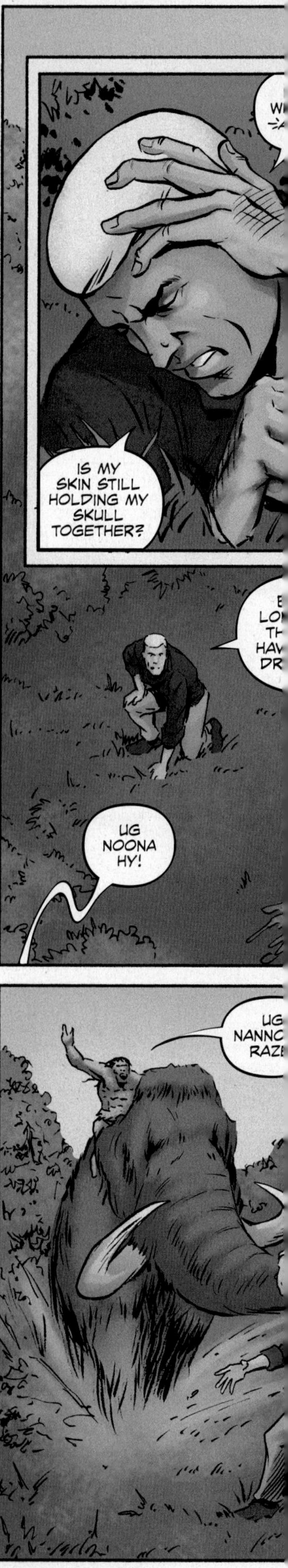
IS MY SKIN STILL HOLDING MY SKULL TOGETHER?
UG NOONA HY!

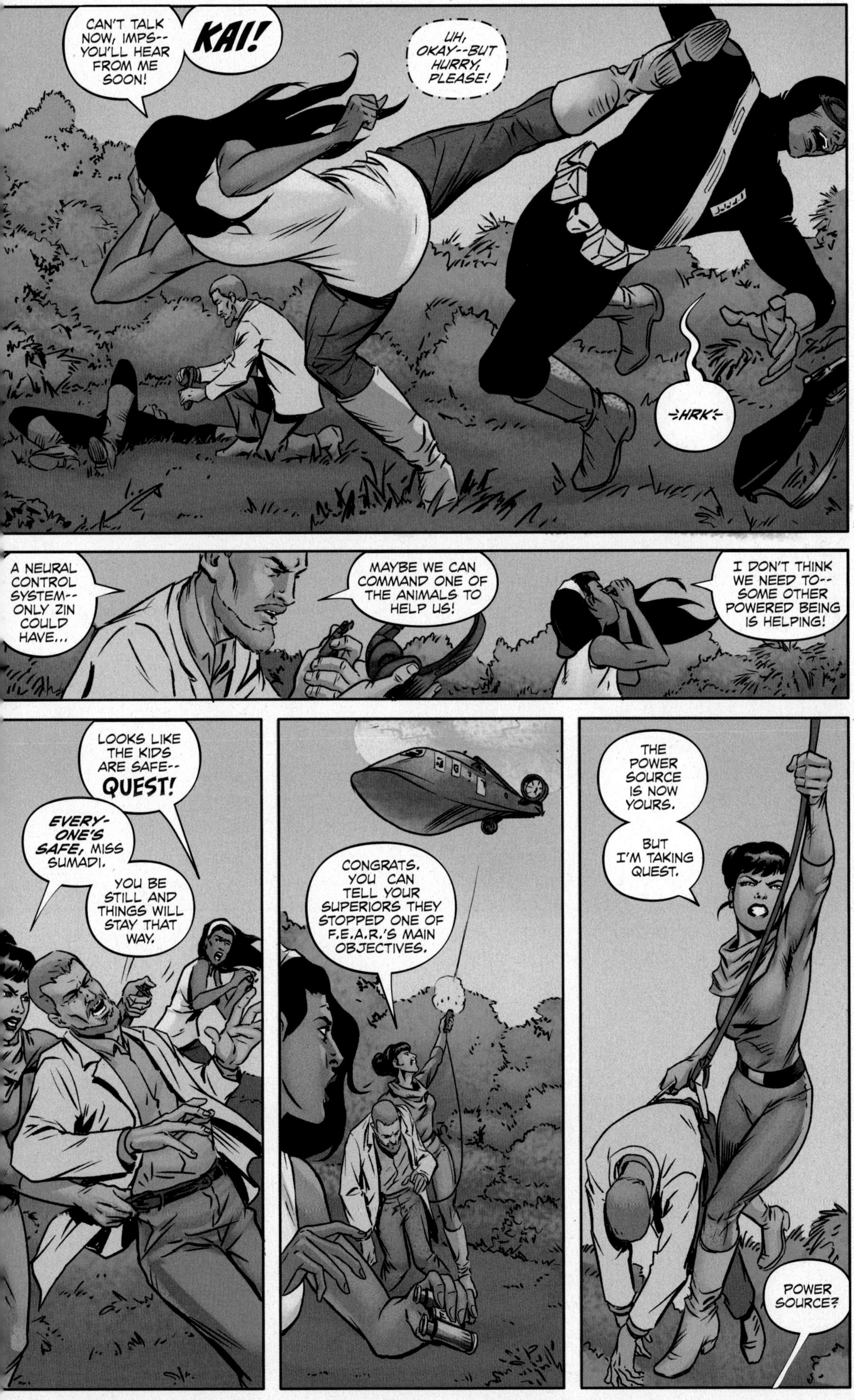
CAN'T TALK NOW, IMPS--YOU'LL HEAR FROM ME SOON!
KAI!
UH, OKAY--BUT HURRY, PLEASE!
HRK
A NEURAL CONTROL SYSTEM--ONLY ZIN COULD HAVE...
MAYBE WE CAN COMMAND ONE OF THE ANIMALS TO HELP US!
I DON'T THINK WE NEED TO--SOME OTHER POWERED BEING IS HELPING!
LOOKS LIKE THE KIDS ARE SAFE--QUEST!
EVERY-ONE'S SAFE, MISS SUMADI.
YOU BE STILL AND THINGS WILL STAY THAT WAY.
CONGRATS. YOU CAN TELL YOUR SUPERIORS THEY STOPPED ONE OF F.E.A.R.'S MAIN OBJECTIVES.
THE POWER SOURCE IS NOW YOURS.
BUT I'M TAKING QUEST.
POWER SOURCE?

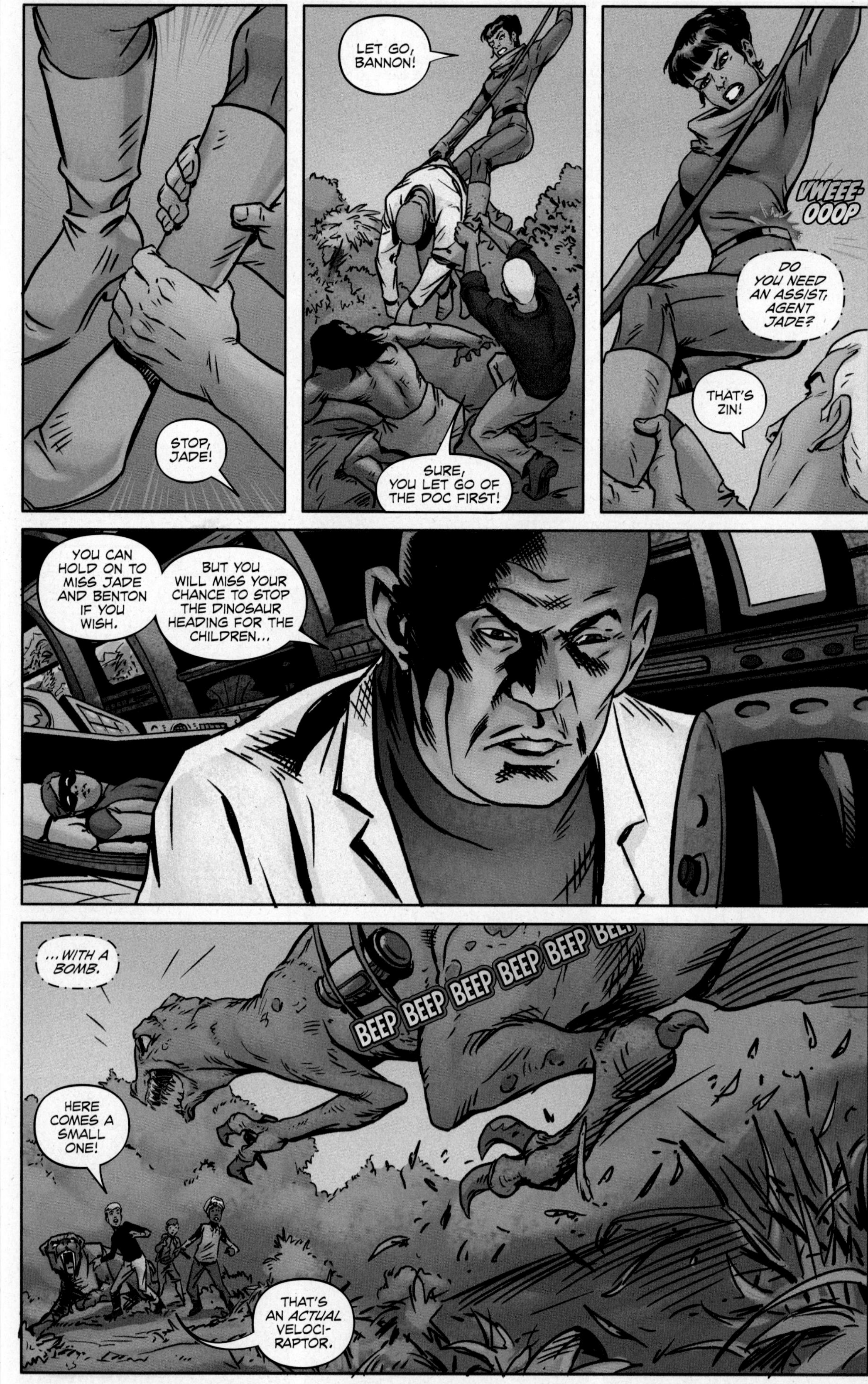
STOP, JADE!
LET GO, BANNON!
SURE, YOU LET GO OF THE DOC FIRST!
UWEEE-OOOP
DO YOU NEED AN ASSIST, AGENT JADE?
THAT'S ZIN!
YOU CAN HOLD ON TO MISS JADE AND BENTON IF YOU WISH.
BUT YOU WILL MISS YOUR CHANCE TO STOP THE DINOSAUR HEADING FOR THE CHILDREN...
...WITH A BOMB.
BEEP BEEP BEEP BEEP BEEP BEEP
HERE COMES A SMALL ONE!
THAT'S AN *ACTUAL* VELOCI-RAPTOR.

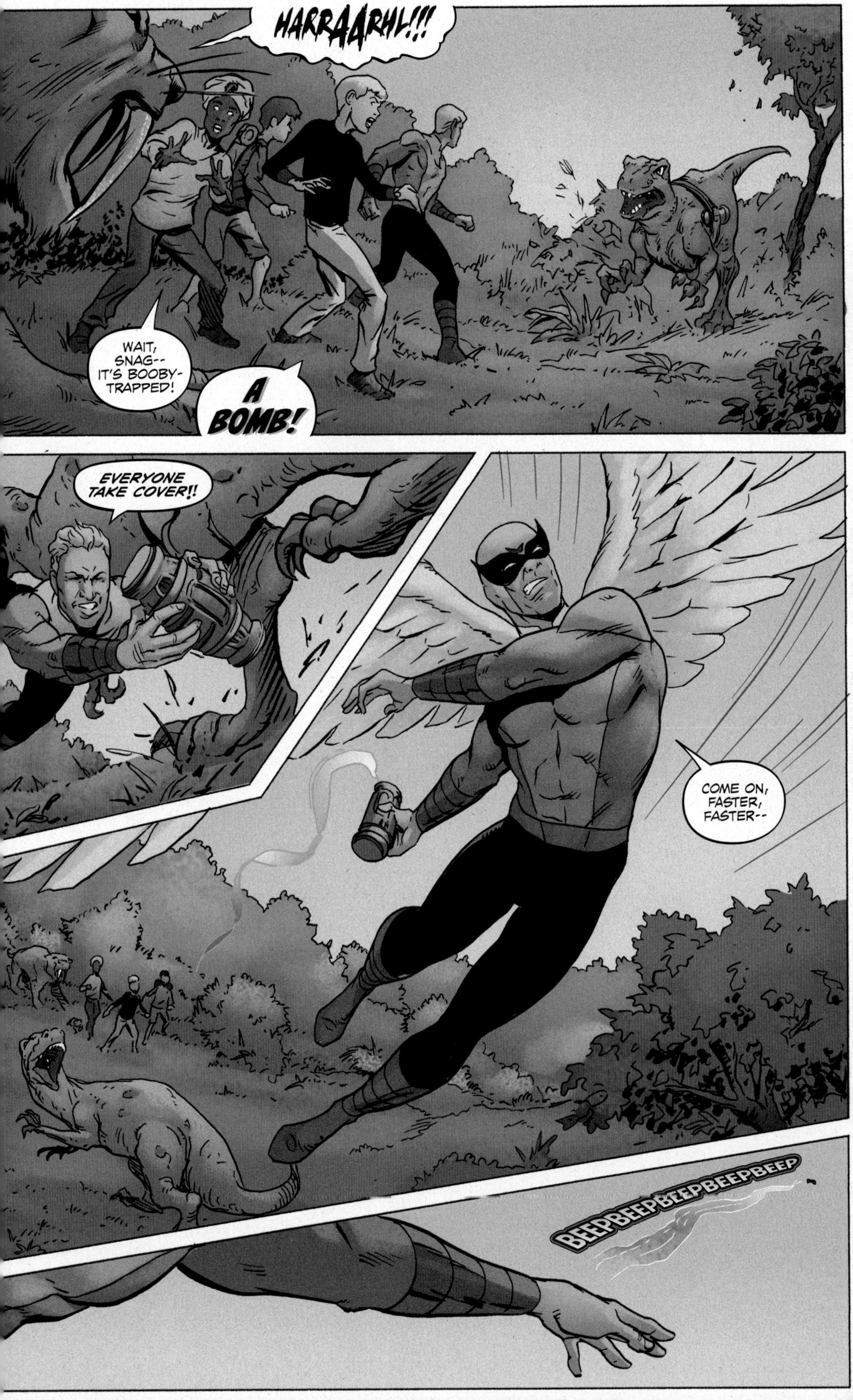
HARRAARHL!!!
WAIT, SNAG-- IT'S BOOBY-TRAPPED!
A BOMB!
EVERYONE TAKE COVER!!
COME ON, FASTER, FASTER--
BEEPBEEPBEEPBEEPBEEP

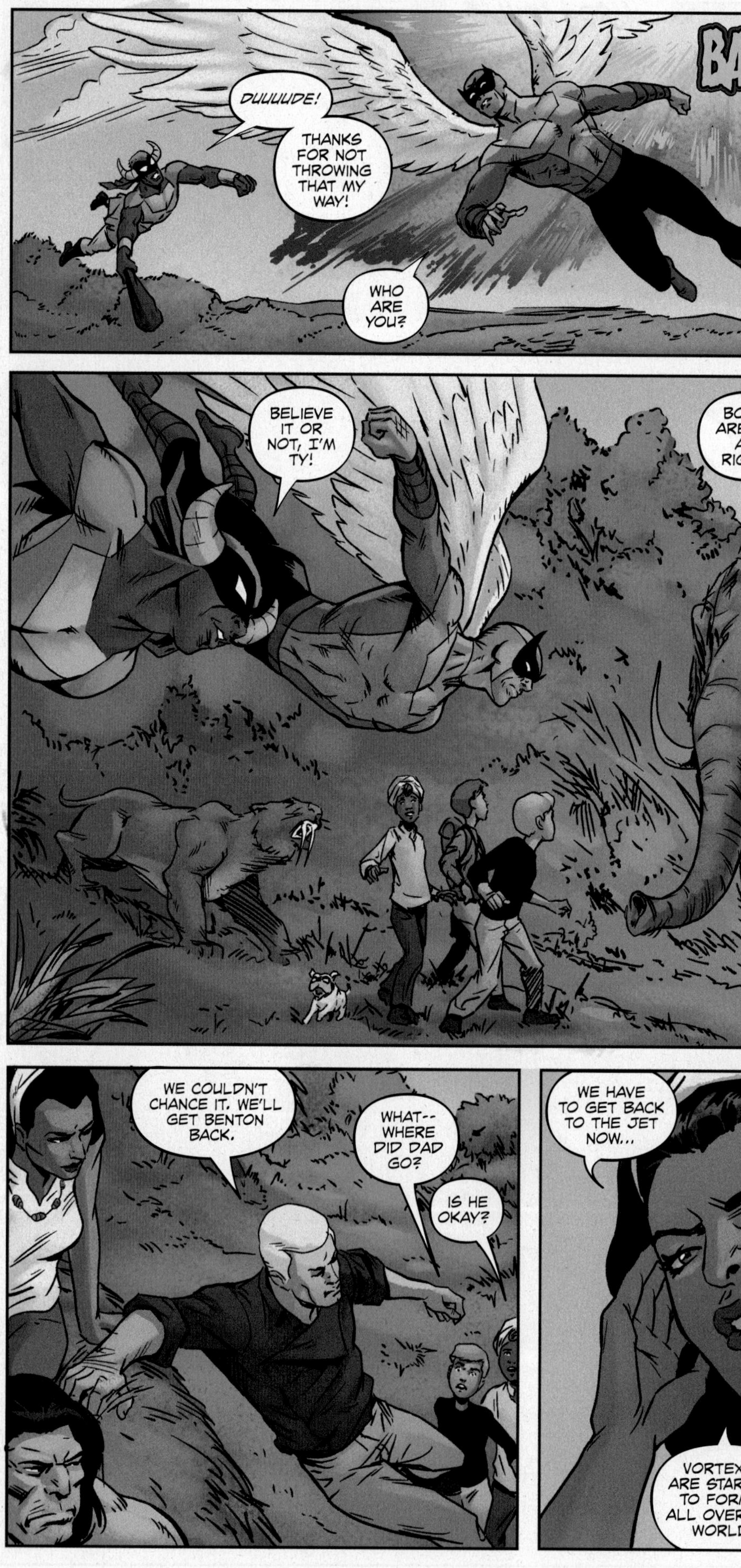

DUUUUDE!
THANKS FOR NOT THROWING THAT MY WAY!
WHO ARE YOU?
BELIEVE IT OR NOT, I'M TY!
WE COULDN'T CHANCE IT. WE'LL GET BENTON BACK.
WHAT-- WHERE DID DAD GO?
IS HE OKAY?
WE HAVE TO GET BACK TO THE JET NOW...

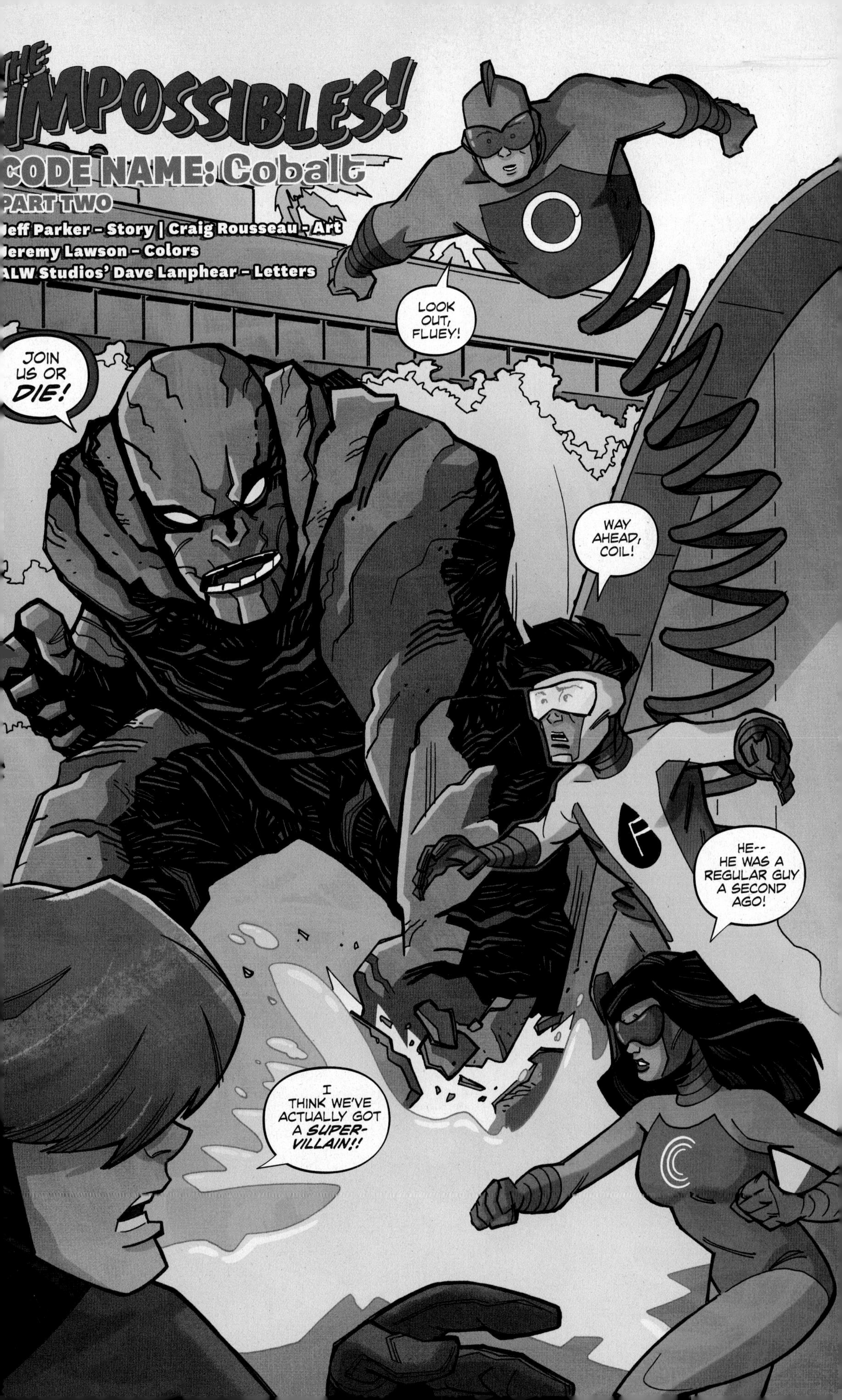

THE IMPOSSIBLES!
CODE NAME: Cobalt
PART TWO
Jeff Parker – Story | Craig Rousseau – Art
Jeremy Lawson – Colors
ALW Studios' Dave Lanphear – Letters
LOOK OUT, FLUEY!
JOIN US OR DIE!
WAY AHEAD, COIL!
HE-- HE WAS A REGULAR GUY A SECOND AGO!
I THINK WE'VE ACTUALLY GOT A SUPER-VILLAIN!!

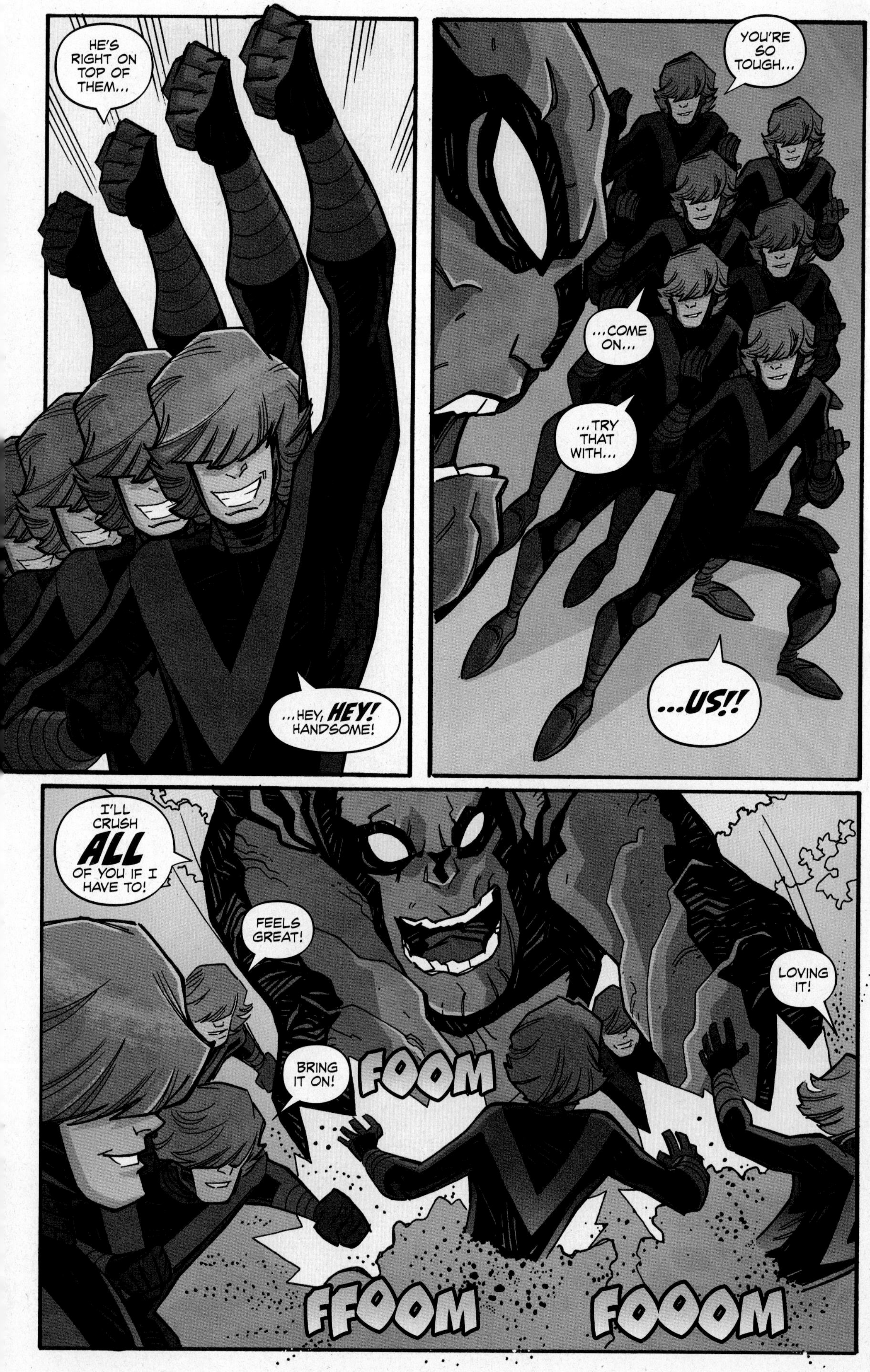
HE'S RIGHT ON TOP OF THEM...
...HEY, HEY! HANDSOME!
YOU'RE SO TOUGH...
...COME ON...
...TRY THAT WITH...
...US!!
I'LL CRUSH ALL OF YOU IF I HAVE TO!
FEELS GREAT!
BRING IT ON!
FOOM
LOVING IT!
FFOOM
FOOOM

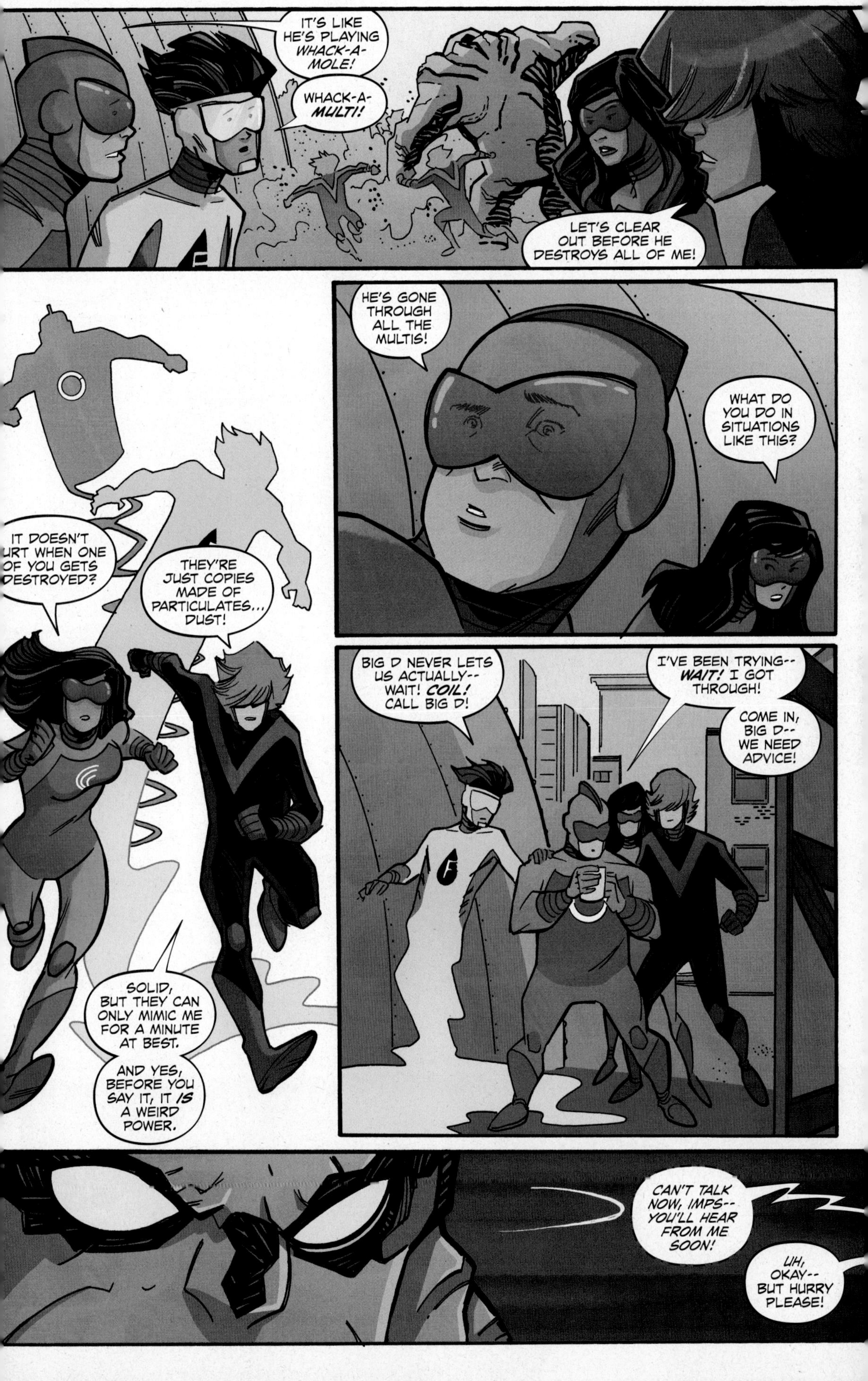
IT'S LIKE HE'S PLAYING *WHACK-A-MOLE!*
WHACK-A-*MULTI!*
LET'S CLEAR OUT BEFORE HE DESTROYS ALL OF ME!
HE'S GONE THROUGH ALL THE MULTIS!
WHAT DO YOU DO IN SITUATIONS LIKE THIS?
IT DOESN'T HURT WHEN ONE OF YOU GETS DESTROYED?
THEY'RE JUST COPIES MADE OF PARTICULATES... DUST!
SOLID, BUT THEY CAN ONLY MIMIC ME FOR A MINUTE AT BEST.
AND YES, BEFORE YOU SAY IT, IT *IS* A WEIRD POWER.
BIG D NEVER LETS US ACTUALLY-- WAIT! *COIL!* CALL BIG D!
I'VE BEEN TRYING-- *WAIT!* I GOT THROUGH!
COME IN, BIG D-- WE NEED ADVICE!
CAN'T TALK NOW, IMPS-- YOU'LL HEAR FROM ME SOON!
UH, OKAY-- BUT HURRY PLEASE!

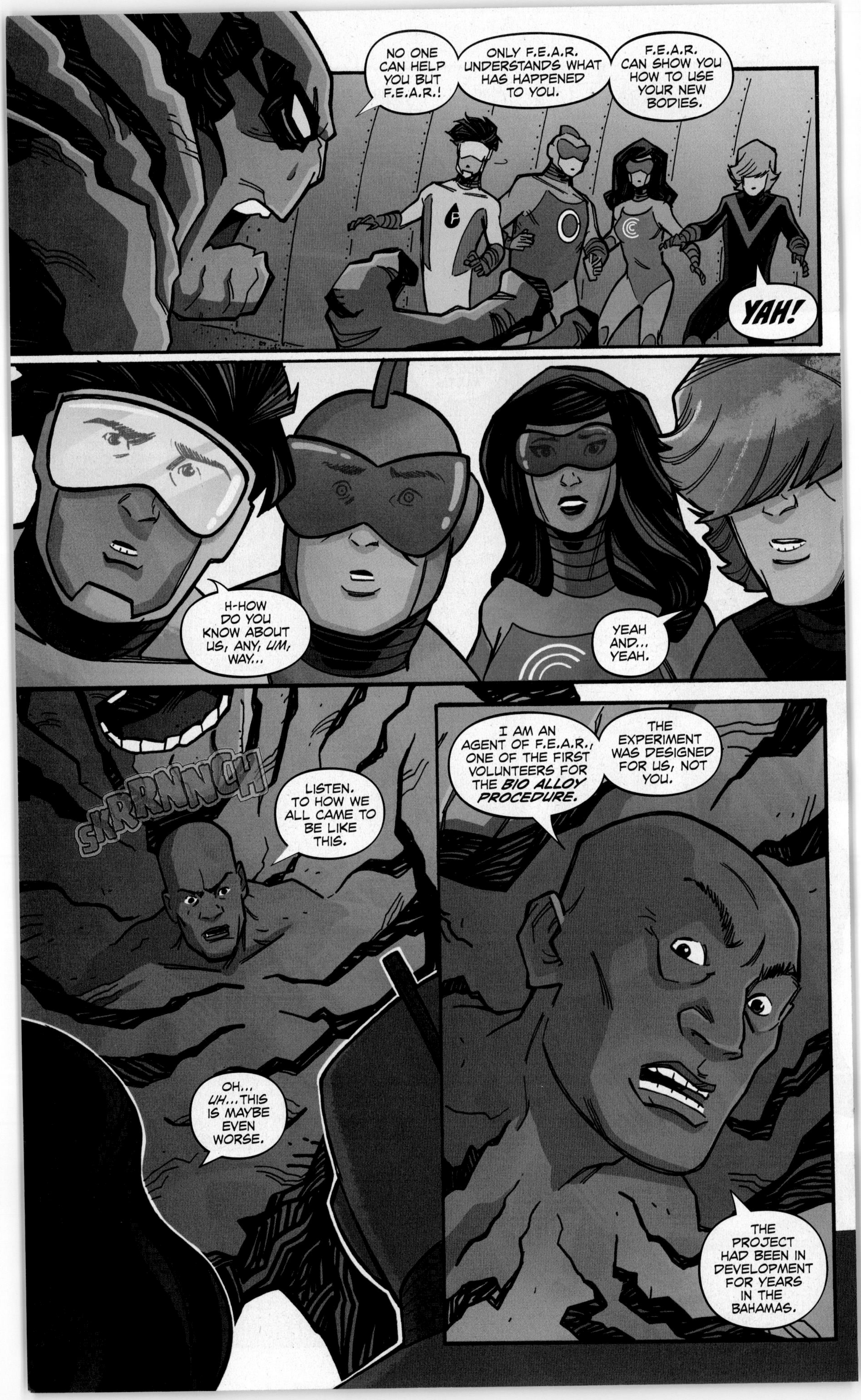
NO ONE CAN HELP YOU BUT F.E.A.R.!
ONLY F.E.A.R. UNDERSTANDS WHAT HAS HAPPENED TO YOU.
F.E.A.R. CAN SHOW YOU HOW TO USE YOUR NEW BODIES.
YAH!
H-HOW DO YOU KNOW ABOUT US, ANY, UM, WAY...
YEAH AND... YEAH.
SKRRNNCH
LISTEN. TO HOW WE ALL CAME TO BE LIKE THIS.
OH... UH...THIS IS MAYBE EVEN WORSE.
I AM AN AGENT OF F.E.A.R., ONE OF THE FIRST VOLUNTEERS FOR THE BIO ALLOY PROCEDURE.
THE EXPERIMENT WAS DESIGNED FOR US, NOT YOU.
THE PROJECT HAD BEEN IN DEVELOPMENT FOR YEARS IN THE BAHAMAS.

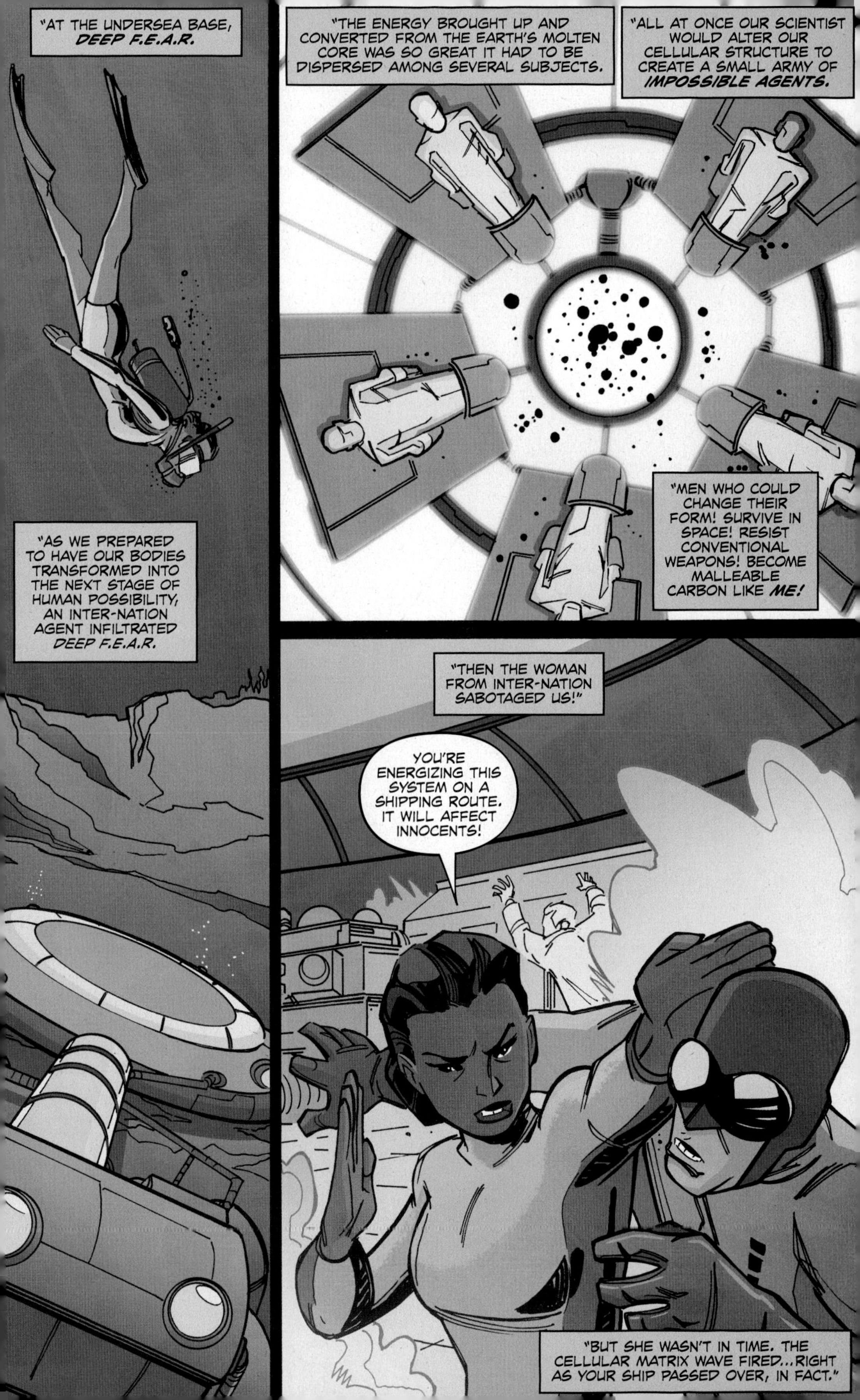
"AT THE UNDERSEA BASE, *DEEP F.E.A.R.*
"THE ENERGY BROUGHT UP AND CONVERTED FROM THE EARTH'S MOLTEN CORE WAS SO GREAT IT HAD TO BE DISPERSED AMONG SEVERAL SUBJECTS.
"ALL AT ONCE OUR SCIENTIST WOULD ALTER OUR CELLULAR STRUCTURE TO CREATE A SMALL ARMY OF *IMPOSSIBLE AGENTS.*
"MEN WHO COULD CHANGE THEIR FORM! SURVIVE IN SPACE! RESIST CONVENTIONAL WEAPONS! BECOME MALLEABLE CARBON LIKE *ME!*
"AS WE PREPARED TO HAVE OUR BODIES TRANSFORMED INTO THE NEXT STAGE OF HUMAN POSSIBILITY, AN INTER-NATION AGENT INFILTRATED *DEEP F.E.A.R.*
"THEN THE WOMAN FROM INTER-NATION SABOTAGED US!"
YOU'RE ENERGIZING THIS SYSTEM ON A SHIPPING ROUTE. IT WILL AFFECT INNOCENTS!
"BUT SHE WASN'T IN TIME. THE CELLULAR MATRIX WAVE FIRED...RIGHT AS YOUR SHIP PASSED OVER, IN FACT."

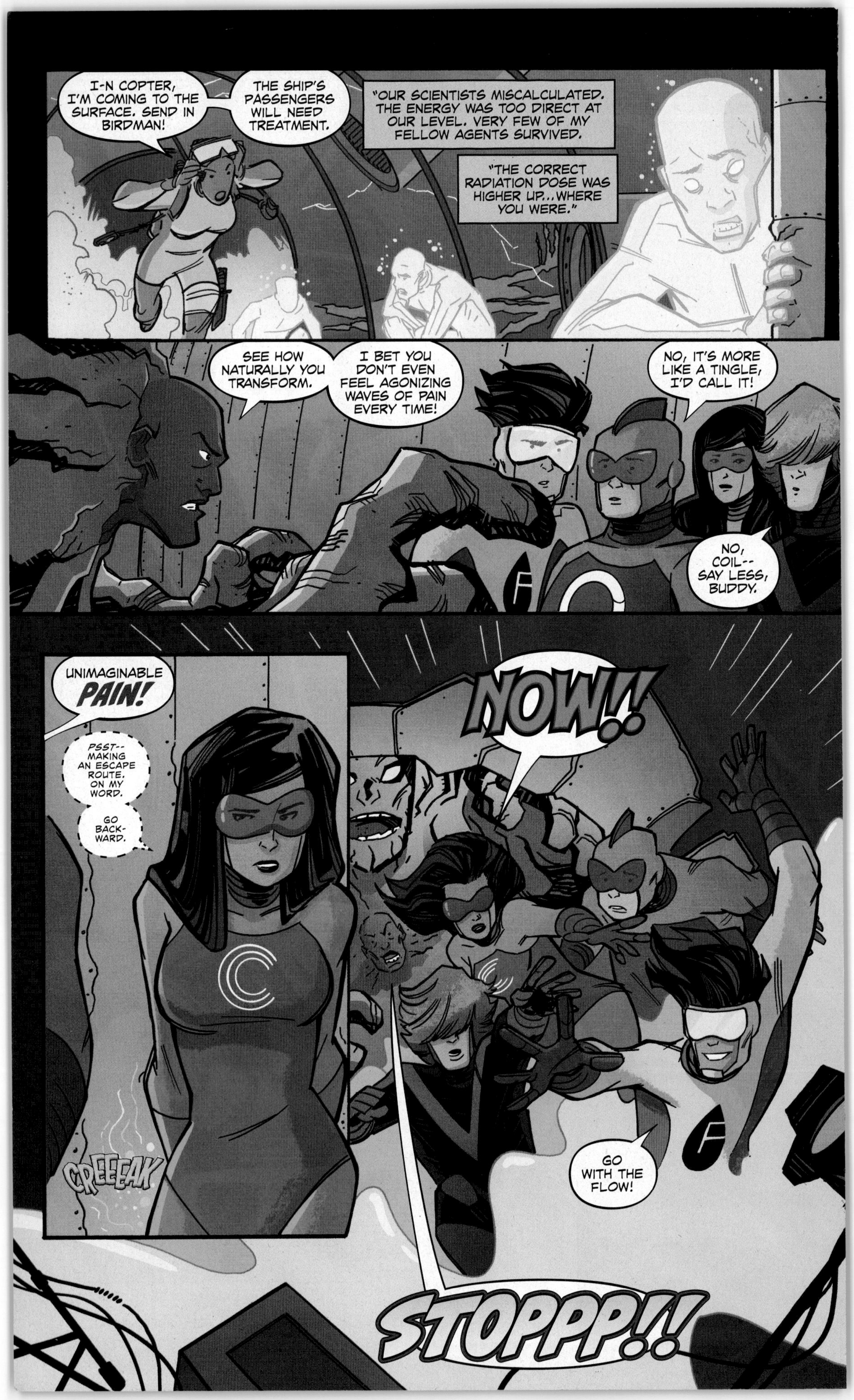
I-N COPTER, I'M COMING TO THE SURFACE. SEND IN BIRDMAN!
THE SHIP'S PASSENGERS WILL NEED TREATMENT.
"OUR SCIENTISTS MISCALCULATED. THE ENERGY WAS TOO DIRECT AT OUR LEVEL. VERY FEW OF MY FELLOW AGENTS SURVIVED.
"THE CORRECT RADIATION DOSE WAS HIGHER UP...WHERE YOU WERE."
SEE HOW NATURALLY YOU TRANSFORM.
I BET YOU DON'T EVEN FEEL AGONIZING WAVES OF PAIN EVERY TIME!
NO, IT'S MORE LIKE A TINGLE, I'D CALL IT!
NO, COIL-- SAY LESS, BUDDY.
UNIMAGINABLE PAIN!
PSST-- MAKING AN ESCAPE ROUTE. ON MY WORD.
GO BACK-WARD.
CREEEAK
NOW!!
GO WITH THE FLOW!
STOPPP!!

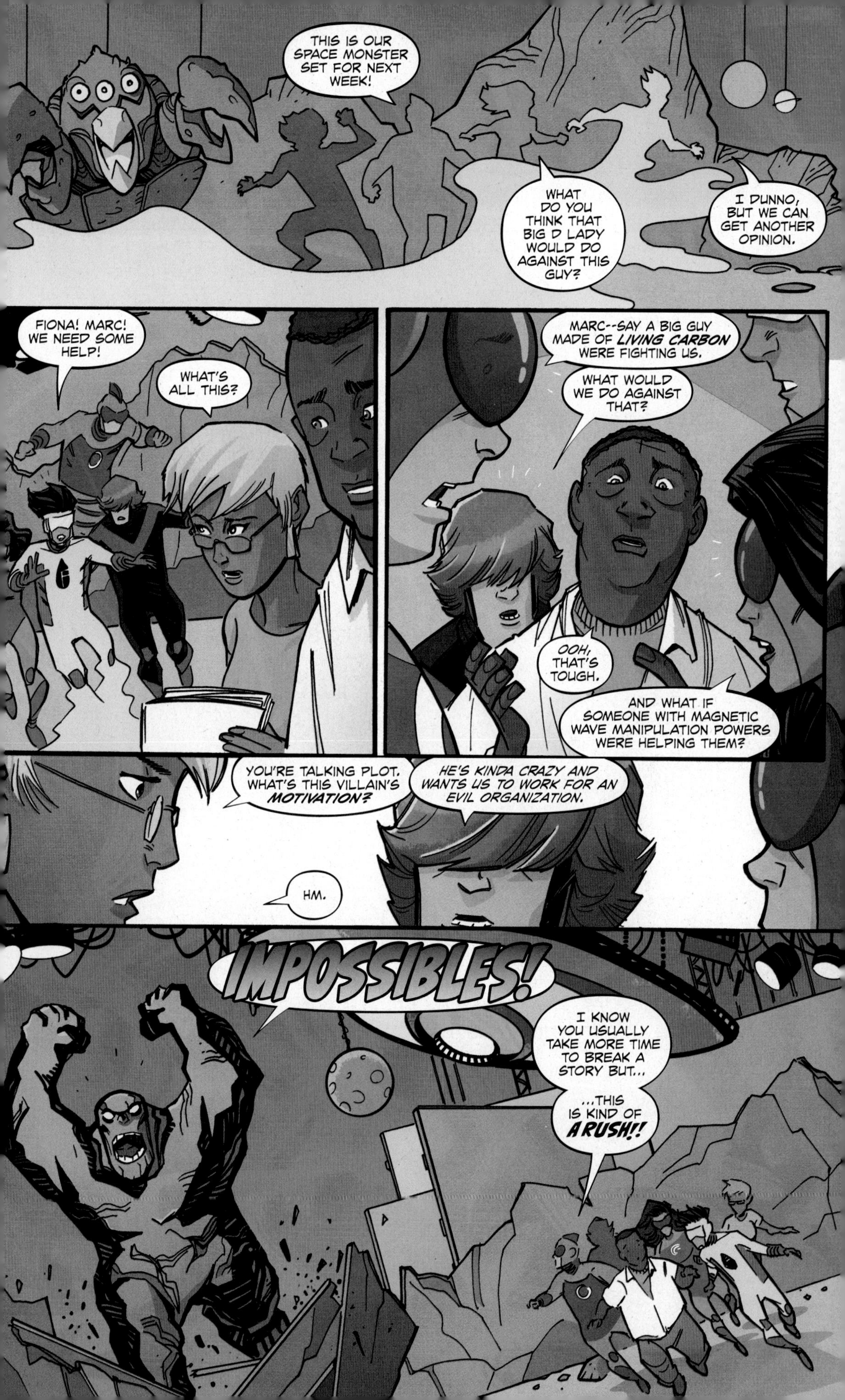
THIS IS OUR SPACE MONSTER SET FOR NEXT WEEK!
WHAT DO YOU THINK THAT BIG D LADY WOULD DO AGAINST THIS GUY?
I DUNNO, BUT WE CAN GET ANOTHER OPINION.
FIONA! MARC! WE NEED SOME HELP!
WHAT'S ALL THIS?
MARC--SAY A BIG GUY MADE OF *LIVING CARBON* WERE FIGHTING US.
WHAT WOULD WE DO AGAINST THAT?
OOH, THAT'S TOUGH.
AND WHAT IF SOMEONE WITH MAGNETIC WAVE MANIPULATION POWERS WERE HELPING THEM?
YOU'RE TALKING PLOT. WHAT'S THIS VILLAIN'S ***MOTIVATION?***
HE'S KINDA CRAZY AND WANTS US TO WORK FOR AN EVIL ORGANIZATION.
HM.
IMPOSSIBLES!
I KNOW YOU USUALLY TAKE MORE TIME TO BREAK A STORY BUT...
...THIS IS KIND OF ***A RUSH!!***

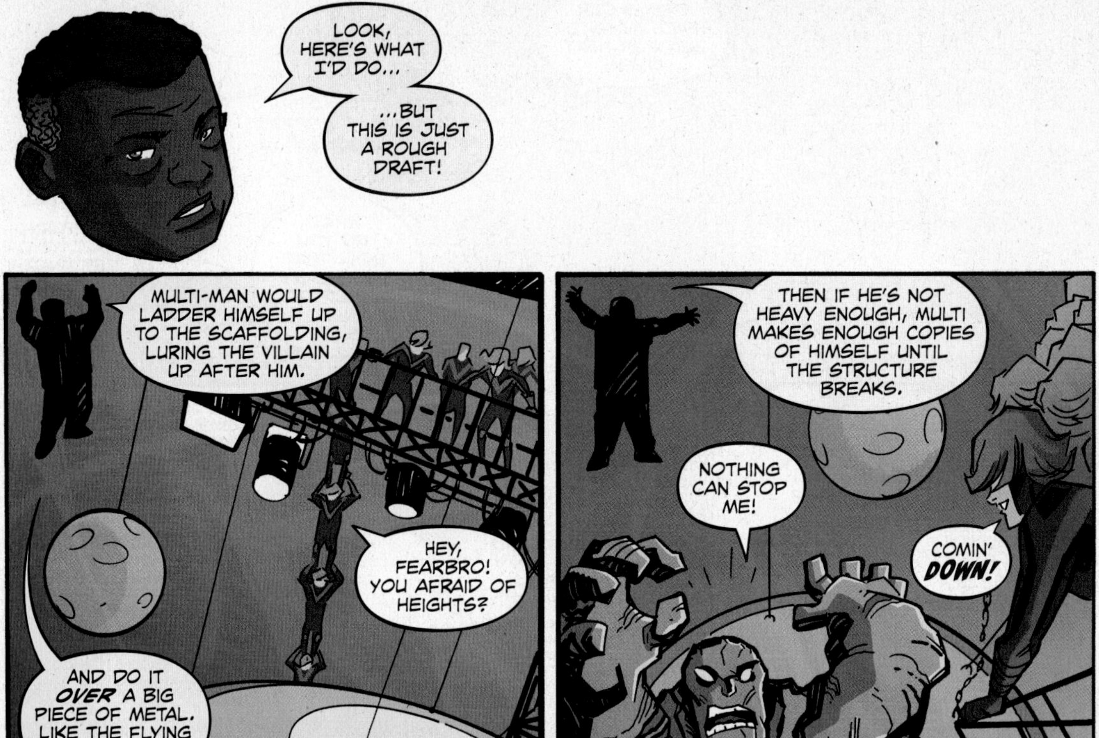
LOOK, HERE'S WHAT I'D DO...
...BUT THIS IS JUST A ROUGH DRAFT!
MULTI-MAN WOULD LADDER HIMSELF UP TO THE SCAFFOLDING, LURING THE VILLAIN UP AFTER HIM.
HEY, FEARBRO! YOU AFRAID OF HEIGHTS?
AND DO IT *OVER* A BIG PIECE OF METAL. LIKE THE FLYING
THEN IF HE'S NOT HEAVY ENOUGH, MULTI MAKES ENOUGH COPIES OF HIMSELF UNTIL THE STRUCTURE BREAKS.
NOTHING CAN STOP ME!
COMIN' **DOWN!**

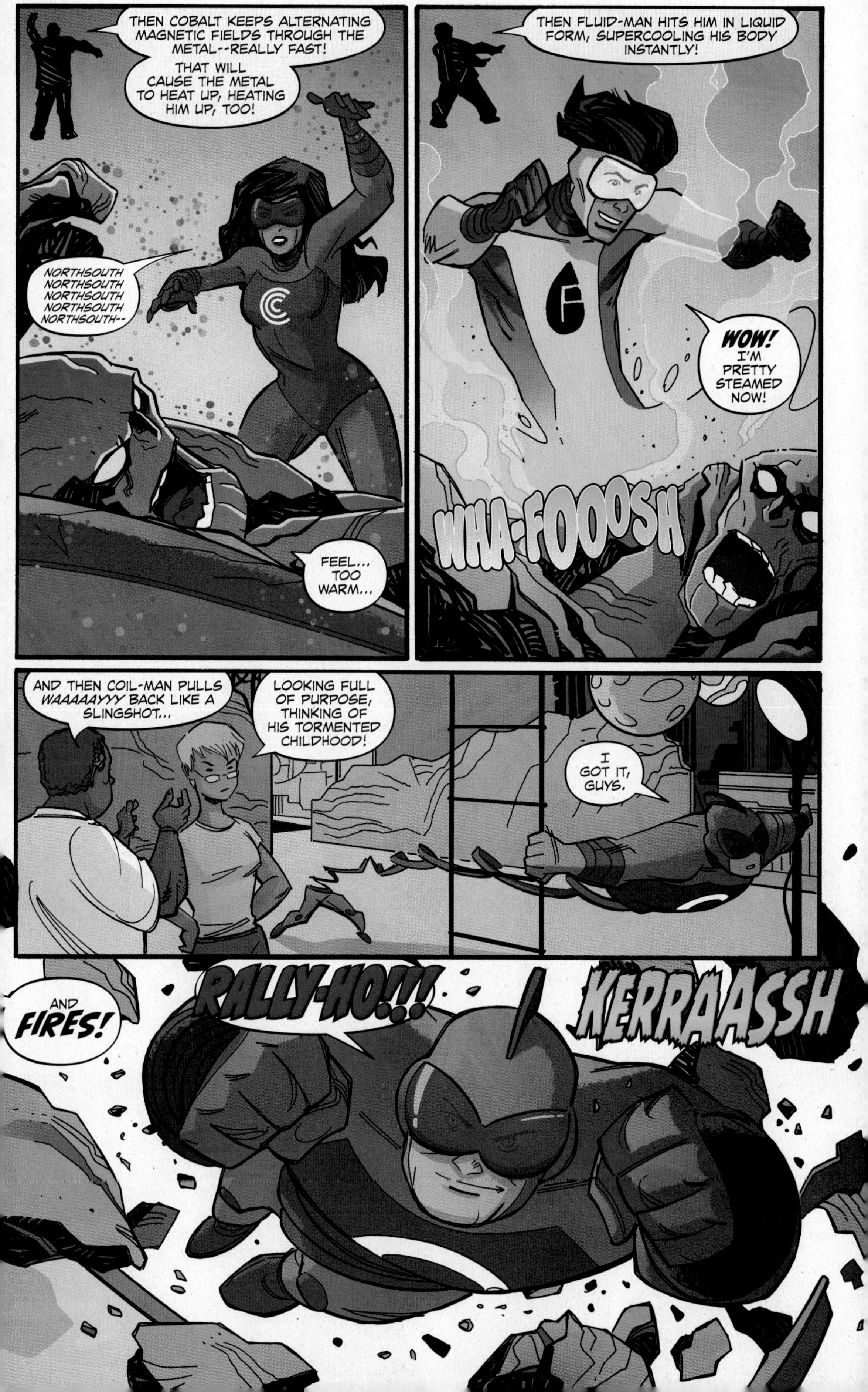

THEN COBALT KEEPS ALTERNATING MAGNETIC FIELDS THROUGH THE METAL--REALLY FAST!
THAT WILL CAUSE THE METAL TO HEAT UP, HEATING HIM UP, TOO!
NORTHSOUTH NORTHSOUTH NORTHSOUTH NORTHSOUTH NORTHSOUTH--
FEEL... TOO WARM...
THEN FLUID-MAN HITS HIM IN LIQUID FORM, SUPERCOOLING HIS BODY INSTANTLY!
WOW! I'M PRETTY STEAMED NOW!
WHA-FOOOSH
AND THEN COIL-MAN PULLS WAAAAAYYY BACK LIKE A SLINGSHOT...
LOOKING FULL OF PURPOSE, THINKING OF HIS TORMENTED CHILDHOOD!
I GOT IT, GUYS.
AND FIRES!
RALLY-HO!!!
KERRAASSH

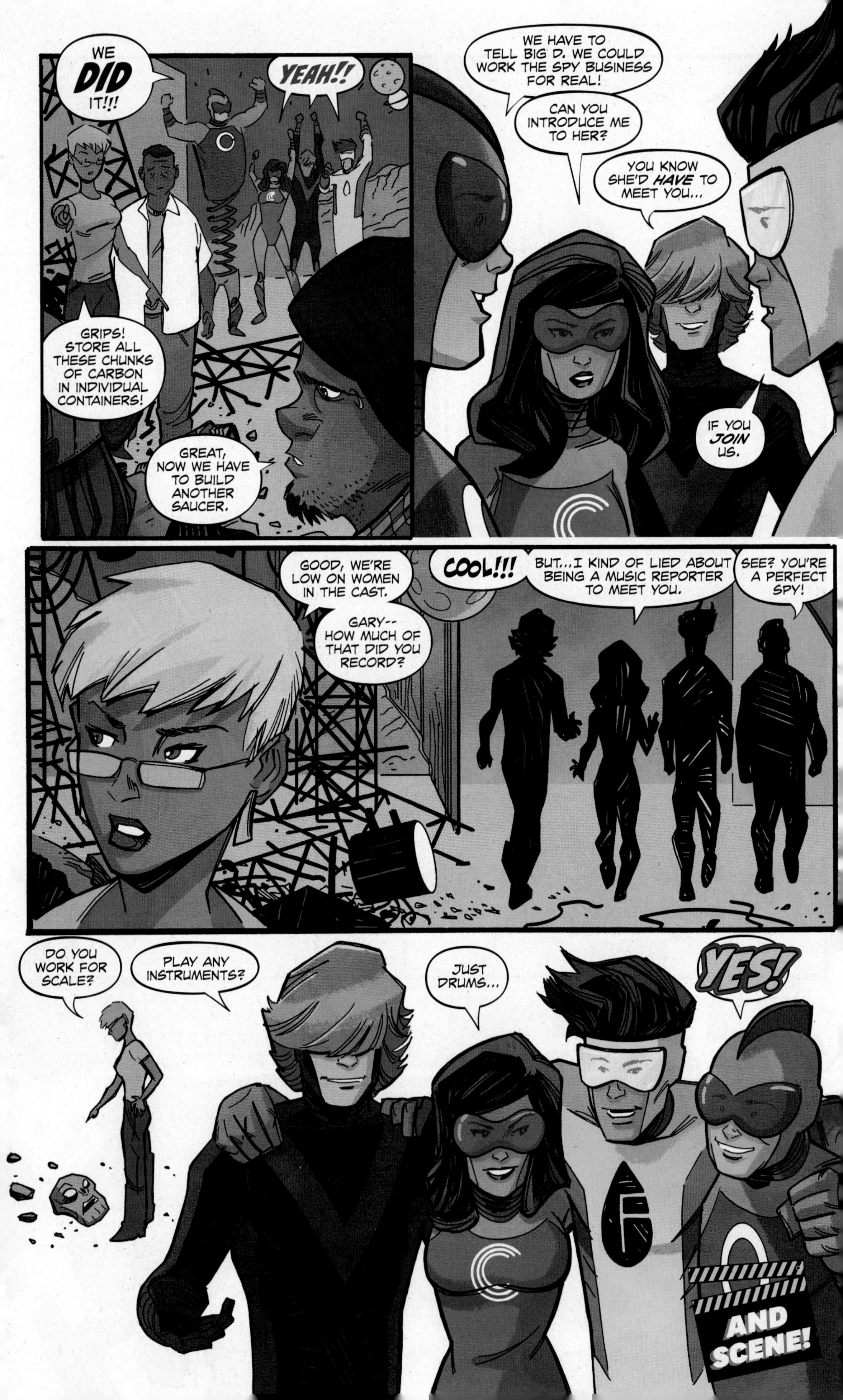
WE DID IT!!!
YEAH!!
GRIPS! STORE ALL THESE CHUNKS OF CARBON IN INDIVIDUAL CONTAINERS!
GREAT, NOW WE HAVE TO BUILD ANOTHER SAUCER.
WE HAVE TO TELL BIG D. WE COULD WORK THE SPY BUSINESS FOR REAL!
CAN YOU INTRODUCE ME TO HER?
YOU KNOW SHE'D HAVE TO MEET YOU...
IF YOU JOIN US.
GOOD, WE'RE LOW ON WOMEN IN THE CAST.
GARY-- HOW MUCH OF THAT DID YOU RECORD?
COOL!!!
BUT...I KIND OF LIED ABOUT BEING A MUSIC REPORTER TO MEET YOU.
SEE? YOU'RE A PERFECT SPY!
DO YOU WORK FOR SCALE?
PLAY ANY INSTRUMENTS?
JUST DRUMS...
YES!
AND SCENE!

ON THE ORIGIN OF COMICS:
The Theories of Darwyn

In 2015, after much pursuit, DC publishers Dan DiDio and Jim Lee got the blessing from Warner Bros. to dive into the rich catalogue of Hanna-Barbera and Scooby-Doo to put them in front of modern readers.

Scooby would be updated, Wacky Races wildly reimagined, and the Flintstones would come back as subversive social commentary. But for the action-adventure characters, DiDio wanted an event book that could bring together the heroes from the heyday of the studio—in essence a "new frontier" of the H-B universe. DC: THE NEW FRONTIER, by the way, is my favorite story from DC so far in the twenty-first century. A retro '50s/'60s take on the DC heroes could have easily been a navel-gazing nostalgia-fest in most hands, but it was written and drawn by a comet that blazed through our industry for a short time—**Darwyn Cooke**. DC: THE NEW FRONTIER made the characters feel fresh and full of purpose and embraced classic aspects that often got dropped in revamps; in short, Darwyn took all the strengths and stripped away everything else to cast a captivating world of adventurers. This was the perfect North Star for plotting the course of FUTURE QUEST.

So Dan went to the source to see how *he* would make this happen. I'll always be grateful that they agreed about bringing me and Evan "Doc" Shaner in to launch this. My first awareness of what they'd discussed came in an email containing only an image—all the heroes in this book in one setting. Jonny Quest and Space Ghost were front and center, drawn by Darwyn. Dan had already prepped me slightly by saying there could be a project *with* Darwyn, and I blurted, "whatever it is, I'll do it!" because I drive a hard bargain. But I wasn't expecting anything like this—what was clearly going to be a *big* story.

A big story at whose heart was *Jonny Quest*, the show that had such an impact on my childhood and beyond. I've been lucky with meeting my heroes, and I was friendly with both Doug Wildey and Alex Toth, who were generous with their time and insights when I'd written or called. Now, I had a chance to break a story full of their creations with direction from an artist in their league.

What followed was a brief time that will always be important to me—brainstorming with Darwyn. In a happy coincidence, we were both guests the following week at Baltimore Comic-Con, and he broke away from the long lines at his table to sneak outside and catch me up. Once out in the sun where he could pace, rant, joke and wave his arms around, he shared some amorphous scenes that were playing out in his head. He saw the story opening in his own second home of Florida—also the home of the Quests, with their secret lab on one of the Florida Keys. Jonny and Hadji would chase down a UFO they saw crash in the Everglades. Heavies sent by Dr. Zin would show up shooting, and then the danger would kick in. Secret agent Race Bannon would certainly be cracking skulls. A cyclopean Spider-Bot from the cartoon would show up. The boys would flee for their lives and run right into a bizarre dead animal the size of a dinosaur—a creature they've never seen before—Tundro the Herculoid. And the whole thing would leave off with the big reveal of a crashed spaceship, Space Ghost's Phantom Cruiser. "That's what I got so far," Darwyn finished.

This was huge for me. I'd known Darwyn for years—we'd met when we'd both worked at Sony Animation in Los Angeles. I'd been a new storyboard artist on *Big Guy and Rusty the Boy Robot* and he'd been a director on the *Men In Black* cartoon. I'd been hyperaware that he had worked on *Batman: The Animated Series*. So I would bug him for details on that whenever he wasn't locked away in his office boarding scenes. And I'd catch up with him at conventions, but we never got the chance to discuss the actual making of comics.

Now, here on a summer day in Baltimore, it was hitting me that one of our best went through the same process I do! He talked more in terms of images, moments that would make an impression on the reader. Things that set mood and tone. There was no story logic yet, no unifying concept, no key question that the series asked—all the stuff that writing advice is full of. He remembered what he liked about the shows and let his mind wander, the story eventually bubbling up to the surface. Plot and structure arrived later. Comics is a visual medium and that's where Darwyn began. We talked about bringing more women to the cast, and created Ty on the spot for the new Mightor. These dreamlike scenes were now in my head, too, and I needed to start figuring out how it all fit together.

That happened surprisingly fast. On my flight back to Oregon, I got another break—an exit-row seat with room to open up my laptop and put down ideas that were now rolling out of me. I soon had the basics—Space Ghost was the last of the Space Force protectors; the Herculoids and the Galaxy Trio would all be from the same solar system; and the galactic threat would escape them by going to Earth, where it would create Mightor. I emailed and waited. And waited. Then I got nervous. Did he hate my ideas? Was he regretting bringing me in on this? I hadn't considered that the part of Nova Scotia Darwyn lived in had frequent power outages and one of them was happening that week. When he was able to write back, he was feeling great about what he'd read, and I'm still exhaling to this day.

This led to *the pitch*, which still had to be approved around the halls of Warner. Pitches were never my strength—lucky for me Darwyn was writing it. He cleanly, quickly got across the story points in ways that suggested thrills and cool developments abounding. Tonally, it would be like *Jonny Quest* had been—nothing kids couldn't enjoy but heavy and conceptual enough for adults to stay engaged, too. He suggested more of those profound visual moments, stressing the emotional impact. I kept gas-lighting Shaner by texting him about bits he might draw without sharing any context. The process has influenced how I approach pitches since. I now finally get that they can be fun without spoiling the story.

While we waited on approvals and schedules, Darwyn had to move on. Other projects beckoned, like the excellent THE TWILIGHT CHILDREN with Gilbert Hernandez. I hated losing the world's greatest safety net and the chance for more collaboration—and the possibility he might draw some of the short stories—but we had a good foundation to build on. Doc Shaner was turning in one excellent design after another for the cast, keeping everything classic and breathing in new life. (He also wouldn't stop drawing Dino Boy until we finally got permission to put him in the series.) Marie Javins and Brittany Holzherr were setting things in motion, interviews were recorded and fans started hearing that many of their long-gone favorites were returning to action.

And like most of fandom, right as we reached the series launch months later, I learned Darwyn was succumbing to cancer. Then it was all glaringly clear why he pulled back when he did. I didn't get to tell him what his help and his work meant to me, but I can tell you. When a story is *really working,* you're not thinking about the people behind it, you're living in that fiction. Later, we can look behind the curtain and find out how it came together, the personalities that shaped the narrative. You need to know that Darwyn's influence and guidance are built into FUTURE QUEST and we would not have gotten here without him. I can't tell him that, but at least I can thank him in his favorite medium—the one he made better in his time with us.

Thanks, buddy.

—**Jeff Parker**

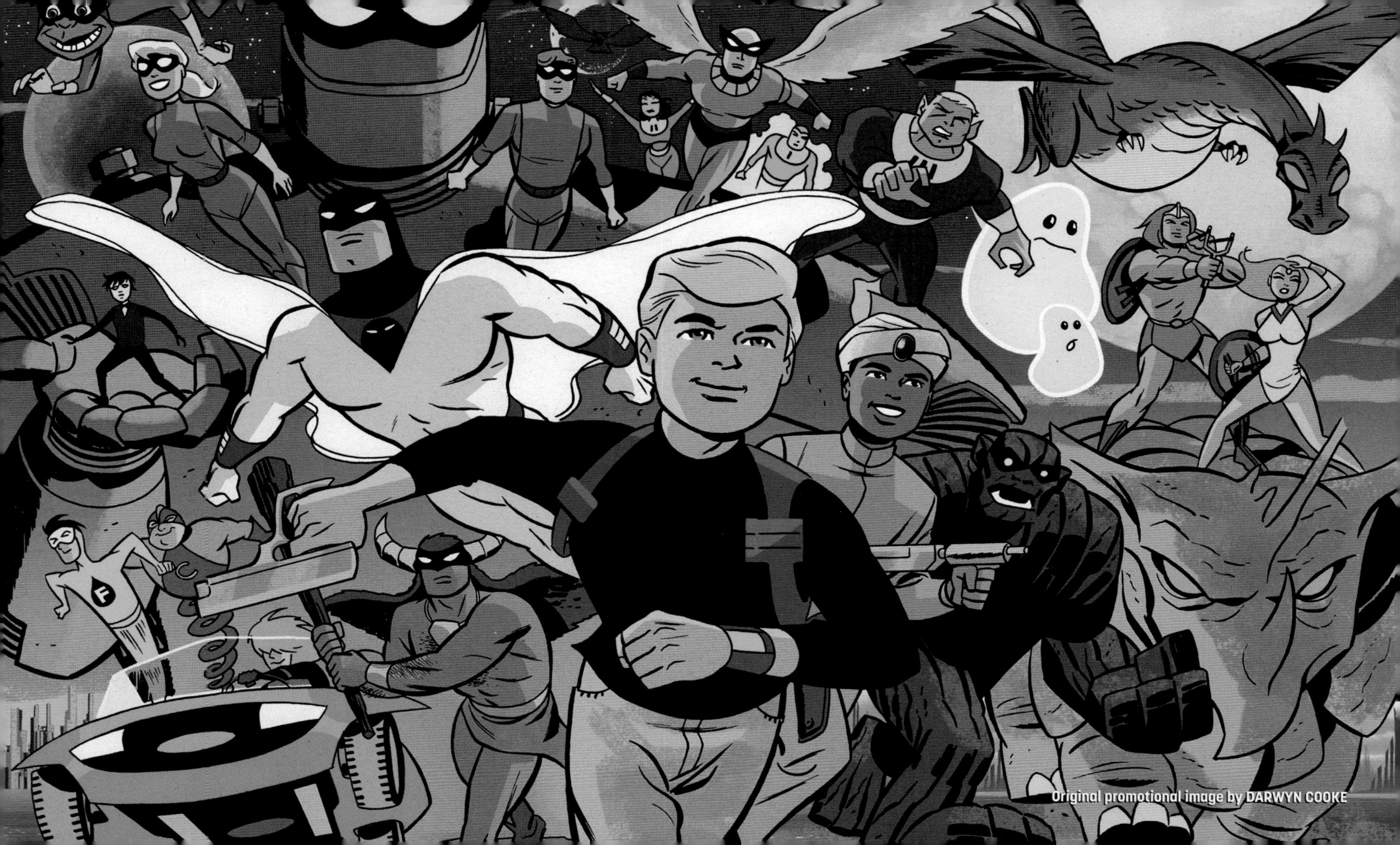

Original promotional image by DARWYN COOKE

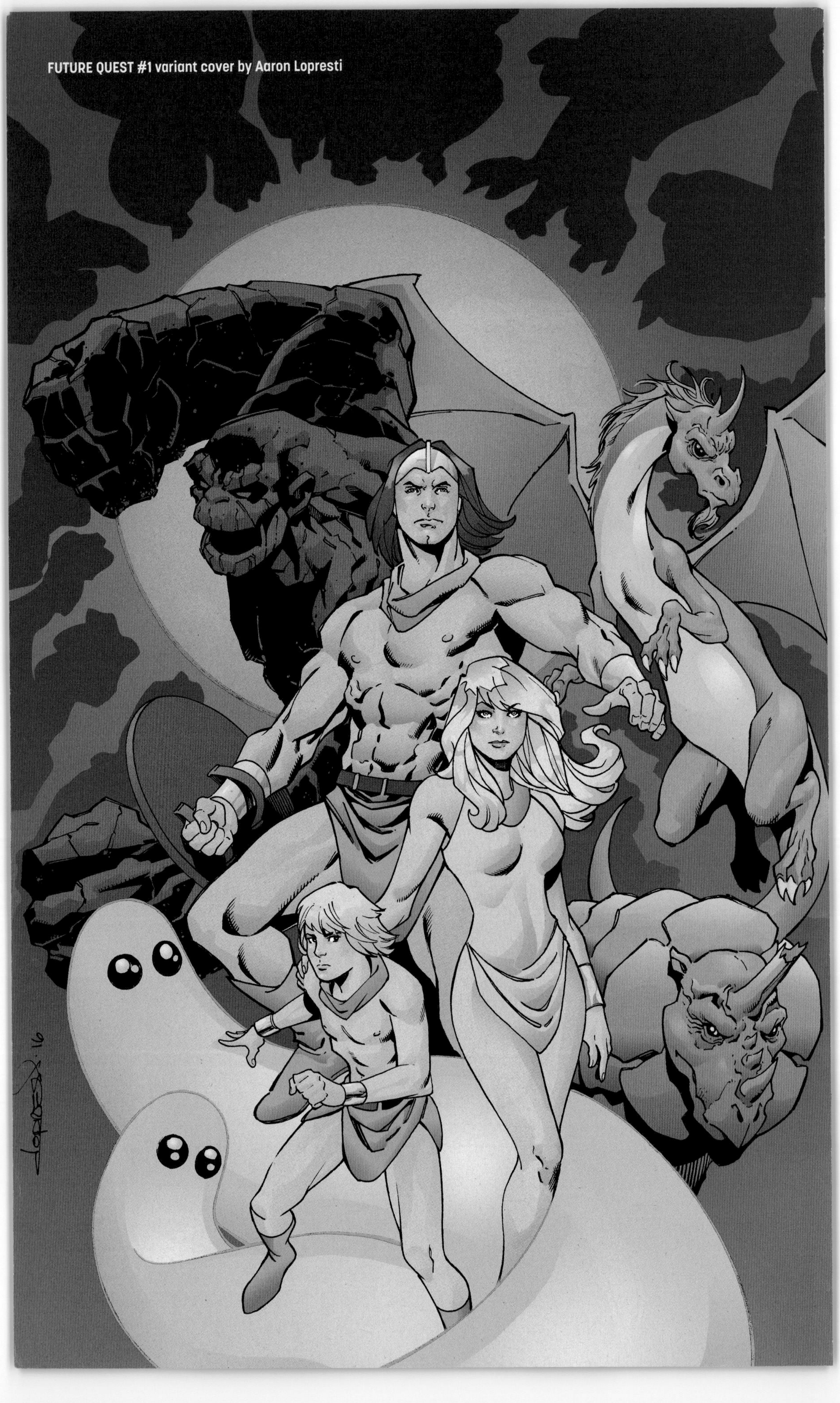

FUTURE QUEST #1 variant cover by Aaron Lopresti

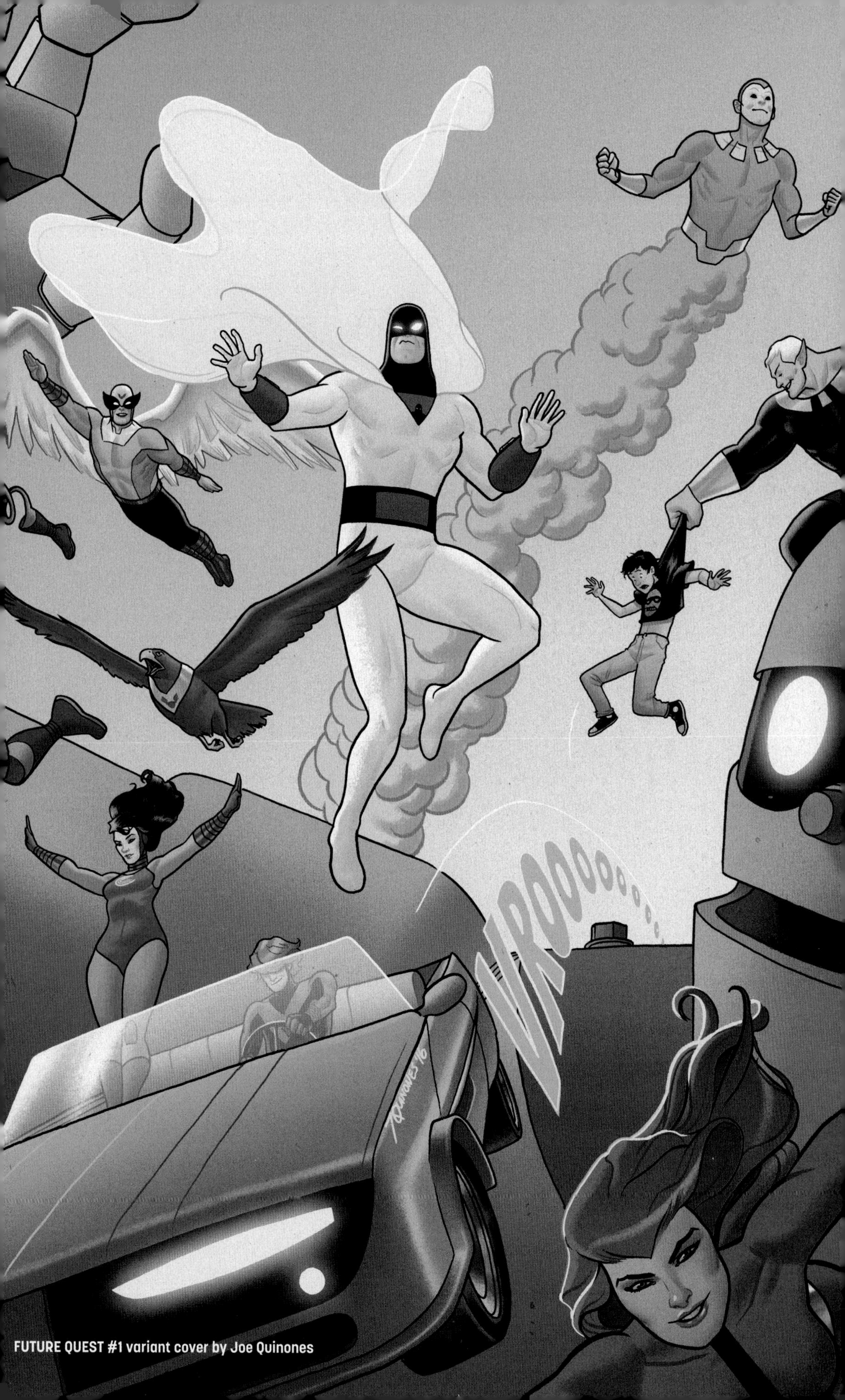
VROOOoooo...

FUTURE QUEST #1 variant cover by Joe Quinones

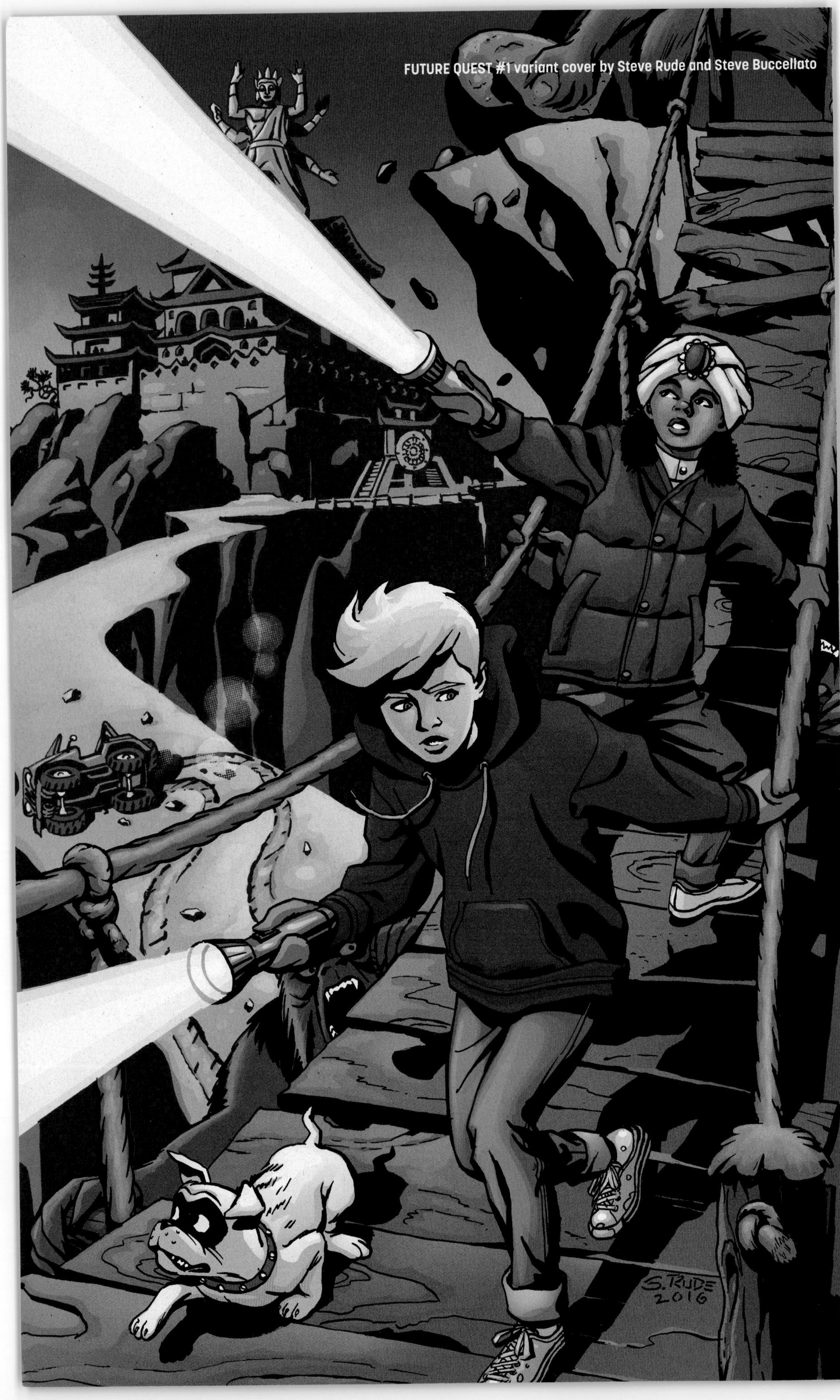
S. RUDE
2016

FUTURE QUEST #1 variant cover by Steve Rude and Steve Buccellato

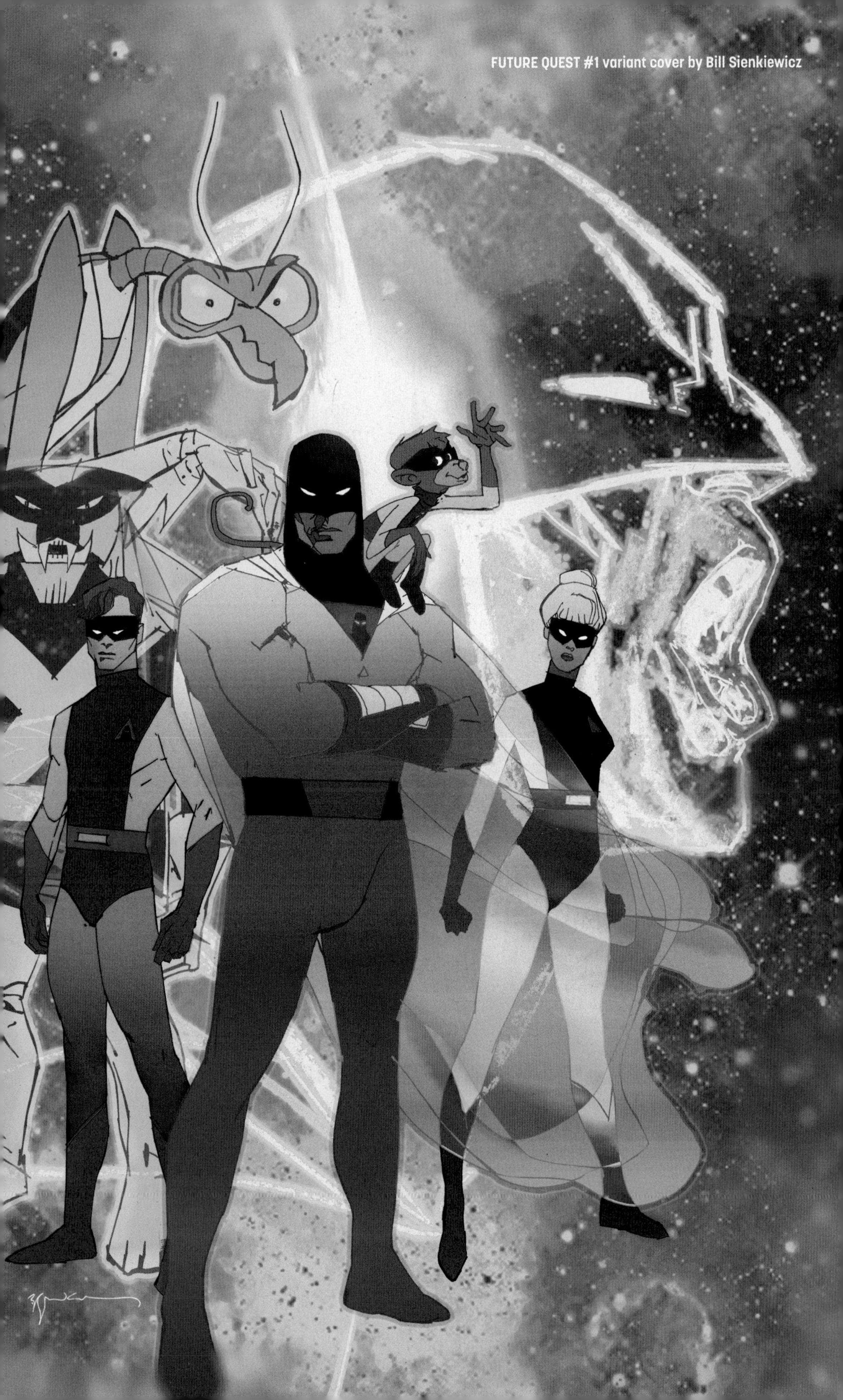

FUTURE QUEST #1 variant cover by Bill Sienkiewicz

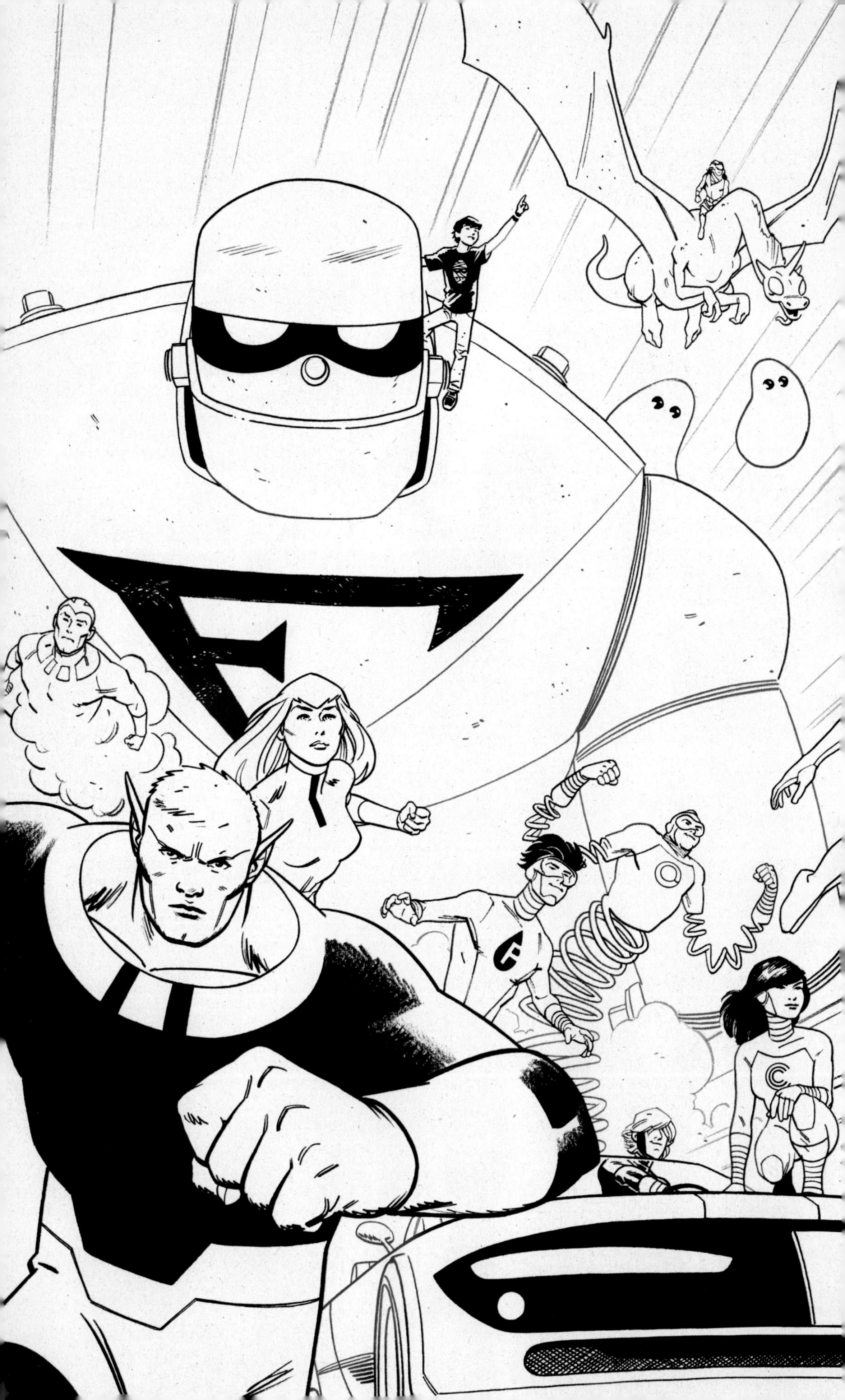

FUTURE QUEST #1 adult coloring book variant cover by Evan "Doc" Shaner

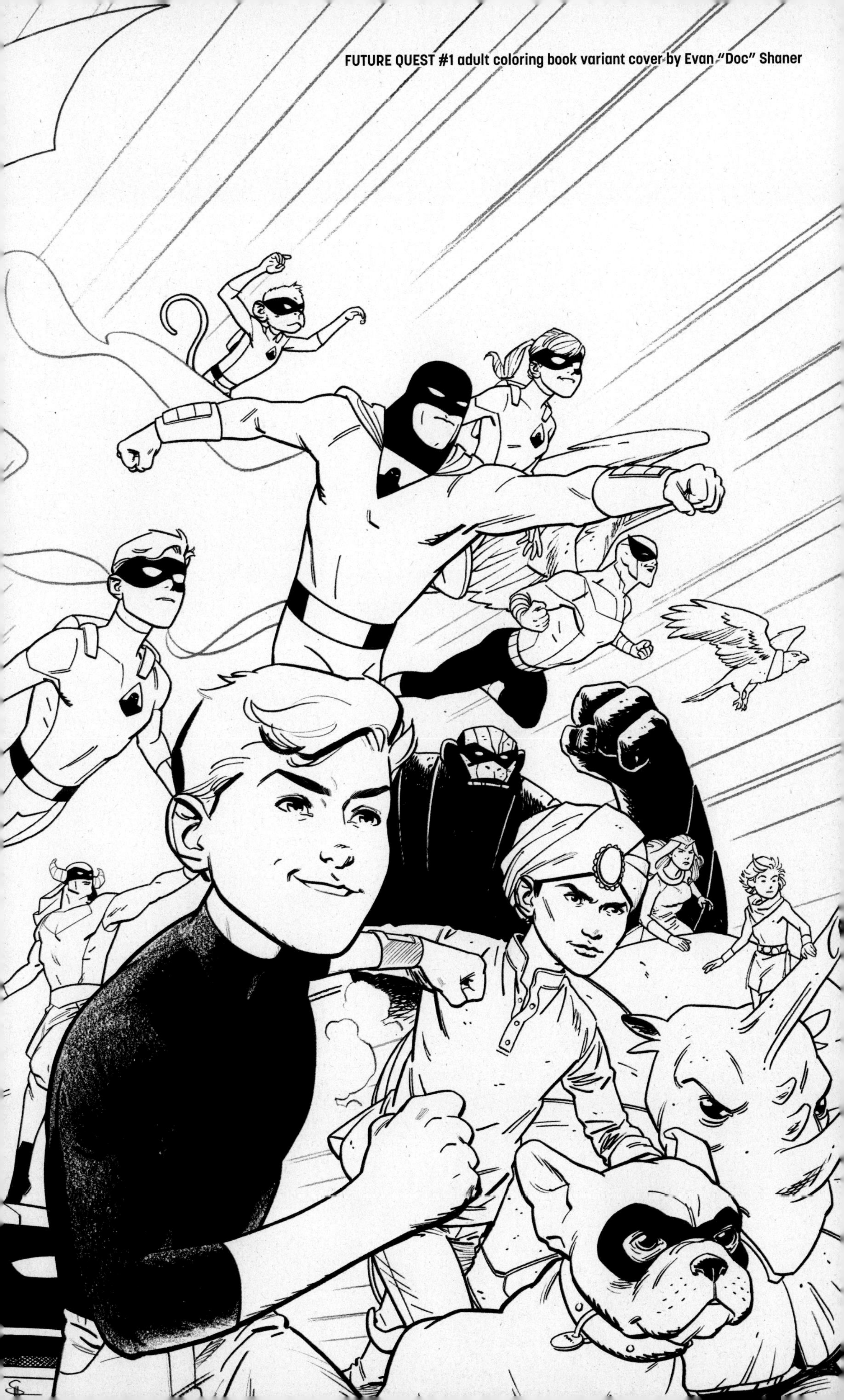

FUTURE QUEST #2 variant cover by Jill Thompson

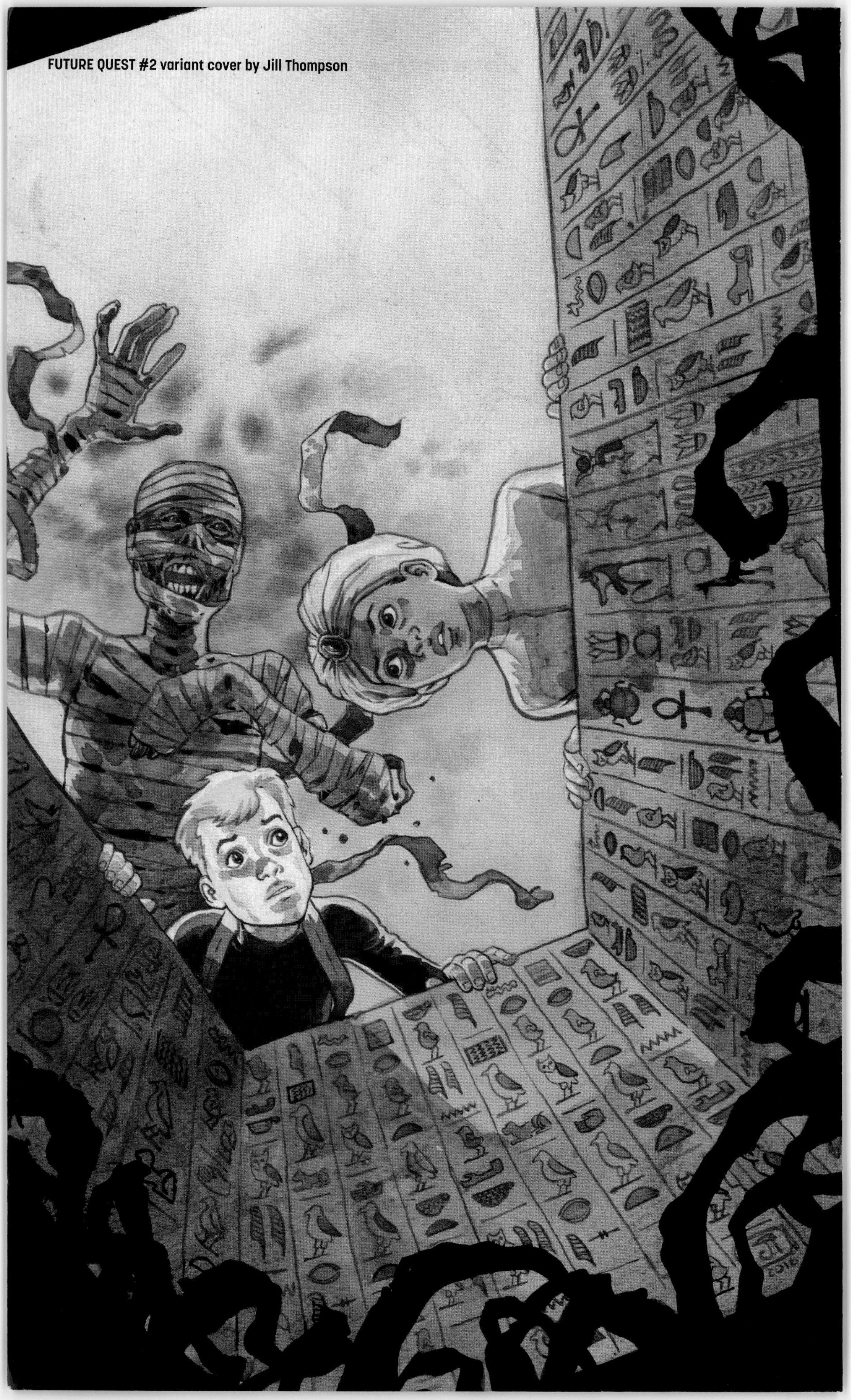

FUTURE QUEST #3 variant cover by Karl Kerschl

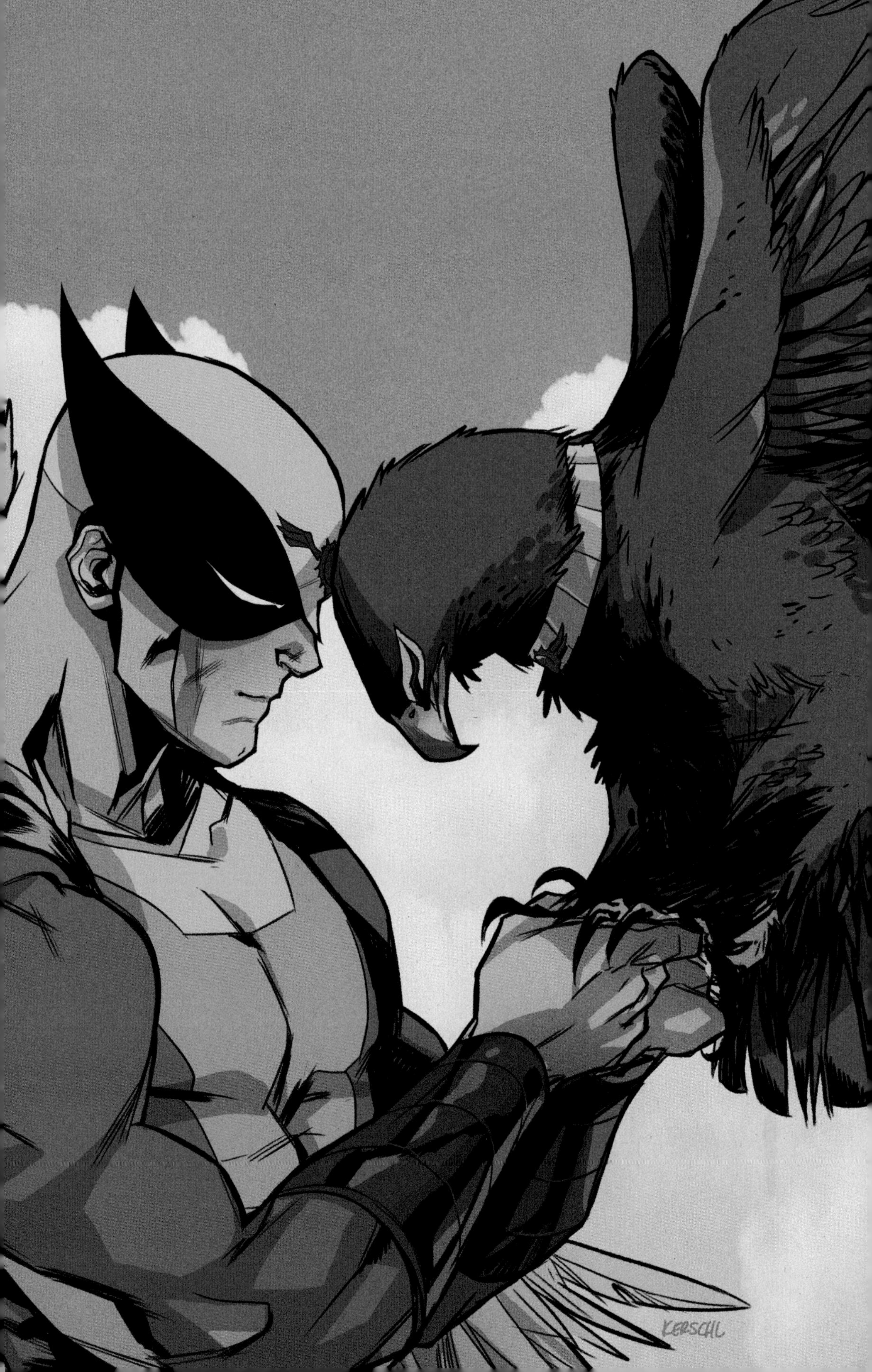
KERSCHL

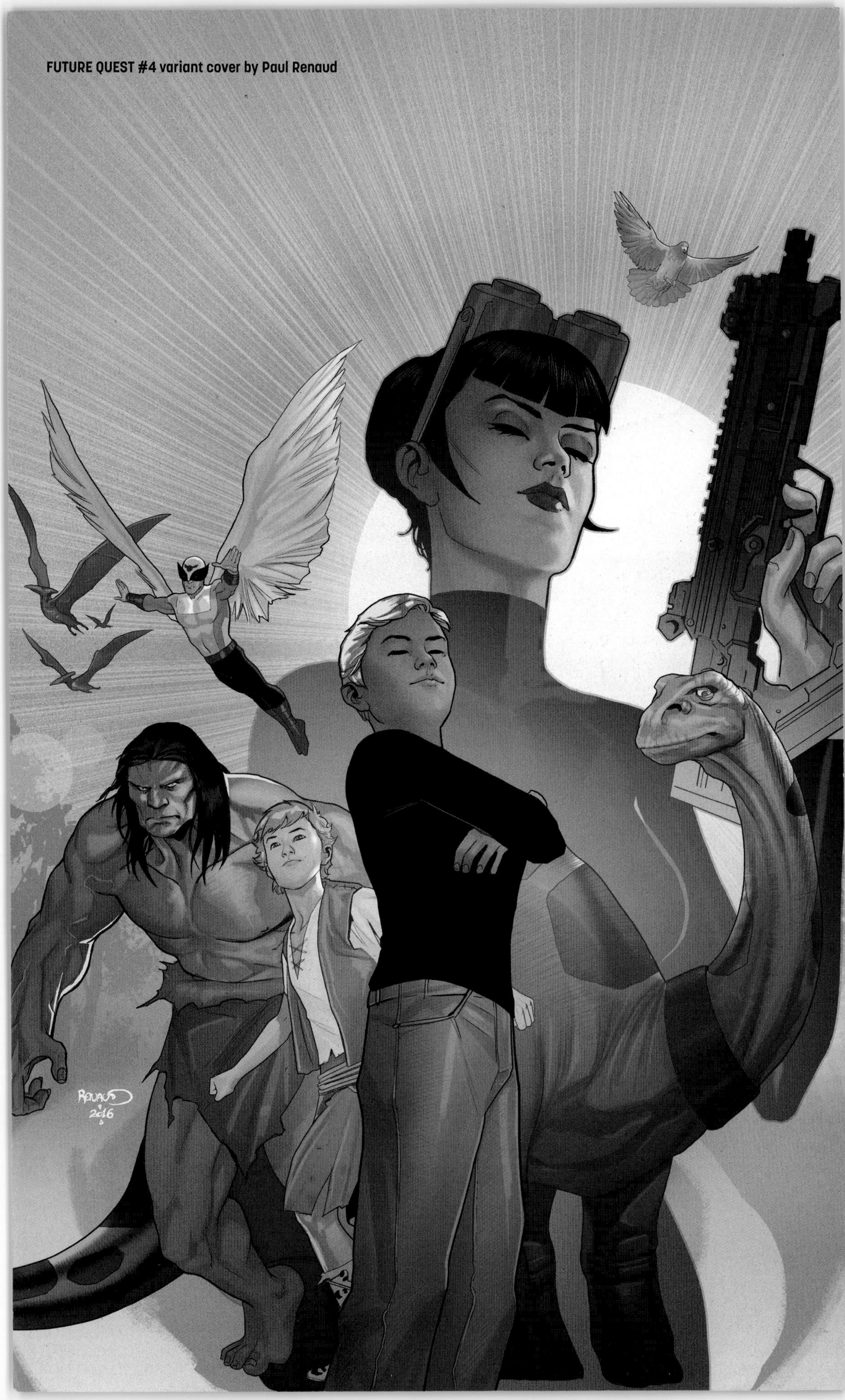

FUTURE QUEST #4 variant cover by Paul Renaud

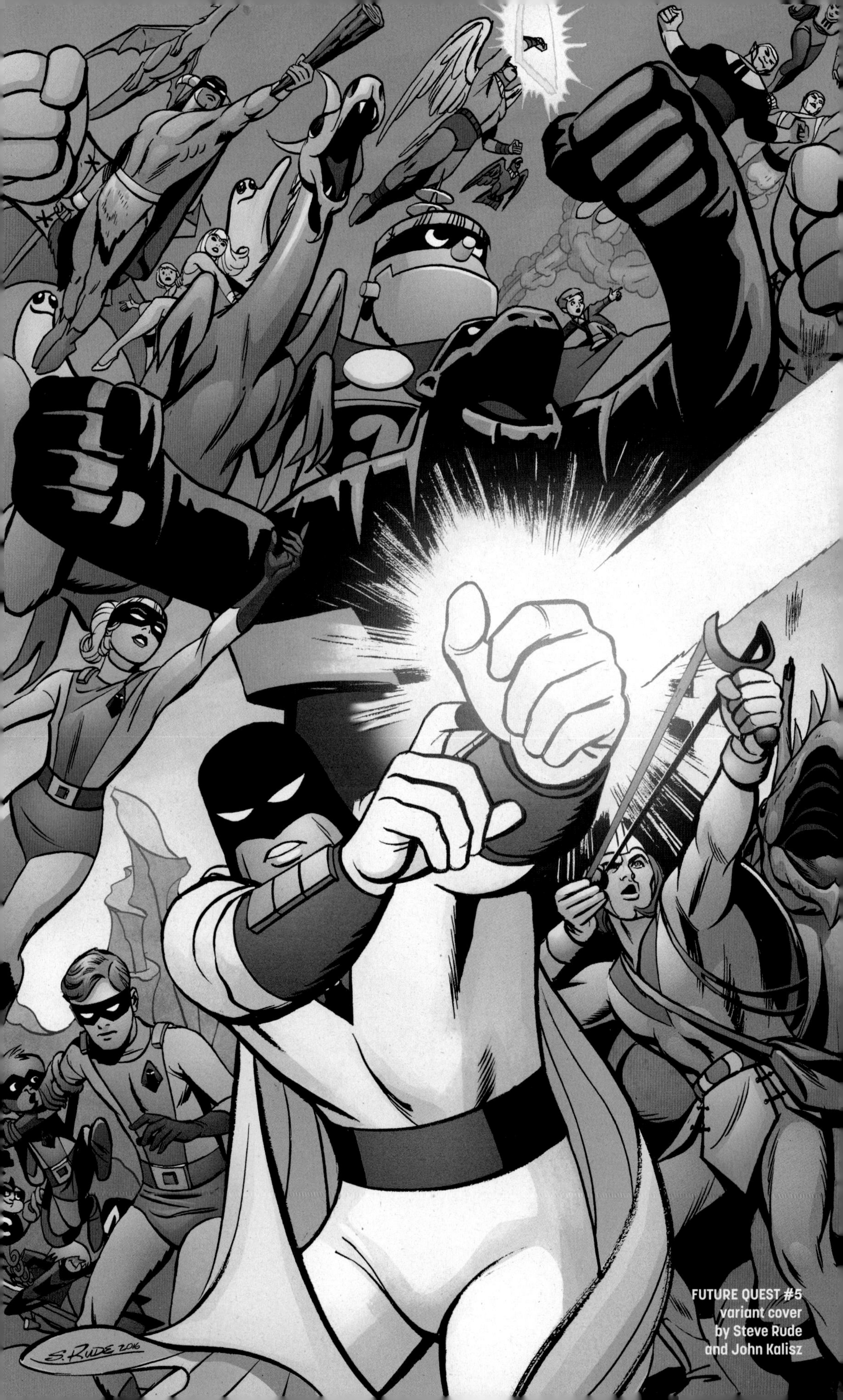
S. RUDE 2016

FUTURE QUEST #5
variant cover
by Steve Rude
and John Kalisz

FUTURE QUEST #6 variant cover by Dan Parent

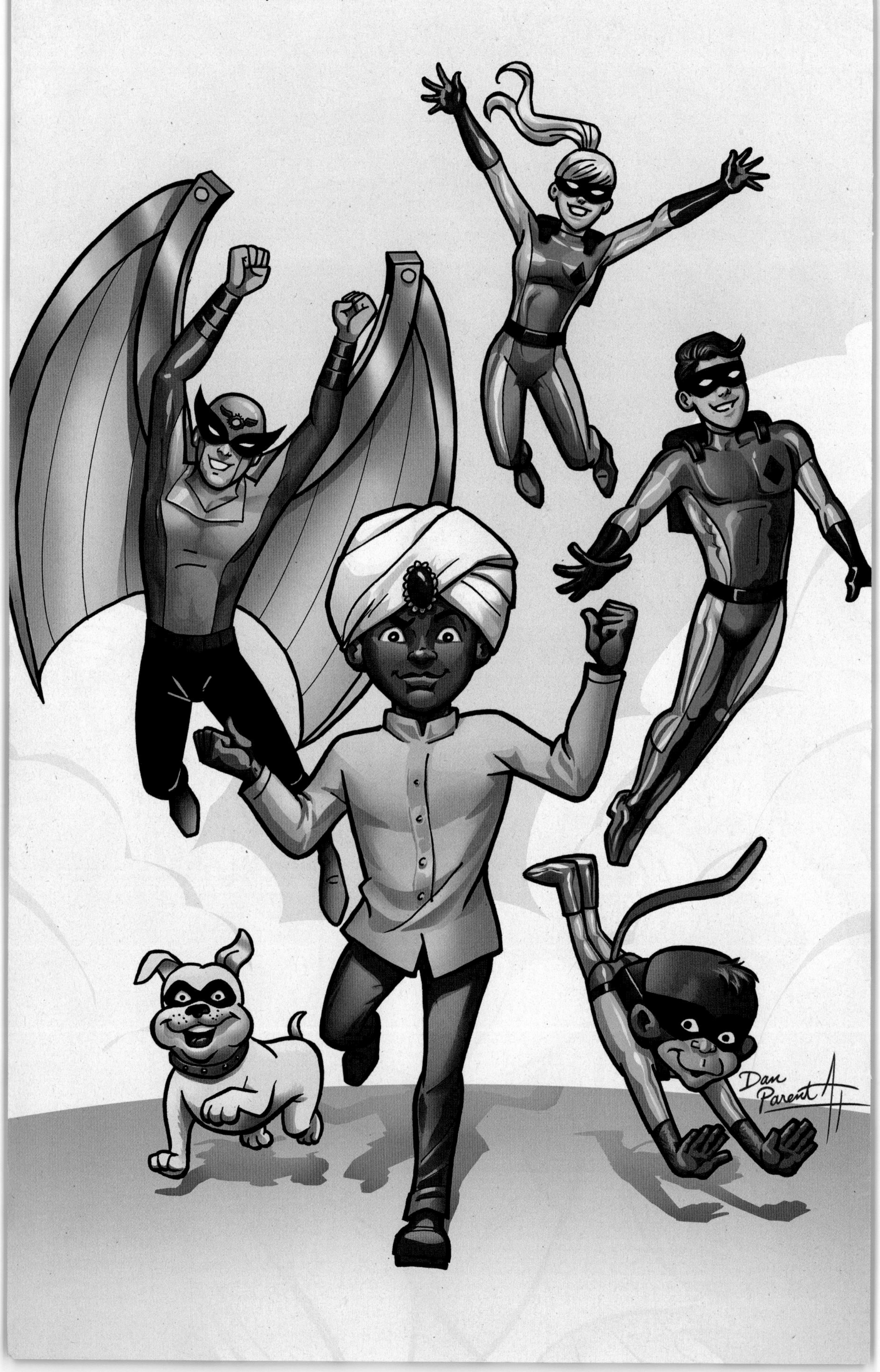
Dan Parent

Original promotional images by EVAN "DOC" SHANER

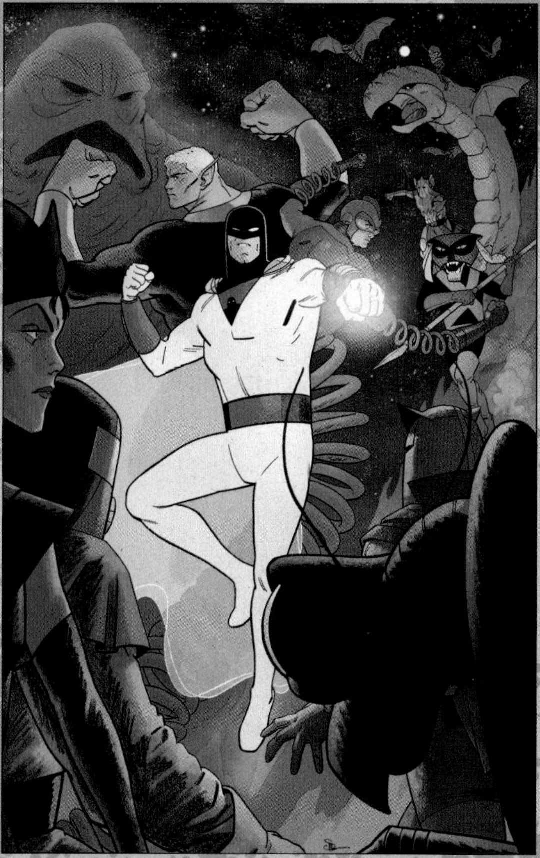

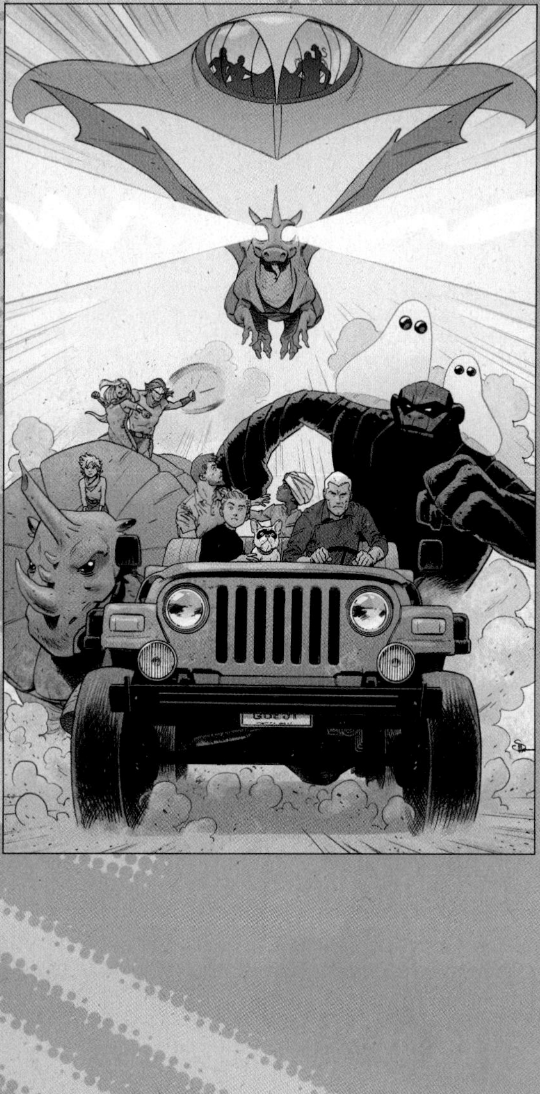

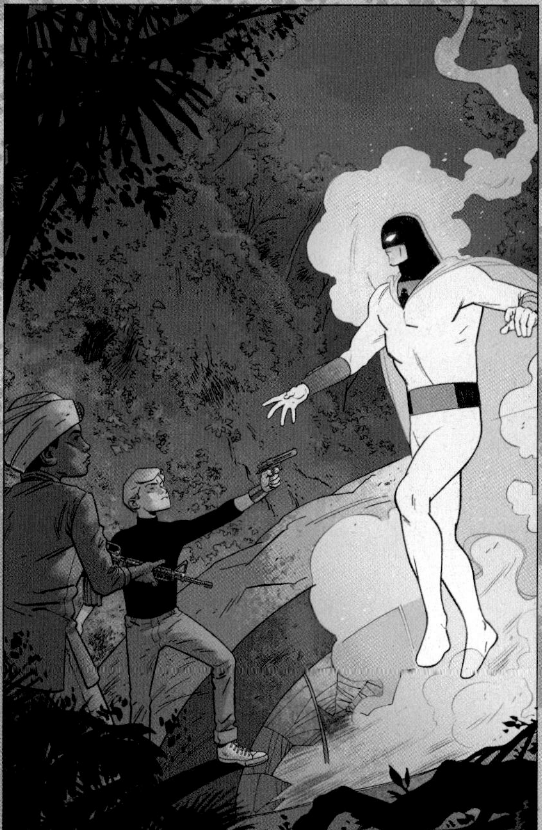

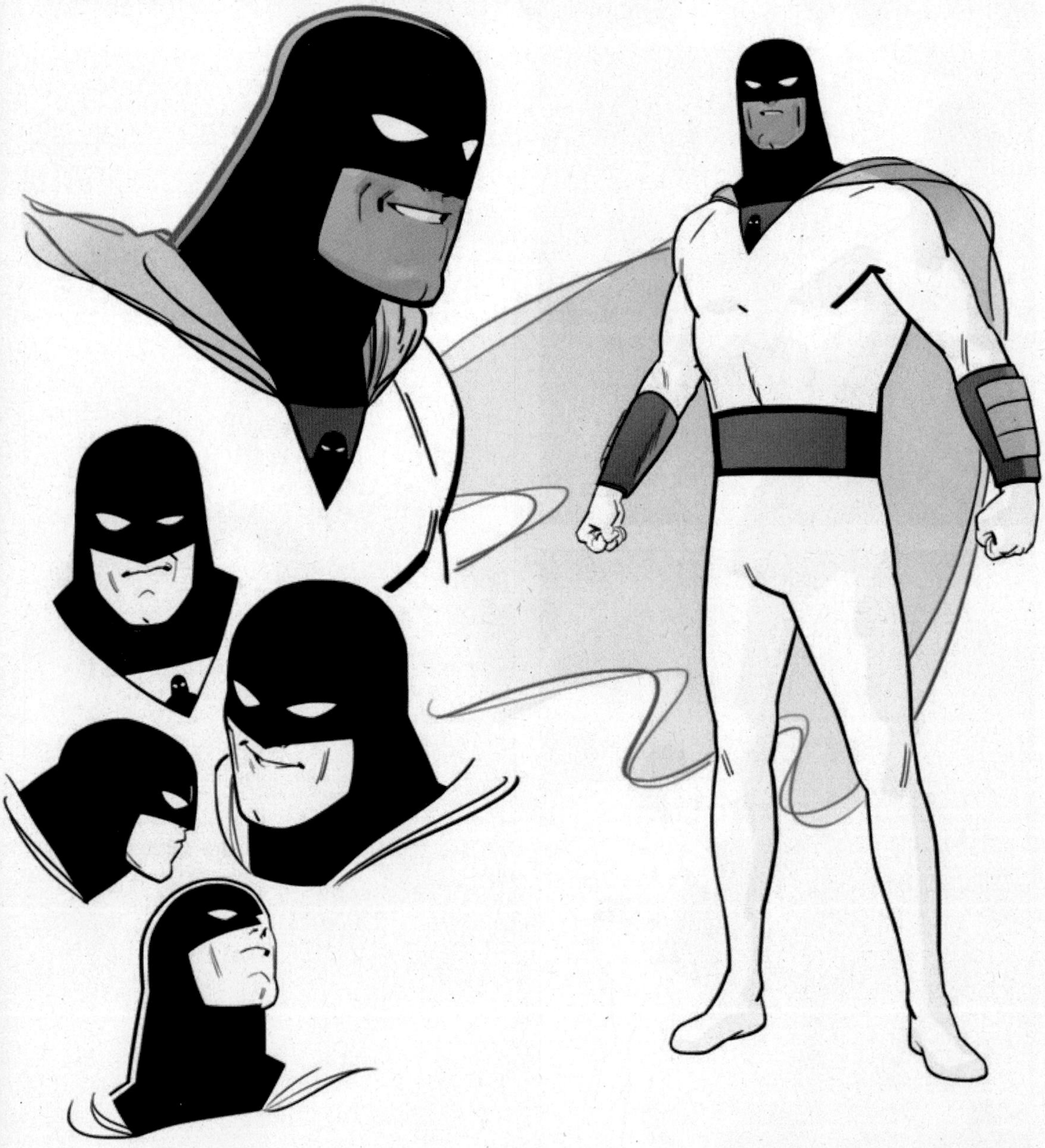

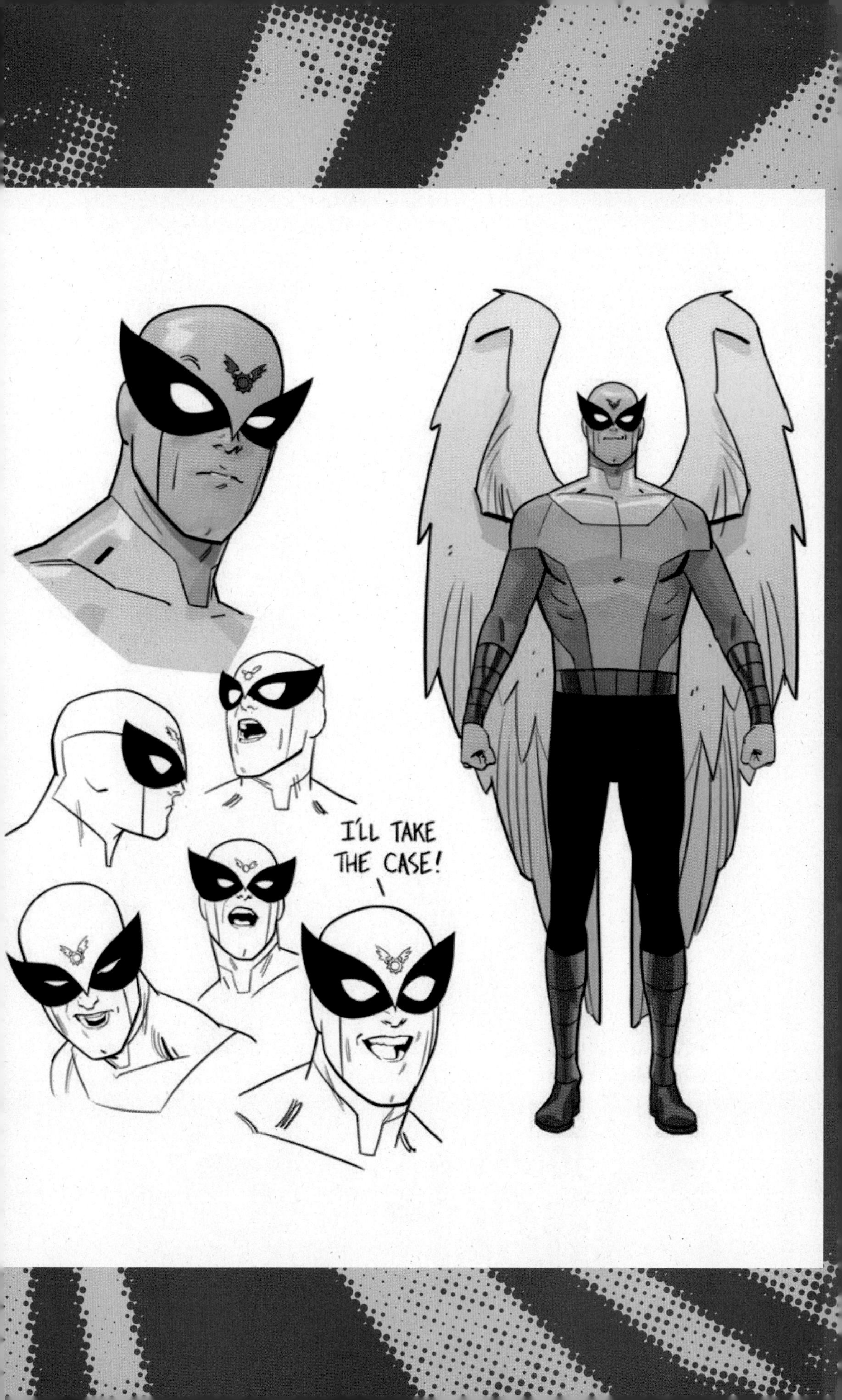
I'LL TAKE THE CASE!

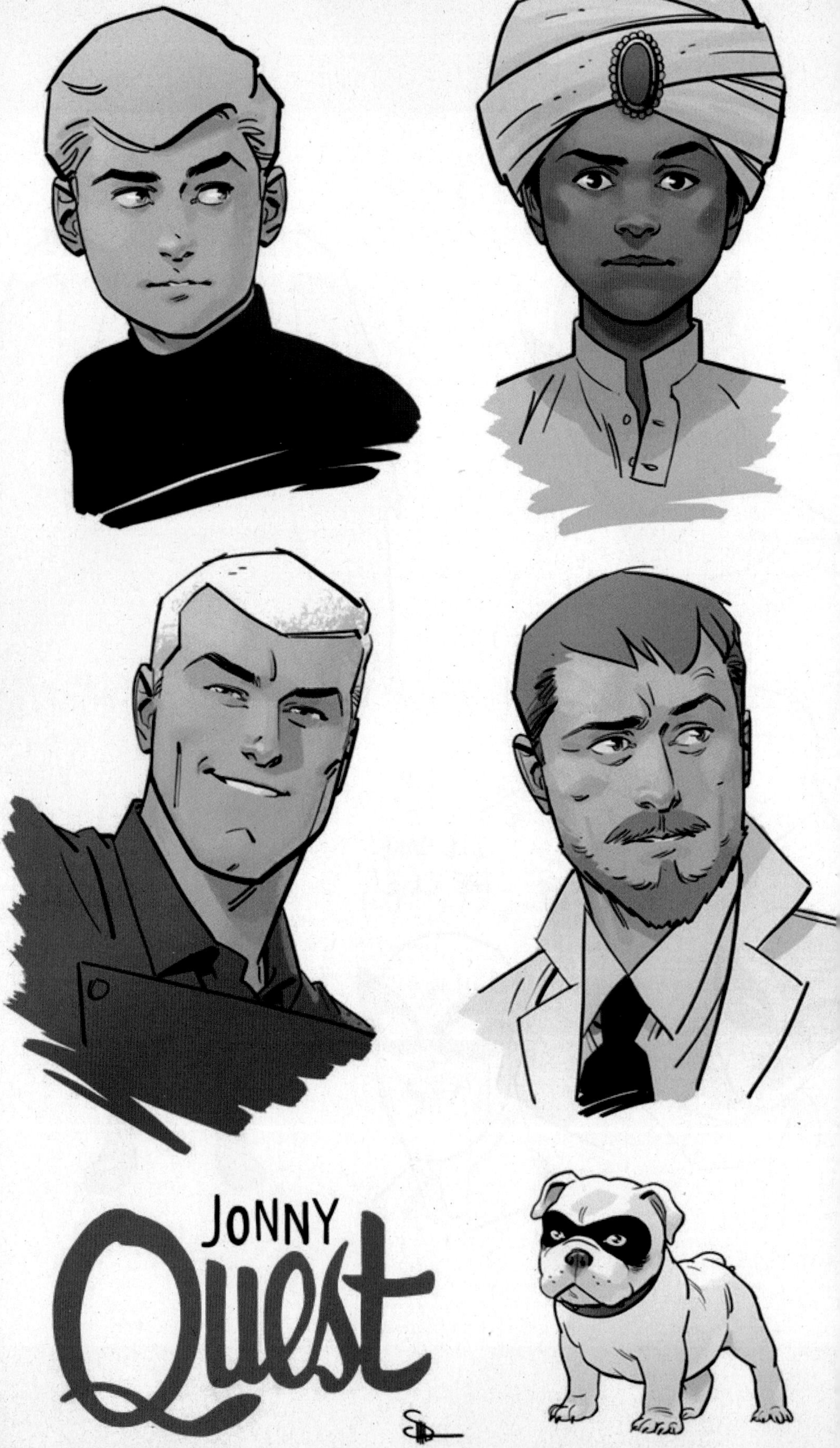
JONNY
Quest

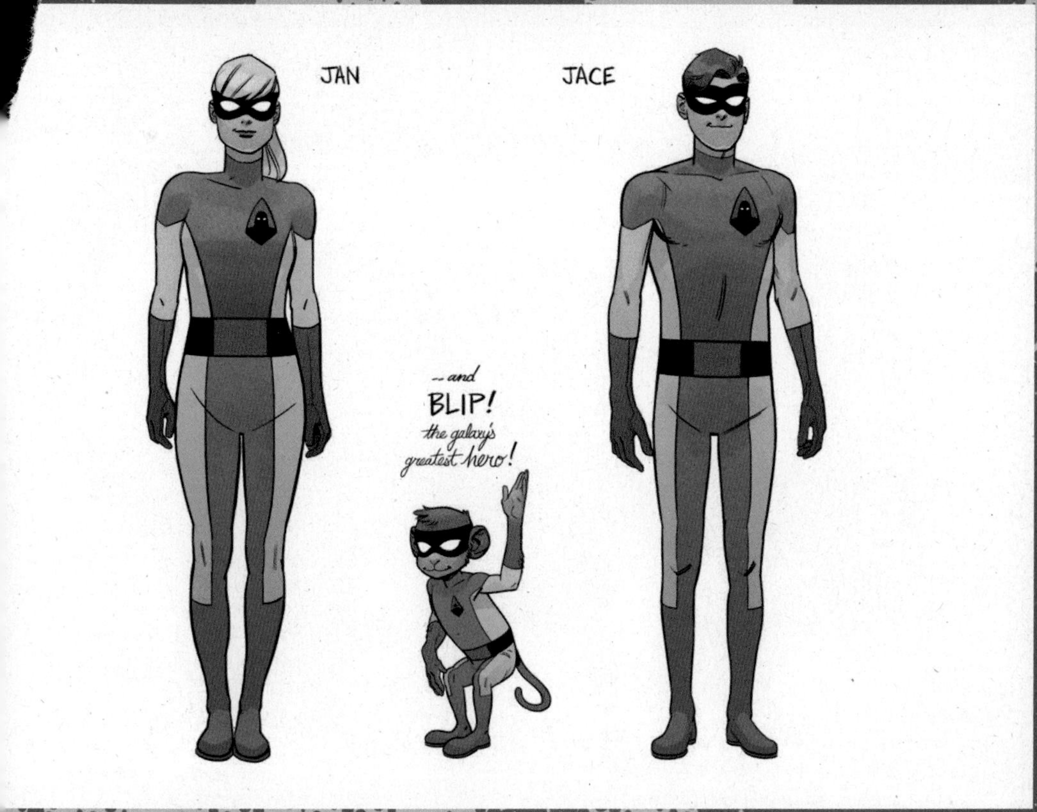
JAN
JACE
-- and BLIP! the galaxy's greatest hero!

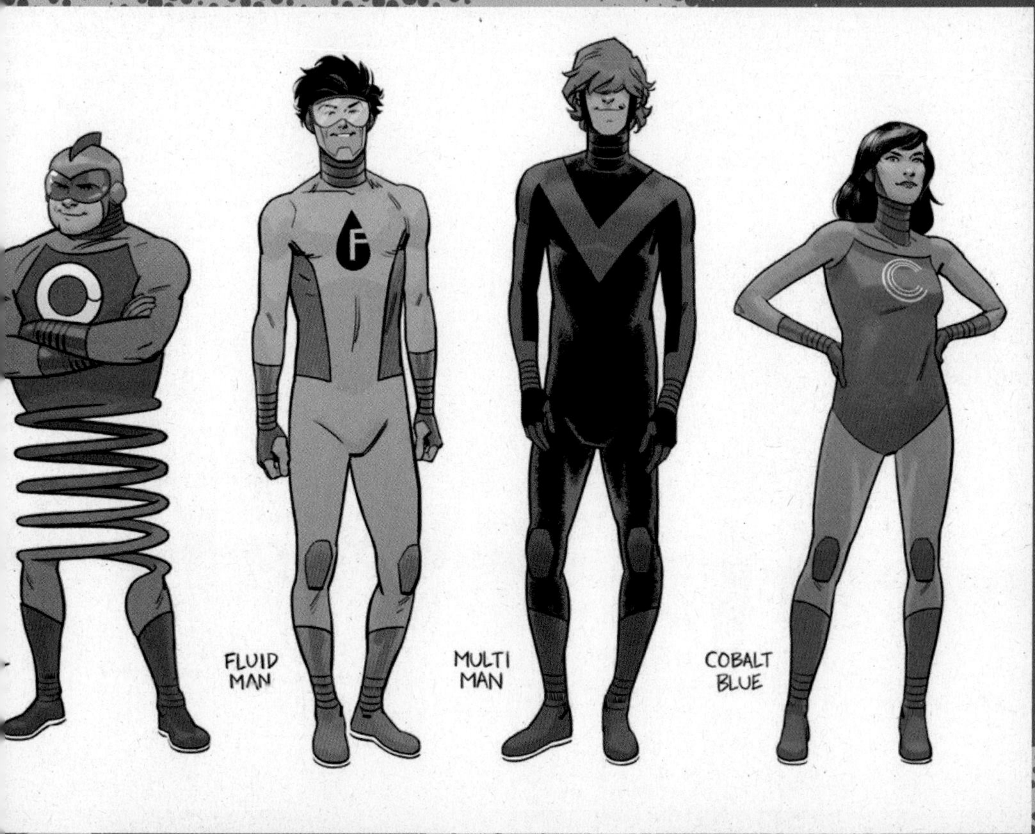
FLUID MAN
MULTI MAN
COBALT BLUE

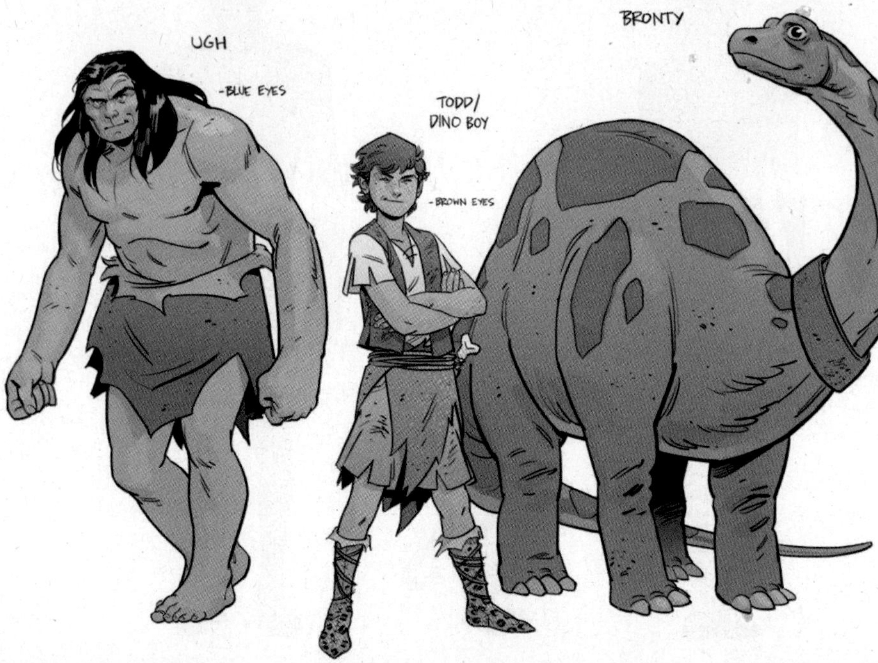
UGH
-BLUE EYES
TODD/
DINO BOY
-BROWN EYES
BRONTY

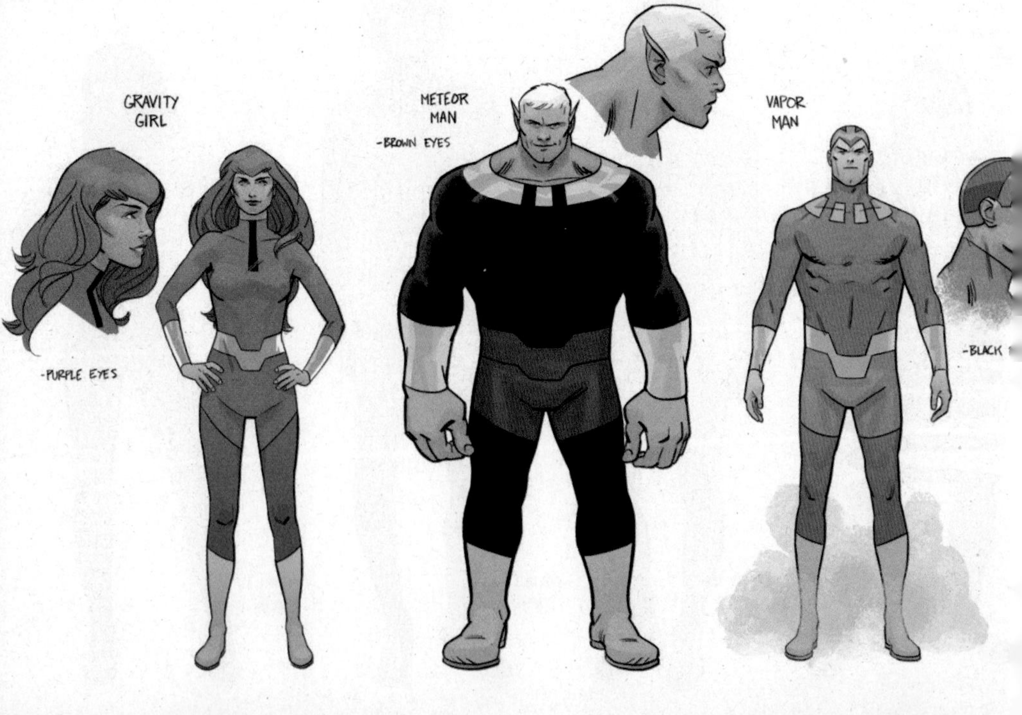
GRAVITY
GIRL
-PURPLE EYES
METEOR
MAN
-BROWN EYES
VAPOR
MAN
-BLACK